LINGUISTIC CATEGORIZATION

LINGUISTIC CATEGORIZATION

Prototypes in Linguistic Theory

JOHN R. TAYLOR

Second Edition

CLARENDON PRESS · OXFORD
1995

Oxford University Press, Walton Street, Oxford OX2 6DP

Oxford New York

Athens Auckland Bangkok Bombay Calcutta Cape Town
Dar es Salaam Delhi Florence Hong Kong Istanbul Karachi
Kuala Lumpur Madras Madrid Melbourne Mexico City Nairobi
Paris Singapore Taipei Tokyo Toronto

and associated companies in
Berlin Ibadan

Oxford is a trade mark of Oxford University Press

Published in the United States
by Oxford University Press Inc., New York

British Library Cataloguing in Publication Data
Data available

Library of Congress Cataloging in Publication Data
Linguistic categorization : prototypes in linguistic theory
John R. Taylor. — 2nd [enl.] ed.
1. Categorization (Linguistics)   2. Linguistic analysis
(Linguistics)   3. Cognitive grammar.   4. Semantics.   I. Title.
P128.C37T38   1995   401'.43—dc20   95–19066
ISBN 0–19–870012–1 (Pbk)
ISBN 0–19–870013–X

1 3 5 7 9 10 8 6 4 2

Typeset by Joshua Associates Limited, Oxford
Printed in Great Britain on acid-free paper by
Bookcraft (Bath) Ltd., Midsomer Norton

For
Genia and Ary

Preface to the Second Edition

FOR the second edition of this book, I have added an extra chapter, Chapter 14, which updates the treatment, especially of issues in lexical semantics. The focus on word meanings reflects a personal interest, but also the belief that a good deal of a person's knowledge of a language resides, precisely, in the knowledge of words, and of their properties. I am grateful, as always, to the many individuals who have encouraged me in my work, including Dirk Geeraerts, Brygida Rudzka-Ostyn, Savas Tsohatzidis, Rob MacLaury, and especially René Dirven. My intellectual debt to Ronald Langacker will be apparent throughout. A special word of thanks, also, to my editor at Oxford University Press, Frances Morphy, who first suggested the expanded second edition. I regret that, because of my translation to the other side of the globe, she had to wait a little longer than promised for the delivery of the additional chapter.

J.R.T.

Preface to the First Edition

THE title of this book is intentionally ambiguous. In one of its senses, 'linguistic categorization' refers to the process by which people, in using language, necessarily categorize the world around them. Whenever we use the word *dog* to refer to two different animals, or describe two different colour sensations by the same word, e.g. *red*, we are undertaking acts of categorization. Although different, the two entities are regarded in each case as the same.

Categorization is fundamental to all higher cognitive activity. Yet the seeing of sameness in difference raises deep philosophical problems. One extreme position, that of nominalism, claims that sameness is merely a matter of linguistic convention; the range of entities which may be called dogs, or the set of colours that may be described as red, have in reality nothing in common but their name. An equally extreme position is that of realism. Realism claims that categories like DOG and RED exist independently of language and its users, and that the words *dog* and *red* merely name these pre-existing categories. An alternative position is conceptualism. Conceptualism postulates that a word and the range of entities to which it may refer are mediated by a mental entity, i.e. a concept. It is in virtue of a speaker's knowledge of the concepts "dog" and "red", i.e. in virtue of his knowledge of the meanings of the words *dog* and *red*, that he is able to categorize different entities as dogs, different colours as red, and so on. Conceptualism may be given a nominalist or a realist orientation. On the one hand, we can claim that concepts merely reflect linguistic convention. The English speaker's concepts "red" and "dog" arise through his observation of how the words *red* and *dog* are conventionally used; once formed, the concepts will govern future linguistic performance. Alternatively, we might claim that concepts mirror really existing properties of the world. On this view, our concepts are not arbitrary creations of language, but constitute part of our understanding of what the world is 'really' like. This book will take a course which is intermediate between these two positions, yet strictly speaking consonant with neither. To the extent that a language is a conventionalized symbolic system, it is indeed the case that a language imposes a set of categories on its users. Conventionalized, however, does not necessarily imply arbitrary. The categories encoded in a language are motivated, to varying degrees, by a number of factors—by actually existing discontinuities in the world, by the manner in which human beings interact, in a given culture, with the world, and by general cognitive processes of concept formation. It is precisely the dialectic of convention and motivation which gives rise to the fact that the categories encoded in one language do not always stand in a one-to-one correspondence with the categories of another language. Languages are indeed diverse in this respect; yet the diversity is not unconstrained.

In the first place, then, this book is about the meanings of linguistic forms, and the categorization of the world which a knowledge of these meanings entails. But language itself is also part of the world. In speaking of nouns, verbs, phonemes, and grammatical sentences, linguists are undertaking acts of categorization. The title of the book is to be understood in this second, reflexive sense. Just as a botanist is concerned with a botanical categorization of plants, so a linguist undertakes a linguistic categorization of linguistic objects. The second half of the book, in particular, will address the parallels between linguistic categorization in this second sense, and the categorization, through language, of the non-linguistic world. If, as will be argued, categories of linguistic objects are structured along the same lines as the more familiar semantic categories, then any insights we may gain into the categorization of the non-linguistic world may be profitably applied to the study of language structure itself.

The theoretical background to the study is a set of principles and assumptions that have recently come to be known as 'cognitive linguistics'. Cognitive linguistics does not (yet) constitute a theoretical paradigm which is able to rival, even less to displace, the (still) dominant generative-transformational approach. The main points of divergence are, however, clear. Whereas generativists regard knowledge of language as an autonomous component of the mind, independent, in principle, from other kinds of knowledge and from other cognitive skills, cognitivists posit an intimate, dialectic relationship between the structure and function of language on the one hand, and non-linguistic skills and knowledge on the other. Language, being at once both the creation of human cognition and an instrument in its service, is thus more likely than not to reflect, in its structure and functioning, more general cognitive abilities. One of the most important of these cognitive abilities is precisely the ability to categorize, i.e. to see similarity in diversity. A study of categorization processes is thus likely to provide valuable insights into the meanings symbolized by linguistic forms. Furthermore, there is every reason to expect that the structural categories of language itself will be analogous, in many ways, to the categories which human beings perceive in the non-linguistic world around them.

The book owes its inception very largely to a suggestion from René Dirven. I am indebted to Professor Dirven, as well as to Maurice Aldridge, Brygida Rudzka-Ostyn, Dirk Geeraerts, and Savas Tsohatzidis for commenting on earlier versions of the manuscript. That the manuscript could be completed at all is due, in no small measure, to the constant encouragement, support, patience, and love, of my wife.

J. R. T.

Contents

Typographical conventions

Linguistic forms are printed in italics: *dog*.

Meanings of linguistic forms, and glosses of foreign language forms, are given between double quotes: "dog".

Citations are marked by single quotes.

Names of categories are printed in small capitals: DOG.

Phonetic and semantic features are printed in small capitals enclosed in square brackets: [VOCALIC], [ANIMAL].

Semantic attributes are printed in normal type enclosed in square brackets: [ability to fly].

Phonemes, and phonemic transcriptions, are enclosed in slashes, phonetic symbols and phonetic transcriptions are enclosed in square brackets.

An asterisk * indicates that a following linguistic expression is unacceptable, on either semantic or syntactic grounds. Expressions of questionable acceptability are preceded by a question mark.

1

The Categorization of Colour

As pointed out in the Preface, linguistics is concerned with categorization on two levels. In the first place, linguists need categories in order to describe the object of investigation. In this, linguists proceed just like practitioners of any other discipline. The noises that people make are categorized as linguistic or non-linguistic; linguistic noises are categorized as instances of a particular language, or of a dialect of a particular language; sentences are categorized as grammatical or ungrammatical; words are categorized as nouns and verbs; sound segments are classified as vowels or consonants, stops or fricatives, and so on.

But linguists are (or should be) concerned with categorization at another level. The things that linguists study—words, morphemes, syntactic structures, etc.—not only constitute categories in themselves, they also stand for categories. The phonetic form [ɹed] can not only be categorized as, variously, an English word, an adjective, a syllable with a consonant–vowel–consonant structure; [ɹed] also designates a range of physically and perceptually distinct properties of the real world (more precisely, a range of distinct visual sensations caused by the real-world properties), and assigns this range of properties to the category RED. The morphosyntactic category PAST TENSE (usually) categorizes states of affairs with respect to their anteriority to the moment of speaking; the preposition *on* (in some of its senses) categorizes the relationship between entities as one of contact, and so on.

Both in its methodology and in its substance, then, linguistics is intimately concerned with categorization. The point has been made by Labov (1973: 342): 'If linguistics can be said to be any one thing it is the study of categories: that is, the study of how language translates meaning into sound through the categorization of reality into discrete units and sets of units.' Questions like: Do categories have any basis in the real world, or are they merely constructs of the human mind? What is their internal structure? How are categories learnt? How do people go about assigning entities to a category? What kinds of relationships exist amongst categories? must inevitably be of vital importance to linguists. Labov, in the passage just referred to, goes on to point out that categorization 'is such a fundamental and obvious part of linguistic activity that the properties of categories are normally assumed rather than studied'. In recent years, however, research in the cognitive sciences, especially cognitive psychology, has forced linguists to make explicit, and in some cases to rethink, their assumptions. In this first chapter, I will introduce some of the issues involved, taking as my cue the linguistic categorization of colour.

1.1 Why colour terms?

There are good reasons for starting with colour terms. In many respects colour terminology provides an ideal testing ground for theories of categorization. It is commonly asserted—by linguists, anthropologists, and others—that categories have neither a real-world nor a perceptual base. Reality is merely a diffuse continuum, and our categorization of it is ultimately a matter of convention, i.e. of learning. This view was expressed very clearly by the anthropologist, Edmund Leach:

I postulate that the physical and social environment of a young child is perceived as a continuum. It does not contain any intrinsically separate 'things'. The child, in due course, is taught to impose upon this environment a kind of discriminating grid which serves to distinguish the world as being composed of a large number of separate things, each labelled with a name. This world is a representation of our language categories, not vice versa. Because my mother tongue is English, it seems self evident that *bushes* and *trees* are different kinds of things. I would not think this unless I had been taught that it was the case. (Leach 1964: 34)

According to Leach, the categories that we perceive in the world are not objectively there. Rather, they have been forced upon us by the categories encoded in the language that we happen to have been brought up with. If categorization is language dependent, as Leach and many others suggest, it is only to be expected that different languages will encode different categorizations, none of them intrinsically any better founded, or more 'correct', than any other.

Intuitively, we would probably want to reject, on common-sense grounds, the idea that *all* categories are merely learnt cultural artefacts, the product of our language, with no objective basis in reality. Surely, the world does contain discrete nameable entities, and in many cases there does seem to be a natural basis for grouping these entities into discrete categories. Tables are one kind of thing, distinct from chairs; elephants are another, and quite different from giraffes. These cases need not concern us at the moment. There is, though, one area of experience where the reality-as-a-continuum hypothesis would seem to hold, and this is colour. It has been estimated that the human eye can discriminate no fewer than 7.5 million just noticeable colour differences (cf. Brown and Lenneberg 1954). This vast range of visible colours constitutes a three-dimensional continuum, defined by the parameters of hue (the wavelength of reflected light), luminosity (the amount of light reflected), and saturation (freedom from dilution with white). Because each of these dimensions constitutes a smooth continuum, there is no physical basis for the demarcation of discrete colour categories. Yet people do recognize discrete categories. It follows—so the argument goes—that these categories are a product of a learning experience, more particularly, of language. This view is supported by the fact that languages differ very considerably, both with regard to the number of colour terms they possess, and with regard to the denotational range of these terms.

There are some well-known examples of non-correspondence of colour terms in different languages (see Lyons 1968: 56f.). Russian has no word for blue; *goluboy* "light, pale blue" and *siniy* "dark, bright blue" are different colours, not different shades of the same colour. *Brown* has no single equivalent in French; the range of colours denoted by *brown* would be described in French as *brun*, *marron*, even *jaune*. Welsh *glas* translates into English as *blue*, *green*, or even *grey*. Very often, it is not just an individual colour term which does not have an exact equivalent in another language. Rather, it is the set of colour terms as a whole which fails to correspond with that of another language. Bantu languages are on the whole rather poor in colour terms; Tsonga, for instance, has only seven basic colour terms.[1] These, with their approximate range of English equivalents, are as follows:

(1) ntima: black
   rikuma: grey
   basa: white, beige

---

[1] The notion of basic colour terms will be elaborated later, in s. 1.3. In addition to their basic colour terms, both Tsonga and Classical Latin (to be discussed below) have a large number of non-basic terms which denote quite precisely the colours characteristically associated with particular kinds of object.

    tshwuka: red, pink, purple
    xitshopana: yellow, orange
    rihlaza: green, blue
    ribungu: dark brown, dull yellowish-brown

Tsonga divides the black–grey–white dimension in essentially the same way as English. However, only three categories are recognized in the hue dimension (*tshwuka*, *xitshopana*, *rihlaza*), whereas English has at least six (*purple*, *red*, *orange*, *yellow*, *green*, *blue*). *Ribungu*, on the other hand, is a special word for colours of low luminosity in the yellow–orange–brown region. Neither do we need go to non-European languages to find cases of extensive non-correspondence with English terms. Older European languages typically exhibit rather restricted colour vocabularies, which contrast strikingly with the modern English system. Consider the colour terms in Classical Latin (André 1949):

    (2) albus: white
         candidus: brilliant, bright white
         ater: black
         niger: shiny black
         ruber: red, pink, purple, orange, some shades of brown
         flavus: yellow, light brown, golden red
         viridis: green
         caeruleus: blue

We find here, as in Tsonga, a rather restricted range of terms for the hue dimension. On the other hand, Latin made a distinction, lacking in English, between blacks and whites of high and low luminosity.

Linguists have not been slow to recognize the theoretical significance of colour terminology. Consider the following passage from Bloomfield's classic volume *Language*:

Physicists view the color-spectrum as a continuous scale of light-waves of different lengths, ranging from 40 to 72 hundred-thousandths of a millimetre, but languages mark off different parts of this scale quite arbitrarily and without precise limits, in the meanings of such color-names as *violet*, *blue*, *green*, *yellow*, *orange*, *red*, and the color-names of different languages do not embrace the same gradations. (Bloomfield 1933: 140)

This passage by Bloomfield could have been the model for Gleason's treatment of the same topic in his once very influential *Introduction to Descriptive Linguistics*:

Consider a rainbow or a spectrum from a prism. There is a continuous gradation of color from one end to the other. That is, at any point there is only a small difference in the colors immediately adjacent at either side. Yet an American describing it will list the hues as *red, orange, yellow, green, blue, purple*, or something of the kind. The continuous gradation of color which exists in nature is represented in language by a series of discrete categories. . . . There is nothing inherent either in the spectrum or the human perception of it which would compel its division in this way. The specific method of division is part of the structure of English. (Gleason 1955: 4).

Other statements in the same vein could be quoted from other scholars. Indeed, many textbooks and surveys of linguistic theory (the present work is no exception!) have an obligatory paragraph, even a whole section or chapter, devoted to colour.

I would like to draw attention to one particularly important detail in the passage from Bloomfield, namely the assertion that colour categorization is *arbitrary*. Gleason, a few pages after the above quotation, makes the same point. What is more, Gleason puts his discussion of colour in the very first chapter of his textbook, as if to suggest that the arbitrariness of colour terms is paradigmatic for the arbitrariness of language as a whole. The arbitrariness of colour terms follows from the facts outlined above, namely the physical continuity of the colour space, and the human ability to make an incredibly large number of perceptual discriminations. There are, no doubt, other areas of experience which, like colour, constitute a smooth continuum: length, height, temperature, speed, perhaps even emotions like love, hatred, anger. Human beings can also make a large number of perceptual discriminations in these domains (but presumably nothing like the alleged 7.5 million colour discriminations). Languages are typically rather poor in their categorization of these domains. For length, English has only two terms, *long* and *short*. Colour, with its rich and language-specific terminology, is indeed an ideal hunting ground for anyone wishing to argue the arbitrariness of linguistic categories.

1.2 Arbitrariness

Arbitrariness, as I have used the term in the preceding paragraph, has been a fundamental concept in twentieth-century linguistics. Its status as a quasi-technical term goes back to Saussure, who, in his *Cours de linguistique générale* (1916) proclaimed as a first principle of linguistic description that 'the linguistic sign is arbitrary': 'le signe linguistique est arbitraire' (Saussure 1964: 100).

The linguistic sign, for Saussure, is the association of a form (or signifier) with a meaning (or signified). There are two respects in which the linguistic sign is arbitrary (see Culler 1976: 19 ff.). In the first place, the association of a particular form with a particular meaning is arbitrary. There is no reason (other than convention) why the phonetic form [ɹed] should be associated with the meaning "red" in English; any other phonetic form, provided it was accepted by the generality of English speakers, would do equally well. It is therefore to be expected that different languages will associate quite different phonetic forms with a particular meaning; were the relationship not arbitrary, words with the same meaning in different languages would all have a recognizably similar form. With this characterization of arbitrariness, few would disagree.[2] But there is another, more subtle aspect to arbitrariness, as Saussure conceived it. This is that the signified itself—the meaning associated with a linguistic form—is arbitrary. Saussure vigorously denied that there are pre-existing meanings (such as "red", "orange", etc.), which are there, independent of language, waiting to be named. The lexicon of a language is not simply a nomenclature for some universally valid inventory of concepts. There is no reason, therefore, why any portion of the colour space should have a privileged status for categorization in the colour vocabulary of a language; indeed, strictly speaking, there is no reason why colour should be lexicalized at all. We return, then, to the theme of Section 1.1. Reality is a diffuse continuum, and our categorization of it is merely an artefact of culture and language.

The arbitrariness of the linguistic sign is closely linked to another Saussurian principle, namely the notion of language as a self-contained, autonomous system. 'La langue', according to Saussure, 'est un système dont tous les termes sont solidaires et où la valeur de l'un ne résulte que de la présence simultanée des autres' (1964: 159). The meaning of a linguistic sign is not a fixed property of the linguistic sign considered in and of itself; rather, meaning is a function of the value of the sign within the sign system which constitutes a language.

---

[2] The doctrine of the arbitrariness of the signifier–signified relationship disregards, of course, the relatively rare phenomena of onomatopoeia and sound symbolism. It is worth mentioning that Rhodes and Lawler (1981) have recently suggested that the phonetic motivation of the signifier might be much more extensive than is traditionally believed.

Thus concepts, i.e. the values associated with linguistic signs, are purely differential; they are defined 'non pas positivement par leur contenu, mais négativement par leurs rapports avec les autres termes du système' (p. 162). This means that while the word *red* is obviously used by speakers of the language to refer to properties of the world, and might well evoke in the mind of a speaker a mental image of the concept "red", the meaning of the word is not given by any properties of the world, nor does it reflect any act of non-linguistic cognition on the part of a speaker. The meaning of *red* results from the value of the word within the system (more precisely, the subsystem) of English colour vocabulary. The fact that English possesses words like *orange*, *pink*, and *purple* effectively limits the denotational range of *red* in contrast with, say, Tsonga, which has only one word for the red–pink–purple area of the spectrum. Should English acquire a new colour term, or should one of the existing colour terms fall into disuse, the whole subsystem would change, and each term in the subsystem would acquire a new value.

There are a number of implications for the study of colour terms which follow from the structuralist approach to word meaning. Amongst these are the following:

(*a*) All colour terms in a system have equal status. Some colour terms might be used more frequently than others, but since the value of any one term is determined by its relation to all the other terms in the system, no one term can have a privileged status.

(*b*) All referents of a colour term have equal status. Admittedly, the structuralist view does allow for the possibility of boundary colours. Recall the earlier quotation from Bloomfield, in which he stated that languages mark off different parts of the colour space 'without precise limits'. There will be regions between adjacent colour categories where unambiguous categorization will be difficult. Discounting such marginal cases, the structuralist view assigns to each exemplar of a colour category equal status within that category. If two colours are both categorized as red, i.e. as the same colour, linguistically speaking, then there is no sense in which one is redder than the other. This does not mean, of course, that an English speaker cannot perceive any difference between the two colours; only that for the purposes of linguistic categorization the difference is ignored.

(*c*) The only legitimate object of linguistic study is the language system, not individual terms in a system. Neither can one legitimately compare single lexical items across different languages. Rather, one must compare entire systems, and the values of the items within those systems.

1.3 An alternative approach: focal colours

In Sections 1.1 and 1.2 I have tried to give as objective and sympathetic an account as possible of the structuralist approach to colour terminology. I now want to present some arguments against the structuralist view. The pioneering work in this regard is *Basic Color Terms* (1969), by the linguist-anthropologists Berlin and Kay. On the basis of an investigation of the colour terms in ninety-eight languages, Berlin and Kay state:

> Our results ... cast doubt on the commonly held belief that each language segments the three-dimensional color continuum arbitrarily and independently of each other language. It appears now that, although different languages encode in their vocabularies different *numbers* of basic color categories, a total universal inventory of exactly eleven basic color categories exists from which the eleven or fewer basic color terms of any language are always drawn. (Berlin and Kay 1969: 2)

Berlin and Kay restricted their investigation to what they called basic colour terms. I shall have more to say about basic level terms in Chapter 3. Here, we can content ourselves with Berlin and Kay's operational definition. Amongst the characteristics of basic colour terms, as understood by Berlin and Kay, are the following. Basic colour terms

- (a) are not subsumed under other terms. *Crimson* and *scarlet* are not basic terms in English, since they are varieties of *red*. *Orange* is a basic term, since it is not subordinate to any other colour term;
- (b) are morphologically simple. Terms like *bluish*, *bluish-green* and *chocolate-coloured*, even *golden*, are excluded;
- (c) are not collocationally restricted. *Blond*, which describes only hair, is not a basic colour term;
- (d) are of frequent use. Rare words like *puce*, and technical words like *xanthic*, are excluded.[3]

---

[3] It might be observed that these 4 criteria do not necessarily give unambiguous results. For some speakers, terms like *mauve*, *lavender*, *lime*, *burgundy* seem to have

Berlin and Kay make two especially interesting claims. The first concerns so-called 'focal' colours. If people of different language backgrounds are shown a colour chart or an array of colour chips and are asked to trace the boundaries of the colour terms in their respective languages, one gets an impression of enormous cross-language variability (as well as of considerable variability between speakers of the same language; even the same speaker might perform differently on different occasions). Thus, two colour samples might well be categorized as the same by speakers of one language, but as different by speakers of another. If, on the other hand, people are asked to select good examples of the basic colour terms in their language, cross-language (and within-language) variability largely disappears. Although the range of colours that are designated by *red* (or its equivalent in other languages) might vary from person to person, there is a remarkable unanimity on what constitutes a good red. Paying attention to the denotational range of colour terms highlights the language specificity of colour terminology; eliciting good examples of colour terms highlights what is common between languages.

By studying the focal reference of basic colour terms, Berlin and Kay were able to make their second, and somewhat more controversial claim. They noted that the ninety-eight languages in their survey appeared to select their basic colour terms from an inventory of only eleven focal colours. Furthermore, the languages did not select randomly from this inventory. If a language has only two colour terms (no language, apparently, has fewer than two), these will designate focal black and focal white. If there is a third term, this will always be red. The fourth term will be either yellow or green, while the fifth will be the other member of the pair yellow and green. The sixth term will be blue, and the seventh, brown. The remaining four colours (grey, orange, purple, and pink) do not show any special ordering. These generalizations may be expressed in the form of an implicational hierarchy:

basic level status, for others not. Interesting in this connection is Robin Lakoff's (1975) claim that women tend to employ a more precise and more differentiated colour vocabulary than men. If this claim is true, women might in general possess a larger number of basic colour terms than men.

(3)

					grey
black	yellow				orange
< red <		< blue	< brown	<	
white	green				purple
					pink

(3) is to be interpreted as follows: the existence in a language of a category to the right of an arrow implies the existence of all the categories to its left; the reverse implication does not necessarily hold. If a language has a colour term designating, say, focal blue, we can predict that the language will also possess the five colour terms to the left of blue; we cannot, however, predict whether it will have the colour terms to the right.

Both in its methodology and substance, Berlin and Kay's work is not immune to criticism; see, for example, McNeill (1972) and Sampson (1980*b*: 96 ff.). For twenty of the languages investigated, Berlin and Kay had access to bilingual informants who happened to be available in the San Francisco region. The responses of these informants could well have been influenced by their knowledge of English and by their exposure to a technological culture. Even more suspect are the data for the remaining seventy-eight languages in the survey; these were gleaned from dictionaries, anthropologists' reports (some dating from the last century), and oral reports from field-workers. No doubt, these deficiencies are part of the price one has to pay for a study of such breadth and generality as Berlin and Kay's. Even so, before we can discuss the linguistic implications of Berlin and Kay's work, it is necessary to see whether their basic insights concerning focal colours stand up to more rigorous experimental testing. With this in mind, let us turn to the work on colour terms conducted in the early 1970s by the cognitive psychologist Eleanor Rosch (published under her former name, Eleanor Heider).

Heider (1972) reports four experiments which both confirm and elaborate some of Berlin and Kay's claims. The first experiment tested the stability of focal colours across languages. It was found that when subjects from eleven different language backgrounds were asked to pick out good examples of the colour terms in their respective languages, there was indeed a high degree of agreement concerning which colours were selected. When asked to point to a good example of red (or its equivalent in other languages), subjects tended to pick out the same shade, irrespective of which language they spoke. The second experiment investigated some of the behavioural correlates of colour focality. Subjects from twenty-three language backgrounds were presented with samples of focal and non-focal colours, which they were asked to name. Subjects responded in their native language, and it was found that focal colours were named more rapidly, and that the names given to focal colours were shorter (when written out, the names contained fewer letters), than was the case with non-focal colours. This strongly suggests that focal colours are perceptually and cognitively more salient than non-focal colours. Experiment three was a short-term memory task. Subjects were shown a colour sample for a period of five seconds. Then, after an interval of thirty seconds, they had to identify from an array of colours the colour that they had just seen. At issue was whether focal colours would be recognized more rapidly and more accurately than non-focal colours. Two groups of subjects participated in this experiment. One group consisted of twenty native speakers of English. The other was made up of twenty-one monolingual speakers of Dani. The Dani are a Stone Age people of New Guinea, whose language is one of the very few in the world which have only two colour terms. Between them, these two terms categorize the whole of the colour space, *mola* referring both to focal white and to warm colours (red, orange, yellow, pink, purple), while *mili* designates focal black and cool colours (blue, green). It was found that, overall, the English speakers could recognize the colours they had seen more accurately than the Dani. This suggests that colour memory is indeed aided by the existence of the relevant colour terms in one's language. (Another possibility, of course, is that a Stone Age culture, in which such things as traffic lights and colour-coded electric wires are unknown, provides little practice and few incentives for the memorization of colours.) More interesting was the finding that although the Dani's overall performance was poorer than that of the English speakers, they nevertheless performed better on the focal than on the non-focal colours. In this respect, the Dani did not differ from the English speakers. This aspect of the Dani's performance could not have been a consequence of the greater codability of focal colours, since the subjects did not possess separate lexical items in their language for designating these colours. Additional support for this view comes from Heider's fourth experiment. Here, Dani speakers were tested for long-term colour memory in a paired-association learning task. As expected, the subjects learned names for focal colours faster than names for non-focal colours. Further evidence for the perceptual and cognitive salience of focal colours comes from Heider (1971). Here it was found that three-year-old children, who had not yet acquired the full range of English colour terms, were more attentive to focal colours than to non-focal colours; also, three- and four-year-olds were able to match focal colours better than non-focal colours.

The evidence for Berlin and Kay's other claim, concerning the implicational hierarchy of focal colours, is less robust. (3) suggests that while focal colours as a whole have greater perceptual and cognitive salience than non-focal colours, some focal colours (namely those on the left of the hierarchy) are more salient than others. Heider addressed this issue in one of the experiments already referred to. In the second experiment reported in Heider (1972), focal colours could be named more rapidly than non-focal colours. There were also differences in the speed with which focal colours could be named. Black was named most rapidly of all, followed by (in order of increasing delay) yellow, white, purple, blue, red, pink, brown, green, and orange. This ordering does not correlate significantly with the ordering of the colour terms in (3), neither was there any significant correlation between the implicational hierarchy and the relative salience of focal colours for the three- and four-year-old children studied in Heider (1971). Indirect evidence, whose significance is however difficult to evaluate, for the implicational hierarchy may be sought in other places. Position on the hierarchy tends to correlate with the productivity of certain derivational processes. Only terms at the very left of the hierarchy undergo derivation by means of the causative–inchoative suffix -*en*: *whiten*, *blacken*, *redden* (cf. **bluen*, **yellowen*, **pinken*, etc.); terms at the very right do not readily form abstract nouns in -*ness*: **purpleness*, **orangeness* (cf. *whiteness*, *blueness*, *greyness*). We also note a weak correlation between position on the hierarchy and frequency of usage. Data in Kučera and Francis (1967) give black and white as the most frequently used terms, followed, in order of decreasing frequency, by red, brown, blue, green, grey, yellow, pink, orange, and purple.

The empirical claims made by Berlin and Kay (1965) with regard to the implicational hierarchy are probably too strong. Firstly, the proposal that all languages in the world select from a universal inventory of just eleven focal colours needs relaxing. Russian, with words for light and dark blue, has twelve basic level terms. Arguably, some English speakers too have additional basic level terms (*mauve*, *turquoise*, etc.). We can also find languages whose inventory of colour terms does not conform to (3). Languages which do not have separate terms for blue and green, but which nevertheless have terms to the right of blue, are by no means infrequent. As may be seen from (1), Tsonga, with a term for grey, fails to conform. The same is true of Zulu. Zulu, like most Bantu languages, does not distinguish between green and blue, yet the language possesses a term for focal brown, *nsundu*. Interestingly, however, terms for green–blue—a category which Kay and McDaniel (1978) call 'grue'—often turn out to be bifocal, that is to say, the grue term refers both to focal blue *and* to focal green, rather than to one or the other of the two focal colours (or to an in-between colour). Certainly, Zulu speakers think of blue and green as different colours, and, if necessary, distinguish them formally by means of the expressions *luhlaza njengesibhakabhaka* "grue like the sky" and *luhlaza njengotshani* "grue like the grass".

The years following the publication of *Basic Color Terms* saw a great deal of research on colour terminology (for a review, see Bornstein 1975). This led, amongst other things, to modifications of the implicational hierarchy (Kay 1975; Kay and McDaniel 1978). The details need not concern us here. Suffice it to say that this body of colour research presents a serious challenge to the structuralist approach to colour terminology. It is not that Berlin and Kay, or subsequent researchers, attempted to minimize the sometimes very different denotational ranges of colour terms in different languages, nor did anyone take issue with the notion of colour space as a physical continuum. But a factor was introduced which the structuralists had ignored, namely perception. It will be recalled that Gleason, in the passage cited earlier, explicitly stated that 'there is nothing inherent either in the spectrum *or the human perception of it* which would compel its division' (Gleason 1955: 4; emphasis added).

At least since the researches of Helmholz, in the middle of the last century, it has been known that colour perception begins in the retina, with the stimulation of light-sensitive cells known as rods and cones. There are three kinds of cone. These react selectively to light in the red, green, and blue regions, while the rods are activated by the brightness dimension. More recent research has studied colour processing beyond the retina. (For a summary and discussion of the implications for colour terminology, see Kay and McDaniel 1978; von Wattenwyl and Zollinger 1979). It seems that green and red, and yellow and blue, stimulate complementary patterns of cell responses in the neural pathways between the retina and the brain. So, while it may be valid to talk of the colour spectrum as a smooth continuum, it does not follow that perception of the spectrum is equally smooth. From a perceptual point of view, it certainly does make sense to speak of an optimum red. An optimum red would be light of a wavelength which produces a maximum rate of firing in those cells which are responsive to light in the red region.

Gleason, Bloomfield, and others not only leave the physiological basis of colour perception out of account, they also ignore environmental factors. Colour perception is not only a function of properties of the light waves entering the eye (Miller and Johnson-Laird 1976: 336). Just as objects are perceived to retain a constant size and shape, irrespective of their location and orientation with respect to the viewer, so the human visual system normalizes variations in the visual stimulus caused by changes in illumination of the perceived object. It might well be valid, at a certain level of theoretical abstraction, to speak of colour as a three-dimensional space. But people do not encounter colours as points in mathematical space, colours come as relatively stable properties of things. It is only in comparatively recent times, and only in technologically advanced societies, that it has been possible for a vast range of diverse colours to be applied, through industrial processing, to things. In the world of nature, things are typically associated with quite narrow segments of the colour continuum. Blood is, within a rather narrow range, red, milk is white, charcoal is black, lemons are yellow. By reversing the terms on either side of the copula, we obtain ostensive definitions of the colours: red is the colour of blood, white is the colour of milk, and so on. (Note, by the way, that many colour terms, in English and other languages, were originally names for objects. Examples from English include *pink* and *orange*, as well as *violet*, *burgundy*, and *lime*.) Also from an ecological point of view, then, it is not really surprising that colour terms should refer, primarily, to rather restricted portions of the spectrum. Equally, the cross-language stability of colour focality may well have as much to do with the stability of the attributes of certain kinds of things, as with neurological processes of perception (cf. Wierzbicka 1980 *b*: 42 f.). It is along these lines, also, that we might attempt to explain the highly puzzling merging of blue and green in many languages of the world.[4]

[4] Such languages are particularly frequent in Africa and the Americas, and examples have been reported from Europe. Certain conservative dialects of southern Italy, for

Why is it that just these colour categories should coalesce into a bifocal category? Blue is, of course, the colour of the sky, and green is the colour of grass. Yet unlike the red of blood and the yellow of lemons, the blue of the sky and the green of grass are highly variable; furthermore, the sky is not a tangible object whose surface can be touched. Blue and green thus lack the referential stability which nature provides for other focal colours, a fact which may go some way towards explaining the somewhat special status of these two categories.

Given the focality of colour categories—whether this be the consequence of neurological processes of perception, of environmental factors, or of both—the structuralist account of colour terminology turns out to be grossly inadequate. Two characteristics of colour terms, in particular, are at variance with the assumptions of structuralism:

(*a*) Colour categories have a centre and a periphery. This means that, contrary to structuralist principles, members of a category do not all have the same status. A colour term denotes, first and foremost, a focal colour, and it is only through 'generalization from focal exemplars' (Heider 1971: 455) that colour terms acquire their full denotational range. Obviously, if a language has relatively few colour terms, the denotational range of each term could well expand to take in a relatively large portion of the colour space. The centre, however, will remain constant.

(*b*) Because of the primacy of focal reference, colour terms do not form a system, in the Saussurian sense. The focal reference of a colour term, e.g. *red*, is independent of whether yellow, orange, purple, etc., are lexicalized in the language. The addition of a new term, such as *orange*, might cause the total denotational range of *red* to contract, but the centre of the category will remain unchanged.

In brief, colour terminology turns out to be much less arbitrary than the structuralists maintained. Colour, far from being ideally suited to demonstrating the arbitrariness of linguistic categories, is instead 'a prime example of the influence of underlying perceptual–cognitive [and perhaps also environmental: J.T.] factors on the formation and reference of linguistic categories' (Heider 1971: 447).

instance, lack a term for blue, *verde* (or its cognates) serving for both blue and green (Kristol 1980).

1.4 Autonomous linguistics vs. cognitive linguistics

In this chapter I have outlined two radically divergent approaches to colour terminology. Although we have been concerned with a minute segment of any one language (we are dealing with, at most, a dozen or so words in any one case), the two approaches are symptomatic of two equally divergent conceptions of the nature of language. The contrast between the two conceptions will, in its various guises, constitute one of the themes of this book. At this point, therefore, it would be appropriate to highlight the basic issues dividing the two approaches.

Structuralism maintained that the meaning of a linguistic form is determined by the language system itself. The world out there and how people interact with it, how they perceive and conceptualize it, are, in the structuralist view, extra-linguistic factors which do not impinge on the language system itself. Of course, people use language to talk about, to interpret, and to manipulate the world, but language remains a self-contained system, with its own structure, its own constitutive principles, its own dynamics. Language, in a word, is autonomous.

With the advent of Chomsky's generative–transformational paradigm, the notion of the autonomy of language acquired a rather different sense. In the first place, language was no longer regarded as a self-contained system, independent of its users; rather, the object of investigation is a 'system of knowledge' (Chomsky 1986: 24) residing in a person's brain. In Chomsky's work, this mentalistic conception of language (which the present writer fully endorses) goes with the much more controversial claim of the modularity of mind: 'What is currently understood even in a limited way seems to me to indicate that the mind is a highly differentiated structure, with quite distinct subsystems' (Chomsky 1980: 27). Just as the human body consists of various parts, each with its own function and developmental history, so the human mind consists of components which, though interacting, nevertheless develop and operate independently. One such component is the language faculty. The language faculty is viewed as a computational device which generates the sentences of a language through the recursive operation of rules on structured strings of symbols, assigning to each sentence thus generated a phonetic representation and a semantic interpretation, or logical form. It is the language faculty, thus understood, which determines a person's grammatical competence, i.e. linguistic competence in the narrow sense. Language is autonomous in the sense that the language faculty itself is an autonomous component of mind, in principle independent of other mental faculties. The main concern of linguistics, in the Chomskyan mould, is the study of grammatical competence, i.e. the strictly linguistic knowledge which a speaker has acquired in virtue of the properties of the language faculty.

As Chomsky is well aware, one can only maintain the thesis of the autonomy of language at the cost of extreme idealization:

The actual systems called 'languages' in ordinary discourse are undoubtedly not 'languages' in the sense of our idealizations. ... [They] might ... be 'impure' in the sense that they incorporate elements derived by faculties other than the language faculty. (Chomsky 1980: 28)

The 'impurity' of actual languages results from the interaction of the language faculty proper with at least two other components of mind, pragmatic competence and the conceptual system. The former has to do with 'knowledge of conditions and manner of appropriate use, in conformity with various purposes' (Chomsky 1980: 224). If grammatical competence characterizes the tool, pragmatic competence as it were determines how the tool is to be put to use. The conceptual system, on the other hand, has to do with matters of knowledge and belief; it permits us to 'perceive, and categorize, and symbolize, maybe even to reason in an elementary way' (Chomsky 1982: 20). It is, in Chomsky's view, the yoking of the conceptual system with the computational resources of language faculty that gives human language its rich expressive power and which makes human language qualitatively different from animal communication systems.

Where, in the Chomskyan scheme, do the facts of colour categorization that we have considered in this chapter belong, to the conceptual system, or to the language faculty? Presumably, the answer most in keeping with the doctrine of modularity is: the conceptual system. This answer implies that the meanings of colour terms in a language are not, in effect, facts of language at all, in the narrow sense. Language, as a computational system for generating sentences, has nothing to do with how a person conceptualizes his world, how he perceives it and how he interacts with it.[5] The issue is by no means so clear-cut, however. Especially in his more recent writings, Chomsky allows for the possibility that 'the state of knowledge attained may itself include

---

[5] Here, and elsewhere in the text, 'he' is used as a 3rd-person pronoun unmarked for gender.

18   *The Categorization of Colour*

some kind of reference to the social nature of language' (Chomsky 1986: 18). He has also conceded that it is not always an easy matter to distinguish between 'intrinsic meanings', i.e. meanings assigned by the operation of grammatical competence alone, and the interpretation given to sentences on the basis of beliefs about the world:

Knowledge of language is intimately related to other systems of knowledge and belief. When we identify and name an object, we tacitly assume that it will obey natural laws. It will not suddenly disappear, turn into something else, or behave in some other 'unnatural' way; if it does, we might conclude that we have misidentified and misnamed it. It is no easy matter to determine how our beliefs about the world of objects relate to the assignment of meanings to expressions. Indeed, it has often been argued that no principled distinction can be drawn. (Chomsky 1980: 225)

Chomsky (1986: 18) states that the blurring of the distinction between the purely linguistic and non-linguistic components of language knowledge does not give rise to 'conflicts of principle or practice' for proponents of the modularity hypothesis. In this book, I shall take the reverse position, i.e. that no distinction needs to be drawn between linguistic and non-linguistic knowledge. The facts of colour categorization as manifested in the meanings of colour terms are at once both facts about human cognition *and* about human language. Informing the content of the following chapters will be a conception of language as a non-autonomous system, which hypothesizes an intimate, dialectic relationship between language on the one hand and more general cognitive faculties on the other, and which places language in the context of man's interaction with his environment and with others of his species. On this view, a clean division between linguistic and non-linguistic faculties, between linguistic facts and non-linguistic facts, between a speaker's linguistic knowledge proper and his non-linguistic knowledge, between competence and per-formance, may ultimately prove to be both unrealistic and misleading.

Criticism of the autonomy hypothesis, both in its structuralist and generative–transformational guises, is not new. More than half a century ago, Malinowski wrote:

Can we treat language as an independent subject of study? Is there a legitimate science of words alone, of phonetics, grammar and lexicography? Or must all study of speaking lead to the treatment of linguistics as a branch of the general science of culture? ... The distinction between *language* and *speech*, still supported by such writers as Bühler and Gardiner, but dating back to De

Saussure and Wegener, will have to be dropped. Language cannot remain an independent and self-contained subject of study. (Malinowski 1937: 172)

The same point has been made by George Lakoff (1978: 274), who maintains that it is unrealistic to speak of a language faculty independent of 'sensory-motor and cognitive development, perception, memory, attention, social interaction, personality and other aspects of experience'.

In recent years, a number of linguists who are sceptical of the autonomy hypothesis, who believe, with Lakoff, that aspects of experience and cognition are crucially implicated in the structure and functioning of language, have given the term 'cognitive' to their approach. With the publication in 1987 of two monumental monographs—Langacker's *Foundations of Cognitive Grammar* and Lakoff's *Women, Fire, and Dangerous Things*—the approach is likely to exert an increasing influence on the direction of linguistic research for some years to come. This said, it should not be forgotten that the cognitive approach is much older than the work of the self-styled cognitive linguists. Scholars standing outside the mainstream of autonomous linguistics, whether structuralist or generative, have frequently worked on assumptions which present-day cognitive linguists would readily support. Important in this respect is Geeraerts's recent reappraisal of the now largely ignored work of the great European historical philologists (Geeraerts 1988*a*). Cognitivist assumptions also inform the work of many present-day linguists who, in spite of large differences in outlook, nevertheless search for an explanation of language structure outside a narrowly defined language faculty. Important contributions have been made by Jackendoff (1983), Hudson (1984), Wierzbicka (1985), and Givón (1979), as well as by a number of researchers into language acquisition (Slobin, Schlesinger, and others).

The aim of this book is to explore some aspects of linguistic categorization, given the assumptions of the cognitive approach. Probably little of what I will have to say can be construed as decisive evidence against the autonomy hypothesis and the modularity hypothesis to which it is related. As Botha (1987) has wittily shown, the imposing intellectual construct erected by Chomsky is in a very real sense impregnable. Evidence on how people categorize the world through language can always be shunted off to the non-language faculties of the mind or dismissed as instances of the 'impurity' of 'actual languages', with little consequence for the autonomy of the language faculty proper. Yet differences in approach are real enough. Given the theoretical question of whether language behaviour needs to be explained in terms of a purely linguistic faculty, or whether language behaviour follows from more general cognitive abilities, the natural starting-point, as Lakoff (1977) has pointed out, is surely the null hypothesis, i.e. the assumption that there are no purely linguistic abilities at all. Only when the null hypothesis has been shown to be inadequate does the need arise to posit language-specific principles. Hopefully, the following chapters will show, not perhaps that the null hypothesis is fully adequate, but that it does, at least, permit a coherent account of a wide range of linguistic phenomena.

2

The Classical Approach to Categorization

In Chapter 1 I contrasted two very different theoretical approaches to colour categorization in language. On the one hand, one can appeal to the physical continuity of colour space as evidence for the view that it is the language system itself that arbitrarily cuts up reality into discrete categories. Alternatively, one may focus on the role played by non-linguistic factors (perceptual and environmental) in the structuring of colour categories. But whichever standpoint one sympathizes with, it is clear that one can hardly base a theory of linguistic categorization on the evidence of, at most, a dozen or so lexical items in a given language. Even the most convinced structuralist must concede that a physical continuum, which contains no natural breaks for categorization (as is the case with three-dimensional colour space), is probably the exception rather than the rule. Conversely, there are going to be very few categories that have such an obviously physiological and neurological base as colours. Berlin and Kay (1969: 13) themselves observe that colour terms, and perhaps also words for some other perceptual domains like taste, smell, and noise, might be atypical of language as a whole. In the following chapters, as we extend the scope of our investigation, we shall see that many of the characteristics of colour categorization that were highlighted in Chapter 1 also, in fact, hold for the categorization of other kinds of entity, even for the categories of linguistic structure itself. Especially important, in this respect, will be the phenomenon of focal designation. One might even say that just as the structuralists saw the arbitrariness of colour terms as symptomatic of the arbitrariness of linguistic categories in general, so for the cognitive linguist colour terms are paradigmatic for the prototype structure of linguistic categories.

This, however, is to anticipate. It is necessary, before proceeding, to place the cognitive approach in its proper context. We must, in other words, begin by looking at what cognitive linguists have sometimes referred to as the 'classical theory' of categorization (e.g. Lakoff 1987:

5 and *passim*). It is, namely, with respect to the classical theory that cognitive linguistics claims to offer a viable, and descriptively more adequate alternative. A brief overview, like that attempted in this chapter, is obviously open to criticism on several points; not only does it grossly oversimplify a vast and complex subject-matter, it also exaggerates the hegemony of the classical theory. Nevertheless, a grasp of the basic principles of the classical theory, and an appreciation of the role it has played in twentieth-century linguistics, form the essential background for a proper understanding of the remainder of this book.

2.1 Aristotle

In speaking of the classical approach to categories, I am using the term 'classical' in two senses. The approach is classical in that it goes back ultimately to Greek antiquity; it is classical also in that it has dominated psychology, philosophy, and linguistics (especially autonomous linguistics, both structuralist and generative) throughout much of the twentieth century.

Let us begin with Aristotle. Aristotle, as is well known, distinguished between the essence of a thing and its accidents. The essence is that which makes a thing what it is: essence is 'all parts immanent in things which define and indicate their individuality, and whose destruction causes the destruction of the whole' (*Metaphysics* 5. 8. 3). Accidents are incidental properties, which play no part in determining what a thing is: ' "Accident" means that which applies to something and is truly stated, but neither necessarily nor usually' (5. 30. 1). To take one of Aristotle's examples: the essence of man is 'two-footed animal'. That a man might be white, or cultured, is accidental; these attributes might be true of an individual, but they are irrelevant in determining whether an entity is indeed a man. For Aristotle, both the concept MAN and the meaning of the word *man* are defined by a 'formula ("logos") of the essence' (7. 5. 7):

If 'man' has one meaning, let this be 'two-footed animal'. By 'has one meaning' I mean this: if X means 'man', then if anything is a man, its humanity will consist in being X. (4. 4. 8)

In order to be able to say that an entity 'is a man', we must know the meaning of the word *man*, which in turn means knowing the 'essence of man':

If anything can be truly said to be 'man', it must be 'two-footed animal'; for this is what 'man' is intended to mean. (4. 4. 14–15)

Let us put this into modern terminology. To say that an X is a Y, is to assign an entity X to the category Y. We do this by checking off the properties of X against the features which define the essence of the category Y; our knowledge of this set of features characterizes our knowledge of the meaning of the word Y. In the passage quoted above, Aristotle singled out two defining features of the category MAN (and hence two features in the definition of the word *man*), namely [TWO-FOOTED] and [ANIMAL]. These two features are, individually, necessary for the definition of the category (the destruction of either causes 'the destruction of the whole'); if any of the defining features is not exhibited by the entity, then the entity is not a member of the category. Jointly, the two features are sufficient; any entity which exhibits each of the defining features is *ipso facto* a member of the category. The basic assumption of the classical approach, then, is as follows:

(1) Categories are defined in terms of a conjunction of necessary and sufficient features.

Further assumptions of the Aristotelian theory follow from the law of contradiction and the law of the excluded middle (*Metaphysics* 4. 4). The law of contradiction states that a thing cannot both be and not be, it cannot both possess a feature and not possess it, it cannot both belong to a category and not belong to it. The law of the excluded middle states that a thing must either be or not be, it must either possess a feature or not possess it, it must either belong to a category or not belong to it. Hence:

(2) Features are binary

Features are a matter of all or nothing. A feature is either involved in the definition of a category, or it is not; an entity either possesses this feature, or it does not. In any given instance a feature is either present or absent, and it can take on only one of two values, either [+] or [-]. (3) and (4) follow from (2):

(3) Categories have clear boundaries

A category, once established, divides the universe into two sets of entities—those that are members of the category, and those that are not. There are no ambiguous cases, no entities which 'in a way' or 'to some extent' belong to the category, but which in another way do not.

(4) All members of a category have equal status

Any entity which exhibits all the defining features of a category is a full member of that category; any entity which does not exhibit all the defining features is not a member. There are no degrees of membership in a category, i.e. there are no entities which are better members of the category than others.

2.2 The classical approach in linguistics: phonology

One can scarcely overestimate the role that the Aristotelian[1] model of categorization has played in mainstream twentieth-century linguistics. Not least, the highly sophisticated formalism associated with much post-war work in phonology, syntax, and semantics rests ultimately on assumptions (1)–(4) of the Aristotelian model. What is more, certain influential schools within modern linguistics have elaborated the Aristotelian model by making a number of further assumptions, especially concerning the nature of the features which define the categories. It is, perhaps, in phonology that the Aristotelian model has been most fruitful. It could be argued that the fortune of the Aristotelian model in syntax and semantics is due, in no small measure, to its success in phonology. And it has been in phonology that the major innovations concerning the nature of features have been made. Let us begin, then, by reviewing some important trends in modern phonology. The following discussion will be highly schematic, and numerous points of detail, some of them highly controversial, have been passed over. I certainly do not wish to imply that all phonologists have subscribed to all the principles of categorization that are set out below. It is probably true to say, however, that most have subscribed to at least some of them.

Phonology is the study of the sound system of a language. A basic assumption of phonology has been that the stream of speech can be exhaustively segmented into a linear sequence of phones. One of its major concerns has been to set up, for a given language, a finite inventory of phonological units, i.e. phonemes, to which these phones can be assigned. Phonemes in turn are analysed into sets of features.

---

[1] The term 'Aristotelian' is being used here as a cover label for a particular model of categorization. It ignores the many subtleties of Aristotle's thought, e.g. regarding metaphor.

The phoneme /i/ of English—the sound of the words *see*, *seat*, etc.—can be described as a vowel which is articulated with a high front tongue position. /i/ may thus be represented by means of the features [VOCALIC], [HIGH], and [FRONT]. /u/ (the vowel in *boot*) contrasts with /i/ with respect to the backness of the tongue. /u/ may thus be represented by the features [VOCALIC], [HIGH], and [BACK]. Phonemes, then, are categories defined in terms of features. The features are binary, cf. (2), i.e. they can take on only one of two values, either present or absent, [+] or [−].[2] Thus a phoneme is either a vowel or not a vowel, i.e. it is either [+VOCALIC] or [−VOCALIC]; a vowel is either [+HIGH] (such as /i/ and /u/ in English) or [−HIGH] (e.g. /e/ or /a/), and so on. Chomsky and Halle explain why it is necessary that features be regarded as binary; the reader will readily appreciate the scholastic flavour of their argument:

> In view of the fact that phonological features are classificatory devices, they are binary . . . for the natural way of indicating whether or not an item belongs to a particular category is by means of binary features. (Chomsky and Halle 1968: 297)

As already mentioned, many phonologists have enriched the Aristotelian model of categories by making some further assumptions concerning features. The first of these is:

(5) Features are primitive

Phonemes, as we have seen, are decomposed into features; but features, it is assumed, are not further decomposable into more basic elements of sound structure. Features are the 'ultimate constituents', the 'atomic components' (Lass 1984: 75) of phonology.

A second, related assumption concerns the universality of features:

(6) Features are universal

By this is meant that the phoneme categories of all human languages are to be defined in terms of features drawn from a universal feature inventory. The set of universal features can be thought of as characterizing the sound-producing capabilities of man (Chomsky and Halle 1968: 297). Perhaps the best known universal feature inventory

---

[2] The reader is reminded of the highly schematic nature of this overview of classical categories in linguistic theory. Ladefoged (1975), amongst others, has proposed multivalued phonological features; multivalued semantic features have also been discussed (e.g. Leech 1981). Even so, the value assigned to a multivalued feature in the definition of a phonological or semantic category remains a matter of either–or.

is that proposed by Chomsky and Halle (1968: ch. 7), which developed the work of Jakobson, Fant, and Halle (1951). Admittedly, the choice of features to go into the universal set has been a controversial issue, and many phonologists have felt it necessary to revise existing inventories and to propose their own (e.g. Ladefoged 1975: chs. 11, 12; Lass 1984: 82ff.). Disagreement on the choice of features, however, does not hide the general consensus concerning the feasibility and desirability of the goal.

The next assumption concerns the ontological status of features:

(7) Features are abstract

Features, as we have seen, can be thought of as representing the speech-producing capabilities of man. And indeed, many of the features that have been proposed such as [VOCALIC] and [HIGH], clearly make reference to aspects of phonation and articulation. Nevertheless, the features do not characterize the observable facts of speech, i.e. its generation in the human vocal apparatus, its acoustic properties, and its perception by the auditory system.

An example will perhaps elucidate this somewhat enigmatic state of affairs. The phonemes /f/ and /v/ in English contrast in virtue of the fact that the former is [-VOICE] and the latter is [+VOICE]. The feature [VOICE] can be given a precise physical characterization, in terms of the quasi-periodic vibration of the vocal cords, which in turn results in a quasi-periodic wave form. Consider, now, the English words *leaf* and *leave*. We would want to say that, phonologically, the contrast between the words resides in the voicing contrast of the final segment: /lif/ vs. /liv/. If, however, we examine the details of articulation of these two words, we find that while the /f/ of *leaf* is indeed voiceless, the so-called voiced /v/ is usually articulated with only initial voicing, or even with no voicing at all. At the articulatory level, then, voicing is not essential for categorization as /v/. Rather, the contrast between *leaf* and *leave* is realized in a number of ways. The vowel in *leave* is perceptibly longer than in *leaf*; the /v/ might well be shorter, and is often associated with less acoustic energy than /f/. (If *leaf* and *leave* are whispered—i.e. they are spoken voiceless throughout—the words can still be distinguished, very largely on the basis of vowel length and consonant intensity.) In spite of the phonetic facts, we would still wish to claim that the essence (to use Aristotle's term) of the *leaf–leave* contrast has to do with the voicing of the final consonant. The voicing feature is abstract precisely in the sense that voicing is not directly observable in the process of articulation or in the acoustic signal. Segment length and consonant intensity—even though these might be important perceptual cues for the discrimination of *leaf* and *leave*— are merely accidental reflexes of the abstract voicing contrast.

But, one might ask, why represent the contrast between *leaf* and *leave* in terms of an abstract feature? Why not claim that the real, essential difference lies in observable, concrete phenomena such as vowel length, e.g. that the vowel in *leaf* is [−LONG] and that in *leave* [+LONG], and that the voicing of the following consonant is an optional, accidental property? If we were to restrict our attention to these two words only, ignoring their status as words of English, there would indeed be no grounds for preferring the abstract account. But once we study the *leaf–leave* contrast within the English language as a whole, the picture changes considerably. The abstract account is preferred, because it permits the linguist to make economical statements about relations between categories within the language system. We already need the /f/–/v/ contrast—which in these cases is really one of voicing, and not of vowel length—to describe the difference between *fairy* and *vary*, *ferry* and *very*, and so on. Precisely the same contrast, i.e. presence or absence of voice, is needed to describe other contrasts, such as *Sue–zoo*, *thigh–thy*, and so on. These contrasts can be represented as proportional relations: /f/ is to /v/ as /s/ is to /z/; *ferry* is to *very* as *Sue* is to *zoo*; *fairy* is to *vary* as *leaf* is to *leave*. The proportional relations do not involve vowel length. Contrasts of vowel length can be described more economically, more elegantly, as a reflex of consonant voicing.

Arguments like those sketched out above lead inevitably to an autonomous conception of phonology. Saussure himself had claimed that the material element of language, i.e. sound, is external to the language system: '[le son] n'est pour [la langue] qu'une chose secondaire, une matière qu'elle met en œuvre' (Saussure 1964: 164). Phonemes are relational entities, whereby it is the relations between the categories, rather than the physical properties of the members of the categories, which establish the value of any one category within the system. The far-reaching implications of Saussure's approach were first worked out by Trubetzkoy and the Prague phonologists of the 1930s (Trubetzkoy 1939), and they have informed subsequent structuralist and generative treatments of phonology. Symptomatic is the fact that phonetics—the study of observable aspects of speech—has generally tended to be regarded more as a sub-branch of physiology, acoustics, and audiology, than as a proper branch of linguistics. Linguistics proper is concerned with the relations between categories, and the abstract features by means of which these relations can be defined. Autonomous phonology, of course, takes its place within the broader thesis of the autonomy of language. Just as autonomous linguistics distinguishes between a speaker's purely linguistic knowledge, determined by the language faculty, and his non-linguistic knowledge, derived from pragmatic competence and the conceptual system, so autonomous phonology splits off the act of speech as an articulatory, acoustic, and perceptual event from the abstract linguistic system which is claimed to underlie the physical data.

Abstract accounts of sound systems are not subject to empirical validation, in any normal sense of the term. The only 'empirical' evidence in their favour is the fact that they seem to work, that is to say, they make possible elegant, economical accounts of a wide range of diverse phenomena. Let us look at a couple of simple examples. Features not only define phonemes and the relations between phonemes. Either singly or in combination, features also define sets of phonemes. These sets are sometimes known as natural classes. The feature [VOICE], for example, defines the natural class of all the voiced phonemes of a language, such as /i/, /u/, /v/, /b/, etc.; [VOICE] and [CONSONANTAL] together define the natural class of all voiced consonants, and so on. A great deal of modern phonology has been concerned with the description of sound systems in terms of rules operating on natural classes of segments. One such rule we have already alluded to—i.e. the lengthening of a vowel before a voiced consonant. Another example concerns plural formation. Regular plurals in English are formed by adding either /s/ or /z/ (or, in a special subclass of cases, /əz/) to the noun stem. /əz/ is added if the final stem consonant belongs to the natural class defined by the features [CORONAL] (roughly, coronal sounds are those produced by a constriction located between the dental and palato-alveolar region of the mouth) and [STRIDENT] (those sounds exhibiting high frequency noise), i.e. /s, z, ʃ, ʒ, tʃ, dʒ/. Otherwise, /s/ is added if the noun ends in a [-VOICE] segment, while /z/ is added if the final segment is [+VOICE]. Without natural classes and the features which define them, a process like plural formation could only be described in very cumbersome and *ad hoc* terms. Feature-based rules have covered a wide range of phenomena—not only morphological processes of inflection and derivation, but also things like historical sound change, slips of the tongue, misarticulations by the speech impaired, and language acquisition by the child and the second language learner.[3]

Phonological theory, then, has enriched the classical model of categories by introducing the feature which is not only binary, but also primitive, universal, and abstract. There is a further, and rather more controversial characteristic, associated especially with the generative–transformational tradition:

(8) Features are innate

This property follows logically from the preceding ones. If features are abstract (i.e. they bear only an indirect relationship to the physical facts of speech), and at the same time universal (i.e. each language selects from a fixed finite inventory), and if, furthermore, the linguist attributes some kind of psychological reality to his abstractions (i.e. the abstract account is not just an exercise in formal elegance, but aims to describe, in some sense, aspects of a speaker's knowledge of his language), the problem arises how a child acquiring his mother tongue can come to gain knowledge of the set of features peculiar to his language. He cannot rely only on the physical data available to him— the abstract account goes beyond the physical data. The only logically acceptable solution is to posit a genetically inherited knowledge of the universal inventory.

2.3 The classical approach in semantics

In dealing with syntactic and semantic categories, many linguists have adopted a feature approach which parallels in many respects the assumptions, and even the notation and terminology, of the phonologists. (For instance, a notational convention, taken over from phonology, is the practice of writing features in small capitals and enclosing them between square brackets.) At work here is what has been called, in a different context, the 'structural analogy assumption':

This is simply the assumption, familiar from much post-Saussurian work, that we should expect that the same structural properties recur at different levels. Structural properties which are postulated as being unique to a particular level are unexpected and suspicious if unsupported by firm evidence of their unique appropriateness in that particular instance. (Anderson and Durand 1986: 3)

[3] For an overview, see any good textbook on phonology, e.g. Lass (1984), esp. chs. 8, 9, and 13.

If the categories of phonology can be represented by features which are binary, primitive, universal, abstract, and innate, then it is only to be expected that the categories of syntax (e.g. lexical categories like NOUN, VERB, ADJECTIVE) and semantics (i.e. in the main, word meanings) can also be represented by features which are likewise binary, primitive, universal, abstract, and innate. Indeed, it is not unusual for a linguist to model a feature approach in syntax and semantics explicitly on principles already worked out in phonology. Characteristically, Chomsky (1965: 81) introduces his account of syntactic features by a brief review of the role of features in phonology.

We shall postpone to later chapters a discussion of syntax, and focus here on semantic categories, i.e. on word meanings. An analysis of semantic categories on lines already familiar to us from phonology has been pursued within the transformational–generative paradigm by scholars such as Katz (e.g. Katz and Fodor 1963; Katz and Postal 1964) and Bierwisch (1967, 1970); also (under the name 'componential analysis') by non-generativists such as Nida (1975) and Leech (1981). Let us illustrate with a well-known example—the word *bachelor* in the sense "man who has never married". Katz and Postal (1964: 13 f.) represent the meaning of this word in terms of four semantic features,[4] namely [HUMAN], [MALE], [ADULT], and [NEVER MARRIED]. These four features together define the essence of bachelorhood. In line with (1), any entity in the world which exhibits these four features can be correctly designated by the word *bachelor*; if any (or all) of the four features is missing, or has the wrong value—if an entity is [FEMALE] or [-ADULT]—then the entity does not qualify for bachelorhood.

The 'empirical' justification of a feature approach to semantic categories appeals essentially to the same kinds of argument that were used in phonology, namely, the fact that features enable the linguist to make economical and insightful statements about the structure of a language. There are three ways in which a feature approach pays off. Firstly, one is able to state the proportional relations which exist within the lexicon. The words *bachelor* and *spinster* are obviously related, just as, in a different way, the phonemes /f/ and /v/ are related. Furthermore, the relationship between *bachelor* and *spinster*

---

[4] There is some disagreement in the literature on whether a feature like [HUMAN] is to be regarded as syntactic or semantic. In the following discussion, I follow Katz and Postal in treating it as a semantic feature.

parallels the way the other pairs of words are related, e.g. *boy* and *girl*, *husband* and *wife*, *uncle* and *aunt*, and so on. These word pairs contrast in that one member of the pair has the feature [MALE], while the other is [FEMALE]. Otherwise, the feature specifications for the two words are identical. With a feature analysis we can capture other kinds of relations between words, e.g. relations of inclusion and hyponymy. The meaning of the word *man*, with the features [HUMAN], [ADULT], and [MALE], is included in the meaning of *bachelor*. *Man* is superordinate to *bachelor*, *bachelor* is a hyponym, i.e. is subordinate to *man*.

The second advantage is that features make it possible to define natural classes of items. Thus [HUMAN] defines the class of human nouns, while [-ANIMATE] defines the class of inanimate nouns. Classes such as these are involved in the statement of selection restrictions, i.e. restrictions on the way words may be combined together into phrases. Not any noun, for instance, can be made the subject (or object) of a given verb. The semantic specification of a verb needs to state the class of nouns which may function as its subject. We cannot say *Sincerity admires John*, since *admire* requires as its subject a noun which is [+HUMAN]. Similarly, for adjective–noun combinations, there must be a congruence between the feature specifications of the words in the construction. We cannot speak of an *infant bachelor*, since *infant*, with the feature [-ADULT], contradicts *bachelor*, which has the feature [+ADULT].

A third justification of features is that they throw light on certain kinds of sentence meaning, and on the meaning relationships that exist among sentences. To consider the first issue. Of the three sentences

(9) (a) This man is a bachelor
   (b) This bachelor is a man
   (c) This bachelor is my sister

the first is said to be synthetic, the second analytic, while the third is contradictory. The truth of (9) (a) requires verification from facts holding in the world, i.e. the sentence is true just in case the referent of *this man* is indeed a bachelor. An analytic sentence like (9) (b), on the other hand, is true independent of any states of affairs in the world; its truth is guaranteed by the meanings of the words *bachelor* and *man*. Similarly, (9) (c) is necessarily false, not because of any facts in the world, but because of the incompatibility of the feature [FEMALE] of *sister* and [MALE] of *bachelor*. Furthermore, features make it possible to account for certain kinds of semantic relationship between sentences, e.g. the relationship of entailment in (10) (*a*), of mutual entailment (or synonymy) in (10) (*b*), and of contradiction in (10) (*c*):

(10) (*a*) John is a bachelor
    entails
    John is a man
  (*b*) John is a bachelor
    entails and *is entailed by* (i.e. *is synonymous with*)
    John is a man who has never married
  (*c*) John is a bachelor
    contradicts
    John is married

Other aspects of sentence meaning can be explained with the help of features. Thus the interplay of feature specifications can help account for the effects of conjoining sentences with *because* and *but*:

(11) (*a*) This man can't be a bachelor, because he's been married before
  (*b*) ?This man is a bachelor, but he's never been married before

Kempson (1977: 3 f.) has written that an essential requirement of an adequate semantic theory is that it should provide general principles by which to account for (*a*) relationships between word meanings, i.e. relationships of synonymy, hyponymy, contradiction, and (*b*) relationships between sentence meanings, e.g. entailment, inclusion, contradiction, etc. To its adherents, it looked as if a feature theory of meaning was able to do both these things. (We should note, however, that the data on which feature semanticists worked rarely surpassed the *bachelor* examples in sophistication.) But we can push the analogy with phonological features even further. Just as phonological features have been regarded as the minimal particles of phonology, so it has been claimed that semantic features are the ultimate, atomic constituents of which word meanings are composed, cf. (5). Katz and Postal state that a 'full analysis' of the meaning of a word involves decomposing the meaning 'into its most elementary components' (1964: 13). Bierwisch expresses a similar view, adding that the elementary components have the status of universals, cf. (6), i.e. word meanings in a particular language are composed of 'basic elements, that are true candidates for the universal set of semantic markers'[5] (Bierwisch 1967: 35). Chomsky, too, has made claims for the universality of semantic features. Just as the set of universal phonological features defines the sound-producing capabilities of man, so the set of universal semantic features defines his cognitive capabilities:

It is important to determine the universal, language-independent constraints on semantic features—in traditional terms, the system of possible concepts. The very notion 'lexical entry' presupposes some sort of fixed, universal vocabulary in terms of which these objects are characterized, just as the notion 'phonetic representation' presupposes some sort of universal phonetic theory. It is surely our ignorance of the relevant psychological and physiological facts that makes possible the widely held belief that there is little or no a priori structure to the system of 'attainable concepts'. (Chomsky 1965: 160)

The postulation of universal semantic primitives is not, of course, an innovation of generative linguists. Leibniz, in the seventeenth century, set himself the task of discovering the 'alphabet of human thought'—a set of basic conceptual building blocks, not susceptible to further decomposition, whose combination might underlie all possible concepts in a language (cf. Wierzbicka 1980b: 4). Some present-day linguists working outside the generative paradigm, including Wierzbicka herself, have subscribed to a similar programme. But while the parallels between phonological and semantic features are compelling, there is a fairly obvious, qualitative difference between the alleged universal phonological primitives and the putative 'building blocks of human thought'. In analysing the sound system of a language, the number of phoneme categories that need to be identified is quite small (forty-five or so in English, depending on the dialect analysed, and on one's method of analysis); the number of universal phonological features that are required is also quite manageable (about twenty are suggested by Chomsky and Halle). In contrast, the number of semantic categories in any one language is not only immense, it is also (as shown by the constant coining of new terms) extendible, and it would seem at first sight unrealistic to expect to be able to reduce *all* possible word meanings in *all* human languages to a manageable, finite set of universal primitives.

Katz and Postal (1964: 14) deal with this problem by recognizing two kinds of semantic feature, which they call markers and

---

[5] In speaking of semantic markers, Bierwisch is following Katz, who recognized two kinds of semantic feature, markers and distinguishers. See below.

distinguishers. Markers, like [HUMAN] and [MALE], 'express general semantic properties'. They enter into the analysis of very many items in the vocabulary, and are involved in the statement of syntactic rules and of selection restrictions. Markers, presumably, are candidates for the set of universal primitives. Distinguishers, on the other hand, represent 'what is idiosyncratic about the meaning of a lexical item'. For instance, a second meaning of *bachelor* (as in *bachelor of arts*), is characterized by the marker [HUMAN] and the distinguisher [having the academic degree conferred for completing the first four years of college]. The latter is the kind of meaning component which is not exploited systematically in the language. In no way can it be regarded as primitive. Neither can it reasonably be regarded as universal, since it presupposes a very specific cultural institution (i.e. places of higher education and their system of conferring degrees). (The same, incidentally, applies to [NEVER MARRIED]—in Katz and Postal (1964) a marker, not as a distinguisher—since this feature, too, presupposes a cultural institution, namely marriage.)

To complete the analogy between semantic and phonological features, we need to consider the abstractness and innateness of semantic features, cf. (7) and (8). Just as a phonological feature like [VOICE] is not directly manifested in the periodic vibration of the vocal cords, so, according to some, a semantic feature like [ADULT] is not to be equated with the meaning of the word *adult*, or with any of the attributes of adulthood shared by adults in the real world. Bierwisch postulates that a person's mental representation of objects and situations in the world is extraneous to the semantic structure of his language. While some 'mechanism of reference' must obviously relate word and sentence meaning to the world, the semantic features characterizing word and sentence meaning do not stand for, and are not learnable from, any 'physical properties and relations outside the human organism' (Bierwisch 1970: 181). The innateness of semantic features follows logically from this view. If features are abstract, i.e. they are not derivable from acquaintance with the world, how can the child language-learner come to have knowledge of the features defining the words of his language? For language acquisition to be possible at all, Bierwisch argues, it is necessary to assume that knowledge of the set of universal features is genetically inherited.

Bierwisch embraces a fairly extreme version of the autonomy semantics hypothesis. Probably adherents of the view that word and sentence meanings can be represented by semantic features which are abstract, primitive, universal, and innate, have never constituted more than a small minority, even within the generative community. Certainly many linguists, including Lyons (1977: 317ff.), Kempson (1977: 18ff.), and Pulman (1983: 29ff.), have been highly critical. Yet the rejection of the semantic feature as an abstract universal primitive does not necessarily entail a rejection of the semantic autonomy hypothesis. What one sees, in the case of Lyons, for instance, is a reinforcement of the structuralist view of meaning as a set of relations internal to the language system. A speaker's knowledge of the world remains a factor external to the system. Developing the distinction drawn by Gottlob Frege, Lyons differentiates between the sense of a linguistic expression and its reference. Reference has to do with the designation of entities in the world. Sense, on the other hand, is the abstract linguistic meaning. For Lyons, the sense of a word is to be equated with 'the set of relations [i.e. synonymy, hyponymy, implication, incompatibility, etc.: J. T.] which hold between the item in question and other items in the same lexical system' (1968: 443). Sense is independent of any properties of things outside the language system itself: 'Since sense is to be defined in terms of relationships which hold between vocabulary-items, it carries with it no presuppositions about the existence of objects and properties outside the vocabulary of the language in question' (Lyons 1968: 427). The same, eminently Saussurian line has been taken by Nida:

A meaning [i.e. 'sense', as used by Frege and Lyons: J. T.] is not a thing in itself, but only a set of contrastive relations. ... There is no way to determine a meaning apart from comparisons and contrasts with other meanings within the same semantic area. (Nida 1975: 151).

—and, more recently, although with different emphasis, by Cruse:

We can picture the meaning of a word as a pattern of affinities and disaffinities with all the other words in the language with which it is capable of contrasting [*sic*[6]] semantic relations in grammatical contexts. Affinities are of two kinds, syntagmatic and paradigmatic. A syntagmatic affinity is established by a capacity for normal association in an utterance: there is a syntagmatic affinity, for instance, between *dog* and *barked*, since *The dog barked* is normal ... A syntagmatic disaffinity is revealed by a syntagmatic abnormality that does not infringe grammatical constraints, as in *?The lions are chirruping*. Paradigmatically, a semantic affinity between two grammatically identical words is

---

[6] Presumably, *contracting* is meant.

the greater the more congruent their patterns of syntagmatic normality. So, for instance, *dog* and *cat* share far more normal and abnormal contexts than, say, *dog* and *lamp-post*. (Cruse 1986: 16)

Cruse's monograph is especially worthy of attention, since it is possible to detect in this work symptoms of the disintegration of the classical theory. Cruse's approach to word meaning, as the above quotation shows, is explicitly structuralist. It is also componential. Yet the components which Cruse posits are not the abstract primitives of the classical theory. The components of word meaning are, quite simply, the meanings of other words. Rather than say that [ANIMAL] is a component feature of the meaning of *dog*, Cruse claims merely that the meaning of the word *animal* is 'included', in some not clearly defined sense, in the meaning of the word *dog*. The abandonment of the abstractness dogma opens the way to the incorporation of encyclo-paedic knowledge into word definitions. Cruse, in fact, explicitly states that 'any attempt to draw a line between the meaning of a word and "encyclopaedic" facts concerning the extra-linguistic referents of the word would be quite arbitrary' (1986: 19). A further, highly significant modification of the classical theory lies in the fact that for Cruse components of word meanings do not have to have the status of neces-sary and sufficient conditions. Some components are indeed criterial; being an animal is essential to the meaning of *dog*. Other components are excluded; being a cat, for instance, is an excluded component of *dog*. Between these two extremes, Cruse recognizes a continuum in the manner in which the meaning of one expression participates in the meaning of another. Some components, while not criterial, are nevertheless expected. Being able to bark is one such component of *dog*. (Being unable to bark is not sufficient reason to exclude categorization as a dog.) Other components, while not excluded, are unexpected, e.g. being able to sing. (Again, ability to sing does not exclude categorization as a dog; we might be dealing with a rather unusual dog, or with a rather degraded form of singing.) Some components, on the other hand, are merely possible. Dogs come in a range of colours; being brown is a possible component of *dog*, neither criterial nor excluded, expected nor unexpected.

We see, then, that there are various angles from which the classical theory of categorization, and its elaborations, may be queried. Do all members of a category necessarily share a set of criterial properties? Are word meanings reducible to sets of primitive semantic components? Is it legitimate to make a distinction between a person's linguistic and non-linguistic knowledge? Can one ever know the meaning of a word independently of one's acquaintance with the relevant facts of the world? These are amongst the questions we shall be addressing in the following chapters.

3

Prototype Categories: I

THE past few years have seen considerable debate, especially within cognitive psychology, on the nature and structure of categories. The debate was triggered by an increasing body of empirical evidence which seriously challenged the foundations of the classical, Aristotelian theory of categorization that we reviewed in Chapter 2 (see e.g. Smith and Medin 1981). The purpose of this chapter is to review some of the better known empirical findings which point to the need for a non-Aristotelian theory of categorization. We will also consider, in a preliminary fashion, the potential relevance of these findings to linguistic inquiry.

3.1 Wittgenstein

Many of the inadequacies of the classical theory of categorization that we will review in this chapter were anticipated by Ludwig Wittgenstein in a highly significant passage in the *Philosophical Investigations* (completed by 1945). Wittgenstein addressed the question of how to define the word *Spiel* "game". He notes, first of all, that the various members of the category GAME do not share a set of common properties on whose basis games can be clearly distinguished from non-games. The boundary of the category is fuzzy—a fact which does not, however, detract from the category's communicative usefulness. Thus, contrary to the expectations of the classical theory, the category is not structured in terms of shared criterial features, but rather by a criss-crossing network of similarities. There are indeed attributes typically associated with the category. Some members share some of these attributes, other members share other attributes. Yet there are no attributes common to all the members, and to them alone. It may even be the case that some members have practically nothing in common with others.

This state of affairs is by no means peculiar to the lexical item *game*. Arguably, the meaning of the vast majority of words in the lexicon are structured in a similar way. (For a further example, the reader is referred to the—in style and spirit very Wittgensteinian—account of the meaning of *pin* in Matthews 1979: 70ff.) Wittgenstein used the metaphor of a family resemblance to describe the structure of GAME. It is worth quoting the passage at length.

Consider for example the proceedings that we call 'games'. I mean board-games, card-games, ball-games, Olympic games, and so on. What is common to them all?—Don't say: 'There *must* be something common, or they would not be called "games"'—but *look and see* whether there is anything common to all.—For if you look at them you will not see something that is common to *all*, but similarities, relationships, and a whole series of them at that. To repeat: don't think, but look!—For example at board-games, with their multifarious relationships. Now pass to card-games; here you find many correspondences with the first group, but many common features drop out, and others appear. When we pass next to ball-games, much that is common is retained, but much is lost.—Are they all 'amusing'? Compare chess with noughts and crosses. Or is there always winning and losing, or competition between players? Think of patience. In ball games there is winning and losing; but when a child throws his ball at the wall and catches it again, this feature has disappeared. Look at the parts played by skill and luck; and at the difference between skill in chess and skill in tennis. Think now of games like ring-a-ring-a-roses; here is the element of amusement, but how many other characteristic features have disappeared! And we can go through the many, many other groups of games in the same way; we see how similarities crop up and disappear.

And the result of this examination is: we see a complicated network of similarities overlapping and criss-crossing: sometimes overall similarities, sometimes similarities of detail.

I can think of no better expression to characterise these similarities than 'family resemblances'; for the various resemblances between members of a family: build, features, colour of eyes, gait, temperament, etc. etc. overlap and criss-cross in the same way.—And I shall say: 'games' form a family. . . .

[H]ow is the concept of a game bounded? What still counts as a game and what no longer does? Can you give the boundary? No. You can *draw* one; for none has so far been drawn. (But that never troubled you before when you used the word 'game'.) (Wittgenstein 1978: 31–3)

In a subsequent passage, Wittgenstein discusses how the category GAME might be learnt. Since GAME is not structured according to classical principles, the category cannot be learnt as a conjunction of those criterial features which uniquely distinguish games from non-games. Rather, the category has to be learnt on the basis of exemplars:

How should we explain to someone what a game is? I imagine that we should describe *games* to him, and we might add: 'This *and similar things* are called "games"'. (Wittgenstein 1978: 33)

Unfortunately, Wittgenstein says nothing about the choice of exemplars—although one would presumably not teach the category by pointing only to the borderline instances. It was the task of others to spell out in detail the notion of a central, or 'prototypical' member of a category.

3.2 Prototypes: an alternative to the classical theory

Wittgenstein's insight that the classical theory fails to predict the referential range of at least some words in everyday use received empirical confirmation in a series of experiments reported in Labov (1973). Labov studied the linguistic categorization of household receptacles like cups, mugs, bowls, and vases. His procedure was simple. Line drawings were prepared of receptacles of different shapes. These were shown to subjects, who were asked to name the depicted objects. A receptacle with a circular horizontal cross-sectional area, tapering towards the bottom, whose maximum width was equal to the depth, and which was provided with a handle, was unanimously called a cup. As the ratio of width to depth increased, more and more subjects called the object a bowl. Contrary to the expectations of classical theory, there was no clear dividing line between CUP and BOWL; rather, the one category merged gradually into the other. Removing the handle from the receptacles lowered the tendency for the depicted objects to be designated as cups, but again the effect was not clear-cut. Categorization was also affected by asking subjects to imagine the receptacles filled with different kinds of things. If filled with hot coffee, cup-responses increased, while bowl-judgements increased if the receptacles were thought of as containing mashed potatoes. Similar effects were found if the depth, rather than the width, was increased. In this case, cup-responses gradually gave way to categorization as vase. If the receptacles were of a cylindrical rather than a tapering shape, they tended to be categorized as mugs.

There are several important conclusions that can be drawn from Labov's beautifully simple experiment. I will assume in the following discussion that entities are categorized on the basis of their attributes.[1]

---

[1] From now on I shall restrict the term 'feature' for the abstract features of the

These attributes are not the binary constructs of the classical approach. Consider the ratio of width to depth. This ratio is a continuous variable. Labov's results show that associated with each of the categories CUP, BOWL, VASE, etc., there is a certain optimum value, or range of values, for the width–depth ratio. In categorizing an entity, it is not a question of ascertaining whether the entity possesses this attribute or not, but how closely the dimensions of the entity approximate to the optimum dimensions. Even the presence or absence of a handle is not, strictly speaking, a matter of either–or. One can easily imagine a range of possibilities intermediate between a full-fledged handle and a slight protuberance on the side of the receptacle. Secondly, attributes, far from being the abstract entities of autonomous linguistics, are properties of real-world entities which are readily accessible (how could it be otherwise?) to competent users of a language in virtue of their acquaintance with the world around them. The attributes of cups, bowls, and vases include the characteristic shape, size, and material of the receptacle. Attributes, though, are not limited to tangible properties. Labov showed that one and the same receptacle might be categorized differently according to whether it is used for drinking coffee or for eating mashed potatoes. In other words, attributes might sometimes be functional (they concern the use to which an object is put) or interactional (they concern the way people handle the object). Ultimately, the attributes have to do, not with inherent properties of the object itself, but with the role of the object within a particular culture, a point stressed by Wierzbicka (1985) in her commentary on Labov's work. As such, the attributes cannot reasonably be regarded as semantic primitives. Finally, it emerges very clearly from Labov's experiment that no one single attribute is essential for distinguishing the one category from the other. Presence of a handle, or function in the drinking of coffee, merely raises the probability that an entity will be categorized as a cup. Although cups typically have handles and are typically used for drinking coffee, presence of a handle and use in drinking coffee are not defining features of CUP. There are, of course, some attributes which *are* shared by all cups. For example, all cups are (potential) containers. Being a container, however, cannot be a defining feature of CUP. Many non-cups are also containers.

classical approach, reserving 'attribute' for alternative, non-classical theories of categorization. A more precise explication of attribute will be given in s. 4.1.

What is it, then, that makes a cup a cup, and not a bowl or a vase? What, in Aristotelian terms, is the 'essence of cup'? This question is tantalizingly difficult to answer, at least in Aristotelian terms. At the same time, we have no difficulty visualizing, or recognizing, a typical cup. Even though CUP might merge with categories like BOWL and VASE, there are certain receptacles that are unanimously and uncontroversially described as cups. The analogy with colour categories will be obvious. Just as certain regions of the colour spectrum count as good, even as optimal examples of RED, YELLOW, and so on, so too household receptacles appear to be categorized around good, clear exemplars of CUP, BOWL, etc. These 'prototypes' serve as reference points for the categorization of non-so-clear instances. Prototypes contain a richness of sometimes culturally bound detail which, on a strictly Aristotelian view, would have to be regarded as accidental. Thus, the prototypical cup (in Western societies) has a handle, it is made of porcelain, it comes with a saucer; it has a certain overall shape and a typical size; cups are used for drinking hot tea or coffee, and you usually buy them in sets of six. None of these attributes is essential for membership in the category. A plastic container, with no handle and without a saucer, such as might be delivered from a coffee vending machine, is still a cup, albeit not a typical one.

Labov's experimental procedure, whereby subjects are asked to name line drawings of artefacts, has been employed by the anthropologist Willett Kempton (1981), with very similar results. The main body of Kempton's study was concerned with the categorization of ceramic vessels in rural varieties of Mexican Spanish. It was found that no one category could be defined in terms of a list of criterial, distinctive features. Rather, associated with terms like *jarro*, *jarra*, *olla*, *cazuela* was a prototype representation of a vessel (or a small range of vessels) of a specific shape, with specific characteristics (e.g. with or without a handle or spout), and which fulfilled certain functions (e.g. cooking, drinking, storage, or pouring). Each term was also used to refer to a wide range of non-prototypical instances, and the boundaries between the categories were fuzzy in the extreme. Perhaps the most extensive and systematic empirical exploration of prototypes, however, has been pursued by the psychologist, Eleanor Rosch. We have already encountered Rosch's work on colour categorization in Chapter 1. Rosch claimed that colour terms acquire their denotational range, not through an arbitrary setting of category boundaries, but by generalization from focal (i.e. prototypical) exemplars. Subsequent research indicated that many other natural categories,[2] like FURNITURE and BIRD, are structured in a similar way.

Rosch (1973*b*, 1975*b*) investigated the structure of natural categories by asking subjects to judge to what extent certain kinds of entity could be regarded as good examples of a category. Rosch (1975*b*) deals with the categories FURNITURE, FRUIT, VEHICLE, WEAPON, VEGETABLE, TOOL, BIRD, SPORT, TOY, and CLOTHING. Table 3.1 reproduces the results from some 200 American college students who were asked to judge to what extent each of the sixty household items could be regarded as a good example of the category FURNITURE. Subjects responded using a 7-point scale ranging from 1 (= very good example), through 4 (= moderately good example), to 7 (= very bad example, or not an example at all). Table 3.1 lists the items according to decreasing degree of membership in the category.

Rosch reports that statistically the order in which the items are listed in Table 3.1 is highly reliable. There was, namely, a very high degree of agreement amongst the 200 subjects, particularly with regard to the items showing a higher degree of membership in the category. Even different subgroups of subjects, e.g. those who had lived predominantly on the east coast of the United States, and those who came from the west, gave comparable responses. Quite obviously, subjects had found the task a meaningful one, and had not been putting random crosses on their answer sheets. This fact alone constitutes a highly significant finding. On the strictly classical view, it simply makes no sense to ask 'to what extent' a thing belongs to a category—either it belongs, or it does not belong. Think, for example, of phonology, a branch of linguistics thoroughly permeated by Aristotelian principles. Does it make sense to ask whether /ɑ/ is a better vowel than /i/? (We shall see in Chapter 12 that the question does in fact make sense.) Rosch showed that degree of membership in a category, far from being meaningless, is in fact a psychologically very real notion.

A second important aspect of Rosch's results is that similar kinds of prototype effect showed up on each of the ten categories investigated. Prototype effects, that is, were insensitive to the distinction sometimes made between natural kind categories and nominal kind categories.[3] A

---

[2] By natural categories Rosch means 'concepts designatable by words in natural languages' (Rosch 1975*b*: 193). Natural categories are opposed to the artificial categories, e.g. configurations of dots or sequences of letters and numbers, that are frequently used by psychologists in studies of learning and concept formation.

[3] Nominal kinds and natural kinds are discussed in Pulman (1983: ch. 6).

TABLE 3.1 *Goodness-of-example ratings for sixty members of the category* FURNITURE

Member	Rank	Specific score	Member	Rank	Specific score
chair	1.5	1.04	lamp	31	2.94
sofa	1.5	1.04	stool	32	3.13
couch	3.5	1.10	hassock	33	3.43
table	3.5	1.10	drawers	34	3.63
easy chair	5	1.33	piano	35	3.64
dresser	6.5	1.37	cushion	36	3.70
rocking chair	6.5	1.37	magazine rack	37	4.14
coffee table	8	1.38	hi-fi	38	4.25
rocker	9	1.42	cupboard	39	4.27
love seat	10	1.44	stereo	40	4.32
chest of drawers	11	1.48	mirror	41	4.39
desk	12	1.54	television	42	4.41
bed	13	1.58	bar	43	4.46
bureau	14	1.59	shelf	44	4.52
davenport	15.5	1.61	rug	45	5.00
end table	15.5	1.61	pillow	46	5.03
divan	17	1.70	wastebasket	47	5.34
night table	18	1.83	radio	48	5.37
chest	19	1.98	sewing machine	49	5.39
cedar chest	20	2.11	stove	50	5.40
vanity	21	2.13	counter	51	5.44
bookcase	22	2.15	clock	52	5.48
lounge	23	2.17	drapes	53	5.67
chaise longue	24	2.26	refrigerator	54	5.70
ottoman	25	2.43	picture	55	5.75
footstool	26	2.45	closet	56	5.95
cabinet	27	2.49	vase	57	6.23
china closet	28	2.59	ashtray	58	6.35
bench	29	2.77	fan	59	6.49
buffet	30	2.89	telephone	60	6.68

Source: Rosch 1975*b*: 229. Copyright 1975 by the American Psychological Association. Reprinted by permission of the author.

natural kind term like *bird* is presumed to correspond to some real phenomenon in the world, whose inner constitution determines the range of things in the category. This being the case, natural kind categories might be expected to have clear boundaries, and not to display degrees of category membership. On the other hand, nominal kind terms, like *toy* and *vehicle*, are said to be, in part at least, definable in analytic terms. Thus a toy is something that children play with, a vehicle is a means of locomotion, etc. If analytic statements specify attributes which are necessary (if not perhaps sufficient) for membership in the category, then nominal kind terms might also be presumed to have clear boundaries and either–or membership. Neither of these expectations is valid.

In addition to establishing degree of category membership as a psychologically valid notion, Rosch also showed degree of category membership to be a relevant variable in a number of experimental paradigms. For instance, degree of membership affects verification time for statements of the kind 'An X is a Y'. It takes less time to verify that a robin (a highly central member of the category) is a bird than to verify that a duck is a bird (Rosch 1973*b*).[4] The effect is more pronounced with child subjects than with adults, suggesting that children have not fully assimilated the more marginal instances to the categories. Degree of membership also interacts with the effect of priming. Two words are shown on a screen, and the subject must indicate, as rapidly as possible, whether the two words are the same or different. The presentation of the two words is preceded by the presentation of a superordinate category name. For example, the words *chair–chair* might be preceded by *furniture*. If the stimulus words are good examples of the category, then priming with the category name results in faster response times. If the words are poor examples of the category (e.g. *stove* as an example of *furniture*), then response time is slower. This suggests that the category name activates the names of more prototypical members of the category, and deactivates the more marginal members (Rosch 1975*b*). Particularly striking, also, is the correlation between degree of category member-ship, and the frequency and order with which category members are named (Rosch 1973*b*). If people are asked to name exemplars of a category, they tend to mention the more prototypical members first.

---

[4] Rosch's experiments were performed with American subjects. British readers are reminded that in American English, *robin* refers to a rather larger bird than the British English word.

Data on the naming of exemplars had been obtained by Battig and Montague (1969) for fifty-six categories. When asked to list members of the categories FURNITURE, WEAPON, BIRD, and SPORT, Battig and Montague's subjects named in first place CHAIR, GUN, ROBIN, and FOOTBALL more frequently than other members. These are precisely the members to which Rosch's subjects assigned the highest degree of membership in the respective categories.

Rosch's questionnaire technique, whereby subjects are required to indicate the extent to which exemplars belong in a category, has been applied many times, with a range of category names, and the same kind of graded responses have been obtained (see Rosch 1978: 36, for references). Of special significance is the fact that prototype effects are not restricted to categories denoted by nouns. Coleman and Kay (1981) report prototype effects in the extent to which statements count as instances of telling a lie, while Pulman (1983) found graded membership in the categories denoted by verbs such as *look*, *kill*, *speak*, and *walk*. A more abstract category, i.e. TALLNESS, was investigated by Dirven and Taylor (1988), again with the same kind of results.

3.3 Basic level terms

Prototypicality, as studied by Rosch, is intimately bound up with what we might call the 'two axes of categorization' (Fig. 3.1). A given entity may be categorized in many alternative ways. *Chair*, *piece of furniture*, *artefact*, and indeed *entity*, are all equally true ways of describing the thing I am sitting on as I write this chapter. CHAIR, FURNITURE, ARTEFACT, and ENTITY represent four levels of categorization, each more inclusive than the preceding one. The category CHAIR is included in the superordinate category FURNITURE, which in turn is included in the even higher category ARTEFACT. On the other hand, KITCHEN CHAIR is a subordinate member of the category CHAIR. These different levels of categorization are shown in Fig. 3.1 on the vertical axis. The horizontal axis represents contrasting categories which are included in the next highest category. Thus TOOL, FURNITURE, and DWELLING PLACE are all examples of ARTEFACT; TABLE, CHAIR, BED are instances of FURNITURE, while DINING-ROOM CHAIR, KITCHEN CHAIR, DENTIST'S CHAIR are instances of CHAIR. At the very lowest level of categorization would stand, not so much categories, but rather individual instances. 'The kitchen chair I

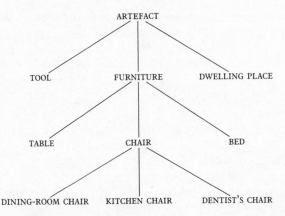

FIG. 3.1 *The two axes of categorization (nominal categories)*

bought last week' might be an instance of KITCHEN CHAIR. Attempts have been made to classify verbal categories in a similar way (although verbal categories turn out to be somewhat more problematic in this respect than noun categories). Figure 3.2 is based on Pulman (1983: 108).

It is, of course, the hierarchical organization of categories, as shown in Figs. 3.1 and 3.2, that provides an important motivation for the classical, feature approach to categories. As we move down the vertical axis, we would say that each category possesses exactly the features of the immediately dominating category, plus one (or more) additional distinguishing features. Items on the same level of categorization all share the features of the immediately dominating category, but each is distinguished from the other categories on the same level by the presence of a unique feature (or set of features).

There are two respects in which the feature model of category hierarchy is open to criticism. Firstly, it is simply not the case that categories at one level of categorization always share a set of features which define the immediately superordinate category. This issue was investigated experimentally by Rosch and Mervis (1975). For each of a number of superordinate categories like FURNITURE, VEHICLE, and FRUIT, the authors selected the names of twenty members in the category. The members exhibited the full range of membership in the higher category. Each of the member names was given to a group of twenty subjects who were asked to list as many of the attributes of the category as possible in a given period of time. It was indeed found that

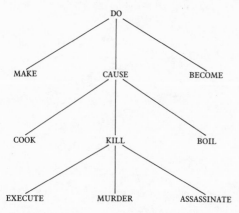

FIG. 3.2 *The two axes of categorization (verbal categories)*

some attributes were associated with several members of the super-ordinate category; other attributes, however, were peculiar to individual members. Very few attributes, it turned out, were common to *all* the members of a superordinate category. Even if common attributes did emerge, e.g. [you eat it] as an attribute of fruits, these were usually so general that they could not be regarded as defining for the superordinate category. It was, however, found that the more central members of a superordinate category did share more attributes than the more marginal members. For instance, the five most central members of FURNITURE had thirteen attributes in common, while the five least central members shared only two attributes. The five most typical members of CLOTHING had twenty-one attributes in common, while the five least typical members shared no attributes at all.

There is a second respect in which the classical view inadequately represents the categories of language. On the classical view, there is no reason for assigning special status to any particular level of categorization, except perhaps to the very highest and the very lowest. (The very highest level is superordinate to all other categories, and thus does not contrast with any other category on that level; while terms on the very lowest level refer to individual instances.) The facts of cognition and language use, however, belie this assumption. There is, namely, a level of categorization which is cognitively and linguistically more salient than the others. This is the 'basic level' of categorization.

It is at the basic level of categorization that people conceptualize things as perceptual and functional gestalts (cf. Rosch *et al.*, 1976).

chair — not furniture or artifact

Try, for example, to visualize or to draw a piece of furniture. The task seems absurd. One feels compelled to ask, 'What kind of furniture? A table, a chair, a bed?' It would not, however, be unreasonable to ask someone to draw a picture of a chair, though in this case it would be equally legitimate to ask, 'What kind of chair? A kitchen chair, a dentist's chair, an armchair?' It is similarly absurd to try to describe how one interacts with a piece of furniture, or to name the parts of which a piece of furniture is composed. We have no difficulty, though, in describing the motor movements we perform when interacting with a chair, or to name the parts of which a chair is composed. It thus comes as no surprise that it is the basic level at which, in the absence of specific reasons to the contrary, people normally talk about reality (Downing 1977*a*). If a foreigner were to point to the object I am now sitting on and ask 'What do you call that in English?', I would almost certainly answer, 'It's a chair.' I would not reply 'It's an artefact', or 'It's a piece of furniture', even though these alternative answers would be equally 'correct'.[5]

On purely formal, language-internal grounds, basic level terms can often be distinguished from non-basic terms. In addition to their high frequency of occurrence, basic level terms are generally short and structurally simple (i.e. monomorphemic). Terms below the basic level are frequently compounds consisting of the basic level term plus a modifier (e.g. *kitchen chair*). Terms above the basic level are sometimes deviant in some way (e.g. *furniture* is morphosyntactically unusual in that it is uncountable, i.e. one cannot say **a furniture* or **furnitures*). It also often happens that superordinate terms are simply missing from the vocabulary of a language. English, for instance, has numerous colour terms which are subordinate to basic colour terms, but has no superordinate colour term. (*Coloured* will not do; this word refers only to the chromatic colours, and excludes black, white, and grey.) Often, if the need for a superordinate term is felt strongly enough, learned terms (such as *sibling* as a superordinate to *brother* and *sister*), or cumbersome circumlocutions, may be coined. A particularly interesting correlation between position in a taxonomic hierarchy and grammatical

[5] As the examples given suggest, the notion of basic level term is generally understood in connection with nominal categories. But the construct is applicable to other kinds of concept. Rosch (1978) reports evidence suggesting that events like 'do the washing up' and 'brush one's teeth' have basic level status, while 'do the household chores' and 'squeeze toothpaste onto the brush' have superordinate and subordinate status, respectively.

gender has been shown to hold in German (Zubin and Köpcke 1986). Terms above the basic level of categorization are 'conceptually vague and undifferentiated'; these terms, with more than chance frequency, are neuter. At the basic level and below, noun meanings are 'richly specified both perceptually and functionally'. These nouns tend to be either masculine or feminine, with neuter appearing more rarely. *Tier* "animal", *Obst* "fruit", *Gemüse* "vegetable", *Metall* "metal" are neuter, while names of specific animals, fruits, vegetables, and metals are generally either masculine or feminine.

What gives basic level terms their privileged status? The answer is to be sought in terms of the usefulness of categories. Categorization makes it possible for an organism to reduce the limitless variation in the world to manageable proportions. A category fulfils this function in virtue of the fact that 'by knowing the category to which a thing belongs, the organism, thereby, knows as many attributes of the thing as possible' (Rosch 1975 c: 197). By the same token, a maximally useful category also makes it possible to exclude as many attributes as possible. That categories can function in this way rests on the fact that attributes do not occur randomly in the world, but tend to be correlated with each other, either positively or negatively. That is to say, the presence of attribute A tends to be associated in the world with the presence of attribute B and with the absence of attribute C. This is the reason for the common-sense rejection of the reality-as-a-continuum hypothesis, mentioned in section 1.1. If we know that an entity is feathered, has wings, and can fly, we can state with some confidence that it also lays eggs. On the other hand, having fur and a tail are attributes which are not associated with laying eggs and the ability to fly. Now, the Aristotelian model of categories assumed a perfect correlation between attributes within a category. On the Aristotelian view, by knowing the category to which a thing belongs, one knows with complete certainty that certain attributes will co-occur; these are the attributes that are necessary conditions for category membership. Experience tells us, however, that such perfect correlations are rare. There are cups with no handles (Chinese cups), birds which don't fly (penguins), cats without tails (Manx cats), chairs which aren't for sitting on (dentist's chairs), and so on.

Rosch argues that it is the basic level categories that most fully exploit the real-world correlation of attributes. Basic level terms cut up reality into maximally informative categories. More precisely, Rosch hypothesizes that basic level categories both (*a*) maximize the number of attributes shared by members of the category; and

(*b*) minimize the number of attributes shared with members of other categories.

Consider once again the members of the category FURNITURE. Glancing at Table 3.1, one would have a hard task to identify any essential defining attributes of the category. Even if we restrict our attention to the thirty or so more typical members of the category, there do not appear to be any attributes which uniquely distinguish articles of furniture from other household artefacts. (This impression was confirmed, as we have seen, by Rosch and Mervis 1975.) Contrary to the assumptions of the classical theory, FURNITURE is probably best thought of, not in terms of a conjunction of defining features, but, as Wierzbicka has argued (1985), in terms of a listing of its more typical members, i.e. *furniture* is more of a collective term for things like tables, beds, sofas, chairs, and so on. With a basic level category, like CHAIR, the situation is different. Chairs have quite a few attributes in common. Furthermore, what chairs have in common is not shared by beds and tables. Members in the categories on the next lowest level, e.g. KITCHEN CHAIR, also share a large number of attributes. Many of the attributes of kitchen chairs, however, are also shared by other kinds of chair, e.g. dining-room chairs. While KITCHEN CHAIR maximizes the attributes shared by members of the category, it is not maximally distinct from other categories on the same level.

It is here, of course, where the notion of basic level terms meshes in with the prototype structure of categories. Categories typically have fuzzy edges and might even merge into each other; some attributes might be shared by only a few members of a category; there might even be categories with no attributes shared by all their members. In order to keep our categories maximally distinct, and hence maximally informative, we need to focus on the basic level of categorization, more specifically, on the more central members of basic level categories.

3.4 Why prototype categories?

There can be little question of the psychological reality of the prototype structure of categories. Degree of category membership can be readily

elicited from speakers of a language; degree of membership characterizes many different kinds of category; and it is a variable which determines performance on a wide range of diverse experimental tasks.
Given the reality of graded membership in a category, the question
arises as to why it is that certain exemplars of a category come to have
the privileged status of prototypical members, while other exemplars
are marginal members. Why is it that chairs, sofas, and tables, and not
mirrors, shelves, and clocks, are prototypical articles of furniture, or
that murder is a better instance of killing than sacrificing? As Geeraerts
(1988b) asks: Where do prototypes come from?

Rosch (1975c) considers a number of possible answers to this
question. For a limited number of categories, prototypicality is very
plausibly a consequence of inherent properties of human perception.
We saw in Chapter 1 that the prototypicality of focal colours very
probably has a natural basis in the neurology of colour perception; in a
sense, colour categories pre-exist their linguistic encoding. There is
evidence that certain geometrical forms (the good forms of gestalt
psychology, e.g. circle, square, triangle) and certain spatial orientations
(e.g. vertical and horizontal rather than oblique), like focal colours, are
perceptually more salient than deviations from these forms, and
thereby also acquire prototype status (Rosch 1973a). Presumably,
there are going to be relatively few categories of this nature. There can
be no question of a neurological basis to the perception of prototypical
cups and furniture, since these are 'artificial' categories, a product of
our cultural environment. Other explanations must therefore be
sought for the prototype structure of these categories.

One possible explanation—and one that is intuitively quite
appealing—is that members of a category achieve prototypical status
because we encounter them more frequently. Rosch, in her empirical
research, carefully controlled for word frequency; degree of membership in a category, as reported in her various publications, is
independent of the frequency of occurrence of member names. In fact,
she warns us to be suspicious of frequency as an explanation of prototypicality. Interestingly, the impression of a higher frequency of
occurrence of prototypical members may well be a *symptom* of
prototypicality, and not its cause. As already noted, when asked to
name examples of a category people tend to mention prototypical
members first. It is thus natural that, when considering the category
FURNITURE, we think immediately of tables and chairs, not of mirrors
and clocks, and may thus conclude—erroneously, perhaps—that we

encounter tables and chairs more frequently than mirrors and clocks.
It is worth mentioning that it is along these lines that Rosch accounts
for what she calls the 'good old days effect' (1976). In recalling earlier
episodes in our lives, we tend to exaggerate the frequency of
prototypical, and underestimate the frequency of non-prototypical
components of those situations. Thus the past is remembered, without
differentiation, as pleasant (or unpleasant, as the case may be).[6]
Another factor that Rosch proposes is order of learning, a possibility
which Pulman (1983) also embraces. (It seems unlikely, however, that
children brought up with a Pekinese would go through life with a
Pekinese as their dog prototype.) A further possibility is that in some
instances the prototype might embody the mean values of variable
attributes. Prototypical birds, for instance, seem to be birds of average
size and average predacity (Rips *et al.* 1973). Alternatively, certain
attributes might be particularly salient, e.g. because they are especially
important in a society, with the result that these attributes cluster in
prototypes. Thus, Wierzbicka (1985) accounts for the characteristics
of prototypical cups in terms of norms for social tea-drinking. Even the
focal reference of certain colour terms may well be a consequence of
the importance of certain objects within a culture (see McNeill 1972
on colour terms in Japanese).

While each of the above factors may no doubt play some role in the
emergence of prototypes, a more general explanation is to be found in
terms of the greater efficiency of prototype categories. Prototype
categories have a flexibility, unknown to Aristotelian categories, in
being able to accommodate new, hitherto unfamiliar data. With only
Aristotelian categories at our disposal, new data would often demand,
for their categorization, the creation of new categories, or a redefinition of existing categories. On the other hand, new entities and new
experiences can be readily associated, perhaps as peripheral members,
to a prototype category, without necessarily causing any fundamental
restructuring of the category system:

Cognition should have a tendency towards structural stability: the categorial
system can only work efficiently if it does not change drastically any time new

[6] This kind of explanation may be offered for the fact that children's drawings
generally depict the grass as an undifferentiated green and the sky as a constant blue,
even though in some environments, the sky is more often grey than blue, and grass for
most of the year might be brown. The children's drawings depict the colour of prototypical grass and a prototypical sky. Prototypically, grass is green, which is not the same
as saying that grass is usually green.

data crop up. But at the same time, it should be flexible enough to adapt itself to changing circumstances. To prevent it from becoming chaotic, it should have a built-in tendency towards structural stability, but this stability should not become rigidity, lest the system stops being able to adapt itself to the ever-changing circumstances of the outside world. ... It will be clear that proto-typical categories are eminently suited to fulfil the joint requirements of structural stability and flexible adaptability. On the one hand, the develop-ment of nuances within concepts indicates their dynamic ability to cope with changing conditions and changing expressive needs. On the other hand, the fact that marginally deviant concepts can be incorporated into existing categories as peripheral instantiations of the latter, proves that these categories have a tendency to maintain themselves as holistic entities, thus maintaining the overall structure of the categorial system. (Geeraerts 1985a: 141)

The epistemological consequences of this characteristic of prototype categories are explored in Geeraerts (1985b).

Certainly, from one point of view, the most efficient categories—categories based on a perfect correlation of attributes over their members—are classical categories. Yet, as Geeraerts argues, the very rigidity of classical categories would make them highly inefficient for human cognition, since the flux of experience rarely presents us with the perfect correlation of attributes which classical categories require. In a sense, prototype categories give us the best of both worlds. The central members of a prototype category do share a large number of attributes (cf. Rosch and Mervis 1975)—in this respect, the centre of a prototype category approaches the ideal of a classical category. At the same time, prototype categories permit membership to entities which share only few attributes with the more central members. In this respect, prototype categories achieve the flexibility required by an ever-changing environment.

3.5 A note on fuzziness

Perhaps the most obvious difference between a classical and a prototype category is the fact that the former permits only two degrees of membership, i.e. member and non-member, while membership in a prototype category is a matter of gradience. It is worth mentioning at this point that attempts have been made to modify the strict assumptions of the classical model, in order to accommodate varying degrees of category membership. The claim is that at least some semantic features are gradable, i.e. they can take on a range of values between 1 and 0. A good candidate for the status of a fuzzy feature would be [TALL]. To the extent that a fuzzy feature enters into the definition of a word meaning (e.g. the meaning of the adjective *tall*), that word would also exhibit fuzziness. Thus, an entity might display the feature [TALL] only to a certain degree, say 0.75, i.e. the entity would count as 'fairly tall', not 'very tall'. Another entity might display the feature to a greater degree, say 0.95. Thus, of two tall entities, one could be described as taller than the other.

At one time, Lakoff (1972) was optimistic about the potential contribution of fuzzy set theory to linguistic semantics. Recently, however, he has expressed the view that the approach is of only marginal interest to the cognitive linguist (1987: 196). The reason is that the kind of fuzziness said to be associated with the category TALL is only superficially comparable with the prototype effects exhibited by the categories studied in this chapter. The fuzziness of GAME, CUP, FURNITURE, etc. is not the consequence of the fuzziness of any of the semantic features whose conjunction can be said to define the essence of the categories. These categories are structured by a criss-crossing of similarities, not by a set of necessary and sufficient conditions. On closer inspection, even TALL turns out not to be a fuzzy classical category. The meaning of *tall* displays a complex interplay of sometimes quite complex components (cf. Dirven and Taylor 1988). Tallness is not only a function of the measured height of an entity. The way an entity is conceptualized, and the context in which it is perceived, also play an important role. While the former aspect could well be a candidate for a fuzzy feature, the latter certainly are not.

3.6 Some applications

I will delay until the next chapter a more detailed elaboration of the prototype model of categories. Then, in the remainder of this book I will explore some of the far-reaching implications of prototype categorization, not only for the study of word meaning, but also for syntax and phonology. In the meantime, we can pause to glance at one area of linguistic research where the prototype category has an obvious and immediate application. This is in the study of semantic equivalence, both between and within languages. Let us begin with the case of intra-language synonyms. It is a common observation that perfect synonyms—lexical items with the same meaning and which are therefore interchangeable in all contexts—are exceedingly rare. Geeraerts (1988*b*) offers as possible candidates the two verbs *vernielen* and *vernietigen* "to destroy, bring to nought" in nineteenth-century Dutch. The two words appear to have referred to exactly the same range of situations and exhibited identical selection restrictions, even in the writings of one and the same author. Were the words, then, perfect synonyms? Geeraerts argues that they were not. Differences emerged when the frequencies of different senses were compared, *vernietigen* being used predominantly in an abstract sense, while *vernielen* referred predominantly to an act of physical destruction. Remarks in contemporary handbooks of good usage also pointed to a difference in the conceptual centres of the two words.

This example suggests that while two words may be distributionally and referentially equivalent, they may nevertheless be associated with distinct prototypes. Such a state of affairs can occur with regard to the 'same' word as used by speakers of different varieties of a language. Kempton (1981) reports a small-scale experiment in which he assembled fifty articles of footwear and asked people to classify these as boots, shoes, slippers, etc. He found that his American (Texan) and British informants showed considerable agreement as to which articles were the boots, i.e. the referential range of *boot* was comparable for the two dialect groups. Yet the two groups of speakers seemed to operate with markedly different prototypes. For the Texans, the prototypical boot came high above the ankle, like a cowboy boot; for the British, the prototype was an army boot, which did not come above the ankle. To what extent this phenomenon is characteristic of a wide range of pan-dialectal items, or even whether speakers of one and the same dialect also operate with divergent prototypes, is a matter which would merit further research. Kempton, for instance, does report on different prototype representations of Mexican ceramics, mainly as a function of the degree of Westernization and urbanization of the speakers. It is worth noting in this connection that for Langacker, it is 'self-evident' that 'no two speakers share precisely the same linguistic system' (1987: 376). Presumably, in day-to-day exchanges, differences in conceptual centre are likely to pass unnoticed, especially if the lexical items in question can be applied to an identical range of referents. It is an open question, however, to what extent such differences in the conceptual centre might sometimes hinder communication, or even lead to gross misunderstandings.

TABLE 3.2 *Goodness-of-example ratings for fifty-five members of the category* MÖBEL *"furniture"*

Member	Rank	Specific score	Member	Rank	Specific score
bed	1.5	1.00	bar	29	3.70
table	1.5	1.0	counter	30	3.73
sofa	3	1.13	mirror	31	4.20
cupboard	5	1.20	drawers	32	4.38
desk	5	1.20	dresser	33	4.47
closet	5	1.20	lamp	34	4.79
chair	5	1.20	piano	35	5.07
love seat	8	1.40	clock	36	5.20
chest of drawers	9	1.43	stove	37	5.33
bookcase	10	1.47	wastebasket	38	5.42
night table	11	1.53	refrigerator	39	5.73
coffee table	12.5	1.67	rug	40	5.80
couch	12.5	1.67	picture	41	5.93
china closet	14	1.70	hassock	42.5	6.00
cabinet	16	1.73	drapes	42.5	6.00
divan	16	1.73	TV	45	6.07
bureau	16	1.73	rocker	45	6.07
buffet	18	1.80	footstool	45	6.07
davenport	19	1.93	hi-fi	47	6.33
shelf	20.5	2.00	vase	48	6.40
rocking chair	20.5	2.00	radio	49.5	6.47
bench	22	2.10	sewing machine	49.5	6.47
lounge	23	2.27	fan	51	6.54
stool	23	2.27	stereo	52	6.64
vanity	23	2.27	pillow	54	6.80
ottoman	26	2.43	telephone	54	6.80
end table	27	2.80	ashtray	54	6.80
magazine rack	28	3.40			

Whatever the variation in category representation between speakers of a given language or dialect, there can be little doubt that the prototype representations of many categories change dramatically over time. The prototypical bicycles and automobiles of fifty years ago are now fairly marginal exemplars of their categories. Possibly, more abstract concepts, like love and beauty, have undergone even more dramatic changes. A final area of interest concerns the presumed translation equivalence of words in different languages. Some data relevant to this issue are given in Table 3.2. Table 3.2 (reproduced by kind permission of René Dirven) summarizes the results of a small-scale replication of Rosch's investigation of the category FURNITURE. German-speaking subjects were asked to assign a degree of membership in the category MÖBEL ("furniture") to German names of fifty-five household items. Dirven (personal communication) suggests that the differences between Table 3.2 and Table 3.1 indicate that the German students were perhaps assessing category membership on the basis of the furnishings of a typical student's room, while Rosch's American subjects may have been visualizing their parents' lounge. If this is the case, *Möbel* and *furniture* cannot be considered exact translation equivalents, at least for the populations tested, even though the referential range of the two words would appear to coincide.

4

Prototype Categories: II

THIS chapter continues the discussion of prototype categories begun in Chapter 3. A number of issues need to be dealt with. Firstly, the notion of prototype itself needs to be given more substance. What exactly are prototypes? The discussion will lead us to reconsider the status of classical categories. If all kinds of entities—natural and arte-factual, those denoted by nouns as well as those denoted by verbs and adjectives, even, as we shall see in later chapters, the categories of linguistic structure itself—are categorized by prototype, what, if anything, is left of the classical model? Do all categories have a proto-type structure, or are there still categories which conform with Aristo-telian principles, i.e. categories with necessary and sufficient conditions for membership, with clear-cut boundaries, and with only two degrees of membership, i.e. member and non-member? We shall see that Aristotelian categories do need to be recognized, although their status will need to be reassessed. First, though, I shall spell out in more detail exactly what is meant by a prototype, and consider some of the difficulties associated with prototype categorization.

4.1 Prototypes

There are two ways in which to understand the term 'prototype'. We can apply the term to the central member, or perhaps to the cluster of central members, of a category. Thus, one could refer to a particular artefact as the prototype of CUP. Alternatively, the prototype can be understood as a schematic representation of the conceptual core of a category. On this approach, we would say, not that a particular entity *is* the prototype, but that it *instantiates* the prototype.

Of the two possibilities, there are, I think, good reasons for adopting the more abstract approach.[1] Even on the prototype-as-exemplar view,

---

[1] Rosch, in her later work at least (e.g. Rosch 1978), appears to reject both options (i.e. prototypes as central members and prototypes as schematic representations). She declines to extrapolate her experimental findings to mental models of category

one still needs to posit a mental representation of the prototype, in order for a speaker to be able to identify the prototype on different occasions. Furthermore, this mental representation may well be unspecified with respect to certain attributes of category members. It is conceivable that the prototype of DOG will be unspecified for sex; yet each exemplar of the category is necessarily either male or female. To this extent, the internal representation of the prototype is in any case schematic. The equation of the prototype with a specific exemplar would also preclude the possibility that the members of a category might themselves be categories. We want to be able to say, not only that individual robins are members of BIRD, but also that BIRD has as one of its members the category ROBIN. A further difficulty arises with more abstract categories. If prototypes are exemplars, where would we expect to find the prototype of COWARDICE and TALLNESS? Events can be described as (more or less) prototypical instances of COWARDICE, objects exhibit a (more or less) prototypical TALLNESS. One could not, on the other hand, say that an event *is* the prototype of COWARDICE, nor could one pick out an object as *the* prototype of TALLNESS.

Entities are assigned membership in a category in virtue of their similarity to the prototype; the closer an entity to the prototype, the more central its status within the category. The notion of similarity thus underlies all categorization processes. Yet similarity is one of the most difficult of psychological constructs, for two reasons. Firstly, as already implied, similarity is a graded concept. Things can be more similar, or less similar. But how different do two things have to be for them to cease to be similar? The second difficulty has to do with the fact that similarity is also a subjective notion. Similarity, like beauty, lies in the eye of the beholder. Once we invoke similarity as a basis for categorization, we inevitably bring language users, with their beliefs, interests, and past experience, into the picture. Things are similar to the extent that a human being, in some context and for some purpose, chooses to regard them as similar.

In measuring similarity, classical semanticists had it (relatively) easy. On the classical view, things are similar in proportion to the number of features they share. To the extent that features are taken to be universal primitives, similarity judgements are not tainted with subjectivity. In a sense, similarity is reduced to an objectively verifiable partial identity. But in rejecting the classical approach, we have also

structure, contenting herself with a characterization of prototypicality merely in terms of its experimental effects (membership judgements, reaction times, etc.).

rejected the primitive binary feature as a theoretical construct, and have spoken instead of attributes. In point of fact, the classical view of similarity was never quite so unproblematic. For instance, should all features count equally as criteria for similarity, or should the sharing of a feature like [ANIMATE] carry less weight than the common presence of a feature like [MARRIED] (cf. Lyons 1977: 553)? This and other problems of the classical view find a highly sophisticated resolution in Tversky's (1977) attribute model of similarity. The model computes the similarity of two entities not only on the basis of the number of attributes they share, the number of attributes not shared by the two entities is also taken into consideration. Furthermore, attributes are differentially weighted. Some attributes receive a high weighting on account of their perceptual salience, others because of their high diagnostic value. Perceptual salience is relatively constant, while diagnostic value is variable, and depends crucially on the context of comparison.

It is easy to see how prototype effects could be accommodated within Tversky's model. The model would compute, for any given entity, a numerical value of similarity with the prototype representation. For an entity to achieve membership in a category, a certain threshold value, specified for that category, would have to be exceeded, while values above the threshold would determine increasing degrees of membership. This kind of approach, however, betrays a serious weakness, in that it ignores the fact that attributes can be cognitively quite complex. Consider again Wittgenstein's discussion of games. Characteristic of a number of games is the need for skill on the part of the players. But skill is not a primitive semantic feature. It is not just that skill is a graded concept, in the sense that some games might require more skill than others. More important is the fact that the skill needed in tennis is a very different kind of entity to the skill needed in chess. To say that tennis and chess are similar on account of the common attribute [skill] itself presupposes a categorization, namely a set of similarity judgements between each kind of skill and a mental representation of prototypical skill. As René Dirven has remarked (personal communication), prototypicality is recursive, in that the very attributes on whose basis membership in a category is determined are more often than not themselves prototype categories. Take, as a further example, [ability to fly] as an attribute of birds. A prototypical instance of this attribute is exhibited by robins. Hens, on the other hand, while certainly able to lift themselves off the ground by energetically flapping their wings, cannot fly in the same way as robins. They exhibit a rather marginal [ability to fly]. This example points to another problem. Prototypical instances of [ability to fly] are exhibited by the prototypical members of the very category which the attribute is supposed to characterize. This state of affairs is not unusual. Other attributes of the BIRD prototype, such as the presence of feathers, wings, and a beak, the building of nests, and the laying of eggs, would appear prima facie to require, for their characterization, a prior understanding of what birds are.

Decomposing an attribute into its constituent attributes might go some way towards solving the second of these problems; it does not necessarily free an attribute from its prototype structure. Suppose we define [ability to fly] as the ability for fairly rapid self-propelled motion through the air. Let us take each of these sub-attributes in turn. How much external assistance does an object have to have before it loses its capacity for self-propelled motion? Does a stone thrown into the air possess this attribute? Presumably it does, but not in the required sense. And if motion through the air is not self-propelled, is [ability to fly] thereby precluded? Consider the case of gliders and hot air balloons. Secondly, how fast does an object have to move before its motion can be described as fairly rapid? Does a hot air balloon satisfy the requirement? Finally, for how long does an object have to be airborne, and what distance does it have to be from the ground, for one to be able to say that it moves through the air? Does an athlete doing the high jump qualify? To what extent, then, can one say that gliders, hot air balloons, stones thrown into the air, and jumping athletes exhibit the attribute [ability to fly]?

It is one of the myths of the classical theory that complex concepts are ultimately reducible to sets of binary primitives. Underlying the above attempt to characterize the attributes of an attribute is the assumption that a complex cognitive structure can be exhaustively represented by means of a listing of its components, the assumption, in other words, that a whole is nothing more than the sum of its parts. Langacker (1987: 19ff.) has questioned this assumption. Cognitive structures often need to be understood more as holistic, gestalt configurations, than as attribute bundles. Especially when we are dealing with basic level categories, the whole might well be per-ceptually and cognitively simpler than any of its individual parts, such that the parts are understood in terms of the whole, rather than vice versa. Such a view follows, in fact, from Rosch's characterization of the basic level (cf. Lakoff 1987: 56 and *passim*). These considerations do not mean that it is illegitimate to speak of attributes, provided one does not intend by this term the atomic (or even molecular) semantic components of the classical theory. Attributes are simply the dimensions along which different entities are regarded as similar. They embody 'the commonality [that speakers] perceive in arrays of fully specified, integrated units' (Langacker 1987: 22).

Bearing in mind this proviso on the nature of attributes, let us now address some of the more controversial aspects of prototype categorization. Firstly, it needs to be stressed that a mental representation of a prototype constitutes but one component of a person's knowledge of a category. To see why this should be so, we need only consider some of the fairly obvious similarities which exist between, for example, cats and dogs. In spite of these similarities, we do not want to say that cats are members, not even highly marginal members, of the category DOG. If unrestricted, a category could eventually encompass the whole universe of entities, since it is possible to establish some kind of tenuous similarity between virtually any pair of objects. Clearly, our representation of DOG imposes a category boundary, beyond which certain kinds of things cannot get associated, even loosely, with the category. For at least some categories, this boundary is guaranteed by the requirement that all members of the category share at least one criterial attribute. Of special significance in this connection are so-called nominal kind categories which, as we have seen, are in part definable in terms of essential attributes. A full characterization of the meaning of *murder* would probably extend over several pages. A minimal definition of the word, however, would surely include the information (*a*) that a person dies, and (*b*) that this death is a result of the behaviour of some person or persons. The death of a victim is an essential attribute of murder.

But is not the presence of essential attributes—attributes which are necessarily shared by all members of a category—inconsistent with the prototype approach? The answer, I think, must be no. Attributes *are* differentially weighted; some might be essential, others can be overridden with varying degrees of facility. Yet the existence of an essential attribute, perhaps even of a set of essential attributes, does not of itself lead to all-or-nothing membership in a category. The criterial attributes themselves might display degrees of membership. Murder, as we have said, requires a death. While it is a relatively clear-cut matter (barring obviously marginal cases) to state whether or not a person has died, it is far from clear-cut to determine, in any particular instance, whether death occurs as a result of the behaviour of an aggressor. If the victim dies instantly of injuries inflicted on him, there would be little doubt about whether a death, in the required sense, has occurred. But as the causal chain linking the act of aggression and the death of the victim grows more tenuous, it becomes less and less clear what value to assign to the attribute. Suppose a person dies only many years after having been injured. Can we state with confidence that an essential attribute of murder (i.e. the death of a victim) has been fulfilled? Or consider, as a further example, what constitutes a triangle. One tends to think of geometrical figures as Aristotelian categories *par excellence*. Thus a triangle is a figure enclosed by three straight lines. That this definition deals in essential attributes does not of itself guarantee that membership in the category will be clear-cut. While the number of sides to the figure might well be a matter of either–or, the straightness of these sides is a matter of similarity to a prototype. Suppose I draw a triangle, freehand. The sides will almost certainly not be straight; they might not even join up. The figure would not be a very good example of a triangle. Yet it could still be called a triangle, and could serve as an adequate illustration of the meaning of the word *triangle* in a foreign language classroom.

Does then the existence of a clear boundary to a category preclude prototype categorization? Again, the answer must be, not necessarily. If the essentiality of attributes is invoked in nominal kind categories, the presence of a clear boundary is often typical of natural kind categories. We have seen that DOG does not merge at its periphery with CAT. Similarly, what counts as gold or silver clearly is a matter of either–or; the one substance does not merge into the other, in the manner of Labov's cups and bowls. Arguably, BIRD is also clearly circumscribed. While penguins might not be very good examples of the category, they are birds none the less. In this connection, Lakoff (1987) has spoken of degrees of 'representativity' within a category, rather than degrees of membership; prototype effects superimpose a 'secondary gradience' on what is essentially a clear-cut category. However, the apparently clear-cut nature of (some) natural kind categories is clearly contingent on a number of factors. Firstly, there are our prevailing beliefs about what natural kinds are. The very notion of a natural kind implies a scientific (or folk-scientific), taxonomic division of certain naturally occurring phenomena—plants, birds, minerals, etc.—into discrete categories. Secondly, the clear boundary of a natural kind category is dependent both on the way the world happens to be, and on what we happen to know about it. It may be the case that what are called birds do constitute a clearly circumscribed category. But if now extinct species had survived (how can we be certain that they haven't?), it could have been otherwise. And, certainly, some natural kinds are not discrete. Consider the phenomenon of ring species, discussed by Lakoff (1987: 190) and briefly mentioned by Cruse (1986: 71f.). The ability of members of a population to interbreed is usually taken as a defining characteristic of a species. On this criterion, species usually do emerge as clear-cut entities. Suppose, however, that members of a population A can interbreed with members of a territorially contiguous population B; members of B can interbreed with members of C, C with D, and so on. But members of A cannot interbreed with members of D. Where, in such a case, would one say that the one species ends and the other begins? Neither have our beliefs about the discreteness of natural kinds always been as strong as they are today. Consider the boundary between man and not-man. Edmund Leach (1982) points out that a major driving force for anthropology over the centuries has been precisely the question whether or not human beings fall into a discrete category.

Perhaps the most appropriate way to end this section is to suggest, with Geeraerts (1989), that prototypicality is itself a prototype category (the recursivity of prototypes again!). Categories with clear boundaries (many natural kinds) and categories with essential conditions for membership (nominal kinds) can certainly show prototype effects, although they are perhaps not optimal exemplars of prototype categories.

4.2 Prototypes and schemas

The importance of extension from a prototype as a principle of category structure has been recognized by a number of linguists in recent years (e.g. Jackendoff 1983). Here, I want to focus on the position taken by Langacker (1987). For Langacker, extension from a prototype coexists with a second structuring principle, namely elaboration of a schema.[2] The difference is explained as follows:

[2] Langacker's schemas appear to coincide, in many respects, with Hudson's (1984) models, Langacker's 'elaboration of a schema' being paralleled by Hudson's 'inheritance from a model'.

A prototype is a typical instance of a category, and other elements are assimilated to the category on the basis of their perceived resemblance to the prototype; there are degrees of membership based on degrees of similarity. A schema, by contrast, is an abstract characterization that is fully compatible with all the members of the category it defines (so membership is not a matter of degree); it is an integrated structure that embodies the commonality of its members, which are conceptions of greater specificity and detail that elaborate the schema in contrasting ways. (Langacker 1987: 371)

Schemas may be hierarchically organized within a category, in conjunction with extension from prototypes. Consider Langacker's account of how the concept "tree" might be acquired (1987: 373 ff.). Langacker speculates that initially, the language learner associates the word *tree* with specific instances of large, deciduous leafed plants, e.g. with oaks, elms, and maples. He then extracts from these instances a schematic representation of what they have in common. We may call this representation TREE^1. This representation now functions as a prototype. Pine trees get associated with the category on the basis of similarity along some dimensions with the prototype, even though pine trees are not fully compatible with the TREE^1 schema, e.g. they don't have leaves. Once pines are associated with the category, the learner can now extract a further schema, TREE^2, which represents what is common to TREE^1 and pines, e.g. a tall central trunk with branches. TREE^2 now functions as a prototype for extension of the category to palm trees; palms share with the prototype a tall central trunk, they do not, however, branch. The commonalities between TREE^2 and palms permit the extraction of a more abstract schema still, TREE^3. Further elaboration of the category is possible. FRUIT TREE, for example, may emerge as a sub-schema of TREE^1, while TREE^2 may function as a prototype for metaphorical extension, i.e. genealogical trees and the phrase structure trees of linguistic description get associated with TREE^2 on the basis of their branching structure.

If one examines more closely the distinction between categorization by prototype and categorization by schema, it becomes clear that categorization by schema and categorization by prototype are in reality aspects of the same phenomenon. In the former case, an entity happens to be fully compatible with an abstract representation, in the latter case, it is only partially compatible.[3] Whether in any particular instance the analyst invokes a prototype or a schema would appear to

[3] Cf. Hudson: 'the "fuzziness" of a prototype-based concept lies ... in the deviations which the world allows between it and its instances' (1984: 40).

depend on the degree of abstractness which he is willing to attribute to a speaker's mental representation. Possibly, all trees *can* be subsumed under a highly abstract representation TREE[3]. Equally, the category could be structured around a rather more concrete prototype representation. Langacker does indeed envisage the possibility of alternative structures. He writes that 'it is possible in principle to conceive of a shape specification schematic enough to neutralize the differences between an Alsatian and a poodle, while still being recognizable as that of a dog' (Langacker 1987: 136f.), mentioning in a footnote the alternative option that 'a person may rely on the more precise shape specification of a prototypical dog, recognizing other shapes as extensions from the prototype'.

In this book I shall emphasize categorization by prototype rather than categorization by schema. In this, I come rather close to the admittedly extreme position which Bolinger appears to adopt, when he writes that 'every equation that does not express identity (a dog is a dog) is an extension' (1980: 145). There are a number of reasons for my focus on prototypes to the neglect of schemas. Firstly, for many categories of natural language, it is just not possible to abstract a schema which is compatible with *all* the members of the category. Some striking examples will be discussed in later chapters. Even if a schema of sufficient generality can be extracted, the schema might not be restrictive enough. Consider the possibility of an abstract tree-schema which encompasses oak trees, pine trees, family trees, and phrase structure trees. What these different kinds of tree have in common is the fact that they branch, in some literal or metaphorical sense. Yet not everything that branches is a tree; one could not, for instance, refer to a road branching at a Y-junction as a tree. Yet the tree-schema is elaborated by a branching road just as much as by a branching syntactic structure. My second reason for focusing on prototypes has to do with Langacker's observation that categorization by prototype and categorization by schema give rise to different predictions concerning degree of membership judgements, i.e. with categorization by schema 'membership is not a matter of degree'. We have seen in the last chapter, however, that for very many categories, membership clearly *is* a matter of degree. Thirdly, while recognizing that speakers can and do structure categories by schema, I would suggest that categorization by prototype occurs developmentally prior to categorization by schema. (See Chapter 13, Section 4, for further discussion.) The increasing abstractness required of schematic representations suggests that schemas may only be accessible to more sophisticated, reflective language users. Possibly, one of the hall-marks of formal education is precisely that it encourages an individual to reflect consciously on the commonality of category members.

4.3　Folk categories and expert categories

In this section I would like to discuss some empirical data which would appear to jeopardize the prototype view of categories I am putting forward, and to consider some of the ways in which the data can be accommodated within the present approach. The data in question are reported in Armstrong *et al.* (1983). Employing Rosch's technique for eliciting degree of membership judgements, Armstrong *et al.* investig-ated the structure of the categories ODD NUMBER and EVEN NUMBER. Subjects were given a series of odd and even numbers, and were asked to rate these numbers for their degree of membership in the respective categories.

If there do exist categories which are structured according to the assumptions of the classical theory—i.e. categories which are defined in terms of necessary and sufficient conditions, which exhibit clear-cut boundaries, and which permit only two degrees of membership (i.e. member and non-member)—then ODD NUMBER and EVEN NUMBER are surely amongst them. An even number is a natural number which is divisible by 2 without a remainder; odd numbers, when divided by 2, leave a remainder of 1. Clearly, a natural number must be either odd or even; one even number cannot reasonably be considered more even than another. One would therefore expect that subjects, given the task of assigning degrees of membership in the categories ODD NUMBER and EVEN NUMBER, would judge all numbers to be optimal members of the respective categories.

This is not what Armstrong *et al.* found. Of the various odd numbers tested, 3 was assigned the highest degree of membership in the category, with a mean value of 1.6; 447 and 91 had the lowest degree of membership, with a value of 3.7. Even numbers showed the same effect: 2 and 4 had the highest degrees of membership in the category EVEN NUMBER, with degrees of membership of 1.0 and 1.1; while 106 and 806 had lowest membership, with a value of 3.9. Admittedly, none of the numbers tested scored less than 4 (= moderately good example) on Rosch's scale. (ODD NUMBER and EVEN NUMBER are therefore not particularly good examples of prototype categories.) Yet the fact that graded responses were obtained at all for what seem to be undeniably clear-cut categories, puts in question the validity of one of the primary sources of evidence for prototype categories.

Armstrong *et al.*'s explanation of their findings is worth considering in some detail. Following Osherson and Smith (1981)—who had also questioned the theoretical import of prototype effects—Armstrong *et al.* propose, Rosch's research notwithstanding, that categories continue to be defined in terms of core, or categorial features. These features define the 'real essence' of a category. The real essence of ODD NUMBER—what an odd number 'really is'—is given by the mathematical definition. Alongside the core definition, however, there exists an 'identification procedure', or 'recognition procedure'. The identification procedure might well rely on properties of an entity which are accidental to its real essence. As Osherson and Smith put it:

the core [of a concept] is concerned with those aspects of a concept that explicate its relations to other concepts, and to thoughts, while the identification procedure specifies the kind of information used to make rapid decisions about membership. ... We can illustrate with the concept *woman*. Its core might contain information about the presence of a reproductive system, while its identification procedures might contain information about body shape, hair length, and voice pitch. (Osherson and Smith 1981: 57)

Let us pursue the implications of this distinction by considering, first, the category NUMBER. Although, from the point of view of a mathematician, any number is just as much a number as any other number, i.e. NUMBER is an ungraded category, non-mathematicians in the course of their daily lives do not experience numbers as having equal status (cf. Lakoff 1987: 150f.). We speak of small numbers more frequently than large numbers; we compute with high numbers by dealing with them on a digit by digit basis; high numbers are generally understood in terms of their proximity to the 'cognitive reference points', such as 500, 1,000, 5,000, of our decimal counting system (cf. Rosch 1975 a); and to determine whether a number is odd or even we know that all we have to do is look at the final digit. It is also important to remember that numbers as such are abstractions. We encounter numbers, not of themselves, but as attributes of groupings of objects. An odd number of objects is one that cannot be divided equally amongst two persons. Taking into account how people normally interact with numbers, it is really not so surprising that a single digit like 3 should be judged a better example of ODD NUMBER than 447—one can readily visualize the impossibility of dividing a set of three objects equally between two people. Nor, given the way we compute with our decimal counting system, is it at all strange that a cognitive reference point like 1,000 should be considered a better even number than 806.

The distinction between core definition and recognition procedures makes it possible, in principle, to preserve the classical theory of categorization without at the same time ignoring the empirical evidence for prototype categorization. We simply say that prototype effects are a consequence of recognition procedures, while the classical theory looks after the core definition. The distinction also fits in nicely, of course, with the modularity assumption of the generative paradigm. The core definition deals in abstract linguistic features, and can thus be said to constitute the purely linguistic meaning of a word. The reader will have perhaps noticed, in the passage from Osherson and Smith quoted above, the eminently structuralist statement that it is the core which explicates the relation of a concept to other concepts (although what Osherson and Smith meant by saying that the core definition has to do with the relation of a concept to 'thoughts', is more obscure). Prototype effects, on the other hand, arise from an inter-action of core meaning with non-linguistic factors like perception and world knowledge, and can thus be assigned to other components of the mind.

A nice illustration of how autonomous linguistics can remain impervious to empirical evidence which threatens the categorization principles on which it is grounded is provided by Geoffrey Leech's *Semantics*. The first edition of the book, published in 1974, makes no reference to Rosch's work on categorization. Leech is aware that many natural categories do have fuzzy boundaries, and recognizes the potential damage of this fact for his structuralist-oriented com-ponential analysis. As a 'dedicated componentialist' (1974: 124) Leech therefore feels obliged to account for fuzziness within a componential model. One of his proposals invokes the only partial overlap of closely related polysemous senses. Thus, addressing the question whether *boast* does or does not contain the component [UNJUSTIFIED (SELF-PRAISE)], Leech suggests two componential analyses, one with the component, the other without. Fuzziness results from uncertainty as to which of the two senses is meant. In the second edition of the book, published in 1981, this highly unsatisfactory account has been deleted. Leech takes cognizance of Rosch's work and is able to state that fuzziness is merely a matter of 'referential vagueness', having to do with 'category recognition' (1981: 120); the core definition of categories remains intact.

Armstrong *et al.* were surely correct to attribute the prototype effects of odd and even numbers to identification procedures. What is questionable is the proposition that there exists a core definition independent of recognition procedures. Chomsky surely put his finger on the heart of the problem when he wrote that word meaning is intimately bound up with matters of knowledge and belief (1980: 225). Inevitably, matters of knowledge and belief are involved in a speaker's identification and recognition of an entity as a member of a certain category. But can one legitimately claim that there exists a definition of a category independent of such factors? Could one legitimately define *odd number* independently of the attributes of odd numbers that people appeal to when identifying something as an odd number?

Even accepting the validity of this argument, we are still left with the task of explaining the tension between the prototype effects shown by odd and even numbers and the clear intuition that odd numbers and even numbers do not constitute fuzzy categories. In point of fact, the same kind of tension shows up with other categories, as well. As noted earlier, penguins are more marginal members of BIRD than robins; at the same time penguins are just as much birds as robins. We can approach this issue by returning to Langacker's distinction between categorization by prototype and categorization by schema. Categorization by schema does not give rise to degree of membership judgements. We might hypothesize, therefore, that the intuition of all-or-nothing membership in certain categories reflects the existence of an abstract schematic representation of the category. The coexistence, within one and the same speaker, of alternative representations of a category, one involving a prototype, the other involving a schema, would thus account for the tension mentioned in the preceding paragraph.

I suggested in Section 4.2 that categorization by prototype occurs developmentally prior to categorization by schema. Categorization by schema presupposes a fairly sophisticated ability on the part of a language user to extract from diverse members of a category an abstract representation of what the members have in common. But schemas can not only be extracted from categories, schemas can also be imposed. Consider, for example, the word *adult*. On the one hand, we determine whether someone is an adult by appealing to such criteria as emotional maturity, financial independence, and, within a rather broad range of values, age. But coexisting with this rather fuzzy understanding of what it means to be an adult is an imposed definition, that of the bureaucrats, according to which a person becomes an adult on his eighteenth birthday, or whenever. Categories defined by the imposition of a set of criteria for category membership I shall refer to as 'expert categories', in contrast to the 'folk categories', or 'natural categories' of everyday use. Folk categories are structured around prototypical instances and are grounded in the way people normally perceive and interact with the things in their environment. On the other hand, expert categories (what Kempton 1981 calls 'devised classification systems'—note that I am using the word 'expert' in its folk sense: experts are people who, because of their professional standing, are 'supposed to know' about their relevant field) have been specifically created, usually in conformity with Aristotelian principles, i.e. the categories have necessary and sufficient conditions for membership, such that the relevant experts are competent to say whether, and on what grounds, any particular instance is or is not a member of the category. Indeed, one of the main activities of experts in many walks of life is precisely the 'drawing of boundaries' (cf. Wittgenstein 1978: 33) around essentially fuzzy categories, and the formulation of criteria on which membership is to be decided. The discipline of linguistics is no exception. Think, for example, of the technical definitions, put forward within the generative tradition, of grammaticality and language. (Grammaticality is a property of those sentences generated by the grammar of a language, while a language is defined as the set of sentences generated by the grammar.) The definitions serve to eliminate the fuzzy edges from the categories, giving them the status of technical, rather than merely pre-theoretical constructs.[4]

Relevant to the distinction I am drawing between expert and folk categories is Putnam's notion of the division of linguistic labour within

[4] Fascinating attempts to remove the fuzziness from the folk categories of natural language may be observed in the daily practice of the legal profession. Arguably, most legal decisions have to do, essentially, with the categorization of entities on the fuzzy borders of natural categories. On what basis, for example, does one decide whether a particular sequence of events constitutes an accident (a matter of obvious concern to the insurance industry); are abortion and euthanasia instances of murder? Confronted with such questions, it is the job of the legal profession to stipulate whether the category is instantiated or not, i.e., in Wittgenstein's words, to 'draw a boundary' around the category.

a speech community (1975). Most speakers of English know, through the general diffusion of scientific knowledge, that water is H_2O and that gold is an element with a particular atomic structure. But a person can use the words *water* and *gold* correctly and appropriately, without having first to acquire the skills necessary for determining whether something 'really is' H_2O or Au. The ordinary speaker of English identifies something as water and gold largely on the basis of what Putnam calls a 'stereotype'.[5] Water is a clear tasteless liquid, gold is a yellow malleable metal; water comes out of taps and is found in rivers and lakes, gold is a component of certain items of jewelry bought from reputable dealers. At the same time, the English speaker knows that there is a body of experts in society, namely chemists and metallurgists, who are professionally competent to determine whether something 'really is' water or gold or whatever. If knowledge of the 'real essence' of water and gold were a prerequisite for the use of the words *water* and *gold*, then only a few specially trained experts would be competent to use these words. And how could the words have been used before the rise of modern chemistry? Of course, some words are indeed restricted to use by experts—words like *phoneme* and *allophone* occur only in the expert discourse of phoneticians and linguists. Other words do not have expert definitions at all—words like *chair* and *cup*. Before the rise of modern science, *water* and *gold* were also words without expert definitions.

Putnam, then, is proposing that at least some words in our vocabulary are subject to both expert and folk definitions, the former having to do with necessary and sufficient conditions for category membership, the latter relying on our knowledge of perceptual and interactional attributes of prototypical instances. Generally, there is a 'structured co-operation' between expert and non-expert usage, in that the experts' definitions provide a kind of guarantee for appropriate linguistic usage in the speech community as a whole. This co-operation does not preclude the possibility of conflict. The folk definition of gold would probably refer to its yellow colour. The yellow colour, though, is not an essential attribute of the metal. On the contrary, it is the presence of impurities that gives what we call gold its yellow colour.

[5] Putnam's stereotypes appear to be rather broader constructs than what I have been calling prototype representations, in that they comprise, not only the prototype, but also frame and script based information which provides the context for a prototype representation. See s. 5.1.

We can now return to the starting-point of this discussion. Odd and even numbers can be characterized in two ways. On the one hand there are the expert definitions, those of the mathematicians. Speakers with only the most basic education have been made familiar with the expert definitions. In their daily encounters with numbers and with groupings of objects, however, people normally operate with a more informal, experience-based understanding of odd and even numbers. The expert and the folk characterizations coexist, not only in different sections of the speech community, but, typically, within individual members of the community. This state of affairs, I have suggested, is by no means unusual; cf. the earlier remarks on BIRD and ADULT. For a final example, consider Langacker's highly pertinent remarks on the concept "circle". On the one hand there is the expert definition, involving the notion of a series of points in a plane all equidistant from a central point. But coexisting with the expert definition is a more naïve understanding of what a circle is:

Anyone who has studied geometry is familiar with [the] definition [of circle] as the set of points in a plane that lie at a specified distance from a reference point. ... But despite the mathematical elegance of this characterization, it is doubtful that it reflects a person's naive or primary understanding of [CIRCLE]. Many people (e.g. young children) acquire [CIRCLE] as a salient and deeply entrenched concept without ever being exposed to the mathematical definition or focusing their attention specifically on the length of line segments from the center to the circumference. [CIRCLE] is probably first learned as a shape gestalt: it is the simplest or minimal closed curve, lacking any dimensional asymmetries or any departures from a smooth trajectory as one traces along its perimeter. (Langacker 1987: 86)

Of the two characterizations of circle, it is the naïve understanding that is developmentally basic. As Langacker observes in a footnote, 'the mathematical definition may be irrelevant to how the concept [CIRCLE] is learned and represented by the geometrically naive' (1987: 87). Subsequent exposure to the mathematical definition does not displace the naïve understanding, although it might enrich a person's encyclopaedic understanding of the notion. So it is with odd and even numbers. Even though we can all state the expert definitions of odd and even numbers, we still operate, in some contexts, with the naïve understanding. It is the tension between the naïve and expert understandings which gives rise to the (at first sight highly bizarre) experimental findings of Armstrong *et al.*

4.4 Hedges

The belief that categories *are* definable in terms of what their members have in common is deeply engrained; it is not only the dominant expert theory of the nature of categories, it also constitutes 'our everyday folk theory of what a category is' (Lakoff 1987: 5). There are many reasons for the persistence of this belief. I have already mentioned the role of formal education in imposing expert definitions. Another probable factor is the authority of the biblical creation story. Genesis teaches us that 'species are fixed entities established by God' (Leach 1982: 72); the creatures were created 'after their kind', and the kinds were given names by Adam. Adam's naming of the kinds points to the role of language itself in the enduring fortune of the classical theory. In the real world of objects, as Labov's (1973) experiment showed, cups might well merge into bowls, yet the lexical items *cup* and *bowl* do not merge into each other. Either one uses the word *cup* to refer to a particular receptacle, or one does not. Similarly, the pastness of an event from the present (a factor involved in the selection of the past tense, in one of its senses, in English), is a continuum, yet a speaker of English must make a discrete choice between the past tense and a non-past tense. One cannot convey degrees of pastness by varying the pastness of the past tense. In other words, the lexical and syntactic resources of a language can be said to impose a digital, rather than an analog, encoding of experience.

Wittgenstein alluded to this matter in the *Philosophical Investigations* (1978: 48): 'A *picture* held us captive. . . . It lay in our language and language seemed to repeat it to us inexorably.' The very fact that the word *game* is used to refer to a range of different activities easily creates in us the belief that the activities *must* have something in common, otherwise why call them the same?[6]

But it is not the case that language in all circumstances inexorably compels us to undertake an all-or-nothing categorization. Language

---

[6] An interesting sidelight on this issue is given by Edmund Leach (1964). Leach argues that while language imposes discrete categories on the continuity of the world, there are nevertheless certain phenomena in the world that refuse to be neatly categorized, as demanded by language. One of the most basic distinctions is between 'me' and 'not-me'. The distinction, in general clear enough, is threatened by certain substances of ambiguous status. Is excrement, for example, me or not-me? In order that we may keep our categories distinct, these ambiguous phenomena have to be suppressed, i.e. they become subject to taboo.

possesses its own resources for expressing degree of category member-ship. Kempton (1981: 27 ff.), in his study of the categorization of footwear, noted that it was not necessary to devise sophisticated exper-iments in order to elicit prototype effects; the evidence was there in the way his informants spoke about the objects. Some shoes were 'typical' (i.e. prototypical) shoes, some boots were not as 'booty' as other boots, but boots nevertheless (i.e. they were more marginal members of the category), one particular shoe could be singled out as 'the most typi-cal'. Some examples from his protocols:

> The most typical shoe is [item 38]; it has been the same through the ages, you can always get a black, lace-up shoe

> [Item 29] is a boot, but in the context of these big boots, you wouldn't say it was as booty, even though it is of the same style

> [Item 38] is really the most typical shoe, it's the kind you would expect to see in a children's book, with 'shoe' written under it.

> [Item 27] is a boot's boot

Amongst the resources of a language which enable a speaker to express degree of category membership are the words and expressions that Lakoff (1972) has called hedges. Lakoff lists over sixty English hedges in his paper. (The list is not exhaustive.) From a formal point of view, hedges form a highly heterogeneous group. They include sentence adjuncts like *loosely speaking* and *strictly speaking*, con-junctions like *in that*, modifiers like *so-called*, and even graphological devices like inverted commas, as well as certain intonation patterns (as when one talks of *a 'liberal' politician*). Semantically, we can characterize hedges as linguistic expressions which speakers have at their disposal to comment on the language they are using. Just as the word *chair* is 'about' chairs, so hedges are 'about' language (Kay 1983). For this reason, a careful study of hedges is likely to turn up valuable information on the nature of language itself. The remaining part of this chapter will examine some of the hedges discussed by Lakoff, and discuss their role in structuring categories.

Compare the following sentences:

(1) A robin is a bird *par excellence*

(2) ?A turkey is a bird *par excellence*

Sentence (2) is odd. It is not that a turkey is not a bird, only that it is not a bird *par excellence*. Turkeys exhibit a range of attributes not shared by prototypical birds: they can't fly, they don't sing, they are quite large, and they are raised in captivity for food. *Par excellence* is a hedge, whose function is to pick out only the central members of a category. One could say that the hedge restructures BIRD in such a way that the category consists only of prototypical, or close to prototypical members. To this extent (2) is false, since turkeys are not prototypical birds. That *par excellence* functions in this way at all, of course, presupposes that BIRD is a category with different degrees of membership.

Other hedges restructure categories by excluding the central members. *Loosely speaking* is an example:

(3) ?Loosely speaking, a chair is a piece of furniture

(4) Loosely speaking, a telephone is a piece of furniture

(5) *Loosely speaking, a six-sided figure is hexagonal

(6) Loosely speaking, France is hexagonal

Here it is (3) and (5) that are odd, since chairs are a pretty good example of furniture, and a six-sided figure *is* hexagonal, period. A telephone, on the other hand, is a pretty marginal example of furniture (if indeed it is a piece of furniture at all), while the frontiers of France trace only a very rough approximation to a hexagon.

Strictly speaking is similar, in that this hedge also excludes more central members of a category:

(7) ?Strictly speaking, beans are vegetables

(8) Strictly speaking, rhubarb is a vegetable.

In a sense, *strictly speaking* tightens up a category. It removes the fuzziness from category boundaries, by picking out non-prototypical entities and giving them full status. *Loosely speaking*, on the other hand, as it were extends the category by picking out things that would not ordinarily be considered members, but which might nevertheless be associated with the category on the basis of one or two non-essential attributes which they share with it. The contrast between the two can be seen in (10) and (11):

(9) A bat is a bird (false)

(10) Strictly speaking, a bat is a bird (false)

(11) Loosely speaking, a bat is a bird
(true, or at least not patently false)

We see from (11) that it is possible to hedge a statement in such a way that what would normally be considered a falsehood becomes true, or at least true to a certain extent. Some readers still might not accept (11), in spite of the hedge. (11) can be improved by making explicit the reasons for the loose categorization:

(12) Loosely speaking a bat is a bird, in that it has wings and can fly

In that spells out the reasons for assigning an entity to a category. In (12), it picks out attributes (i.e. flying and having wings) which, although typically associated with a category, would not normally of themselves grant membership to it. At the same time, membership in the category is released from otherwise highly entrenched, one might even say essential, attributes (e.g. laying eggs and having feathers). *In that* has been studied by Herrmann (1975). Although Herrmann makes no reference to prototypes, her examples can be readily interpreted in prototype terms. Consider the following sentences:

(13) *He killed Alice in that he murdered her
(14) He killed Alice in that he did nothing to keep her alive
(15) She's a friend of mind in that I've known her for years, but we're really not that close

(13) is odd, since it is not usually necessary to state the reasons for categorizing murder as killing. *Kill* prototypically denotes an action which directly causes loss of life, and murder is a central instance (cf. Pulman 1983: 113). (14), however, refers to a non-prototypical instance of killing, i.e. a non-event which leads indirectly to loss of life. Indeed, one might argue whether doing nothing to keep someone alive is an instance of killing at all. (14), as it were, restructures the category, overriding attributes typically associated with it. Similarly, (15) focuses on a single attribute which is frequently associated with friendship (i.e. long acquaintance), but which does not normally guarantee friendship; a highly entrenched attribute of friendship, i.e. close personal relationship, is cancelled.

So far, I have dealt only with hedges in terms of the status of members in a category. Hedges also serve to differentiate between various non-members of a category. (Recall that in the classical theory, not only do all members of a category have equal status, so do all non-members of a category.) Some entities, while not belonging to a category, are nevertheless felt to be closer to it than other non-members:

(16) Strictly speaking, a bat is not a bird
(17) *Strictly speaking, a TV set is not a bird

Neither bats nor TV sets are birds. Bats nevertheless exhibit some attributes of birds (but not enough attributes, or attributes of sufficient weight, for them to qualify strictly as birds), such that an inattentive or naïve observer might possibly categorize a bat incorrectly. TV sets, on the other hand, have nothing whatsoever in common with birds. The hedge *as such* functions in a similar way:

(18) An octopus is not a fish as such
(19) *A bicycle is not a fish as such

The fact that an octopus lives in the sea is not sufficient for it to be categorized as a fish. On the other hand, there is no way in which a bicycle might be categorized, even loosely, as a fish.

Consider, finally, the hedge *technically (speaking)*. *Technically*, like *strictly*, removes the fuzziness from a category, and in many contexts the two hedges are interchangeable. There is, though, an important difference. This is that *technically* invokes a technical, or expert definition of a category, setting it off against the folk definition. Consider the following example, from Lakoff's 1972 paper:

(20) Ronald Reagan is technically a cattle rancher

When Lakoff wrote this paper, Ronald Reagan was Governor of California. In order to take advantage of tax concessions, he bought cattle stocks. From the point of view of the experts (i.e. the tax authorities), Reagan was a cattle rancher. He was just as much a cattle rancher as any other registered cattle rancher. But he was not a cattle rancher in terms of the folk definition, i.e. he did not engage in the kinds of activities that people normally associate with cattle ranching. Indeed, it is doubtful whether one could say that Reagan, either *loosely speaking* or *strictly speaking*, was ever a cattle rancher.

Let us take stock of the discussion so far. According to the classical theory of categorization

(*a*) all members of a category have equal status
(*b*) all non-members of a category have equal status
(*c*) there is a fixed set of necessary and sufficient conditions defining membership to each category

   (*d*) all necessary and sufficient features defining a category have
       equal status

   (*e*) category boundaries are fixed

Hedges have provided evidence, from within the language itself, that none of these assumptions is true. Hedges require us to distinguish between central and peripheral members of a category (*par excellence*, *strictly speaking*), as well as between different degrees of non-membership in a category (*strictly speaking*). They show that category boundaries are flexible (*loosely speaking*), and that categories can be redefined by an *ad hoc* selection and re-weighting of attributes (*in that*). Furthermore, hedges can pick out cases where, exceptionally, categories *are* being defined by classical principles (*technically*), although in doing so they at the same time imply a contrast with non-classical categorization. In a very important sense, then, hedges both confirm and complement the psycholinguistic evidence reviewed in the preceding chapter.

5

Linguistic and Encyclopaedic Knowledge

In previous chapters we have encountered a number of instances where it seemed that the meaning of a linguistic form could only be characterized against specific cultural norms or practices. Various attributes of cups have to do with cultural norms for drinking hot liquids; *bachelor of arts* only makes sense in the context of institutions of higher learning and their procedures for granting degrees; even in the sense "man who has never married" *bachelor* needs to be understood against the cultural institution of marriage. The understanding of terms like *cup* and *bachelor* thus presupposes a certain amount of world knowledge on the part of the language user. In this chapter, we explore in more detail the relevance of background knowledge, and consider the ways in which this kind of knowledge can be incorporated into the characterization of word meanings.

Autonomous linguistics assumes a clean separation between a speaker's world knowledge and his purely linguistic knowledge. 'Meaning *per se*' (Leech 1981: 70) is held to be independent of whatever states of affairs might hold in real or imaginary worlds, and independent of whatever a speaker of a language might know about these states of affairs. The mental dictionary, the slogan goes, is not an encyclopaedia. There are many problems associated with this approach (for a critique, see Haiman 1980), not the least of which is the problem of demarcation. Where, and on what criteria, do we draw the line between what a speaker knows in virtue of his knowledge of a language and what he knows in virtue of his acquaintance with the world? The problem shows up in a particularly acute form in connection with the analytic–synthetic distinction. In terms of this distinction, one would presumably say that sentence (1) is analytic:

(1) Dogs are animals

(2) Dogs have four legs/have a tail/bark/do not miaow/do not have horns, etc.

i.e. that the sentence is true in virtue of the conjunction of semantic features[1] which define the (purely linguistic) meanings of the words *dog* and *animal*. But what about (2)? Are these sentences true in virtue of the meaning of *dog*, or in virtue of our knowledge of what dogs happen to be like? Leech (1981: 83f.) argues that to say that the sentences in (2) are analytic, would amount to adding the features [POSSESS FOUR LEGS], [POSSESS TAIL], [−POSSESS HORNS], etc. to the set of necessary and sufficient features defining the category DOG. But to add these features is to make way for an indefinitely long definition of the category; the definition would have to include the features [POSSESS FUR], [POSSESS SNOUT], [−POSSESS WINGS], and many, many more. The solution, for Leech, is to restrict the purely linguistic, dictionary definition of *dog* to "animal of the canine species", i.e. to the feature set [ANIMAL] and [CANINE], and to leave everything else one knows about dogs to the zoologist.

And, indeed, it would seem to make sense to claim that dogs do not *have* to have four legs in order to be dogs. Possession of four legs is merely an expected attribute of dogs, not a defining feature of the category. (Thus a dog, one of whose legs has been amputated, is still a dog.) But is the situation with regard to (1) really any different? The extended discussion of analycity conducted by the philosophers Quine, Kripke, and Putnam (see Pulman 1983 for an overview) suggests that it is not. Our conviction that (1) is necessarily true is merely a consequence of deeply entrenched beliefs about the inner constitution of the natural kinds dog and animal, and about the manner in which the kinds are related in a taxonomic hierarchy. In the highly unlikely, but not totally inconceivable, event of dogs being discovered to be self-reproducing automata controlled by extraterrestrial minds, (1) would cease to be true. (1) cannot therefore be analytic, in that its truth is not independent of our understanding of real-world contingencies.

These considerations inevitably lead to a view of word meaning which is broadly encyclopaedic in scope. Our concept "dog" is not independent of our knowledge about dogs—about the status of dogs as a species within the animal kingdom, about different breeds of dog, about their appearance and behaviour, their relationship with humans, and so on. This kind of knowledge is the matrix for our mental representation of the prototypical dog, and provides a rationale

---

[1] Recall (ch. 3 n. 1) that I am using the term 'feature' to refer exclusively to conditions for membership in classical, Aristotelian categories.

for delimiting the range of creatures that can be referred to as dogs. Admittedly, an encyclopaedist approach also brings with it a demarcation problem. We do not, presumably, want to say that everything an individual happens to know about dogs will be relevant for a characterization of his concept "dog". To say that the dictionary is encyclopaedic is not equivalent to saying that the dictionary *is* an encyclopaedia. At the same time, we should not exclude a priori the possibility that different speakers of a language may have slightly different representations of "dog". The specialized knowledge of the dog breeder or the veterinarian, or the idiosyncratic knowledge of the dog lover (as well as the strongly felt aversion of the dog hater) may well enter into an individual's characterization of "dog". In general, however, we can regard the relevant background information for the characterization of word meanings as a network of shared, conventionalized, to some extent perhaps idealized knowledge, embedded in a pattern of cultural beliefs and practices.

5.1 Domains and schemas

We can begin with what is, I think, a fairly unproblematic assertion: meanings do not exist in themselves. In denying that meanings of linguistic forms constitute independently existing entities, cognitive and structuralist linguistics are in agreement. For both cognitivists and structuralists, meanings are context dependent. For the structuralist, however, context dependency is a matter of the syntagmatic and paradigmatic relations between signs within the linguistic system, i.e. the context for the definition of a meaning is language internal. We saw at the close of Chapter 2 how this eminently Saussurian notion has been implemented to the present day, as shown by the citations from Lyons, Nida, and Cruse. For cognitivists, on the other hand, the context against which meanings are characterized is external to the language system as such. Meanings are cognitive structures, embedded in patterns of knowledge and belief. In stark contrast to the structuralist approach, a meaning is, in principle, independent of whatever other cognitive structures happen to be lexicalized in a particular language. Bickerton (1981: 230f.) claimed that the meaning of *toothbrush* is delimited by the meanings of other items in the linguistic system, such as *nailbrush* and *hairbrush*. But is it really plausible that a person who does not have the words *nailbrush* and *hairbrush* in his vocabulary would understand *toothbrush* differently from those people who do know what nailbrushes and hairbrushes are? Surely, *toothbrush* derives its meaning from the role of toothbrushes in dental hygiene, and not from paradigmatic contrasts with other terms in the language system. The concept "toothbrush" has nothing whatever to do with the way people clean their nails, adjust their hair, or sweep their floors.

In general, we can only understand the meaning of a linguistic form in the context of other cognitive structures; whether these other cognitive structures happen to be lexicalized in the language is in principle irrelevant. To take a simple, though telling example: what is the meaning of the word *Monday*? Clearly, *Monday* can only be explicated in the context of the concept "week"; someone unfamiliar with the notion of the seven-day week would have no basis for an understanding of *Monday*. "Week", in turn, must be understood in terms of the recurring day–night cycle. Ultimately, the concepts "day", "week", and "Monday" are understood against the concept of time. Similarly, *up* and *down*, *high* and *low*, *rise* and *fall* can only be explicated against the notion of three-dimensional, gravitational space; *in* and *out*, *enter* and *exit* require the notion of a three-dimensional container; *wing* presupposes "bird' (or "aeroplane"), *birth*, *old age*, and *death* presuppose a knowledge of the life cycle, *heavy* requires reference to the notion of "weight", and so on, throughout the dictionary.

We shall say, following Langacker (1987: 147 ff.), that the seven-day week is the semantic 'domain' against which *Monday* is understood, and that the day–night cycle is the domain for an understanding of *week*. Similarly, three-dimensional space is the domain against which *up* and *down* are understood, while a three-dimensional container is the domain of *in* and *out*. In principle, any conceptualization or knowledge configuration, no matter how simple or complex, can serve as the cognitive domain for the characterization of meanings. Neither should we restrict ourselves, in this discussion, to the meanings of lexical items. Morphological and syntactic categories also need to be understood against the relevant domain. For instance, the diminutive (in its basic sense) presupposes the domain of physical size, the domain for the understanding of the past tense (in its past-time reference) is time, and so on.

A linguistic form gets its meaning by 'profiling', or highlighting, a particular region or configuration in the relevant domain. Profiling entails the structuring of a domain by means of an appropriate 'schema', or set of schemas.[2] The concepts "week", "day", and "Monday" emerge when a bounding schema profiles bounded regions in the domain of time; a sequencing schema structures the concept "week" into a succession of discrete bounded entities; and a further schema profiles the first of these successive units. *Up* and *down* impose an up–down schema on the domain of vertical space; *in* and *out* get their meanings through a containment, or, respectively, an exclusion schema; *wing* profiles a particular region of its domain by means of the part–whole schema; and so on.

Time and three-dimensional space, in the above examples, constitute what Langacker (1987: 148) calls 'basic domains', i.e. the concepts of time and space are not reducible to other, more primitive cognitive structures. Other basic domains include sensory experiences like temperature, colour, taste, and pitch, and perhaps certain psychological states like pleasure and enthusiasm. Lakoff (1987) has drawn attention to the role of a small number of basic schemas in the structuring of domains. In addition to those already mentioned (boundedness, part–whole, containment, up–down), Lakoff mentions the journey schema with its constituent parts of source, path, and goal, and the schemas of linkage and separation, and of proximity and distance. As we shall see in Chapter 7, these and other schemas are crucially involved in any proper understanding of processes of metaphorization.

Some of the examples given so far, like *up* and *in*, can be explicated very simply with reference to a single domain. Very often a linguistic form needs to be characterized against a number of different domains simultaneously. *Golfball* is understood partly in terms of typical shape (i.e. golfballs are bounded entities in three-dimensional space), as well as colour, size, material, texture, etc. A full understanding of the word also requires reference to the set of rules and activities which together constitute the game of golf. Similarly *Monday* is not only the first day of the week; a full understanding of the word needs to make reference to the division of the week into periods of leisure (i.e. the weekend) and periods of work, Monday being the first day of the working week after the weekend. Sometimes one of the domains associated with a lexical item might be more salient than others. In this connection, Langacker (1987: 165) distinguishes between primary and

---

[2] The term 'schema', or 'image schema', is taken from Lakoff (1987). Lakoff's schemas are not to be confused with Langacker's use of the word to refer to the abstract representation of what is common to the members of a category.

secondary domains. *Salt*, in its everyday sense (i.e. "table salt"), is primarily associated with the domain of food: salt is a substance added to certain kinds of food in order to enhance their flavour; only secondarily is its chemical composition at issue. *Sodium chloride*, an expression with the same reference, is understood against the domain of chemical composition, and only secondarily in terms of its role as a food additive. Other near synonyms may be distinguished with respect to the different domains against which they are understood. *On land* evokes the domain of a sea voyage; *on the ground*, in contrast, evokes the domain of a flight through the air (cf. Fillmore 1979*b*: 97).

A rather more complex example of a lexical item being characterized against several domains simultaneously has been provided by Lakoff (although Lakoff does not use the term 'domain') in his discussion of the word *mother* (Lakoff 1987: 74 ff.). Lakoff points out that we need to take into consideration at least five domains (in addition to those which characterize *mother* as a human female) for any adequate understanding of the word. These are:

(*a*) the genetic domain. A mother is a female who contributes genetic material to a child;
(*b*) the birth domain. A mother is a female who gives birth to the child;
(*c*) the nurturance domain. A mother is a female adult who nurtures and raises a child;
(*d*) the genealogical domain. A mother is the closest female ancestor;
(*e*) the marital domain. The mother is the wife of the father.

We can compare the domains against which *mother* is understood with the domains necessary for a full understanding of *father*. Again, five domains seem to be implicated:

(*a*) the genetic domain. A father is a male who contributes genetic material to a child;
(*b*) the responsibility domain. The father is financially responsible for the well-being of the mother and the child;
(*c*) the authority domain. The father is a figure of authority, responsible for the discipline of the child;
(*d*) the genealogical domain. The father is the closest male ancestor;
(*e*) the marital domain. The father is the husband of the mother.

It is clear from this account that the meaning of *father* is not, as the componentialists and structuralists would maintain, identical to *mother*, but for the feature [MALE] rather than [FEMALE]. Only with respect to the genetic, genealogical, and marital domains are the two concepts at all comparable.

5.2 Frames and scripts

Langacker has pointed out that his construct of domain—especially in cases where the domain is cognitively quite complex, or where a linguistic form needs to be characterized against several domains simultaneously—overlaps to a large extent with what others have referred to variously as frames, scripts, schemata, scenes, scenarios, idealized cognitive models, and so on; Putnam's stereotypes also appear to coincide with our notion of a prototype seen in the context of the relevant domain matrix. The terminology in this area is confusing, partly because different terms may be used by different authors (or even by the same author in different publications) to refer to what seems to be the same construct, or the same term may be used to refer to very different constructs. Furthermore, it is not at all clear that it is possible to make clean conceptual distinctions in this area. Nevertheless, I have found the term 'frame' to be metatheoretically useful in addition to 'domain'. In the following, 'frame' will refer to the knowledge network linking the multiple domains associated with a given linguistic form. We can reserve the term 'script' for the temporal sequencing and causal relations which link events and states within certain action frames.

Frames and scripts are constructs which were originally developed by researchers in the field of artificial intelligence. The constructs made it possible to represent in computer memory those aspects of world knowledge which appear to be involved in the natural processing of texts. The constructs have also proved invaluable in studies of natural comprehension. According to de Beaugrande and Dressler (1981: 90), frames constitute 'global patterns' of 'common sense knowledge about some central concept', such that the lexical item denoting the concept typically evokes the whole frame. In essence, frames are static configurations of knowledge. Scripts, on the other hand, are more dynamic in nature. Typically, scripts are associated with what we have referred to earlier as basic level events such as 'do the washing up' and 'visit the doctor', which are structured according to the expected sequencing of subordinate events (cf. Rosch 1978).

As an illustration of the notion of frame, let us reconsider Lakoff's discussion of *mother*. The five domains against which this word needs to be characterized do not constitute a random set. It is the structured whole that I shall call the 'mother frame'. According to the mother frame, a mother is a woman who has sexual relations with the father, falls pregnant, gives birth, and then, for the following decade or so, devotes the greater part of her time to nurturing and raising the child, remaining all the while married to the father. In such a situation, all five domains converge. Clearly, such a scenario is highly idealized, in that the frame abstracts away from its many untypical instantiations. Unmarried mothers renounce, for whatever reasons, the marriage relationship with the father; in the case of children given for adoption, there is a split between the genetic and birth domains on the one hand and the nurturance domain on the other; surrogate motherhood results in a splitting off of the genetic domain from the birth domain; alternatively the nurturance domain might undergo a split, in that the birth-giving mother remains responsible for nurturance, while the actual job of nurturing is taken over by someone else, e.g. a nanny or a grandparent. It is, of course, against the background of the idealized scenario that we characterize a prototypical mother. Adoptive mothers, surrogate mothers, stepmothers, unmarried mothers, widowed mothers, uncaring mothers, even perhaps so-called working mothers, are more marginal members of the category. Ultimately, the frame embodies deeply held beliefs about the status and role of the family in society. To this extent, it is irrelevant to ask whether prototypical mothers are in fact of more frequent occurrence than less prototypical members of the category. Some people might well believe that the idealized scenario does in fact constitute the norm; others might be more sceptical, but might at the same time believe in the desirability, at least, of the idealized scenario, while others vehemently reject it for its sexist assumptions. Neither is the idealized scenario immune to change. Some readers might feel that my account of prototypical motherhood is already outdated.

Clearly, then, frames do not necessarily incorporate scientifically validated knowledge of the world. Take again the example of *Monday*. We would want to include in the frame the knowledge that Monday is the first working day after a culturally institutionalized weekend, that on Mondays people reluctantly return to the routine of work after their weekend leisure, and that it generally takes them a little time to readjust to the work pattern. Again, the knowledge is idealized. It is hardly relevant to housewives, or to people who work at weekends and have Mondays free. Other people are only too happy to return to work after the boredom of their weekend, while people on vacation have both weekends and Mondays free. And, just as with the *mother* example, the idealization of the frame seems to rest, ultimately, on deeply entrenched cultural beliefs and practices. In this case we have to do with the division (inherited from the Jewish tradition) of one's waking life into periods of work and periods of rest.

As mentioned in the introduction to this chapter, the mental lexicon, although encyclopaedic in nature, includes but a subset of a person's total knowledge. But where, and on what basis, does one draw the line? Brown and Yule consider that the outstanding problem for frame and script theory is to find 'a *principled* means' for distinguishing between those aspects of world knowledge that are relevant to text processing, and those which are not (1983: 244; authors' emphasis). Wierzbicka (1985) also recognizes the importance of this issue by consistently making a distinction between knowledge *of* a concept and knowledge *about* a concept. Relevant to this distinction is whether a particular piece of knowledge associated with a concept shows up in linguistic expressions. Thus Wierzbicka's definition of *elephant* includes the encyclopaedic information that elephants are reputed to have long memories, presumably because of the existence of the catch phrase in English *Elephants never forget*. On the other hand, other facts about elephants—e.g. that they are a threatened species—are not included in her definition. But, it might be objected, does not this distinction, assuming we agree on the means for drawing it, merely reinstate the old distinction between linguistic and non-linguistic knowledge? Admittedly, the boundary is drawn in a different place, but is it not the same kind of distinction that is being made?

The objection is unjustified, as it presupposes a clear dividing line between linguistically relevant and linguistically irrelevant knowledge. Frames, as I have stressed, are configurations of culture-based, conventionalized knowledge. Most importantly, the knowledge encapsulated in a frame is knowledge which is shared, or which is believed to be shared, by at least some segment of a speech community. In principle, *any* scrap of knowledge, even the most bizarre, can get absorbed into a frame, provided the association is shared by a sufficient number of people. Langacker (1987: 160) notes that Jimmy

Carter's presidency had a substantial, albeit transient, effect on the meaning of *peanut*.

5.3 Perspectivization

I would like at this point briefly to introduce a further construct which will prove valuable in the following discussion, namely perspectivization. (The term is taken from Dirven *et al*. 1982.) It frequently happens that different uses of a word whose semantic structure is rather complex tend to highlight different components of frame-based knowledge. Thus, if I say that my birthday falls this year on a Monday, I am using the word *Monday* to refer simply to a position in the seven-day week. Suppose, on the other hand, that I complain of a Monday-morning feeling. What is at issue here is not primarily the position of Monday in the week, but rather the fact that Monday follows the weekend. What is perspectivized is only one component of the Monday frame, i.e. the reluctance with which one returns to work after the leisure of the weekend. Again, if I remark that my car must have been made on a Monday, I am perspectivizing the shoddy workmanship associated, within the Monday frame, with the reluctant return to the work-place after the weekend. Other examples are provided by some of the mother expressions cited earlier. *Birth mother* perspectivizes the birth domain, while *working mother* invokes the belief associated with the nurturance domain that a mother should devote a major part of her time to caring for her children.

As will be discussed more fully in the next chapter, perspectivization gradually shades into metonymic extension. In many instances, the perspectivization of one component of a frame not only backgrounds other components, the other components are suppressed completely. I can complain of a Monday-morning feeling even if it is not Monday, while the remark *This car was made on a Monday* need not entail any commitment regarding the actual day of the week on which the car was assembled, or even whether it was in fact assembled on a single day. Similarly, when a Zulu uses the word *umama* "mother" as a term of respect to an older female, the genetic, birth, and other domains are irrelevant to the word's meaning; only certain components of the genealogical domain are in focus.

5.4 Frames and scripts in language comprehension

If, as I have argued, the meanings of all linguistic forms can only be characterized relative to a speaker's background knowledge, it follows that the comprehension of any linguistic expression, even the most banal, requires the activation of appropriate encyclopaedic knowledge. The thesis is well illustrated by the formation and understanding of compound nouns, especially so-called 'root compounds' (Botha 1984: 2), in English. In the early years of generative syntax, it used to be thought that nominal compounds could be derived through trans-formation from an underlying phrasal structure. Thus, *girlfriend* was derived from *The friend is a girl*, *arrow head* was seen as a transforma-tion of *The arrow has a head*, and so on (Lees 1960). This approach assumed, among other things, a finite number of underlying syntactic relationships between the elements of nominal compounds, and, associated with these underlying syntactic relationships, an equal number of compounding transformations. Since the number of under-lying relationships seemed to be rather large, it followed that any single nominal compound was multiply ambiguous, i.e. it was derivable from many different underlying phrases. It was, of course, left to the language user's encyclopaedic knowledge to select the pragmatically most reasonable derivation (cf. Katz and Fodor 1963). It is on the basis of what we happen to know about the manufacture and use of shoes that *alligator shoes* are taken to be "shoes made from alligator skin", rather than "shoes worn by alligators" (cf. *horse shoes*), "shoes for walking on alligators" (cf. *beach shoes*), or even "shoes for wearing during the alligator time" (cf. *winter shoes*). Our purely grammatical competence, however, makes each of these interpretations (and many more) equally available to us.

Downing (1977*b*) has questioned the assumption of a finite number of relationships underlying nominal compounds. She distinguishes between nonce formations and conventionalized compounds. In the former, practically any kind of association between entities can be the basis for a descriptive phrase, as when a hostess tells her guest to sit in 'the apple-juice seat'. Conventionalized compounds, on the other hand, depend on the recognition of relatively permanent, non-predictable relationships of varying semantic types. The nature of the relationship, in any specific instance, is determined through the activa-tion of an appropriate frame. The matter has been discussed by Lakoff

(1977) in connection with expressions like *topless dress*, *topless bar*, *topless district*, *topless judge*. Our understanding of these expressions presupposes, firstly, the knowledge that women are required to cover their breasts in public. We know that women who do not do so serve in certain kinds of bars; that such bars are found in restricted areas of a city; and that such practices, being subject to legislation, are liable to be commented on by judges. Accordingly, we construe a topless bar as a bar in which women wearing topless dresses work as waitresses, a topless district as a district in which topless bars are to be found, and a topless judge as a judge who has made pronouncements on the phenomenon of topless bars, districts, etc. By the same token, an expression like *topless chair* is virtually uninterpretable. It could mean "a chair on which women wearing topless dresses sit", but the knowledge encapsulated in our topless frame has no place for such an object. The expression is to all intents and purposes ill-formed.

These considerations lead to an important conclusion. On the classical, feature theory, sequences of words (e.g. adjective-plus-noun combinations) are either grammatical or ungrammatical, depending on the compatibility of their feature specifications; because features are binary, the grammaticality of word combinations is strictly a matter of either–or. It seems, however, that the acceptability (i.e. grammaticality) of an expression is not merely a function of the semantic and syntactic properties of its component parts. Acceptability is also a function of interpretability, given certain background knowledge. To the extent that an expression is interpretable, it will be accepted as well formed; otherwise it will be rejected.

5.5 Fake

In this and the following section I would like to explore the above thesis by considering two words whose semantics, and whose combinatorial possibilities, are difficult to account for without reference to frames. In this section I take the word *fake*.

It is well known that the semantics of *fake* create problems for the classical theory of categorization. The difficulties have been noted by Lakoff and Johnson (1980) in connection with sentence (3):

(3) This is a fake gun

The problem is whether a fake gun is or is not a gun. In some respects it is, in other respects it isn't. (Recall the Aristotelian law of contradiction!) A fake gun is a gun to the extent that it possesses many of the attributes of a real gun; it looks like one, and performs at least some of the functions of a gun, e.g. it can be used to intimidate people. Yet a fake gun fails to perform a presumably essential function of a gun, i.e. it doesn't shoot. However, a real gun which fails to shoot, e.g. because it is rusty, or simply because it is unloaded, does not for this reason become a fake gun. Neither is a toy gun, which also fails to shoot, a fake gun. A fake gun has to have been constructed so that its appearance is such that it can be used with the intention of deceiving.

Thus only things that have been fabricated by man can qualify as fakes. Even if *fake* modifies a noun that normally refers to a non-artefact, as in the expression *fake gold*, the noun would be understood as referring to a fabricated substance.[3] The problem is, not all artefacts come in fake versions. It is difficult to imagine what would be meant by *fake bed*, *fake newspaper*, or *fake examination paper*. On the other hand, *fake Louis XIV chair*, *fake first edition*, and *fake Ph.D. certificate* are readily interpretable. In each case an essential attribute of the real thing is missing—the fake chair is not really an antique, the certificate does not really testify to the holder having obtained an academic degree, the book was not really published on the date stated on its title page. Deception in these cases is possible because the fake possesses all (or a very large number) of the perceptual attributes of the genuine article. But there is another important property of fakes. This is that the stakes involved in a successful deception are potentially high. Dealers who can pass off fake antiques as real antiques stand to make a good deal of money; conversely, if the fakes are discovered, the dealers stand to lose both money and their reputation. On the other hand, not much is to be gained from the construction of, say, a bed which looks in all respects like a bed but which fails to perform an essential function of a bed (what might this be?). In this respect, *fake* contrasts with *false*. Consider what would be meant by *false teeth* and *fake teeth*. False teeth have been fabricated to look like teeth and to perform most of the functions of teeth, e.g. one can chew with them,

---

[3] Some uses of *fake* might appear not to refer to artefacts, e.g. *That man is a fake*. This sentence, however, does not mean that the man, as a biological entity, is a fake, only that his personality, or the identity that he presents to the world, is a deception. Admittedly, a personality is not a prototypical artefact. Yet a person can consciously 'construct' his persona, and do so with the intention of deceiving.

yet not much is at stake in passing off false teeth as genuine teeth. On the other hand, in view of the fact that the examination of teeth has played an important role in the study of primate evolution, one can easily imagine unscrupulous palaeontologists presenting fake teeth to the academic world. At stake here are their professional reputations and their careers.

At this point, we might consider how these facts about the combinatorial possibilities of *fake* could be accommodated within a feature-based description. That *fake* can only be applied to a certain range of nouns is an instance of a selection restriction. We could capture some very general properties of the word by saying that *fake* is restricted to occurring with nouns possessing the feature [+ARTEFACT] (or alternatively, to account for cases like *fake gold*, that *fake* transfers this feature to the noun), and that *fake* is distinguished from *false* in that the former possesses the feature [+DECEPTION], while the latter is marked [-DECEPTION]. There are two, related problems. How can we delimit the range of nouns to which the feature [+ARTEFACT] can be transferrred, i.e. why can we have *fake gold* but not, presumably, **fake vermin*? And how do we represent the fact that *fake* readily combines with the names of some artefacts (e.g. *gun* and *antique*) but not with others (e.g. *bed* and *newspaper*)?

In contrast with the componentialist view, I would maintain that the possibility of combining with *fake* has nothing to do with any properties of the nouns *gun*, *newspaper*, *tooth*, etc. as such. What is at issue is certain properties of the entities to which these nouns refer.[4] These properties are not inherent to the entities, but rather have to do with the role of the entities in a particular cultural context. More precisely, the appropriate use of *fake* requires the activation of an appropriate frame. To understand the expression *fake antique*, we need to draw on what we know about antiques. We need to know that the age of certain artefacts can in some instances greatly affect their monetary value, that there are people in our society who make their living by buying and selling such artefacts, that some people invest in them, that others collect them, that there are people with professional expertise for estimating their age and value, and so on. This knowledge comes together in what we might call the antique trade frame. It is only in the context of this frame that we can know what is at stake in constructing an artefact so that it looks old. Otherwise, the expression

[4] A similar point has been made by Dirven and Taylor (1988) in their discussion of Bierwisch's example **hohe Zigarette*.

would be simply uninterpretable. Similarly, to understand *fake Ph.D. certificate*, we need to know about the role of academic degrees as a formal qualification for certain kinds of employment, while *fake gun* only makes sense in the context of generally held knowledge about bank robberies and plane-hijackings. If *fake gun* were to activate only a game safari frame, the expression would be virtually uninterpretable, since it would be difficult to imagine someone intimidating wild animals with a gun which did not shoot. By the same token, *fake bed* is unacceptable simply because we cannot activate a frame in which beds can be associated with any kind of high-stake deception.

5.6 Real

Real, in one of its senses, is the converse of *fake* and *false*. We can contrast a *fake gun* with a *real gun*, a *real moustache* with a *false moustache*. *Real* can also function as a kind of hedge. Let us illustrate with the word *bachelor*. In Chapter 2 we discussed a componential analysis of *bachelor*. A componential analysis, and the related notion of analytic truth, neatly account for the semantic anomaly (in this case, contradiction) of a sentence like (4):

(4) *This married man is a bachelor

Yet, if we hedge the word *bachelor* with *real*, sentences like (4) cease to be contradictory

(5) Mary's husband is a real bachelor

Paradoxically (5) is not only non-anomalous, it is also quite informative. It tells us quite a lot about Mary's husband, e.g. that he is an inveterate womanizer. A *real bachelor*, then, does not have to exhibit each of the four defining features of *bachelor*, as analysed by Katz and Postal. Conversely, in some situations it is inappropriate to use the word *bachelor* of someone who clearly does exhibit each of the defining features. In one of his papers, Fillmore raises the question whether the Pope can be considered a bachelor (Fillmore 1982: 34). The question seems bizarre. The Pope is surely a very marginal instance of the category, cf. (6). Even worse is a description of the Pope as a *real bachelor* (7):

(6) ?The Pope is a bachelor

(7) ??The Pope is a real bachelor

Not surprisingly, a description of the Pope as a bachelor becomes much more acceptable if it is hedged with *strictly speaking* (recall that *strictly speaking* removes the fuzziness from a category: s. 4.4):

(8) Strictly speaking, the Pope is a bachelor

Strictly speaking, however, cannot be combined with *real*:

(9) *Strictly speaking, Mary's husband is a real bachelor

(10) *Strictly speaking, the Pope is a real bachelor

An explanation of these (according to a classical feature theory of meaning) highly bizarre facts is to be found, once again, in terms of world knowledge systematized in frames. In Chapter 2 I mentioned in passing that the concept of bachelorhood presupposes the cultural institution of marriage. But the background knowledge is much more complex than this. In the first place, what we might call the bachelor frame (as well as, *mutatis mutandis*, the spinster frame) includes the notion of a marriageable age. People who have passed this age are expected to have married; only those who fail to do so are normally referred to as bachelors (or spinsters, as the case may be). People below the marriageable age are not normally categorized in terms of their unmarried status. One consequence is that while one may readily say that a man will cease to be a bachelor on his wedding-day, one does not normally speak of a youth becoming a bachelor on reaching adult-hood:

(11) *On your eighteenth birthday, you'll become a bachelor

Like some examples discussed earlier in this chapter, the bachelor frame is highly selective, not to say stereotyped. It certainly does not present a scientifically accurate picture of marriage practices in our society. Most obviously, the frame leaves out of account various minority groups, like celibate priests and nuns, who go through life unmarried. It also ignores homosexuals, and people who have long-term unmarried relationships. These people, like persons below the marriageable age, just do not qualify for bachelor- or spinsterhood; they are not covered by the frame. Hence the oddity of referring to a Catholic priest, just as to an eighteen-year-old school pupil, as a bachelor. We can, however, appropriately refer to these people as bachelors if we hedge our statements with *strictly speaking* or *technically*. *Technically* invokes a bureaucratic definition of bachelor-hood, while *strictly speaking*, as we have seen, gives a more central status to marginal members.

There are further ramifications of the frames activated by the words *bachelor* and *spinster*. We have seen that, in terms of the frames, a person who has passed the marriageable age is expected to have married. But some people (we are not considering those groups of people, like priests, nuns, and homosexuals, who are not covered by the frame) do not marry. The frames attribute different motives to men and women who fail to marry. A man who does not marry does so from choice; he decides against the 'commitments' of marriage. A woman who does not marry does so from necessity. Thus *eligible spinster* is almost a contradiction, while *eligible bachelor* is a normal collocation. As Robin Lakoff put it, in her study of sexism in language, the spinster 'has had her chance, and been passed by'; she is 'old unwanted goods' (1975: 32f.). *Real* activates these dormant, rarely explicated components of frame logic. *Real bachelor* highlights the man's irresponsibility, while *real spinster* focuses on the woman's sexual unattractiveness. The words *bachelor* and *spinster* thus differ in many more ways than just the feature specification [MALE] vs. [FEMALE]. No doubt it is the sexist bias implicit in the spinster frame that accounts for the relatively infrequent use of the word *spinster*, as well as the coinage of the expression *bachelor girl*. The expression attributes to single adult females the same motives for not marrying as to their male counterparts.[5]

In a sense, *real* and *technically/strictly speaking* have opposite semantic effects. *Technically* and *strictly* dissociate a category from its conventionalized frame. *Real*, on the other hand, highlights attributes conventionally associated with a frame, while at the same time releasing the category from otherwise necessary conditions for membership. A *real man* exhibits to a high degree stereotyped attributes of masculinity; his gender is not at issue. Colloquially, a *real moron* is someone who conforms pretty well with our stereotype of slow-wittedness; his mental age on the Binet test (the technical definition of *moron*) is irrelevant. Significantly, given the classical structure of most expert categories, terms restricted to technical discourse are difficult

[5] It hardly needs pointing out that on Katz and Postal's analysis of *bachelor*, *bachelor girl* is doubly contradictory: *girl*, being [FEMALE] and [-ADULT], contradicts *bachelor*, which is [MALE] and [+ADULT]. The fact that *girl*, to a greater extent than *boy*, can be used of adults, can also be explained in terms of stereotyped sex-role frames.

to hedge with *real*. It would be very odd to speak of a 'real bilabial plosive' (although we shall see in Chapter 10 that one linguist has written of 'copperclad, brass-bottomed Noun Phrases'). It simply goes counter to the very function of a technical term to release it from its criterial definition, and to highlight its conventional associations.

6

Polysemy and Meaning Chains

THE discussion so far in this book has been restricted to what we might call monocentric categories, that is to say, degree of membership in the category is a function of similarity to a single prototype representation. This chapter extends the prototype model, so as to render it applicable to a wider range of linguistic data. Many natural language categories, perhaps even the majority, exhibit a polycentric, rather than a monocentric structure, i.e. category membership is a function of similarity to one of several prototype representations. The multiple prototypes associated with the category are themselves related in what I shall call, adapting Wittgenstein's metaphor, a family resemblance structure. Family resemblance categories will be illustrated on the examples of the lexical items *climb* (briefly discussed in Fillmore 1982) and *over* (the topic of Brugman's 1981 thesis). To conclude the chapter, some theoretical problems associated with the family resemblance model will be discussed.

6.1 Monosemous and polysemous categories

The distinction between monocentric and polycentric categories corresponds to the traditional distinction between monosemy and polysemy. A monosemous lexical item has a single sense, while polysemy is the association of two or more related senses with a single linguistic form.[1] Intuitively, the distinction is clear enough. The word *bird* can refer to many different kinds of creature—robins, penguins, ostriches, etc. These different kinds of creature are members of the category in virtue of similarity to a single prototype representation. *School* can likewise refer to many kinds of entity. In this case we would want to recognize a number of distinct, though related, conceptual centres, according to whether we are talking about the education of

---

[1] Here, as elsewhere in this book, I am using the term 'sense' as a stylistic variant of 'meaning'.

children, an administrative division of a university, an intellectual trend, or even a group of whales.

In view of the importance of the monosemy–polysemy distinction, we need to give more substance to the intuitive characterization given above. Of some help in this respect is our earlier account of meaning in terms of the structuring of a domain, or set of domains, by means of a schema, or set of schemas (Section 5.2). If different uses of a lexical item require, for their explication, reference to two different domains, or two different sets of domains, this is a strong indication that the lexical item in question is polysemous. *School*, which can be understood against a number of alternative domains (the education of children, the administrative structure of a university, etc.), is a case in point. Another clear example is provided by the word *pig*. Some uses of the word have to do with the classification of animals; alternatively, the word is understood in terms of the eating habits of humans. An item can still be polysemous even if its different meanings need to be characterized against the same domain. In such cases one and the same domain may be structured by means of alternative schemas. Compare the two senses of *high* in *high ceiling*, and *high building*. In both expressions, *high* needs to be characterized against the domain of vertical space. In *high ceiling*, however, *high* profiles the position of an entity in vertical space, while in *high building* it is the vertical extent of an entity that is being profiled. The two expressions thus exemplify two different—though obviously closely related—senses of *high*.

Even though the distinction between monosemy and polysemy is in principle clear enough, it is in many cases tantalizingly difficult to decide if two uses of a linguistic form instantiate two different senses, or whether they represent two exemplars, one perhaps more central than the other, of a single sense. Consider some uses of the word *mother*, discussed in the preceding chapter. An adopted child could use the word to refer either to the adoptive, nurturing mother, or to the natural, birth-giving mother. Do these uses represent two different senses? On the one hand, the two uses do indeed perspectivize different domains. On the other hand, it could be argued that the perspectivized domains are still understood against the context of the whole matrix of domains characterizing prototypical mothers. Adoptive mothers and birth-giving mothers are merely different kinds of mother.

To deal with the numerous not-so-clear cases, semanticists over the years have proposed a variety of tests for diagnosing polysemy. The tests rest on the fact that the polysemy or monosemy of a lexical item can affect the interpretation of a sentence in different ways. In (1):

(1) I don't want to have a pig in the house

the word *pig* is polysemous, and gives rise to an ambiguity; either the word refers to a certain kind of animal, or it refers to a person with gluttonous eating habits. To understand the sentence requires that we select one of these senses, and reject the other. Likewise, it is legitimate to suppose that anyone who utters (1) had one of the two senses in mind, to the exclusion of the other. Monosemous items, on the other hand, merely give rise to vagueness, or indeterminacy, rather than ambiguity. In (2):

(2) There's a bird in the garden

bird is vague; any member of the category could be meant, including its more marginal members. While one could, in principle, question the speaker of (2) as to what kind of bird he was talking about, an understanding of the sentence does not require such specification, nor does the utterance of (2) presuppose that the speaker is interested in, or even capable of, undertaking such a specification.

The distinction between monosemy and polysemy thus resolves into a question of distinguishing vagueness from ambiguity. Three ambiguity tests will be mentioned here.[2] An ambiguous sentence has more than one reading. It is thus possible, in principle, to assert one of the readings while denying the others. Thus one can readily assert that there is a pig (i.e. a gluttonous person) in the house, while denying the presence of a pig (i.e. a farm animal). One could not, however, say there is a bird (i.e. a robin) on the lawn and at the same time deny that there is a bird (i.e. a penguin) on the lawn. A second test concerns the possibility of co-ordinating the putatively distinct senses of a word in a single construction. If the senses are distinct, the resulting sentence exhibits the kind of oddity, popular with punsters, which traditional rhetoric called zeugma. Cruse (1986: 13) gives the following example:

(3) Arthur and his driving licence expired last Thursday

The oddity can be removed by unyoking the two senses of *expire*:

(4) Arthur expired last Thursday; his driving licence also expired

---

[2] For detailed discussion and exemplification, see Zwicky and Sadock (1975), Kempson (1977: 123 ff.), and Cruse (1986: 54 ff.).

A third, closely related test exploits the fact that an anaphoric expression like *do so too* requires for its interpretation the same sense as its antecedent. To the extent that an anaphoric expression and its antecedent can refer to different states of affairs, we are dealing with a case of vagueness; if crossed interpretation is impossible, we have an instance of ambiguity. Sentence (5) would be appropriate if I had seen a robin and Jane had seen an ostrich; *bird* is therefore vague.

(5) I saw a bird in the garden, and so did Jane

Punning aside, (6) could not mean that I did not want a farm animal in the house, and Jane did not want a gluttonous person; *pig* is therefore ambiguous.

(6) I don't want a pig in the house, and neither does Jane

Unfortunately, the results from ambiguity tests are frequently far from unambiguous themselves. The test sentences need to be constructed with great care. For some putatively ambiguous linguistic forms, suitably co-ordinated structures are difficult to devise; also, factors other than the monosemy–polysemy of a lexical item (such as definiteness of reference, quantification, or pragmatic oddity) can all too easily interfere with the results. Perhaps the major methodological drawback is that in the last analysis the tests rely, for their success, on the sometimes very fine intuitive judgements which they were designed to replace. I suggested earlier that *high*, as a spatial term, has two distinct senses. It does indeed seem possible to assert that a window is high (i.e. far from the ground) while denying that it is high (i.e. of greater than average vertical extent). But it needs a sophisticated (and co-operative!) informant to detect the zeugma in (7):

(7) (*a*) Both the ceiling and the bookcase are high
(*b*) The ceiling is high; so is the bookcase.

While it is possible, then, to identify clear instances of monosemy and clear instances of polysemy, the not-so-clear cases suggest that the boundary between monosemy and polysemy is fuzzy. In later chapters I shall develop the thesis that we need to approach the categories of linguistic description in the same manner as we approach real-world entities like cups and bowls. Cruse, for one, has suggested that the separateness of different senses of a lexical item might be more a matter of points on a continuum than of a dichotomy (1986: 71). This kind of approach would also make sense on a diachronic perspective.

Suppose, in the course of time, that a non-central member of a monosemous category increases in salience to the point where it constitutes a secondary conceptual centre of the category. (Developments of this nature have been traced by Geeraerts 1985*a*.) Such a process will, inevitably, be gradual. Before the full establishment of the secondary prototype within the category, there will be uncertainty as to whether the category is no longer monosemous or not yet polysemous.

So far we have been concerned with the distinction between monosemy and polysemy. A second distinction that is often made is between polysemy and homonymy. The different meanings of a polysemous lexical item are felt to be related in some non-trivial way. Homonymy is when unrelated meanings attach to the same phonological form. There are in principle two ways in which homonymy can come about. Firstly, related meanings of a once polysemous word have drifted so far apart that there is no perceived relationship between them. This is the case with the two meanings of *pupil*: "scholar" and "iris of the eye". The word, in both its senses, derives from Latin *pupillus/pupilla*, a diminutive of *pupus* "child". (The pupil of the eye was so called because of the tiny reflection of a human being that can be observed in a person's eye.) Alternatively, unrelated words which were once phonologically distinct have been subject to the 'blind' operation of sound change, and in the course of time have become phonologically identical. An example is the word *die*. The verb ("to expire") derives from Old English *dīegan*, while the noun ("the cube thrown in games of chance") comes from Old French *dé*.

As with the distinction between monosemy and polysemy, the dividing line between polysemy and homonymy is not always easy to draw. We can readily cite clear cases of polysemy (the *neck* of the human body and the *neck* of a bottle) and clear cases of homonymy (*die*). Not-so-clear cases are also numerous. Are the two meanings of *eye* ("organ of sight" and "aperture in a needle") and the two meanings of *ear* ("organ of hearing" and "grain-holding part of a cereal plant") instances of polysemy or homonymy? In fact, the two meanings of *ear* reflect a merging of two distinct words in Old English, while the two meanings of *eye* are related through metaphorical extension. The problem, of course, is that relatedness of meaning is both a gradient and a subjective notion. Perhaps some speakers do perceive a tenuous sense relation between the two meanings of *ear*, while others fail to notice any relation between the two meanings of *eye*. Yet it is doubtful whether speakers' intuitions in this respect correlate with any observable differences in language use (Lyons 1977: 552). If such is the case, it may be questioned whether in the last analysis the distinction between polysemy and homonymy is of any theoretical significance. Consistent with this view is the fact that there are no readily available tests for diagnosing homonymy as opposed to polysemy. Even so, I would suggest that the distinction is of importance. Some evidence comes from cross-language comparisons. Homonymy is in a very real sense an accidental phenomenon, and is thus highly language specific. It would be pure coincidence if a phonological form in another language happened to share the two meanings of English *die*, and we would certainly not expect the phenomenon to recur in language after language. The attestation of similar senses in different, and, especially, in historically unrelated languages, thus virtually rules out the possibility of chance homonymy, and strongly points to the presence of motivated, polysemous categories.

The distinction between polysemy and homonymy is complicated by a factor which up to now I have left out of account, namely the syntactic behaviour of the linguistic form in question. The feeling that *die* is homonymous is strengthened by the fact that the two senses are associated with two different syntactic categories; in one sense the word is a noun, in the other sense it is a verb. Should we then stipulate that polysemy requires constancy of grammatical function over the different senses? On the face of it, this seems a reasonable approach; if different senses are associated with different parts of speech, we are dealing prima facie with different words. Certainly, the diagnostic tests for ambiguity reviewed earlier presuppose that the various senses of a putatively polysemous word are associated with a single grammatical category. Accordingly, we should not regard the two senses of *drink*— the one associated with the noun, the other with the verb—as an instance of polysemy. The senses are obviously very closely related, but syntactically we are dealing with two different words. But how different, syntactically, do two instances of a linguistic form have to be in order for polysemy to be excluded? Are transitive and intransitive uses of the verb *drink* (as in *He drank a glass of milk* and *He used to drink*) instances of two syntactically different lexical items?

As already mentioned, it is possible to argue that the distinction between polysemy and homonymy is of no theoretical significance. Not surprisingly, therefore, some linguists have attempted to conflate the two phenomena. One approach (cf. Lyons 1977: 553) is to maximize homonymy at the expense of polysemy. This is the line taken by Kempson (1977). Kempson envisages a 'constant semantic value' (1977: 82) for each lexical item in a language. If a phonological form has more than one identifiable sense, then each sense, irrespective of its relation to the other senses, is characterized separately. A treatment of polysemy as if it were homonymy avoids the demarcation problem that we have been discussing. But the approach is open to serious criticism. Firstly, and rather obviously, prototype categorization rules out the possibility that each individuated sense can be assigned a 'constant' semantic value. Secondly, and more to the point, to give the different senses of a polysemous word the same status as the different senses of a homonym, is rather like treating the regular plurals of English in the same manner as the irregular ones. Polysemy is thereby reduced to an arbitrary, unmotivated phenomenon, and the study of recurring patterns of category structure, both within a given language and across different languages, is rendered theoretically and descriptively inaccessible. In contrast, cognitive linguists have perhaps tended to err in the opposite direction, maximizing polysemy at the expense of homonymy, even, as we shall see, relaxing the requirement that the senses of a polysemous item are associated with a single syntactic category.

6.2 An illustration: Climb

The family resemblance approach to polysemy contrasts strikingly with what we might call the core meaning approach. A typical statement may be found in Allerton (1979: 51). For Allerton, one criterion for the recognition of polysemy as opposed to homonymy is the presence of a shared meaning core. Thus the three 'main meanings' of *a paper*, i.e. "newspaper", "document", and "academic lecture", all share the core meaning "important written or printed material for public use". It is in virtue of this core meaning that the three senses of *a paper* are to be associated with a single lexical item. Cases where a core meaning cannot be extracted—examples mentioned by Allerton include *race* (in the senses "ethnic group" and "speed competition") and *look* (as in *John looked at the professor* and *John looked after the professor*)—must be classified as instances of homonymy.[3]

---

[3] Strictly speaking, of course, disjunctive glosses, like Allerton's 'important printed *or* written material', already point to the absence of an invariant meaning core.

The requirement that all senses of a polysemous item share a core meaning clearly stems from the classical definition of a category in terms of a set of necessary and sufficient conditions for membership. But just as the range of things that can be designated as cups do not share a set of cup-defining properties, so the related senses of a polysemous item do not have to share an invariant meaning core. This is not to say that the different senses of a polysemous item *never* share a set of common attributes, nor that an abstract schema (in Langacker's sense) can never be extracted. But to make the presence of a common semantic component a defining feature of polysemy is unduly restrictive. In cases where a common semantic core cannot be postulated, one is forced to regard the recalcitrant meanings as instances of chance homonymy. This defeats any attempt to offer a motivated account of meaning extension.

In this section, I will look at a fairly typical example of a polysemous lexical item, elaborating on Fillmore's remarks on the word *climb* (Fillmore 1982). We will individuate a number of discrete senses of the word, and explicate the relations which hold between them. In the course of the discussion the impossibility of subsuming the various senses under a more general core sense will hopefully become apparent.

One of the meanings of *climb* is exemplified in (8):

(8) The boy climbed the tree

Climb, in (8), designates a rather complex process, involving locomotion from a lower to a higher level by means of a fairly laborious manipulation of the limbs. The process can be readily predicated of human beings, as well as of four-legged animals. Following Fillmore, we may characterize the process in terms of the attributes [ascend] and [clamber]. It is significant that when asked to give a sentence illustrating the meaning of the verb *climb*, native speakers invariably come up with examples like (8), which strongly suggests that we are here dealing with the central sense of the word.

Now consider sentence (9):

(9) The locomotive climbed the mountainside

Clearly, locomotives cannot clamber. The upward ascent of the locomotive proceeds, not through the manipulation of limbs, but with the turning of wheels. Yet there are similarities between the ascending motion profiled in (8) and (9). The motion in each case is self-propelled; the wheels of the locomotive establish contact with the mountainside, just as the limbs of the climbing boy establish contact with the tree; the motion in both cases is fairly slow, and proceeds with difficulty. Other self-propelled wheeled vehicles, like automobiles, can climb in this sense. In the next sentence, virtually nothing is left of the original notion of clambering. *Climb* merely profiles the powerful upward motion of the plane with respect to the vertical dimension.

(10) The plane climbed to 30,000 feet

We note, however, that not everything which ascends can be said to climb. Planes climb into the sky, as do perhaps eagles soaring upwards. But robins and balls thrown into the air do not climb, neither does steam issuing from a kettle, in contrast with, perhaps, smoke rising from a chimney. It is also questionable whether one can speak of an elevator climbing from one floor to another.

The notion of ascending is prominent in other uses of the verb:

(11) (*a*) The temperature climbed into the 90s
      (*b*) Prices are climbing day by day

Here, [ascend] is optionally combined (perhaps) with the idea of gradualness, which in turn has a tenuous relation to the notion of laboriousness present in [clamber]. But whereas in examples (8)–(10) ascending takes place within the spatial dimension, in (11) ascending is on a numerical value scale. These uses of *climb* are made possible by a process of metaphorization. The sentences in (11) share a common attribute with (8)–(10); what has changed is the domain in which the attribute applies. Extension to further domains is also possible, e.g. the domain of social organization, as in the expression *social climber*.

On the evidence of the examples cited so far, it does look as if it might be possible to extract a common core from the different meanings of *climb*, namely [ascend]. Even so, the schematic nature of this attribute scarcely does justice to the complexity and subtlety of the individual senses; neither, of course, does a core meaning account provide any adequate basis for distinguishing *climb* from other verbs which also profile the upward movement of an entity, such as *ascend*, *rise*, *go up*, etc. But not all uses of *climb* have to do with ascending. Consider the sentences in (12). *Climb*, as used in these sentences, is related to the use in sentence (8). The verb perspectivizes only the notion of clambering, with prepositional phrases specifying the path followed by the subject of the verb:

(12) (*a*) The boy climbed down the tree and over the wall
     (*b*) We climbed along the cliff edge

Predictably, the clambering sense of *climb* is not applicable to entities without limbs:

(13) (*a*) *The plane climbed (down) from 30,000 to 20,000 feet
     (*b*) *The locomotive climbed over the mountain
     (*c*) *The snail climbed along the top of the wall

Very many activities which involve a laborious use of one's limbs can be described as climbing. As well as climbing down a tree, one can also climb into a car, under a table, and out of a sleeping-bag. One can even climb into and out of certain articles of clothing, particularly if the article of clothing completely encloses a part of the body and getting into and out of it involves considerable inconvenience. Examples might be a boiler suit or track-suit pants. One cannot, however, climb into a shirt or jacket, although one might—as a very marginal instance—climb into a pair of boots (though hardly into a pair of shoes).

From these examples, CLIMB emerges as a polysemous category consisting of several relatively discrete senses. The different senses cannot be unified on the basis of a common semantic denominator. Rather, the different meanings are related through 'meaning chains'. Schematically: Meaning A is related to meaning B in virtue of some shared attribute(s), or other kind of similarity. Meaning B in turn becomes the source for a further extension to meaning C, which is likewise chained to meanings D and E, and so on. The process may be illustrated as follows:

(14) $A \rightarrow B \rightarrow C \rightarrow D$ etc.

Within the category, meaning relations exist, in the first instance, between adjacent members, while members which are not adjacent might well have very little in common with each other. For instance, given only the sentences in (15):

(15) (*a*) Prices are climbing day by day
     (*b*) John climbed out of his clothes

one might conclude, erroneously, that *climb* is homonymous, rather than polysemous. Yet the meanings *are* related, but only in virtue of intervening links. Adapting Wittgenstein's metaphor, I shall refer to categories with this kind of structure as family resemblance categories.[4] In principle, any node in a meaning chain can be the source of any number of meaning extensions. Consequently, as we shall see in the next section, family resemblance categories can sometimes exhibit immense structural complexity.[5]

6.3 Over

Amongst the most polysemous words in English, and in other languages, are the prepositions. As any foreign learner of English will confirm, the polysemy of prepositions verges on the chaotic. This impression is strengthened by the fact that the range of uses associated with any one preposition in one language rarely overlaps with the meanings of any single linguistic form in another language. In English you put gloves *on* your hands and a ring *on* your finger; in Italian gloves go *sulle mani*, but a ring goes *al dito*. In German, you go *auf Urlaub*, you live *auf dem Lande*, and you meet people *auf einer Party*, while in English you go *on* holiday, you live *in* the country, and you meet people *at* a party. Confronted with facts like these, language teachers and writers of textbooks and pedagogical grammars have generally despaired of giving a reasoned account of prepositions. Prepositional usage is idiomatic, and 'just has to be learnt'. Prepositional polysemy, in other words, is reduced to homonymy. Mainstream linguistics seems to have taken a similar line. To the extent that structuralist and generative linguists have had anything at all to say about prepositions, attention has been largely restricted to a small range of central senses. The staggering complexity of prepositional polysemy, not being subject to obvious rule, has been ignored.

---

[4] Wittgenstein used the metaphor of a family resemblance to refer to certain characteristics of a monosemous prototype category (see s. 3.1). What I am calling a family resemblance category corresponds to Lakoff's (1987) 'radial category'.

[5] Lakoff (1987: 17 ff.) cites, as a precursor of the family resemblance construct, a passage from a 1940 paper by J. L. Austin. The idea that the different senses of a polysemous item are linked through chaining relationships was also anticipated by John Stewart Mill, in his discussion of the logic of folk categories ('Of definition', in *System of Logic* 1843): '[T]he established grouping of objects under a common name, even when founded only on a gross and general resemblance, is evidence, in the first place, that the resemblance is obvious, and therefore considerable; and, in the next place, that it is a resemblance which has struck great numbers of persons during a series of years and ages. Even when a name, by successive extensions, has come to be applied to things among which there does not exist this gross resemblance common to them all, still at every step in its progress we shall find such a resemblance' (quoted from Hayden and Alworth 1965: 126).

In contrast, cognitive linguists have taken up the challenge of the alleged arbitrariness of prepositional usage. In fact, the demonstration that prepositional usage is highly structured has probably been one of the major achievements of the cognitive paradigm. Amongst the outstanding contributions that should be mentioned are the dissertations by Brugman (1981), Vandeloise (1984), and Hawkins (1984), as well as shorter treatments by Dirven (1981), Radden (1985), and Hawkins (1988). Important also is Lindner's (1981) account of the verb particles *in* and *out*. In the following, I will illustrate the approach on what is perhaps the most polysemous of the English prepositions, *over*. The account draws heavily on Brugman's (1981) monograph, and on Lakoff's (1987) re-presentation of Brugman's data.

The discussion, which does not pretend to be exhaustive, will be limited mainly to the spatial meanings of the preposition. First, it is appropriate to make a few remarks about prepositions in general. Prepositions, in their spatial sense, serve to locate spatially one entity with reference to another. Following terminology introduced by Langacker (1987: 231 ff.), the entity which is located will be referred to as the trajector, or TR, while the entity which serves as a reference point will be referred to as the landmark, or LM. Prepositions may highlight many different aspects of the TR–LM relationship. An important distinction is between a static and a dynamic relationship. If the relationship is a static one, the preposition denotes the place of the TR. Alternatively, the relationship may be a dynamic one of goal (the end-point of the TR's movement is highlighted), source (the starting-point of the TR's movement is highlighted), or path (some or all of the trajectory followed by the TR is denoted). Other aspects that may be relevant are the shape, size, and dimensionality of the LM and the TR; the presence or absence of contact between the TR and the LM; the distance between the TR and the LM; the orientation (e.g. superior/ inferior, inclusion/exclusion) of the TR with respect to the LM, and so on. We should also bear in mind the possibility that a particular preposition may encode some highly idiosyncratic, language-specific aspect of the TR–LM relation.

With these general characteristics of prepositions in mind, let us examine the following sentences with *over*:

(16) (*a*) The lamp hangs over the table
    (*b*) The plane flew over the city
    (*c*) He walked over the street

(*d*) He walked over the hill
(*e*) He jumped over the wall
(*f*) He turned over the page
(*g*) He turned over the stone
(*h*) He fell over a stone
(*i*) He pushed her over the balcony
(*j*) The water flowed over the rim of the bathtub
(*k*) He lives over the hill
(*l*) Come over here
(*m*) Pull the lamp down over the table
(*n*) He walked all over the city
(*o*) The child threw his toys (all) over the floor
(*p*) He laid the tablecloth over the table
(*q*) He put his hands over his face

The great diversity of meanings associated with *over* scarcely needs comment. Some meanings, in fact, such as (*a*), (*g*), and (*l*), appear to have practically nothing in common with one another. To attempt to extract a common meaning core from all the sentences in (16) would thus be a fruitless undertaking. Our task will be to systematize nevertheless the data in (16)—to show, in fact, that OVER constitutes a complex family of related meanings.

In the first of the above sentences (*The lamp hangs over the table*), *over* denotes a static relationship of place. The TR is located vertical to, but not in contact with, the LM. In (*b*) (*The plane flew over the city*), the TR is again vertical to, and not in contact with, the LM. The relationship, however, has changed from static to dynamic. The expression *over the city* denotes (part of) the path followed by the TR. (*c*) (*He walked over the street*) is similar, except that now there is contact between the TR and the LM. (*d*) (*He walked over the hill*) is closely related to (*c*), that is, the TR traces a path vertical to, and in contact with, the LM. A new element, however, has been introduced, namely the shape of the path. In walking over a hill, a person first ascends, reaches the highest point, and then descends. In (*e*) (*He jumped over the wall*) this curved, arc-like path of the TR is again in evidence. Here a further element is making its appearance, namely, the notion of the LM as an obstacle that the TR must surmount by first ascending, then descending. The next few examples exploit the idea of a curved path, introduced in (*d*). In (*f*), the page moves through 180° as it is turned. (Note that in this and the next few examples, *over* is more of an adverb than a preposition. As mentioned earlier, our view of polysemy does not require absolute identity of syntactic function.) In (g), the stone, in being turned over, likewise rotates on its axis. In (h) (*He fell over a stone*), the subject of the verb traces a more limited arc-like path (say, through 90°), while the unfortunate victim in (i) (*He pushed her over the balcony*) traces a curved, downward path. In (j), water, in flowing over the rim of a bathtub, traces a path of a similar shape.

So far, we have identified a fairly extensive chain originating with (a) and leading, via intermediate links, to (j). Notice in particular how the notion of a curved path, introduced in (d), motivates a set of uses of *over* which at first sight are quite unrelated to the *over* of sentence (a).

It is possible to identify other meaning chains in the sentences in (16). Let us return to (16) (d). In (16) (d) (*He walked over the hill*), *over the hill* denotes the path of the TR, with, as already observed, the LM as a kind of obstacle along the path. A related use is (16) (k) (*He lives over the hill*), where *over* is again a place preposition, denoting not the path traced by the TR, but the end-point of the path which an observer would have to follow in order to arrive at the TR, while the LM is construed as an obstacle that the traveller would have to surmount. (l) (*Come over here*) is an extension of (k). *Over here* again denotes the end-point of a path, only now the path is an imaginary one which originates at the addressee and finishes in the region of the speaker.

Further uses of *over* denote a covering relationship, as in (p) (*He laid the tablecloth over the table*). We can relate sentence (p) to (c), via the intermediate uses in (n) and (o). A person who walks *over the street* (c) traces a path in the street. If he walks *all over the city* (n) we can think of the path as being so convoluted that it virtually covers the total area of the LM. Cases like (n) motivate sentences like (o) (*The child threw his toys (all) over the floor*), where the notion of covering comes more strongly to the fore. In (p), the covering is complete; the LM has become invisible to an observer. In sentences like (o) and (p), the TR, in covering the LM, is still located vertical to it. The verticality of the TR to the LM is not essential, however, as shown by sentence (q) (*He put his hands over his face*).

Over in the sense of covering can be derived by another route, starting from sentence (a). As we have already seen, (a) denotes the superior location of the TR, and absence of contact with the LM. The sentence has a further meaning nuance. Although the TR is not in contact with the LM, it is nevertheless construed as being fairly close to it, and can, in appropriate circumstances, exert an influence over it. In this respect, *over* contrasts with *above*. I am much more likely to be disturbed by noise from people living over me, than by people merely living above me. The idea of the TR influencing the LM comes out in (*m*): *Pull the lamp down over the table* (i.e. so that the table is illuminated by the lamp). Significantly, *over* in (*m*) cannot be replaced by *above*, a preposition which suggests, if anything, an absence of interaction between the TR and the LM. It is perhaps not too fanciful to see covering as a special instance of influencing. Certainly, the relative closeness of the TR to the LM, in (16) (*a*), seems a pre-condition for the semantic extension to covering.

So far, we have restricted our attention to some of the spatial uses of *over*. There are, in addition, a vast number of non-spatial, meta-phorical uses. We shall deal with metaphor more fully in the next chapter, but a few examples will be appropriate at this point. A meta-phorical use of *over* is exemplified in (17):

(17) He has no authority over me

This sentence is a metaphorization of (16) (*a*). The relationship between the TR and the LM is one of power, not of spatial orientation. In other words, we witness a transfer of the TR–LM relationship from the domain of vertical space to the domain of power relations. Power relations (like social organization, mentioned earlier) are typically conceptualized in terms of vertical space. Someone with power is 'higher' than someone without power. Hence a preposition denoting a higher vertical location comes to be employed to encode a position of greater power. *Over* is a particularly appropriate preposition in this case, since spatial *over*, as we have seen, often conveys that the TR is close enough to the LM to exert some kind of influence over it. Sig-nificantly, *over* in (17) is not replaceable by *above*, a preposition which emphasizes the lack of influence of the TR on the LM. A further metaphorical use is exemplified in (18):

(18) He got over his parents' death

This sentence is related to (16) (*e*), where *over* denotes a path surmounting an obstacle. The metaphorization is made possible by the fact that life itself is often construed as a path, and difficult episodes during one's life as obstacles in the path. Based on (16) (*k*), *over* can also designate the end-point of an activity or state of affairs, as in (19):

(19) (*a*) Our troubles are over
     (*b*) The lesson is over

The various senses of *over* that we have discussed form four major clusters. Firstly, there are the senses which have to do, in one way or another, with the higher location of the TR. Then there are the senses which indicate some kind of covering relationship between TR and LM. Thirdly, *over* designates a curved, arc-like movement. A final cluster of senses has to do with the end-point of a path. At the same time, each individual sense of *over* is itself a category with its own prototype structure. Let us consider the meaning exemplified in (16)(*k*): *He lives over the hill. Over*, in this sentence, is roughly equivalent to *on the other side of*. Some further examples:

(20) (*a*) He has a farm over the river/on the other side of the river
     (*b*) You'll find the bookshop over the street/on the other side of the street
     (*c*) He lives just over the frontier/on the other side of the frontier

Yet *on the other side of* is not replaceable by *over* in all cases. We would not usually speak of a bookcase being over (= on the other side of) the coffee table, or of a greenhouse being over the lawn. *Over* in (16) (*k*) is associated with a very specific 'image'. As already noted, the LM is construed as an obstacle situated between the TR and an observer (usually the speaker), such that the observer, in approaching the TR, would have to surmount the obstacle (e.g. by tracing an ascending–descending path). More abstractly, the LM is construed as a boundary separating the TR from an observer. Hence, we find restrictions on the kinds of entities which can serve as LMs. Hills, mountains, and walls are good instances of obstacles which must be surmounted, while rivers, streets, and national frontiers serve as good instances of boundaries. Lawns and coffee tables, on the other hand, are not (usually) thought of as obstacles to be surmounted, or as boundaries. Hence the strangeness of saying that something is located over (= on the other side of) a lawn or table. The wider applicability of *on the other side of* results from the fact that this expression does not share the image of *over*.

The details of the family resemblance structure of OVER that we have been discussing are, needless to say, conventionalizations (albeit motivated conventionalizations) of the English language. There is no reason to expect that prepositional categories in other languages will be structured in a similar way, and indeed, a preposition in one language rarely has a single translation equivalent in another language. Yet the non-equivalence of prepositions across languages is no reason for accepting the view that prepositional usage is essentially arbitrary. Non-equivalence can be explained very simply in terms of different structurings of the categories, and in fact cross-language data even support the family resemblance approach advocated here. Let us suppose that a language has a lexical item with the meanings A, B, C, and D, as represented in (14). According to the meaning chain model of polysemy, the association of meanings A and D within the same category is dependent on the existence of the intervening links in the chain, B and C. We can predict that if another language has a polysemous word with meanings A^1 and D^1 (i.e. with meanings identical to, or very close to, meanings A and D), that word will also have meanings B^1 and C^1. (I ignore here the possibility that meanings B^1 and C^1 might have fallen into disuse, leaving A^1 and D^1 stranded as (relatively) unrelated meanings of a single linguistic form.) Conversely, if A^1 has not extended in the direction of B^1, meanings C^1 and D^1 will be absent. The presence of meaning B^1, however, does not necessarily imply the existence of C^1 and D^1.

These predictions were confirmed in a small-scale comparison of English and Italian prepositions (Taylor 1988). Italian *sopra*, like English *over*, is a place preposition one of whose meanings is "vertical to, not in contact with", cf. (16) (*a*):

(21) La lampada pende sopra il tavolo
"The lamp hangs over the table"

Sopra, like *over*, can also imply a certain influence of the TR on the LM, cf. (16) (*m*):

(22) Abbassa la lampada sopra il tavolo
"Pull the lamp down over the table"

(16) (*m*), we argued, can be regarded as a link in the chain which permits *over* to acquire the sense of covering, as in (16) (*p*) and (*q*). Significantly, *sopra*, like *over*, can also encode a covering relation:

(23) Si mise le mani sopra il viso (cf. (16) (*q*))
"He put his hands over his face"

So far, *sopra* closely parallels the semantic extension of *over*. But unlike *over*, *sopra* has not developed into a path preposition. Crucially, (24)

    (24) L'aereo volò sopra la città
        "The plane flew over the city"

does not mean that the plane *crossed* the city (a notion which would be expressed by the verb *sorvolare*), only that the plane's flight was located vertical to the city. In other words, in (24) *sopra* is a preposition of place, not of path. As predicted, none of the meanings exemplified in (16) (*c*)–(*i*) can be rendered in Italian by *sopra*. In contrast, the German cognate of *over*, *über*, as a path preposition, has a range of meanings very similar to English *over*, cf. (25) (*a*) and (*b*). In fact, the meaning chain goes further in German than in English. The LM need not be an obstacle or boundary on the path traced by the TR, it can simply be some entity located on the path. *Über*, in this sense, is roughly equivalent to English *via* (25) (*c*):

    (25) (*a*) Er ging über die Straße
            "He walked over the street"
      (*b*) Er wohnt über der Straße
           "He lives over the street"
      (*c*) Ich fahre nach Hamburg über Bremen
           "I'm going to Hamburg via Bremen"

6.4 Some problems

The family resemblance model is a powerful tool for explicating the structure of such highly polysemous lexical items as prepositions. Yet there are a number of matters which will need to be clarified if the model is to come to maturity. I will discuss two particularly pressing issues here, and mention several more. The first concerns the possibility that some members of a family resemblance category might have a more central status within the category than others. If this is the case, what gives them their central status?

Wittgenstein, in his discussion of the category GAME, ignored the possibility that some games might be better examples of the category than others (see Section 3.1). He did recognize the existence of border-line cases, but otherwise he seemed to give all games the same status within the category. In discussing *climb*, I suggested that the sense in (8) might have central status. On the other hand, I have not taken any explicit position on whether some meanings of *over* are more central to the category than others, even though, by placing sentence (16) (*a*) at the top of the list of examples, I have implicitly assigned a central status to this sense of *over*. (We might note that this is the sense of *over* which is often listed first in dictionary entries.) Brugman (1981), in contrast, starts her discussion with the sense exemplified in (16) (*b*).

But the claim that (16) (*a*) instantiates the central sense of *over* runs into difficulties. Recall Rosch's notion of basic level terms (Section 3.3.). Basic level terms maximize category informativity: while categories might merge into each other at their boundaries, proto-typical members of basic level categories are kept maximally distinct. Suppose we regard *over* in the sense "vertical to, not in contact with" as a basic level term for the description of spatial relations. There are good reasons for this view. *Over*, in this sense, enters into a number of simple, and perceptually highly salient contrasts with other place prepositions, which likewise can be said to encode basic level relations. For example, the contrast between "superior to" and "inferior to" is realized by *over* vs. *under*; the contrast being "superior, without contact" and "superior, with contact" distinguishes *over* and *on*. There is, however, a problem, and that is the existence of the preposition *above*. *Above* has a much more restricted range of senses than *over*. But what we would probably want to identify as its central meaning coincides pretty closely with the putatively central meaning of *over*, i.e. "vertical to, not in contact with". Although, as already pointed out, there is a slight difference in nuance between *X is over Y* and *X is above Y* (*over* implies some kind of influence of the TR on the LM, *above* emphasizes the absence of interaction), it is a fact that in some cases the two words are practically interchangeable. The existence of two, partially synonymous lexical items conflicts with the very notion of a basic level term, as discussed by Rosch. It would be unrealistic to claim that *over* and *above* in their presumed central senses maximize category distinctiveness.

These problems would be eliminated by the selection of another sense of *over* as central. Evidence that it is the sense in (16) (*e*) (*He jumped over the wall*), rather than (16) (*a*), that is central, emerged from a small-scale experiment in which thirteen native speakers were asked to write down as many sentences as they could think of containing the word *over*. At issue was which senses would be exemplified most often, and which would be elicited in first place. (Recall that when subjects are asked to list members of a category they tend to mention central members first. See Section 3.2.) Within the five minute time limit that was set, altogether 97 sentences were produced. The most frequent sense was that of (16) (*e*) (17 instances), followed by the deictic sense (16) (*l*) (*Come over here*: 13 instances), and two non-spatial senses (as illustrated by *The lesson is over*: 12 instances, and *Do it over again*: ten instances). The sense in *He jumped over the wall* also occurred more frequently than any other in initial position on subjects' answer sheets (11 occurrences in first position). Only one of the 97 sentences exemplified what we considered earlier to be the central sense of *over*.

What, though, is the theoretical status of this supposedly central sense? In the preceding discussion I have carefully avoided speaking of the prototype of a family resemblance category. The sense exemplified in (16) (*e*)—if indeed this is the central member of the category—is not the prototype in the sense in which this term has been used so far. Membership in the category OVER is not established on the basis of similarity with the central member, but by the chaining process illustrated in (14). The central member of a family resemblance category thus does not have the same psychological status as the pro-totype representation of a monosemous category like BIRD. Neither are the more peripheral senses of the category, such as that illustrated in (16) (*q*), comparable to the marginal members of a prototype category. For some family resemblance categories, especially those with a more limited structure, it might be feasible to claim that the central member shares a maximum number of attributes with other members. On this view, the central member of CLIMB would be that illustrated in (8); this sense exhibits the two attributes [ascend] and [clamber], only one of which is present in each of the other senses. For categories with a more complex structure, this approach is not possible. OVER has such a large number of members, none of which can legitimately be said to maximize attribute correlation within the category.

To some extent, the problem I am addressing is a consequence of terminology. I have spoken of family resemblance categories being structured through a process of extension. The metaphor implies a real-time, dynamic process, which begins at the centre of a category, and proceeds outwards until the periphery is reached. However, as Lakoff and Brugman (1986) have noted, the structure attributed to a family resemblance category is to be interpreted more as a hypothesis concerning the 'synchronic connections in the semantic knowledge of the user' than as a recapitulation of a real-time process. The central member is thus that member from which all others can be most plausibly and most economically related. Fillmore (1982: 32) suggests an analogy between the central member and the reconstructed forms of historical linguistics; the one provides a rationale for describing the current state of polysemy in a language, the other for describing regular phonetic correspondences between related languages. Degree of centrality certainly seems to be a psychologically and linguistically real notion. Colombo and Flores d'Arcais (1984) report evidence for the structuring of Dutch prepositions around central senses, while in Chapters 8 and 10 we shall see that hypothesized degree of centrality has a further linguistic correlate, namely with regard to productivity. To insist on the diachronic nature of category structure does not, however, rule out the possibility of implications for language history. Implications for language acquisition may also be drawn. We shall pursue such a possibility in Chapter 13.

The other problem with family resemblance categories concerns the range of meanings that can get associated within a category. (The problem was also raised, in another context, in Section 4.1.) In recent decades much theoretical work in linguistics has been concerned with the formulation of constraints, i.e. with restricting the notion of what is possible in a natural language. Are there constraints on the poly-semization process (are there, in other words, 'impossible categories'), or can, in principle, anything get associated with anything else? According to Pulman, 'no language, it is safe to assume, has a name for a category consisting of just teacups, treacle and loud noises, or similar heterogeneous collections of things' (1983: 73). As regards the content of monosemous categories, this observation is no doubt correct. Polysemous categories, however, are a different matter. Meaning chains can establish indirect links between very diverse meanings. Take a heterogeneous collection of entities comparable with Pulman's teacups, treacle, and loud noises, namely polishing pads, yellow colour, and amateur enthusiasts. There does exist in English a family resemblance category embracing precisely these objects—that denoted by the polysemous word *buff*.

Approaching this issue intuitively, we might want to say, as a very general constraint, that a category, no matter how extended or rambling, cannot accommodate contraries. One feels, intuitively, that *over* could not mean both "superior to, not in contact with" and "inferior to, not in contact with", i.e. that *over* could not acquire the meaning of *under*. While this proposal seems reasonable enough, we can nevertheless point to many cases where different meanings of a polysemous word are characterized by incompatible attribute specifications. The requirement, in (16) (*a*), that the TR is not in contact with the LM is dropped in (16) (*p*), while (16) (*q*) does not require that the TR be superior to the LM. *Climb*, in (8), obligatorily describes an ascent, while in (11), with an appropriate preposition, the word can describe a *de*scending movement. Even more striking are cases where one and the same word has contradictory senses. *Sanction*, in one of its senses, means "permission, authorization". This sense happily coexists with the contradictory sense "prohibition, embargo". *Fast* usually denotes rapid movement (*He ran fast*), but the word can denote an absence of movement (*Hold fast*). Our first, putative constraint must therefore be rejected.

The feeling that *over* could not extend so as to include the meaning of *under* perhaps reflects the fact that the meaning "under" is already lexicalized in the language. We might thus suggest, as a second constraint, that category extension will be restricted by the existence of neighbouring categories. It seems reasonable that a category will extend in order to fill semantic gaps in the language, i.e. to express meanings not already conventionally lexicalized. By the same token, we might suppose that a meaning chain will be cut short once it begins to encroach on the range of meanings belonging to some other category. Our study of *over* suggests that this putative constraint is also invalid. Nothing has prevented *over* from encroaching on the semantic space of *beyond*, *across*, and *on the other side of*. Although these expressions are far from synonymous with *over*, they are interchangeable with *over* in some contexts (e.g. *He walked over/across the street*). Again, these are not isolated examples. Arguably, the central sense of Italian *sopra* is very similar to one sense of *over*, i.e. "superior to, not in contact with". Yet *sopra* can be used to describe a situation in which the TR and the LM are in contact (*Siediti sopra quella sedia* "Sit on that chair"). Here, *sopra* encroaches on the meaning of *su* "on". Indeed, in a large range of sentences, *sopra* and *su* are virtually interchangeable (Taylor 1988).

Should we therefore conclude that family resemblance categories are not subject to constraints, that, in principle, practically anything can get associated with anything else within a category? This appears to be the position of Langacker (1987: 17): 'an entity [will] be assimilated to a category if a person finds any plausible rationale for relating it to prototypical members.' And on the required degree of similarity with the prototype, Langacker observes that 'there is no specific degree of departure from the prototype beyond which a person is absolutely incapable of perceiving a similarity'. Perhaps, in the last analysis, a search for constraints (in the sense of absolute prohibitions on possible category structure) is merely a relic of what we might call the classical mind-set. Linguists who operate with classical categorization models instinctively look for clear-cut principles, not least in their study of language. A prototype mind-set, on the other hand, leads one to accept, even to expect, fuzziness and gradualness. But if it is not possible to state absolute constraints on the content of family resemblance categories, it might none the less be the case that certain kinds of meaning extension are more frequent, more typical, and more natural, than others. In other words, we should be looking for recurrent processes of meaning extension, both within and across languages, rather than attempting to formulate prohibitions on possible meaning extensions.

A cataloguing of preferred means of category extension might also shed light on a further problem with the approach presented here. A mature model of family resemblance categories needs to have at its disposal some principled means for deciding between alternative descriptions. Given alternative accounts of the relations holding between the meanings of a polysemous category—and alternatives are not difficult to come up with; my account of *over* does not accord in every detail with Brugman and Lakoff—on what basis do we prefer one description rather than another? The final problem with family resemblance categories, indeed with all categorization models, concerns the processes by which different things get associated in the first place. We shall address some aspects of this problem in the next chapter.

7

Category Extension: Metonymy and Metaphor

In the last chapter we examined in some detail the structure of two polysemous lexical categories in English. Polysemous categories exhibit a number of more or less discrete, though related meanings, clustering in a family resemblance category. Of crucial importance in this model of polysemy is the notion of meaning relatedness; it is, namely, relatedness of meaning which permits different meanings to get associated in the first place. In this chapter we look at two of the most important processes whereby different meanings get associated, namely metaphor and metonymy.

Metonymy and metaphor are familiar concepts of traditional rhetoric. Metaphor, especially, has been the object of much research by cognitively oriented linguists (see the contributions in Paprotté and Dirven 1985). I begin, however, with the no less important phenomenon of metonymy.

7.1 Metonymy

Metonymy has received relatively little discussion (at least, in comparison with metaphor) in the linguistic literature, either recently or in the past. (A notable exception is Nunberg 1978; Lakoff 1987 also has some interesting examples.) We may begin by considering the traditional view. Traditional rhetoric defines metonymy as a figure of speech whereby the name of one entity e^1 is used to refer to another entity e^2 which is contiguous to e^1. This process of transferred reference is possible in virtue of what Nunberg (1978) calls a 'referring function'. There is a referring function which permits the name of a container to refer to the contents of the container, as when we say *The kettle's boiling*. Similarly, a referring function permits the name of a producer to refer to the product (*Does he own any Picassos?*, *Dickens is on the top shelf*). A subcategory of metonymy is synecdoche; here, reference to the whole is made by reference to a salient part: *We need some new faces around here*. Alternatively, the name of an institution may stand for an influential person or group of influential persons who work in the institution (*The Government has stated . . .*). Sometimes, double metonymies are in operation. When we talk of *negotiations between Washington and Moscow*, we are using the names of places to refer to important persons associated with institutions located in those places. A further metonymy permits the name of a token to refer to the type. The salesman who comments that *This jacket is our best-selling item* intends to convey, not that the particular jacket has been sold many times, but that jackets made to that design have sold well.

The metonymic expressions cited in the above paragraph are highly conventionalized. The referring functions which make the metonymies possible are also quite productive. Thus one can in general use the name of any well-known creative artist to refer to the artistic creations of the artist. Similarly, a government can in general be referred to by the name of the city in which the government is located. But the referring functions are not fully productive, in that not any product, for example, can be referred to by the name of the person who created the product. I could hardly say *Mary was delicious*, meaning by *Mary* the cheesecake which Mary made, in spite of the analogy between Mary's mixing and processing of ingredients to produce her cake and Picasso's mixing and application of colours to produce his paintings. Any given instance of a referring function needs to be sanctioned by a body of knowledge and beliefs encapsulated in an appropriate frame. It is a widespread belief in our culture that the distinctive value of a work of art is due uniquely to the genius of the individual who created the work of art. No such unique relationship would normally be believed to hold between a cake and the person who baked it. Certain specialized situations do, however, permit the use of referring functions which are not sanctioned outside those situations. A waiter may comment to his colleague that *The pork chop left without paying*. Reference to a customer through the name of the dish which the customer ordered is possible because of certain features of the restaurant situation, in particular the fact that waiters interact with customers principally for the purpose of taking and delivering the customers' orders.

These examples suggest that the essence of metonymy resides in the possibility of establishing connections between entities which co-occur within a given conceptual structure. This characterization suggests a rather broader understanding of metonymy than that given by traditional rhetoric. The entities need not be contiguous, in any spatial sense. Neither is metonymy restricted to the act of reference. On this broader view, metonymy turns out to be one of the most fundamental processes of meaning extension, more basic, perhaps, even than metaphor.

In talking about an entity, we frequently highlight different aspects of its constitution. When we *wash a car* we are thinking of the car's exterior; when we *vacuum-clean the car* we highlight its upholstered interior; while to *service a car* focuses mainly on its moving parts (Cruse 1986: 52f.). We would not, in these examples, claim that *car* is polysemous, merely that, in Cruse's terminology, the meaning of *car* is 'contextually modulated'. Note, for example, that we can easily co-ordinate the different uses, without any hint of zeugma (*They washed, vacuum-cleaned, and serviced the car*). Yet the process of contextual modulation contains the seeds of polysemy. Consider the examples *door* and *window*. Both doors and windows, like cars, may be conceptualized as unitary structures (*I bought a car, The room has two doors, The workmen delivered the window*). Alternatively, we can focus on the moving part of the structure (*Open the door, Close the window*), or on the aperture created when the moving part is opened (*He walked through the door, She put her head through the window*). Here, the contextually modulated meanings are beginning to acquire an independent status. Symptomatic is the potential ambiguity of *He walked through the door*. (Does *he* refer to a real person passing through the door aperture, or to a ghost passing through the solid structure?) As evidence for the polysemous status of *door*, Cruse (1986: 65) notes the zeugmatic effect of co-ordination:

(1) We took the door off its hinges and then walked through it

Zeugma also results from the co-ordination of different senses of *window*:

(2) I painted the window while she was standing in it

The different senses of *door* and *window* illustrated above are related through metonymy, in our understanding of the term. A speaker of English has a good deal of common-sense knowledge about doors and windows. He knows, for example, about their usual shape, size, and manner of construction, and about their function and usual location. This kind of knowledge is held together in what we might call (with apologies for the pun!) our 'door' and 'window frames'. Different uses of *door* and *window* merely perspectivize (cf. Section 5.3) different components of the respective frames. It is perhaps significant that most speakers of English need to think twice before becoming aware of the polysemy of *door* and *window*. This is undoubtedly because the frames, and the background cultural knowledge they embody, are so much taken for granted.

There are countless instances in the lexicon of metonymic extension by the perspectivization of a component of a unitary conceptual structure. (Many of the different meanings of *climb* that were discussed in the preceding chapter are so related.) I will mention a few further examples. The first—the verb *close*—is based on Jongen (1985). The act of closing involves the manœuvring of some device with respect to a container, with the purpose of preventing access to, or escape from, the container. These two components of the act of closing (i.e. manœuvring the closing device, and preventing access to a container) are so intimately associated—the second necessarily pre-supposes the first—that it probably takes a moment's thought to keep them separate. Yet the verb *close*, as well as its translation equivalent in many other languages, is used in two quite distinct ways, which reflect the conceptual distinction that has just been made. Firstly, *close* can profile the closing process in its entirety. In this case, the name of the container functions as the direct object of the verb, as in *close the box*, or, with a less prototypical container, *close the office*. But *close* can also refer only to the first component of the closing process, i.e. to the placing in position of the device which prevents access to (or escape from) the container. Here, the direct object of the verb is the name of the closing device, as in *close the lid*, *close the door*. In some cases, the semantic distinction is indeed blurred. In *close your mouth* is *mouth* construed as a container, or as the device which prevents access to a container? In other cases, there may be uncertainty as to which component of the closing process is implicated. Thus failure to close a container may be due to the non-availability of a closing device, or simply to the bad fit of the closing device:

(3) I couldn't close the jar because I couldn't find the lid

(4) I tried to close the jar, but the lid didn't fit

A further illustration is provided by the word *mother*. As discussed in Chapter 5, a full understanding of *mother* needs to make reference to a number of different domains. Not all uses of *mother* activate each of the domains to the same extent. Sometimes only one domain is involved. When *mother* is used as a verb (*to mother a child*), the nurturance domain is perspectivized, while the other domains (genetic, birth-giving, marital, and genealogical) are eclipsed. Thus one may mother a child of which one is not, in any literal understanding of *mother*, the mother. The verb simply means "treat with caring affection, as a mother". (Note that the analogous expression *to father a child* perspectivizes, in contrast, only the genetic domain.) Other non-literal uses of *mother* typically perspectivize single domains. Thus (5) perspectivizes again the nurturance domain, while (6)—cf. Lakoff (1987: 76)—perspectivizes the birth domain:

(5) He's looking for a girlfriend who'll be a mother to him
(6) Necessity is the mother of invention

Rather more interesting are cases of metonymic extension through what we might call the 'perspectivization of an implication'. Consider two of the meanings of the verb *leave*, as illustrated by the phrases *leave a room* and *leave something in a room*. The first sense profiles the movement of an entity from the inside of an enclosed space; in this case, the direct object of *leave* denotes the enclosure. But if one leaves an enclosure, one distances oneself, by implication, from those entities which do not leave. It is through a perspectivization of this implication that *leave* can also mean "not to be accompanied by", or "not to take with one", i.e. "leave behind". The act of leaving behind can be intentional or unintentional. If the latter, *leave* comes to mean "forget to take with one".

Another fine example of this phenomenon is provided by the French verb *chasser*. (Again, the example is from Jongen 1985.) In one of its senses, *chasser* means "pursue (an animal) with the aim of catching and/or killing", i.e. "hunt". This sense is etymologically basic (< Vulgar Latin *captiare* "try to catch" < *capere* "catch"). Now, our common-sense knowledge of the world includes the information that if we pursue an animal, the animal will run away. A second sense of *chasser* (i.e. "chase away") perspectivizes this common-sense knowledge. Whereas the animal's attempt to run away was merely a troublesome aspect of hunting, we now pursue an animal with the aim of making it run away. Released from the hunting frame, this second meaning can now be applied to all manner of troublesome creatures, like insects, adult humans, and children.[1]

Especially in view of the rather broad definition of metonymy given earlier, it would be an easy matter to fill up the rest of this chapter by a further listing of examples. However, a topic of particular concern must be to identify general processes of metonymic extension. The question needs to be addressed in connection with a matter raised at the close of Chapter 6, namely, the constraining of family resemblance categories. As pointed out in that chapter, it is counter to the spirit of cognitive linguistics to attempt to formulate categorial rules for meaning extension, such that one can predict with complete certainty which meaning extensions will or will not be possible in any particular instance. One may, however, search for preferred patterns of meaning extension, patterns which recur in case after case throughout the lexicon of a particular language, and in different languages.

I will therefore devote the remainder of this section to a discussion of some preferred patterns of meaning extension which are exhibited, especially, by prepositions. The overwhelming majority of spatial senses of *over* which were exemplified in Chapter 6 are related through metonymy. The polysemy of spatial prepositions is of special interest because of the rather abstract sense relations that are involved. Consider, first of all, the notions of path and place (cf. Lakoff and Brugman 1986). There is a natural, metonymic relationship between the path followed by a moving entity, and any one of the infinite number of points located on the path. The relationship is, in essence, an instance of the whole–part relationship traditionally referred to as synecdoche. It frequently happens that a linguistic form which designates a path can also designate a place:

(7) (*a*) The helicopter flew *over* the city (path)
    (*b*) The helicopter hovered *over* the city (place)

(8) (*a*) He drove *by* the post office (path)
    (*b*) He lives *by* the post office (place)

(9) (*a*) The road passes *under* the railway line (path)
    (*b*) The dog is *under* the table (place)

---

[1] Note that *chasser* is an instance of the by no means infrequent phenomenon alluded to in s. 6.4, namely, the association of two partially contradictory senses—"pursue with the aim of catching", "pursue with the aim of chasing away"—with one and the same linguistic form.

A particularly salient point on a path is the end-point. Again, a linguistic form designating a path not infrequently also designates a place construed as the end-point of a path:

(10) (a) He walked *over* the hill (path)
   (b) He lives *over* the hill (place, construed as end-point of a path)

(11) (a) He walked *across* the street (path)
   (b) He lives *across* the street (place)

Somewhat similar is the polysemy of goal and place; the one sense has to do with a static relation construed as the final point of movement, the other with the static relation *tout court*:

(12) (a) We hung the picture *over* the sofa (goal)
   (b) The picture hangs *over* the sofa (place)

(13) (a) I put the money *in* my wallet (goal)
   (b) The money is *in* my wallet (place)

Less frequent is the polysemy of place and source, as illustrated in (14) and (15):

(14) (a) He came *out of* prison (source)
   (b) He is now *out of* prison (place)

(15) (a) The child was taken *away from* his parents (source)
   (b) The child now lives *away from* his parents (place)

More usually, the source relation needs to be specially encoded, e.g. by the use of a complex prepositional phrase:

(16) (a) The book is *under* the table (place)
   (b) He put the book *under* the table (goal)
   (c) He took the book *from under* the table (source)

Another natural metonymic relation exists between what Talmy (1978) and Lakoff (1987: 428 ff.) refer to as mass and multiplex conceptualizations. An assembly of entities may be conceptualized, either in terms of its constituent members, i.e. as a multiplex, or as an undifferentiated mass. The alternative conceptualizations are related by the everyday experience that an assembly of individual entities, if viewed from a sufficient distance, is indeed perceived as an undifferentiated mass. A specific instance of this kind of relationship exists between a one-dimensional line and a series of points which constitute a line. Thus we find that the same linguistic form can invoke both a continuous line, and a linear configuration of entities:

(17) (*a*) There were soldiers posted *along* the road (separate entities)
    (*b*) The railway track ran *along* the road (one-dimensional line)

(18) (*a*) There were trees planted *around* the house (separate entities)
    (*b*) There was a moat *around* the castle (one-dimensional line)

A similar kind of relationship exists between a two-dimensional area and an assembly of entities located within an area:

(19) (*a*) The child threw his toys *all over* the floor (two-dimensional assembly of separate entities)
    (*b*) He spilled water *all over* the floor (two-dimensional area)

—as well as between a two-dimensional area and the points making up a convoluted path which, in the limiting case, can completely 'cover' the area:

(20) (*a*) The cat walked *all over* the floor (convoluted path 'covering' an area)
    (*b*) There was mud *all over* the floor (two-dimensional area)

It is, of course, this relationship which helps to sanction the extension of *over* in the direction of "covering".

In terms of the framework introduced in Section 5.1, place, goal, and path, as well as mass and multiplex conceptualizations, are image schemas which structure a conceptual domain. In the above examples, we have restricted our attention to the spatial domain. But the same image schemas also structure other domains, e.g. the domain of time.[2] A punctual event is the temporal equivalent of a place. In both cases, the internal constitution of the entity is not at issue; both are conceptualized as points. As we have seen, a line may be construed as a series of points; analogously, a series of punctual events may be conceptualized as a single, temporally protracted event. A line may also be construed as the path followed by a moving point; similarly, a temporally protracted event can be seen as an event in progress, i.e. as

[2] For the analogy between spatial things and temporal events, see Langacker (1987: 258 ff.).

an activity, the completion of the event being analogous to the end-point of a path. Significantly, verbs can be polysemous in the same way as prepositions. Thus a verb can denote the single occurrence of a punctual event, or a series of occurrences:

(21) (*a*) The light *flashed* once (punctual event)
     (*b*) The light *flashed* for half an hour (series of punctual events)

(22) (*a*) The boy *kicked* the ball (once)
     (*b*) The boy *kicked* the ball for half an hour

Similarly, the same linguistic form can focus on an activity (equivalent to a path) or on the termination of an event (equivalent to the end-point of a path):

(23) (*a*) We *walked* in the forest (focus on activity)
     (*b*) We *walked* home (focus on end-point of event)

With these examples, we witness the application of spatial schemas to non-spatial domains. In this respect, we are already encroaching on the phenomenon of metaphor. It is to metaphor that we now turn.

7.2 Metaphor

The study of metaphor has been an important site for research within the cognitive paradigm; a significant landmark in this respect was the publication in 1980 of *Metaphors We Live By* by Lakoff and Johnson. It is, in fact, with respect to their approaches to metaphor that the cognitive and the autonomous paradigms contrast most dramatically. Before discussing the cognitive approach, it would be advisable, therefore, to outline briefly some of the salient characteristics and corollaries, as well as some of the problems, of the autonomous approach.

Metaphor has always been something of an embarrassment to generative linguistics. The source of the problem lies in the view that the meanings of words can be represented as bundles of necessary and sufficient features. Meanings, on this approach, emerge as entities with clear-cut boundaries. The possibility of combining words into phrases is then a question of the compatibility of the feature specifications of the component forms, compatibility being formalized in terms of selection restrictions. Again the acceptability of word combinations is a clear-cut matter: either the feature specifications are compatible, or they are not. Within this tradition, the essence of metaphor is captured by the notion of a violation of a selection restriction. The approach taken by Botha (1968) with regard to these violations is representative of a whole generation of linguists. Botha distinguished between novel, creative metaphors, and established, or dead metaphors. Novel metaphors, Botha claimed, lie outside the study of a speaker's competence, and thus outside the scope of linguistics proper. Competence has to do with a speaker's 'rule-governed creativity', not his 'rule-changing creativity' (1968: 200). By violating a rule, a speaker is in effect going beyond his competence, thus changing his grammar. But once a metaphorical expression has been created, the speaker's internalized rule system is thereby modified. Metaphor thus ceases to be an instance of deviance; one might even say, metaphor ceases to be metaphorical. The metaphorical sense of a lexical item is now listed in the lexicon along with its other 'conventional senses' (1968: 201). On the one hand, then, metaphor is declared out of bounds, otherwise it is assimilated to any other instance of polysemy/homonymy.

The view that metaphor lies outside the study of linguistic competence proper underlies Searle's (1979) well-known account. The sentence

(24) Sally is a block of ice

is, if taken literally, semantically anomalous. *Ice* (and *block of ice*) possesses the feature [−ANIMATE]; one cannot therefore predicate 'be a block of ice' of an entity (i.e. *Sally*) which is [+ANIMATE]. The sentence is only acceptable to the extent that a listener/reader can go beyond the literal meaning and construe the speaker/writer's intended meaning. To perform this task, the listener/hearer needs to supplement linguistic competence with proficiency in pragmatics. Searle's account thus presupposes a distinction between semantics and pragmatics, the former having to do with literal, or purely linguistic meaning, the latter with the context-dependent construal of intended meaning. Over the past decade or so, pragmatics has emerged as an important subdiscipline of linguistics, taking its place alongside the more traditional components of linguistic study, such as phonology, syntax, and semantics. Given the basic assumptions of the generative paradigm, the emergence of pragmatics as an independent object of study was perhaps inevitable. If language constitutes an autonomous cognitive system, then, given the self-evident fact that language is an instrument for conceptualizing and interacting with the world, the need arises for an interface that links these otherwise independent systems. Pragmatics functions as precisely such an interface. In rejecting the notion of an autonomous linguistic faculty, cognitive linguistics necessarily removes the need for pragmatics as a separate branch of study. All meaning is, in a sense, pragmatic, as it involves the conceptualizations of human beings in a physical and social environment. As Bosch (1985) has argued, the understanding of *any* utterance requires an act of context-sensitive interpretation by the listener/hearer; metaphorical utterances, on this view, do not form a special set.

A devastating criticism of Searle's account of metaphor may be found in Cooper (1986: 68ff.). I will restrict myself here to a few comments on the notion of metaphor as grammatical deviance. Four objections can be made. Firstly, the supposed deviance of metaphor implies that any competent speaker of a language ought to be able to uniquely 'demetaphorize' each metaphorical expression that he encounters, thereby restoring the expression to full grammaticality. In practice, it is often difficult, if not impossible, to replace a metaphorical expression by a single non-metaphorical equivalent. Secondly, it is highly counter-intuitive to claim that anything as pervasive as metaphor should have to be accounted for in terms of rule-breaking: metaphor is 'such a familiar and ubiquitous ingredient of speech that ... few stretches of everyday conversation would escape the presumption of censure' (Cooper 1986: 78). Furthermore, the very pervasiveness of metaphor argues strongly against the deviance hypothesis; being endemic, metaphor would eventually destroy the norm against which deviance is to be recognized as such. Finally, the question arises why any bona fide communicator should wish to do such a bizarre thing as intentionally to produce utterances which are grammatically deviant, only so that his partner can mobilize all kinds of interpretative principles in order to arrive at the intended meaning. Why don't people say what they mean in the first place?

The cognitive approach to metaphor does not give rise to this conundrum, since metaphor is not understood as a speaker's violation of rules of competence. Rather, the cognitive paradigm sees metaphor as a means whereby ever more abstract and intangible areas of experience can be conceptualized in terms of the familiar and concrete. Metaphor is thus motivated by a search for understanding. It is characterized, not by a violation of selection restrictions, but by the conceptualization of one cognitive domain in terms of components more usually associated with another cognitive domain.[3] It is thus not surprising that metaphor should abound in precisely those kinds of discourse where writers are grappling with the expression of concepts for which no ready-made linguistic formulae are available. Obvious examples are poetic, mystical, and religious texts. Metaphor plays an essential role in scientific enquiry, too (Hoffman 1985). A nice example is discussed at length in the opening chapter of MacCormac (1985). In their studies of cognition, psychologists, some more explicitly than others, have drawn analogies with the functioning of a computer; 'cognition' is merely the 'computation' produced by the 'hardware' of the brain operating under the control of the 'software' of the mind (1985: 9). Salmond (1982) also draws attention to a number of metaphors which underlie the pursuit of anthropology. The discipline of linguistics provides many examples, too. Linguists in the Chomskyan tradition speak of *deep*, *shallow*, and *surface* levels of syntactic description, structures undergo *transformations* and are represented in the form of *tree* diagrams. In this book we distinguish between *central* and *peripheral* exemplars of a category; meanings are *chained* together to form *family resemblance* networks, and so on. These metaphors are more than just pedagogical aids. The conceptualization of the subject-matter entailed by the metaphors constitutes the very essence of the theories in question.

It is not only, of course, in specialized discourse that metaphor abounds. As Lakoff and Johnson (1980) richly document, much of our understanding of everyday experience is structured in terms of metaphor. For an illustration we need go no further than the cluster of metaphors discussed in their opening chapter. Here, Lakoff and Johnson drew attention to the military source of the language we use in talking of intellectual argument. When taking part in an argument, we set up positions, we attack and defend and retreat, and we end up by winning or losing. These metaphorical expressions are made possible in virtue of what Lakoff and Johnson call a 'conceptual metaphor', namely ARGUMENT IS WAR. The domain of intellectual argument is understood in terms of war. Elements from the domain of war—things like attack, defence, retreat, etc. (note that it is not a

---

[3] The cognitive view of metaphor, like many other aspects of cognitive linguistics, is not new. It was already anticipated in Black's interactional theory of metaphor. See e.g. Black (1962).

prerequisite that people have had personal experience of war; they merely need to draw on conventionalized knowledge encapsulated in the war-making frame)—are projected on to the abstract domain of intellectual argument. The basic logic of the donor domain (i.e. war) is applied to a different area of experience, the receptor domain, i.e. argument. The process gives rise to a number of metaphorical entailments. Wars typically end in victory for one party, or at least in a truce. Thus an argument must end in victory, or, in the limiting case, in stalemate. An argument which ends up in amicable agreement has already ceased to be an argument.

Important themes of metaphor research within the cognitive paradigm have included the role of metaphor in word formation (Rudzka-Ostyn 1985), the metaphorical base of grammatical constructions (Claudi and Heine 1986), and the structural parallelisms between donor and receptor domains which facilitate transfer from one to the other (Rudzka-Ostyn 1988*a*). A particularly interesting line of enquiry is suggested by Lakoff (1987: 271 ff.). Lakoff discusses the possibility that many areas of experience are metaphorically structured by means of a rather small number of image schemas. Amongst these image schemas are the following:

(*a*) Containment. The image schema profiles a container, with its inside and outside, in the domain of three-dimensional space. The image schema is applied metaphorically to a large number of non-spatial domains. Linguistic forms are conceptualized as containers (*put ideas into words*, *the contents of an essay*, *empty words*; see Reddy 1979), as are emotional states (*be in love*, *fall out of love*).

(*b*) A journey and its component parts (i.e. origin, path, and destination, with possible obstacles and detours on the way). Life itself is frequently conceptualized as a journey (*My life isn't getting anywhere*, *He's come a long way*, *We're going round in circles*), as is, for instance, the progress (i.e. moving forward) of society (*He's a progressive*, *He's ahead of his time*, *He's a fellow traveller*).

(*c*) Proximity and distance. Once again, a schema based on spatial relations is projected on to non-spatial domains. Thus degree of emotional involvement and the possibility of mutual influence are understood in terms of proximity (*a close friend*, *a close adviser*, *to keep one's distance*).

(*d*) Linkage and separation. Closely related to the proximity–distance schema is the schema of linkage and separation. Again, basically spatial notions can be applied to abstractions. We *make contact* with people, we *keep in touch*, and we *break* social and family *ties*.

(*e*) Front–back orientation. This schema is applied, in the first instance, to the human body. The front of a human body is that side on which major sensory organs, especially the eyes, are located. The front also faces in the direction in which a human being normally moves. A particularly widespread conceptual metaphor applies this schema to orientation in time. The future lies in front (*look forward to the future*), while the past is at one's back (*look back on the past*). Events, too, have fronts and backs. Many languages make no formal distinction between 'in front of' and 'before', and between 'behind' and 'after'. What is in front of an event is what happens before; what is behind, happens after.

(*f*) The part–whole relationship. The whole consists of parts arranged in a specific configuration. The separation or rearrangement of the parts results in the destruction of the whole. Primarily, this schema is applied to discrete, concrete entities. Metaphorically, it can be applied to a range of abstract notions, for example, interpersonal relations. A married couple form a whole; on divorce they *split up*, or *break up*; later, they may *come together* again.

(*g*) Linear order. Primarily, this schema arranges objects in a one-dimensional line in terms of their increasing distance from an observer. Metaphorically, it can be applied to temporal sequence. What occurs *first* happens before, what comes *second* occurs later.

(*h*) Up–down orientation. Primarily, this schema has to do with spatial orientation within a gravitational field. We examine in detail some of its metaphorical applications below.

(*i*) Mass vs. multiplex conceptualizations. Some aspects of these alternative ways of viewing objects and events have already been mentioned.

A particularly intriguing aspect of Lakoff's work is the suggestion that these image schemas might be so deeply grounded in common human experience that they constitute, as it were, universal pre-linguistic cognitive structures. Many of the schemas clearly derive from the most immediate of all our experiences, our experience of the human body. The experiential base of containment is the human body with its surface separating the inside from the outside. The body, with its various parts which make up the whole, and with its front clearly distinct from its back, is also a permanent exemplar of the part–whole and front–back schemas, while our existence in a gravitational field provides the base for the up–down schema.

Let us examine more closely the metaphorical applications of the up–down schema in English, concentrating on the lexical item *high*. In its literal sense (see Dirven and Taylor 1988), *high* is characterized against the domain of three-dimensional space. There are two distinct spatial senses, extensional *high* (*high*^{1}), as in *high building*, and positional *high* (*high*^{2}), as in *high ceiling*. The first sense denotes the greater than average vertical extent of an entity, while the second denotes the above average location of an entity on the vertical dimension. The meanings are related through metonymy. If an entity is *high*^{1}, then its upper surface is *high*^{2}. It is the second sense of *high* which is subject to metaphorical extension in English.

In denoting the position of an entity in vertical space, *high*^{2} normally implies a zero point, or origin, from which vertical distance is measured, as well as a norm with which the high entity is implicitly compared. In many cases, the zero point is provided by ground level (as in *high telegraph wires*) or floor level (as in *high ceiling*), while in *high plateau* the zero point is sea level. In other cases, the zero point is provided by the domain against which the entity is conceptualized. A *high shelf* is located higher than the norm within the domain of, for example, a bookcase, a *high waistline* against the domain of an article of clothing, while in *high shoulders* the domain is the human torso. Possibly, it is the very flexibility of *high*^{2}—the fact that the zero point and the norm are selected according to the domain of the profiled entity—that renders the word so available to metaphorical extension.

Metaphorical extension becomes possible in virtue of conceptual metaphors which map the up–down schema on to other areas of experience. There are three major conceptual metaphors in English which involve the up–down schema. These concern the domains of quantity (MORE IS UP, LESS IS DOWN), evaluation (GOOD IS UP, BAD IS DOWN), and control (POWER IS UP, POWERLESSNESS IS DOWN). There are also one or two minor conceptual metaphors that map the up–down schema on to sensations of pitch and smell, as revealed in expressions like the *high notes* of a piano, and meat which *smells high*.

In accordance with the conceptual metaphor MORE IS UP, *high* lends itself naturally to denoting position on a numerical scale. Examples include *high number*, *high temperature*, *high price*, *high speed*, *high blood pressure*, *high pulse rate*, etc. Here, the numerical scale is the domain for the location of an entity (*number*, *temperature*), the zero point of the scale being the origin from which vertical distance is measured. More generally, the schema can be applied to a non-numerical scale of degree or intensity, as in *high level of violence*, or of sophistication and complexity, as in *high technology*, *higher education*, and *higher forms of life*. It will be observed that, for some of these domains, conceptualization in terms of verticality is so deeply engrained in our consciousness that alternative, non-orientational modes of expression are scarcely available to us. How else can we express position on a scale of price or temperature, other than with *high* and *low*?

The second conceptual metaphor, GOOD IS UP, is the basis for a large number of expressions in which *high* carries a positive evaluation: *high standards*, *high quality*, *high opinion*, *high moral values*, etc. In other expressions, *high* denotes a positive valuation of emotional states, as in *high hopes* and *high expectations*. Connotations of enjoyment and liveliness may be found in *high spirits*, *high life*, *high jinks*. Some metaphorical uses of *high*, e.g. *high technology*, appear to fuse the two conceptual metaphors of quantity and evaluation. *High technology* is not only high on a scale of sophistication, it is also positively valued over *low technology*. In other words, MORE is often also BETTER. A fusing of the two metaphors may be felt in other expressions, e.g. *higher mathematics*, *higher education*, *higher forms of life*. (In *highbrow*, on the other hand, a greater than average intellect is not given a positive evaluation.) Sometimes it is difficult to classify a particular usage. In *get high on drugs*, does *high* refer to a value on a scale of brain stimulation, or does it imply a positive evaluation of a mental state, or both?

The third conceptual metaphor (POWER IS UP) maps the up–down schema on to power relations. A person or group with power is higher than those without power. Frequently, status in human society is conceptualized in terms of the up–down schema: *high society*, *high class*, *high born*, and, of course, the expression *high status* itself. Status within a more limited domain may also be denoted by *high*, as in *high command*, *high priest*, *high position in a company*. Generally, positions of higher status are valued positively (MORE POWER is usually BETTER). This is not always the case, however. Expressions like *high-handed* and *get on one's high horse*[4] imply a negative attitude towards real or assumed power.

---

[4] Note that some metaphoric transfers, like *get on one's high horse*, are mediated by very specific visual images. *Highbrow* is another instance. For the role of images, especially in the understanding of idioms, see Lakoff (1987: 451 ff.).

Metaphor, as we have seen, consists in the mapping of the logic of one domain (usually, but not always, a more concrete domain) on to another (usually more abstract) domain. At this point we need to enquire more deeply into the motivation of this transfer. What is it that permits the association of donor and receptor domain? Why are power relations, for instance, conceptualized in terms of verticality, and not some other domain, such as left–right, front–back, or whatever? And what motivates the particular skewing of the mapping relationship? Why does the powerful end of the power hierarchy get associated with high and the powerlessness end with low, rather than vice versa? Traditionally, of course, metaphor has been explained in terms of the similarity of the tenor and the vehicle. In their discussion of metaphor, Paivio and Begg (1981: 274) comment on the 'theoretical puzzle' of similarity. I have already had occasion to point out the problems associated with the notion of similarity (Section 4.1). On what basis do elements in one domain come to be perceived as 'similar' to elements in another domain?

In some cases, at least, it seems that the possibility of transferring elements from one domain to another is established in virtue of the co-occurrence of the domains within a particular area of experience. Consider the conceptual metaphor MORE IS UP. As you add objects to a pile, the pile gets higher. This experience establishes a natural association between quantity and vertical extent. Strictly speaking, the association is one of metonymy; if one adds objects to a pile, height is literally correlated with quantity. Only when the up–down schema is released from the piling-up image and applied to more abstract instances of addition (as when one speaks of *high prices*) does metaphor take over. The conceptual metaphors GOOD IS UP and POWER IS UP have a similar experiential basis (cf. Lakoff and Johnson 1980). Positively evaluated human attributes like life, health, and consciousness are typically associated with an upright posture. A person who is up is one who is alive, well, and conscious, while someone who is unconscious, ill, dead, or asleep is down. Similarly, a person with the power to control, influence, or physically overcome someone else is typically someone of greater bodily strength, and greater bodily height, than the other person. And in the course of a physical combat the one with the greater power finishes up while the victim is left down. Again, the relationship between verticality and the power domain is a metonymic one. Only when the relationship is generalized beyond the stereotypical situation can one speak of metaphor.

It is tempting to see all metaphorical associations as being grounded in metonymy. (This is the reason why I suggested, earlier in this chapter, that metonymy might be even more basic in meaning extension than metaphor.) This view has been shared by scholars as diverse as Eco and Skinner. Eco (1979: 77) surmises that all associations are first grasped 'as contiguity internal to semantic fields', while Skinner (1957) postulated that verbal responses generalize from the stimulus to salient attributes of the stimulus, and to entities that are contiguous to the stimulus. Thus the verbal response 'eye' would generalize to such attributes as 'recessed', 'oval', 'near top (of head)'. This particular cluster of attributes then facilitates the metaphorical transfer from *eye* "organ of sight" to *eye* "aperture of a needle". If it were the case that metaphor were grounded, ultimately, in metonymy, then we would have gone a long way towards solving the 'theoretical puzzle' of similarity. There are, however, numerous instances of metaphor which cannot reasonably be reduced to contiguity. Particularly recalcitrant are instances of a subcategory of metaphor, synaesthesia. Synaesthesia involves the mapping of one sensory domain on to another. Examples include *loud colour* (where an attribute of the auditory domain is mapped on to the visual domain), *sweet music* (which maps a gustatory sensation on to the auditory domain), and *black mood* (colour transferred to an emotional state). It is doubtful whether attributes of these different domains get associated through metonymy. Neither is it plausible to propose metonymy as the basis for a mapping of the vertical dimension on to sensations of pitch (*the high notes on a piano*)[5] and smell (*the meat smells high*).

Perceived similarity across different domains—of which synaesthesia is an example—was systematically studied by Osgood and his colleagues (e.g. Osgood *et al.* 1957). Osgood postulated a highly abstract 'affective reaction system' which was independent of any particular sensory modality. Three primary dimensions of the affective reaction system were identified: evaluation, potency, and activity. Conceivably, identical reactions on these dimensions to stimuli from different domains could provide the psychological basis for metaphor and synaesthesia. Yet, as Paivio and Begg note, 'when individuals use

---

[5] One could argue that the correlation of high pitch with the high rate of vibration of the sound-producing body provides the metonymic basis for the conceptual metaphor. This correlation, however, does not form part of the world knowledge of the scientifically naïve language user, and cannot therefore provide an experiential grounding for the metaphor.

scales such as *fast–slow*, *hard–soft*, and *weak–strong* to rate such
diverse concepts as MOTHER and DEMOCRACY, they obviously must do so
in a metaphorical way' (1981: 276). The theoretical puzzle of similarity remains.

　The discussion so far has been restricted to examples from English. I
would like to conclude with a cross-language comparison. English and
the Sotho languages of Southern Africa provide an interesting contrast
with regard to the understanding of certain bodily and mental
experiences. In English a range of emotional and physiological states,
especially those involving excessive arousal, such as impatience, anger,
and sexual desire, are understood in terms of heat, cf. expressions like
get hot under the collar, *lose one's cool*, *a bitch on heat*. (Anger
metaphors in English are extensively discussed in Lakoff 1987: 380 ff.)
The metaphors may well have an experiential base in the physiological
changes, such as raised body temperature and increased heart beat,
which accompany states of arousal. The metaphors are thus, once
again, grounded in metonymy. For speakers of the Sotho languages,
on the other hand, 'being hot' is associated with a rather different
range of experiences (Hammond-Tooke 1981). Briefly, any abnormal
or unpleasant condition of the body or psyche is understood in terms
of being hot: bereavement, physical pain, illness (not only fever),
extreme tiredness, insanity, menstruation, pregnancy, childbirth, as
well as (and here the Sotho understanding coincides with English)
agitation, impatience, and anger. A person in one of these conditions
has 'hot blood' which needs 'cooling' (e.g. with cold water, or with cold
ash from a burnt-out fire). Furthermore, he must be kept away from
family and cattle, in case he infects these with his heat. These
metaphors exist not only amongst traditional speakers, but also
amongst urbanized Sothos, and they show up even in their use of
English (Hewson and Hamlyn 1985). The experiential base of the
metaphors is no doubt to be found in the physical environment of the
speakers. The Sothos live in a hot arid plateau, where the search for
water is a major concern. It is not unreasonable to suppose that, in this
environment, heat gets metonymically associated with negatively
valued states (HOT IS BAD) and coolness with positively valued states
(COOL IS GOOD).

　It is the grounding of metaphor in experience that has made it such
a central concern of the cognitive paradigm. For structuralist linguistics, language was an arbitrary system of signs, independent of the
cognition and experience of its users. In contrast, cognitive linguistics

strongly emphasizes the non-arbitrary, motivated nature of language structure. Reference to the experiential base of metaphor thus stimulates meaningful discussion of a question that is often raised in connection with the arbitrary vs. motivated dichotomy, namely the relationship between language and culture. Since, on the one hand, certain experiences are presumably common to all normal, healthy human beings, while others are strongly conditioned by culture and environment, it comes as no surprise that we find both considerable cross-language similarity in metaphorical expression, as well as cross-language diversity. As an example of the former, one might point to the widespread correspondences in the way unrelated languages conceptualize time in terms of space (see Taylor 1987 for a comparison of English and Zulu in this respect). Diversity can be expected if different language communities draw on different experiential bases in their conceptualization of reality. Such is the case with the heat metaphors in English and Sotho.

8

Polysemous Categories in Morphology and Syntax

CHAPTER 6 presented an analysis of polysemous lexical items in terms of family resemblance categories consisting of sometimes quite extensive chains of distinct though related meanings. The major advantage of this approach is that it frees the linguist from the obligation to search for a semantic component unifying all the different uses of a word. It is not that a family resemblance approach is inconsistent with the notion of a common core; rather, a common core would constitute but one possible structuring of a family resemblance category. Where such a common core does not exist—and these cases are probably in the majority—the linguist working with the meaning core hypothesis has to list, in a very *ad hoc* fashion, the numerous 'exceptions' to his semantic analysis. Polysemy thus reduces to homonymy, and multiple meaning emerges as an arbitrary, unprincipled phenomenon. A family resemblance approach, on the other hand, highlights the structured, motivated nature of polysemy.

Polysemy is generally regarded as a property of lexical categories, and it was lexical polysemy that was the focus of Chapter 6. But polysemy is not a property of words alone. Other categories of language structure—morphological categories of number and case, morphosyntactic categories of tense and aspect, the syntactic categories of sentence types, even, as we shall see in Chapter 9, prosodic categories like intonation contours—may also exhibit a cluster of related meanings, and must thus count as instances of polysemy. In this chapter I want to suggest a family resemblance approach to some of these non-lexical categories. As illustrations, I will take examples from morphology (the diminutive) and morphosyntax (the past tense), and conclude with a brief discussion of a syntactic category (the yes–no interrogative).

The semantic content of morphological categories was addressed by Roman Jakobson in his essay on Russian case (1936). The Russian cases, especially the genitive and the instrumental, display a bewildering variety of uses, comparable in range with the variety of meanings associated with the English preposition *over*. Jakobson begins his essay by considering various alternatives. He rejects the idea that cases are purely formal, semantically meaningless categories. Given that cases have meaning, it is not sufficient to make an *ad hoc* list of the different senses of each case. This procedure reduces case categories to pure homonymy, and destroys the unity of the linguistic sign. The only solution, for Jakobson, is to identify each case category uniquely with an abstract general meaning (*Gesamtbedeutung*). 'Local meanings' (*Sonderbedeutungen*) can then be derived through an interaction of the abstract meaning—expressed in terms of binary features like [PERI-PHERAL] and [AFFECTED]—and the particular linguistic context. In this, Jakobson is applying to morphology the descriptive apparatus developed in phonology. The phoneme is considered as an abstract entity, characterized in terms of binary features. The actual realization of a phoneme is a function of the context in which it occurs. Thus the /p/ in *pit* is phonetically different from the /p/s in *tip*, *upper*, and *spit*. The local meanings of any instance of a case category are analogous to these contextually determined positional variants of the abstract phoneme category.

Jakobson's core meaning approach to the Russian cases has been criticized by Wierzbicka in her monograph on the Russian instrumental, *The Case for Surface Case* (1980*a*). Wierzbicka acknowledges the descriptive elegance of Jakobson's analysis. She is led to reject it, however, on the grounds that it is predictively useless: 'A person who does not know Russian *cannot* learn to use the Russian cases on the basis of Jakobson's formulas' (1980*a*: p. xv; author's emphasis). One might similarly question whether Jakobson's highly abstract account can be plausibly taken as a representation of the native speaker's current state of knowledge. Although Wierzbicka makes no reference in her monograph to prototype theory or to Wittgenstein's reflections on the structure of categories, her approach is entirely consonant with the notion of a family resemblance category that we developed in Chapter 6. Indeed, the following passage, *mutatis mutandis*, could easily be taken as a summary of our analysis of *over* given in Chapter 6. It could equally apply to the examples to be discussed in this and the following chapter:

Cases do have meanings; each case has a *large* number of meanings, which, however, can be clearly separated from one another. All the different meanings of each case are interrelated. Since every case meaning is complex (i.e. contains a number of distinct components), most meanings share some components with most of the others; it is possible, and even likely—though by no means necessary—that *all* the meanings of one case may share some of the components (hence the impression that each case has a semantic invariant). But the different 'uses' of a case cannot be regarded as mere contextual variants of one meaning because the formula expressing such a 'common meaning' would be usually too general to have any predictive value; for this reason a number of different, though related, meanings have often to be postulated. (Wierzbicka 1980*a*: p. xix)

8.1 The diminutive

I begin with the morphological category of the diminutive. English is unusual in that it does not possess a productive diminutive affix. Many other languages, in contrast, have not only one, but sometimes several diminutive morphemes. Interesting, for the cognitive linguist, is the fact that these morphemes are used not only to indicate the small size of an entity, but also to express various other kinds of meaning. Diminutive morphemes, in other words, are polysemous. What is more, there is considerable agreement across different languages with regard to the kinds of meaning that can be conveyed by the diminutive.

Since English lacks a diminutive, I shall take most of my examples from Italian. Italian has a large number of diminutive suffixes, three of the most frequent being *-ino*, *-etto*, and *-ello*. Multiple diminutivization is also possible, e.g. *-inello*, *-ettino*, etc. Various factors appear to influence the choice of a particular suffix in any given case. Convention undoubtedly plays some role, as does the phonetic shape of the stem (thus *lettino* "small bed" would be preferred over *lettetto*). There is also evidence for semantic differentiation amongst the different suffixes. Bates and Rankin (1979), while noting considerable between-speaker variation on this issue, report that *-ino* tends to be associated with a greater degree of smallness than the other diminutive suffixes.

For the purpose of the following discussion, I shall disregard the possibility of semantic differences amongst the diminutive suffixes, and consider the various suffixes as instantiations of a single category. The central sense of the category is reasonably self-evident. As suggested by its traditional name, the diminutive expresses the small size of a physical entity: *paese* > *paesino* "small village", *villa* > *villetta* "small villa". But the diminutive is not restricted to the names of physical entities; nouns designating more abstract entities can also be diminutivized, as can parts of speech other than nouns. We can regard these extended uses as instances of metaphorization, in that the notion of smallness is transferred from the spatial to non-spatial domains. Thus, applied to nouns, the diminutive comes to express the short temporal duration, the reduced strength, or the reduced scale of an entity: *sinfonia* > *sinfonietta* "small-scale symphony", *cena* > *cenetta* "small supper", *pioggia* > *pioggerella* "light rain, drizzle". Applied to adjectives and adverbs, the diminutive expresses reduced extent or intensity: *bello* "beautiful" > *bellino* "pretty, cute"; *bene* "well" > *benino* "quite well". Verbs may also be diminutivized. Typical verbal suffixes include *-icchiare* and *-ucchiare*. The diminutivized verbs usually designate a process of intermittent or poor quality: *dormire* "sleep" > *dormicchiare* "snooze", *lavorare* "work" > *lavoricchiare* "work a little, work half-heartedly", *parlare* "speak" > *parlucchiare* "speak (a foreign language) badly".

In these few examples we already have the beginnings of a family resemblance category. As it happens, the different meanings are linked by a common meaning attribute, namely [smallness (on some dimension)]. But the diminutive in Italian (and other languages) may also be used in cases where smallness is not at issue. *Mammina*, a diminutivized form of *mamma* "mother", does not convey small size. Rather, the word is expressing an attitude of affection or tenderness on the part of the speaker. First names may also be diminutivized, for the same purpose. This affectionate use of the diminutive is not restricted to nouns denoting animate creatures. Thus, *vestitino* < *vestito* "dress" and *casella* < *casa* "house" could mean, quite simply, "small dress" and "small house"; the words could also be translated "nice little dress", "nice little house" (note that the English expression *nice little*— but not **nice small*—is roughly equivalent to the affectionate sense of the Italian diminutive; *nice little* does not necessarily indicate small size). If the use of the diminutive to express the reduced scale of an entity or an activity exemplifies a metaphoric transfer from the central meaning, the extension of the diminutive to express an attitude of affection is an instance of metonymic transfer. Human beings have a natural suspicion of large creatures; small animals and small children on the other hand can be cuddled and caressed without embarrassment or fear. The association of smallness with affection is thus grounded in the co-occurrence of elements within an experiential frame.

If smallness is experientially associated with an attitude of affection, smallness also goes with lack of worth. The experiential base is obvious: superior worth correlates with increased size, decreased size with diminished worth. Hence, the diminutive can express, not only affection, but also an attitude of depreciation. Thus, in referring to a person's thesis as a *tesina*, a speaker would probably be conveying by the diminutive his low opinion of the work in question. Sometimes one and the same expression can be ambiguous between the two interpretations. (The metonymic extension of the diminutive can thus give rise to the phenomenon discussed at the end of Chapter 6, namely the accommodation of incompatible, even contradictory meanings within a single category.) According to Lepschy and Lepschy (1977: 167), *alberello* < *albero* "tree" could mean both "nice little tree" or "stunted little tree". The same ambiguity may be found in other languages. Zulu *indodakazana* < *indodakazi* "daughter" can be used both in an affectionate and derogatory sense: *lendodakazana yakho* "this (nice) daughter of yours" or "this (horrible) daughter of yours" (Ziervogel *et al*. 1967: 154).

There are further meanings of the diminutive, each with its own experiential base. Things which are small are of little importance. This association gives rise to what we may call the dismissive sense of the diminutive; hence *fatto* "fact" > *fatterello* "matter of no significance", *storia* "story" > *storiella* "lie, fib". Closely related is the approximative use. The approximative diminutive is restricted to expressions of quantity; it is as if the exact value is unimportant, and the speaker excuses himself (and at the same time covers himself against possible reproaches) for not being precise. Thus, the person who says that he'll return in *un'oretta* (*oretta* is the diminutive of *ora* "hour"), would not usually mean that he'll be back in less than an hour. On the contrary! *Oretta* is more in the nature of an approximate indication of duration, which the speaker can feel free to exceed.

A somewhat less frequent use of the diminutive is as an intensifier; thus *casino*, the diminutive of *caso* "state of affairs", has the meaning "uproar, chaos". Wierzbicka (1980*b*: 55) cites a fine example from Spanish: *Son igualitos* "they are the same (diminutive)" conveys perfect identity, i.e. "they are the very same", rather than just more or less the same (cf. *Son iguales*). The diminutive as an intensifier is also attested in Dutch: *hartje* (<*hart* "heart") can refer not only to a heart of small dimensions (*Een muis heeft een klein hartje* "A mouse has a tiny heart"), but also to the 'very heart', i.e. the centre of something: *in het hartje van de stad* "in the (very) heart of the city" (Dirven 1985). Again we are dealing with a fairly transparent metonymic extension of the central sense; the centre of an entity is necessarily of smaller dimensions that the entity in its totality. Thus the diminutive comes to denote the very essence of a thing, a thing stripped of its non-essential periphery.

From this very brief survey, the diminutive emerges as a polysemous category whose various meanings are linked, some through metaphor, some through metonymy, to a central sense, i.e. "smallness in physical space". The linking of separate senses to a single central sense does not, however, entail the presence of a common meaning core. In this, I take issue with Wierzbicka's analysis (1980*b*: 53 ff.). Wierzbicka attempted to unify the various meanings of the diminutive on the basis of a common semantic component, namely that the speaker is "thinking of an entity as something small, and thinking of it as one would think of something small". Now, thinking of something as one would of something small undoubtedly constitutes the experiential basis for the metonymic extension of the diminutive. Furthermore, the experiential base would appear to be shared by speakers of very different language communities, hence the remarkable similarities in the semantic extension of the diminutive in different languages. Wierzbicka's formula, however, fails to take cognizance of the separateness of the meanings that can be associated with the category. "Thinking of something as something small" can imply a range of different, even inconsistent attitudes. Small things can be regarded with affection or contempt, they can be dismissed as unimportant, or prized because of their essentiality. Each of these nuances need not be conventionally associated with the diminutive in any given language. (The use of the diminutive as an intensifier seems to be more common in Spanish than in Italian, for example.) Wierzbicka's formula thus suffers from the same kind of defect that Wierzbicka noted in Jakobson's account of the Russian cases. On the basis of the formula alone, one cannot predict whether a particular use of the diminutive will be sanctioned in a given language or not.

There are two further aspects of diminutivization that I would like to draw attention to. The first concerns the productivity of the process. In Italian, the diminutive as an expression of small size can be applied more or less across the board to any noun which denotes a physical entity. Leaving aside the question of the choice of a diminutive suffix (Italian, as we have seen, has several), we are able, in principle, on the basis of a semantic characterization of the central sense alone, to predict (or 'generate') a complete set of forms exhibiting the central sense. As we move away from this central sense, diminutive suffixation becomes less productive, i.e. only a subset of the possible candidates for diminutivization actually occurs with a diminutive suffix. While the affectionate use of the diminutive is highly productive, the dismissive and approximative uses are restricted to a smallish number of instances sanctioned by convention. Similarly, only a handful of adverbs can be diminutivized; equally sporadic is the diminutivization of verbs. A complete set of diminutivized verbs and adverbs cannot be predicted. The attested forms are certainly motivated, on the basis of one of the meanings of the diminutive category; the forms must never- theless be listed in the lexicon, and learnt one by one by the language user.

The only limited productivity of certain senses of the diminutive— and the ensuing need for each attested form to be separately learnt— leads to the second characteristic of diminutivization that I would like to mention. Many diminutivized forms, in Italian and other languages, have a tendency to acquire the status of independent lexical items, with more or less specialized meanings. A *sinfonietta* is not just a small- scale symphony; it is a musical form in its own right. These specialized forms, too, need to be learnt one by one. The process of semantic specialization has been studied by Dirven (1987) in connection with diminutivization in Afrikaans. Diminutivization, to the extent that it is a productive morphological process in a language (even more so in a language with more than one diminutive suffix), generates a prolifera- tion of lexical items alongside the base forms. These may come to have the status of 'forms in search of a meaning'. Diminutivization thus becomes an important means whereby a language can extend its lexicon. The specialized meanings can usually be related to the meanings of the base forms by way of one of the meanings of the diminutive suffix; yet the meanings of the diminutivized forms cannot be predicated from the meanings of the constituent parts. Sometimes similar processes of specialization can be found in different languages. Quite common, for instance, is the use of a diminutivized form to refer to the young of an animal: Italian *gattino* (> *gatto* "cat") may be a small cat; it also means "kitten". Otherwise specialization follows quite unpredictable paths. Thus, in Afrikaans, *kaartjie*, the diminutive of *kaart* "map", has come to mean "ticket", and *vuurhoutjie*, from *vuurhout* "firewood", translates as "match".

8.2 The past tense

My next example is the past tense. As was the case with the diminutive, the name traditionally given to this morphosyntactic category points to its central meaning: the past tense is used, first and foremost, to locate an event or state at some point or period in time prior to the moment of speaking (or writing). The past tense is thus, primarily, a deictic tense; not infrequently, adverbials of time (*yesterday*, *a week ago*, *last year*) explicitly locate the past state of affairs with reference to the present. The past tense can also be used non-deictically, as in a historical narrative. In a historical narrative events and states are sequenced with reference to each other, not with reference to the time at which the narrative was composed. By extension, the past tense comes to be used in any kind of narrative, including fictional narrative. Here there can be no question of the past tense locating events prior to the moment of composition, since the events, being imaginary, never took place at all. Even science fiction narratives, in which events are imagined to take place subsequent to the moment of composition, are written in the past tense. In some languages (French is the best-known example) the distinction between the deictic and narrative senses is grammaticalized; the 'passé composé' (*il a vu* "he saw") is employed for deictic reference, while the 'passé historique' (*il vit*) is obligatory in historical and fictional narratives. In English, of course, the same form is used in both instances.

The above paragraph has already sketched out a very simple meaning chain for the past tense: from pastness with respect to the present and the pastness of a historical narrative, the past tense comes to be used as a marker of narrativity *tout court*. The past tense, however, has at least two other very important meanings (or constellation of meanings) in English. These have nothing to do with past time, or with narrativity. Firstly, the past tense indicates the unreality (or counterfactuality) of an event or state. Secondly, the past tense can function as a kind of pragmatic softener.

Typically, the counterfactual use of the past tense is restricted to a small number of environments—*if*-conditionals (1), expressions of wishes and desires (2), and suppositions and suggestions (3):

(1) If I had enough time, …

(2) (*a*) I wish I knew the answer
    (*b*) It would be nice if I knew the answer

(3) (*a*) Suppose we went to see him
    (*b*) It's time we went to see him

The past tense in these sentences denotes counterfactuality at the moment of speaking, and not at some previous point in time. (1) implies that, at the moment of speaking, the speaker does *not* have enough time, the sentences in (2) convey that the speaker does not know the answer, while in (3), the proposition encoded in the past tense, if it is to become true at all, will do so after the moment of speaking, that is to say, the past tense refers to a suggested future action. There are also a number of verbs whose past tense forms, under certain circumstances and with the appropriate intonation, can convey the present-time counterfactuality of a state of affairs represented in a past tense subordinate clause (Oakeshott-Taylor 1984*a*):

(4) (*a*) I thought John was married (… but he apparently isn't)
    (*b*) I had the impression Mary knew (… but it seems she doesn't)

These sentences might occur in a situation in which the speaker has just received information which causes him to doubt the (present-time) factuality of the propositions "John is married", "Mary knows". That it is a present, rather than a past state of affairs, that is at issue is shown by the choice of tense in a tag question. Imagine (5) uttered in a situation in which both speaker and addressee are preparing to go to a concert:

(5) But I thought the concert began at 8, doesn't it?/*didn't it?

The tag *doesn't it* is obligatorily in the present tense. In (5), the speaker is questioning the apparent counterfactuality, at the moment of speaking, of the proposition "The concert begins at 8".

The other use of the past tense that I want to consider is also restricted to a small number of contexts. This is the use of the past tense as a pragmatic softener. By choosing the past tense, a speaker can as it were cushion the effect an utterance might have on the addressee. Thus, (6)(*b*) is a more tactful way of intruding on a person's privacy than (6)(*a*):

(6) (*a*) Excuse me, I want to ask you something
    (*b*) Excuse me, I wanted to ask you something

Tact can also be conveyed by the past tense in association with the progressive aspect, as in (7):

(7) (*a*) Was there anything else you were wanting?
    (*b*) I was wondering if you could help me

This softening function of the past tense has been conventionalized in the meanings of the past tense modals in English. (8) (*b*) and (9) (*b*) are felt to be less direct than the (*a*) sentences; (10) (*b*) expresses greater uncertainty than (10) (*a*), especially with tonic stress on *might*; (11) (*b*) merely gives advice, while (11) (*a*) has the force of a command.

(8) (*a*) Can you help me?
    (*b*) Could you help me?

(9) (*a*) Will you help me?
    (*b*) Would you help me?

(10) (*a*) John may know
     (*b*) John might know

(11) (*a*) You shall speak to him
     (*b*) You should speak to him

Summarizing so far: there are three groups of meanings associated with the past tense: past time (and by extension historical and fictional narrativity), counterfactuality, and pragmatic softening. It is significant that a similar constellation of meanings is found in other languages, too. In Italian, a past tense (the so-called imperfect) can refer to past time (*Ieri pioveva* "it rained yesterday"); it can in addition express both unreality: *Se sapevo* ... "If (only) I knew ...", and tact: *Volevo chiederLe una cosa* "I wanted to ask you something". Zulu children are admonished by their elders not to ask for things with *Ngicela* ... "I want ...". Instead, they must use a past tense: *Bengicela* ... "I was wanting". A past tense is also used in counterfactual conditionals in Zulu: *Uma ebefikile* "If he had come" (Doke 1981: 366; the form *ebefikile* is a 'past in the past'). These remarkable cross-language similarities strongly suggest that the past tense needs to be regarded as a polysemous (rather than a homonymous) category.

But if this is so, how are the different meanings related? Let us begin with the counterfactual sense. Consider sentence (12):

(12) I was ill last week

On hearing this sentence, one could plausibly draw the inference that the speaker is no longer ill. An account of a past-time state of affairs may well carry the implication of the present-time counterfactuality of that state of affairs. By the perspectivization of this common implication, the past tense can come to convey counterfactuality *tout court*. Of interest in this connection is the potential ambiguity of *B*'s response in (13):

(13) *A*: Do you want to come for lunch?
    B: Well, I was expecting an overseas phone call . . .

Speaker *B* may be declining the invitation. The expected phone call has not yet been received, the speaker would therefore prefer not to leave the office. The response could also preface an acceptance. The past tense conveys that the phone call can no longer be expected, and the speaker is therefore free to accept the invitation. This interpretation might impose itself more strongly if *was* receives heavy tonic stress (Oakeshott-Taylor 1984*a*). The process of meaning extension illustrated by this example has been discussed by Östen Dahl in terms of the 'conventionalization of implicatures':

One powerful mechanism for creating secondary foci [of a polysemous category: J. T.] and secondary interpretations is what we can refer to as the *conventionalization of implicatures*. . . . If some condition happens to be fulfilled frequently when a certain category is used, a stronger association may develop between the condition and the category in such a way that the condition comes to be understood as an integral part of the meaning of the category. For instance, the tendency for categories like the English Perfect to develop 'inferential' interpretations might be explained in this way . . . Another example would be the development of Perfects and Pluperfects into recent and remote pasts, respectively. (Dahl 1985: 11 author's emphasis)

We have already encountered this kind of meaning extension in Chapter 6. In terms of the discussion in Chapter 6, the 'conventionalization of an implicature' is an instance of metonymy.

The softening function of the past tense is rather more complex, in that it seems to involve a double metaphorization. Firstly, there is the metaphor which construes the time domain in terms of space. We talk of the *distant past* and the *near future*. The second metaphor applies the schema of distance and proximity to the domain of involvement.

Again this is a metaphor which underlies many everyday expressions: one *distances oneself* from a proposal, one has a *close relationship* with a person, and so on. Thus, by using the past tense, the speaker can as it were distance himself from the speech act that he is performing. Hence the greater tactfulness of the past tense sentences in (6) and (7).

In the preceding section, I mentioned Wierzbicka's attempt to provide a unified account of the diminutive in terms of a common meaning component. Core meaning accounts of the past tense have also been proposed. Palmer writes:

> It has been suggested that the use of unreality and the past time use of the past tense are essentially the same—that the past tense is the 'remote' tense, remote in time or in reality. There is some attractiveness in this idea, for tense could then be seen to have but a single use. (Palmer 1974: 48)

As with the diminutive, however, I believe that it would be mistaken to try to unify the various uses of the past tense on the basis of a common semantic component, such as [REMOTE]—to claim, in fact, that there is really only one meaning of the past tense. Firstly, and rather obviously, the notion of 'remoteness' is far too general to serve as a formula for predicting the distribution of past tense. According to such a formula, the past tense could indicate futurity just as well as pastness, and could refer to present events taking place at some spatial distance from a speaker. More importantly, the formula ignores the fact that the various senses of the past tense are conceptually quite distinct. Remoteness in past time is a very different kind of remoteness from fictional and counterfactual remoteness, while remoteness as a component of pragmatic softening is mediated by a very specific conceptual metaphor associating proximity with involvement, and distance with lack of involvement. Furthermore, assigning a single sense to the past tense fails to take due account of the fact that the different uses of the past tense differ in their productivity. As with the diminutive, the more peripheral members of the past tense tend to be instantiated more sporadically and unpredictably than the central members. With one or two exceptions,[1] any verb in the English language, given an appropriate syntactic and semantic context, can take the past tense as a marker of past time. As a marker of counterfactuality, on the other hand, the past tense is typically restricted to a small number of syntactic environments (*If. . .*, *Suppose. . .*, *I thought. . .*). The use of

---

[1] The exceptions include certain strong verbs preceded by prefixes. A verb like *oversee* does not readily go into the past tense: ?*oversaw*.

the past tense as a pragmatic softener is even more limited. It occurs, primarily, in conjunction with a small set of modal auxiliaries (*could*, *should*, *might*, etc.). Furthermore, some of these past tense auxiliaries have undergone the same kind of semantic specialization that was noted in the discussion of the diminutive. The current meaning of *should*, although motivated by the pragmatic softening function of the past tense, is not entirely predictable from the meaning of present tense *shall*.

8.3 A note on yes–no questions

To conclude this chapter, I would like to comment on the sentences in (8), repeated here as (14):

(14) (*a*) Can you help me?
     (*b*) Could you help me?

These sentences would normally be understood as polite requests. Accordingly, an appropriate hearer response would be an offer to help, or, as the case may be, a refusal. Syntactically, however, the sentences look like yes–no questions, and in this respect appear to be enquiring merely into the listener's present and past ability to help. From this point of view, *Yes, I can/could*, and *No, I can't/couldn't* constitute the only appropriate responses. The kind of split exhibited in (14) between the syntactic form of a sentence and its illocutionary force has frequently been dealt with in terms of the semantics–pragmatics dichotomy (e.g. Searle 1975). As was the case with metaphorical utterances (cf. Section 6.2), it is proposed that a listener first extracts the literal meaning from a sentence. On finding the literal meaning inappropriate, or in some way bizarre, he then draws on principles of pragmatic inferencing in order to compute the probable intended meaning. This account of polite requests is open to the same kind of criticism as the Searlean account of metaphor. Metaphor, being all-pervasive, cannot reasonably be analysed in terms of grammatical deviance. Similarly, it seems more in keeping with the norms of English usage to regard the sentences in (14) as being in no way bizarre or inappropriate. On the contrary, the sentences exemplify two of the most frequent and unexceptional ways of making polite requests in English.

Searlean accounts of sentences like (14) are based on the presupposition that major sentence types like declarative, imperative, WH-interrogative, and yes–no interrogative constitute clear-cut categories, with regard both to their syntactic form and to their semantic value. The sentences in (14) thus have the same syntactic and semantic value as any other yes–no interrogative; subsequently, we need to invoke pragmatic principles to explain the fact that the sentences are not understood like other yes–no questions. Suppose, however, that we regard sentence types as polysemous family resemblance categories. A yes–no interrogative might now have a range of possible senses. It could be a request for the specification of polarity; alternatively, it might have some of the force of a request. Similarly, a declarative sentence need not only make a statement, it could also have some of the force of a question. In their form, too, sentence types might merge into each other. This possibility has been pursued by Givón (1986). Givón cites the following sentences as illustrations of the syntactic and semantic continuum which he claims exists between prototypical imperatives on the one hand, and prototypical yes–no interrogatives on the other:

(15) (*a*) Pass the salt! (most prototypical imperative)
    (*b*) Please pass the salt
    (*c*) Pass the salt, would you please?
    (*d*) Would you please pass the salt?
    (*e*) Could you please pass the salt?
    (*f*) Can you please pass the salt?
    (*g*) Do you see the salt?
    (*h*) Is there any salt around? (most prototypical interrogative)

Givón also sets up a continuum from prototypical declarative to prototypical yes–no interrogative:

(16) (*a*) Joe is at home (most prototypical declarative)
    (*b*) Joe is at home, I think
    (*c*) Joe is at home, right?
    (*d*) Joe is at home, isn't he?
    (*e*) Is Joe at home? (most prototypical interrogative)

Let us posit, as the central member of the yes–no interrogative, a question which requests no more than a specification of polarity. In point of fact, the number of occasions on which one asks a yes–no question for the sole purpose of eliciting the specification of polarity is probably vanishingly rare. Almost invariably, a yes–no question is preliminary to something else. We can distinguish two possibilities. Consider a fairly 'pure' exemplar:

(17) Did you see the Prime Minister on TV last night?

An affirmative response to this question might lead the speaker of (17) to ask additional, more specific questions (*What did she say?*, *What did you think of her?*, etc). (17), that is, functions as a prelude to further requests, in this case for information. On the other hand, the speaker of (17) may be using his question merely as a preliminary to his own comment on the Prime Minister's speech. The question, in this case, serves primarily to introduce the topic of the Prime Minister's speech into the discourse. Through perspectivization of these two components a yes–no interrogative can lose its interrogative force, and come to be used either as a request for information and/or action, or as a statement and/or comment. The first meaning chain can be read off from (15), starting from the bottom, while the second can be traced from the bottom of (16). Thus (18) would invariably be interpreted as a request to the hearer to indicate (if he has the information) where the nearest telephone is, while (19) is merely commenting on the obvious:

(18) Is there a public telephone around here?

(19) Have you lost your keys again?

In support of this approach to the yes–no interrogative we may note that members of the category are sometimes ambiguous, cf. Sadock 1972. (Recall that ambiguity is the hallmark of polysemy.) Thus (20):

(20) Can you play the piano?

could function as a request for polarity specification, or as a request for the hearer to sit down at a piano and to play. Alternatively, the sentence could be a speaker comment; the speaker is expressing surprise at learning that the addressee can play the piano.

One further observation can be made. As with the categories studied earlier in this chapter, some of the instantiations of the more peripheral members of the yes–no interrogative appear to have acquired the status of conventionalized, quasi-independent linguistic forms. It is appropriate, perhaps, to regard certain highly formulaic instances of the yes–no interrogative in this way. The sentences in (21) and (22)—note that one typically experiences uncertainty as to whether to write them with a question mark or not!—have no interrogative force whatsoever; the sentences are little more than formulaic expressions of speaker surprise.

(21) Would you believe it!

(22) Is that a fact?

It is in the context of the yes–no interrogative as a family resemblance category that the sentences in (14) are to be approached. Of course, the semantic extension of the yes–no interrogative is motivated by principles that, in a rather general sense, would be called 'pragmatic'. (But the same is true of any metonymic extension, cf. the metonymic extensions of the diminutive and the past tense.) Yet we do not need a semantics–pragmatics split in order to explain the alleged discrepancy between the form of the sentences and their usual interpretation. That the sentences in (14) are taken as polite requests for action and not as requests for polarity specification, is due to the fact that the yes–no interrogative is a polysemous category with, as one of its members, the *Can you?*-form. That (14) (*b*) is felt to be more deferential than (14) (*a*) results from the interaction of this meaning of the interrogative with one of the meanings of the past tense.

9

Polysemous Categories in Intonation

ALTHOUGH polysemy is generally regarded as a property of lexical items, we have seen (Chapter 8) that the association of more than one meaning with a single linguistic form is not limited to the lexicon. Polysemy also characterizes morphological, morphosyntactic, and even syntactic categories. In this chapter I take the discussion one step further, and explore the polysemy of prosodic categories involved in a description of intonation.

The main burden of the chapter will be, firstly, to demonstrate that the formal categories employed in an analysis of intonation are indeed polysemous, and, secondly, to show the inadequacy of attempts to state the semantic contribution of intonation in terms of core meanings. In conclusion, some data pertinent to an important component of English intonation will be analysed with a view to explicating the family resemblance structure of the category.

9.1 The problem of intonational meaning

Intonation is one of the most difficult areas of linguistic description. Even linguistically naïve speakers are aware that intonation contributes, in some vaguely felt way, to the total meaning of an utterance. It is the task of the linguist to explicate this semantic contribution. This involves setting up a formal descriptive apparatus, associating a meaning, or range of meanings, to each formal element of the descriptive systems.

To this extent, the study of intonation is in principle no different from the study of any other component of linguistic structure. In studying tense, we identify, first of all, the formal elements of the tense system. For English we would identify, at the very least, a present tense and a past tense. Then, for each of these formal elements, we specify a meaning (or range of meanings), such that, for any given sentence, we can state the semantic contribution of the tense form in question. But whereas it is a relatively straightforward matter to identify the formal elements of a tense system, to attempt to state the formal elements of intonation presents us with a different order of difficulty. Any sentence can be spoken with a virtually limitless range of pitch levels and pitch sequences. The first step in any analysis must be to digitalize the phonetic data, i.e. to abstract from the limitless possibilities a small, finite set of meaning-bearing elements. Do we, in accord with the practice of many American linguists (e.g. Pike 1945), analyse intonation in terms of a sequence of discrete pitch levels and terminal contours? Or do we follow the British tradition (e.g. Halliday 1970) and postulate a set of intonation tunes, or contours? If the former, how many distinct pitch levels, and what combinatorial patterns, do we recognize? If the latter, we need an inventory of tunes, perhaps consisting of a small set of basic tunes and a rather larger set of variants. Alternatively, we might try to synthesize the two traditions by adopting an autosegmental approach (e.g. Gussenhoven 1985). Then there is the question of stress, or accent. Do we treat stress, as in the American tradition, independently of pitch, or, in line with Bolinger (e.g. 1986) and the majority of British linguists, in terms of pitch movement? Even assuming that there were agreement (which there is not: see Ladd 1980: ch. 1, for some discussion) on the formal apparatus for intonation description, there remains the second issue, i.e. specifying the semantic contribution of each formal element to the meaning of a given utterance. On this issue, there is even less consensus than on the first. Not only do linguists disagree on the semantic contribution of any formal element, there is even controversy on the very kinds of meaning that intonation can convey. For some, intonation contributes principally to the cohesion of a text; for others, intonation is primarily attitudinal. Alternatively, intonation has been seen as a grammatical phenomenon, while others propose that intonation is exclusively interactional.

It is this second issue—the semantic contribution of the formal elements of intonation—that will concern us in this chapter. In view of the different formal analyses of intonation that have been proposed, I shall base the following discussion, somewhat arbitrarily, on one particular formal model. Although the categories proposed by the model have been criticized on both acoustic and perceptual grounds (Brown *et al*. 1980), I will assume in what follows the general validity of the kind of analysis proposed by a majority of British linguists. According to the British school—a typical exponent is Halliday (1970)—the domain of intonation is a rhythmically and intonationally coherent stretch of speech known as the tone unit. The tone unit contains one or more stressed (in Halliday's terminology: 'salient') syllables. Stressed syllables tend to occur at approximately regular intervals of time; the occurrence of stressed syllables thus determines the rhythm of English speech. Of the stressed syllables in a tone unit, one is especially prominent. This is the tonic syllable. The perceptual prominence of the tonic syllable is largely due to the fact that this syllable is the bearer of tone, i.e. it is the centre of the intonation contour with which the tone unit is spoken. Halliday—along with many others—recognizes five tones in standard British English: falling, high-rising, low-rising, falling-rising, and rising-falling. Again in line with many other students of intonation, Halliday lists numerous variants of these five basic tones.

9.2 The meanings of falling and rising tones

Is it possible to associate a semantic content with the elements of Halliday's intonation model? Let us restrict our attention to the meaning of tone. I shall review three very different approaches to this question. Halliday himself introduces the topic as follows:

Since the falling and rising pitch contours constitute the basic elements of English intonation, it would be useful if we could find some overall meaning for them; if we could say, in general terms, what falling pitch means in English and what rising pitch means. (Halliday 1970: 23)

Clearly, Halliday is here preparing the ground for a core meaning approach. The passage continues:

Basically, a falling contour means certainty and a rising contour means uncertainty. This is true in many languages, though by no means all. In English, it takes this particular form: a falling contour means certainty *with regard to yes or no*. We go down when we know whether something is positive or negative, and we go up when we do not know. In other words we go down when we know the *polarity* of what we are saying. (Halliday 1970: 23, author's emphasis)

Halliday then proceeds to apply these core meanings to the contribution of falling and rising tones to various kinds of sentence. The polarity of a statement is known, it is either affirmative or negative; statements are therefore (usually) spoken with a falling tone. In a yes–

no question, like *Are you coming?*, it is polarity which is at issue; yes–no questions are thus (usually) spoken with a rising tone. WH-questions, on the other hand, are not about polarity. To ask *Where are you going?* is to enquire about a person's destination, not about whether or not he is going somewhere. Consequently, WH-questions are (generally) spoken with falling tone. Halliday draws on the same core meanings to account for tones involving pitch changes, i.e. his tone 4 (falling-rising) and tone 5 (rising–falling). These tones 'contain two components of meaning, with a "change of mind" in the middle'. Tone 4 thus means "it may seem as though all is clear, but in fact there is more involved". Hence the fall-rise is typically used with expressions of reserved agreement, as in ˅MAY*be*, *I sup* ˅POSE *so*. Tone 5, on the other hand, conveys "there may seem to be a doubt, but in fact all is certain". Consequently, the rise-fall is used for expressions of uncompromising finality, as in *That's all there is* ˆTO *it*.[1]

As Halliday points out, the association between falling pitch and certainty, and between rising pitch and uncertainty, exists in many of the world's languages. Very probably, the association has a natural experiential base, and is grounded in a rather intricate web of metaphor and metónymy. Firstly, there is a metaphor which maps the up–down schema from the spatial domain on to the domain of pitch. The very expressions *rising pitch* and *falling pitch* instantiate this metaphor. The up–down schema is also applied to the notions of completion and incompletion, and, by metonymy, to certainty and uncertainty. Matters that have not yet been finalized (in the sense of not having been completed, and therefore still subject to uncertainty) are up, while things that have reached a conclusion are down. Thus we speak of a discussion *getting off the ground*, i.e. getting started, while a discussion which ends *up in the air* is one which has failed to come to a satisfactory end. This second metaphor is very likely based on our experience of flying objects. An object thrown into the air typically describes an arc-like trajectory—first ascending, then descending—before it comes to rest. Thus falling motion heralds the approaching end-point of the trajectory (and falling pitch the approaching end-point of an utterance), while rising motion signals a continuing trajectory (and rising pitch the need to continue the discourse). This

---

[1] Transcription conventions in these and other examples are as follows: Tonic syllables are capitalized; tone-unit boundaries are indicated (where appropriate) by the slash /; tones are represented by ˋ (falling), ´ (high rising), ˌ (low rising), ˅ (falling-rising), and ˆ (rising-falling).

metaphorical association of falling pitch with completion is strengthened by physiological and aerodynamic characteristics of speech production; falling pitch is a natural accompaniment of the decrease in subglottal pressure which occurs as a speaker approaches the end of a breath group (Lieberman 1967).

That the elements of intonation have a natural explanation in metaphor and metonymy (cf. Lakoff and Johnson 1980: 57; Bolinger 1986: 194 ff.) is an attractive hypothesis, entirely consonant with the cognitive approach to language. Yet the natural meanings of intonation contours, postulated by Halliday, do not appear to account for all uses of the contours. It may well be true that yes–no questions are generally spoken with rising tone, and that WH-questions are generally spoken with falling tone, and for the reasons that Halliday mentions. But what about the fact that some yes–no questions are spoken with falling tone, and some WH-questions may be asked with rising tone? Do the proposed meanings of the falling and rising tones (i.e. certainty/uncertainty with respect to polarity) explain, let alone enable us to describe, the different nuances in (1) and (2):

(1) (*a*) Are you ´coming?
  (*b*) Are you `coming?

(2) (*a*) Where are you `going?
  (*b*) Where are you ´going?

Halliday's explication of the rising-falling tone is equally suspect. Consider Halliday's own example—already cited—of a sentence which is nearly always spoken with a rise-fall:

(3) That's all there is ˆto it

It is surely not all that enlightening to claim that the semantic contribution of intonation to this sentence is to convey that 'there may seem to be a doubt, but in fact all is certain'. The formula seems even more irrelevant for utterances where the rise-fall conveys a kind of exaggerated involvement by the speaker, as in (4):

(4) (*a*) The concert was ˆawful
  (*b*) It was fanˆtastic

The problem is a familiar one. Given that a semantically relevant formal contrast has been isolated, the analyst feels compelled to associate each term of the contrast with an invariant meaning, such that it is possible to account in all cases for the unique semantic contribution of the formal element under consideration. It is not that Halliday fails to make interesting and perceptive remarks on *some* of the meanings (perhaps we might even want to say, the central, or prototypical meanings) of the English tones. But to regard these meanings as core meanings is to give up on accounting for the contribution of intonation to a wide range of English utterances. Significantly, Halliday himself is aware of the limitations of his approach: 'There are so many different kinds of combinations of falling and rising pitch that anything which is general enough to apply to all of them is not likely to be very enlightening' (1970: 23). Yet the urge to posit core meanings is so deeply engrained that even a linguist of Halliday's stature pursues the approach none the less.

The same urge characterizes other attempts to explicate intonational meaning. As a further illustration, let us turn to another account of the meanings of the falling and the rising (more precisely: falling-rising) tones, an account that stems from a very different linguistic tradition. I refer to Jackendoff's remarks on intonation in his *Semantic Interpretation in Generative Grammar* (1972: 258 ff.). According to Jackendoff, the (*a*) and (*b*) sentences below select falling and rising tone by the same principles:

(5) (*a*) ˇFRED ate the ˋBEANS
    (*b*) As for ˇFRED, he ate the ˋBEANS

(6) (*a*) ˋFRED ate the ˇBEANS
    (*b*) As for the ˇBEANS, ˋFRED ate them.

Underlying each of these sentences is the proposition "x ate y". Jackendoff claims that of the two variables, x and y, one is assigned a value before the other. In (5), x is first assigned the value *Fred*. Given that x has the value *Fred*, it is asserted that y has the value *beans*. Conversely, in (6), the value assigned to x is dependent on the value *beans* having first been assigned to y, i.e. given that someone ate the beans, it is asserted that that someone is Fred. In brief, the falling-rising tone signals the independent variable, while the falling tone signals the dependent variable.

In support of this analysis, Jackendoff notes that topicalized elements in a sentence are generally spoken with a fall-rise. The topic of a sentence is what the sentence is about, while what is said about the topic constitutes the comment. In English, the topic generally coincides with that constituent of clause structure which is placed in sentence initial position. In the unmarked state of affairs, the topic of a sentence is the subject. Topicalization is the selection of a non-subject constituent for sentence initial position. Jackendoff argues that the topic of a sentence is 'chosen freely' (1972: 262), i.e. it is the independent variable. The comment, on the other hand, is dependent on the prior choice of the topic. Accordingly, topics (especially marked topics) are eligible for the fall-rise tone. In (5)(*b*) and (6)(*b*) the topicalized status of *Fred* and *the beans* is explicitly signalled by the topicalizing phrase *as for*. In (7), on the other hand, the topicalized status of the initial constituents is signalled solely by their position in the sentence. They would typically be spoken with a fall-rise.

(7) (*a*) ˇBAGels / I don't like to ˋEAT
    (*b*) At six o' ˇCLOCK / ˋFRED walked in

So far so good. Jackendoff now proceeds to apply his semantic formulas to a further range of sentences, in particular to sentences with only one tonic syllable. Consider, first, a sentence spoken with a falling tone, e.g. (8).

(8) ˋFRED ate the beans

A falling tone 'marks its focus as a dependent variable, a value chosen not freely, but rather in such a way as to make the sentence true' (1972: 263). This rather tortuous formulation means, in essence, that declarative sentences are spoken with a fall; these sentences are true in virtue of their assigning a particular value to a variable. The case of a sentence with a single falling-rising tone is more difficult. On the assumption that the falling-rising tone signals an independent variable, sentences with a single falling-rising tone ought to be impossible, since such sentences lack a dependent variable. Jackendoff gets out of this difficulty by arguing that in these cases the dependent variable is the affirmation–negation polarity contrast. Underlying the sentences in (9) is the proposition "x ate the beans". Given the prior assignment of the value *Fred* to the variable x, the sentences in (9) select positive and negative polarity respectively as their dependent variables.

(9) (*a*) ˇFRED ate the beans
    (*b*) ˇFRED didn't eat the beans

(9)(*b*) thus receives the interpretation "Given that someone ate the beans, it is asserted that that someone is not Fred". However, it is difficult to see how Jackendoff's highly abstract, not to say casuistic account throws any light whatsoever on any of the meaning nuances that can attach to (9) (*a*), nor does it explicate, in any intelligible way, the different meanings of (9) (*a*) and (8). This criticism should not be taken to imply that the whole of Jackendoff's account is in question. What is in question is the idea that Jackendoff's semantic formulas can serve as core meanings for the falling and falling-rising tones.

A radically different account of the meaning of tone is presented in Brazil *et al.*'s *Discourse Intonation and Language Teaching* (1980). This monograph is one of the most thoroughgoing, and arguably most successful, attempts at providing a core meaning analysis of English intonation. The authors claim that intonational meaning is exclusively interactional, and has to do with the ongoing creation of text by the participants in a discourse. They relate the use of the falling and the falling-rising tones to the extent of 'common ground' between speaker and hearer. Thus a speaker uses a falling tone ('proclaiming tone', in their terminology) to add new information to the common ground, while the falling-rising tone ('referring tone') is used to mark information as part of the common ground. (A rather similar account of the meanings of tone may be found in Gussenhoven 1983). Thus in (10):

(10) He'll be ˇTWENty in ˋAUgust

the hearer is informed when a mutual acquaintance will be twenty, while in (11):

(11) He'll be ˋTWENty in ˇAUgust

he is informed how old the acquaintance will be in August. I will not give an account of the wide range of data which Brazil *et al.*'s formulas can accommodate. (We might note in passing that the notions of proclaiming and referring readily encompass Jackendoff's interpretations of (5), (6), and (7).) But a number of facts cast suspicion on the adequacy of proclaiming and referring as core meanings of the tones. Firstly, the authors concede that in many cases there may be no independent basis for deciding whether the content of a tone unit is or is not part of the common ground between speaker and hearer. Sometimes, a speaker may attempt to insinuate solidarity with the hearer by treating new information as if it were shared. Since the analyst can have no access, other than by observation of intonation, to a speaker's intentions in this regard, the account becomes very much *post hoc* and thus empirically unfalsifiable. In addition, there are cases where appeal to common ground would anyway appear to shed little light on choice of tone. Consider the hesitancy of ˇWELL, compared with the relative confidence of ˋWELL, or the reserved agreement expressed by *I sup* ˊPOSE *so* in contrast with the relatively unreserved agreement of *I su* ˋPOSE *so*. And what has common ground got to do with the well-known semantic contrast in (12)?

(12) (*a*) He doesn't want to marry ˋANYone
i.e. "He wants to marry no one"
(*b*) He doesn't want to marry ˇANYone
i.e. "He wants to marry someone, but not just anyone"

Many years ago, Pike (1945: 23) set down a guiding principle for the study of intonation: 'Once a particular intonation contour has been isolated ... its meaning is determined by finding the least common denominator of the linguistic contexts or physical and emotional situations within which that contour occurs.' The above review suggests that Pike's programme has not been realized. Each of the three proposals for specifying the meanings of English tones turns out to be valid for only a certain range of data. For each approach, one can readily find sentences where the semantic contribution of intonation appears to have little to do with the proposed core meaning. Significantly, Cruttenden (1986) concludes his recent state of the art monograph on intonation by singling out, as one of the areas which is likely to dominate intonation research in the next decade or so, 'the semantics involved in a set of abstract meanings [i.e. core meanings: J. T.] to be matched to the set of tones in an intonational lexicon' (1986: 184). Pessimistically, Cruttenden notes that 'it is not yet even clear what sort of meanings are involved'. Nor is this state of affairs restricted to the study of tone. Attempts to associate the choice of tonic syllable within the tone unit to a single core meaning run into the same kinds of difficulty (Oakeshott-Taylor 1984*b*).

The failure of successive generations of linguists to come up with a satisfactory set of core meanings for the elements of intonation should not really surprise us. After all, a search for the least common denominator of all the various uses of *climb* and *over* would equally come to nothing. Significantly, Pike himself suggested an analogy with lexical polysemy. He noted that just as words may have two or more related meanings, 'so with intonational contours one must sometimes indicate a central meaning with minor variations from it' (1945: 23). A hint of the possibility of intonational polysemy may also be detected in one of Cruttenden's publications. Cruttenden (1981) notes that the core meanings of the tones, if there are any, are likely to be of a very high degree of abstraction. After comparing the contribution of a falling vs. rising intonation to different kinds of sentences, he comes up with the following list of semantic dimensions associated with the two pitch contours:

Fall	*Rise*
reinforcing	limiting
statement	question
finality	continuity
closed-listing	open-listing
conducive	non-conducive
statement	statement with reservations
dogmatic	conciliatory

Cruttenden is aware of the difficulty of abstracting a common core from each of the two lists; he even hints, in the following passage, at the possibility of a family resemblance structure linking the various meanings of the two intonation tunes. Unfortunately, the hint is not followed up. His reservations notwithstanding, Cruttenden proposes common core meanings all the same:

The meanings of each list appear to have something in common; there appear to be metaphorical links between the members of each set (preliminary results from naïve informants on a sorting task support such links). But it is not easy to put a cover label on each group of meanings. It is, indeed, inevitable that any label used will be vague in itself without knowing the various meanings which it covers. The meanings associated with falling intonations are generally assertive and I suggest the label CLOSED as a cover term for such meanings; similarly, the meanings associated with rising intonations are in general non-assertive and the cover term OPEN is suggested. (Cruttenden 1981: 81)

The core meanings [OPEN] and [CLOSED] are subject to precisely the same criticism which Wierzbicka levelled at Jakobson's account of the Russian cases: the meanings are so general as to be predictively useless. On the basis of the features [CLOSED] and [OPEN], or, alternatively, [ASSERTIVE] and [NON-ASSERTIVE], the person who does not know English could not predict the semantic nuances conveyed by falling vs. rising intonation in any particular instance.

9.3 High key

In this section I would like to explore the possibility of a family resemblance approach to intonation, by examining some data taken from Brazil *et al.* (1980). In the main, the formal elements of Brazil's analysis are the familiar ones of the British school: tone unit, tonic syllable, and tone. One innovation concerns the importance attached to key. Key is defined in terms of the relative pitch of the first stressed syllable (which may or may not coincide with the tonic syllable) in a tone unit. The system has three values: high, mid, and low. These values are defined, not in absolute pitch terms, but relative to the terminating pitch of the preceding tone unit. The meanings of high, mid, and low key are identified as "contrastive", "additive", and "equative", respectively. Now, 'contrast' is one of the most misused terms in studies of intonational meaning (see Oakeshott-Taylor 1984*b* for some discussion). To their credit, Brazil *et al.* offer a very precise definition of what they understand by contrast. Consistent with their overall approach of assigning only discourse meanings to intonation, contrastivity is understood as an interactional phenomenon:

We should, at this point, attempt to clarify the way in which we are using the concept of contrastivity. There is of course a generally recognised, Saussurian, sense in which all linguistic items are contrastive; in this description, however, the term is not to be taken as referring primarily to paradigmatic relations existing between items in the language—so that by choosing 'wife', for instance, one is meaningfully not choosing 'daughter', 'mother', 'sister', 'niece', 'aunt' . . . Rather the additional contrastivity which choice of high key conveys is a social construct, a closed set of items created by the participants as part of the common ground and available and intelligible to them at the time and place of utterance—and sometimes only there. (Brazil *et al.* 1980: 29)

Contrast, then, involves the creation, by the participants in an interaction, of a mutually exclusive set of items. The contrasting items constitute 'choice-exhausting features of the world' (1980: 26), such that a speaker, by selecting one item in the set, rejects the others.

This understanding of contrastivity clearly motivates the choice of high key in the following example:

(13) / *p* we're going to MARgate this year / *p* not <u>BOG</u>nor /[2]

---

[2] The notation is based on Brazil *et al.* The slash / indicates tone unit boundaries; *p* and *r* stand for proclaiming (i.e. falling) and referring (i.e. falling-rising) tone; stressed

Here, the speaker has explicitly created a two-member set (Margate and Bognor), and selects one of the terms rather than the other.[3] In the next example, membership in the set is given by the context of the utterance. Imagine the sentence spoken by a member of a two-car family:

(14) / *p* WHY not take the / *p* R̲E̲D̲ car /

By selecting *red car* the speaker is implicitly rejecting the other member of the closed set.

These cases constitute unequivocal instances of contrast, on Brazil's definition of the term. However, as one reads further in the monograph, one cannot fail to notice that Brazil and his co-authors subtly change their understanding of contrastivity. Consider (15):

(15) / *r* S̲O̲M̲E̲ people will like it /

Here, by choosing high key the speaker is said to be emphasizing 'the potential linguistic contrast and opposes "some" to "all" or "none"' (1980: 33). The speaker, then, is not so much creating a closed set of items, as exploiting a closed contrast made available by the linguistic system. A special instance of a linguistically encoded contrast is a contrast of polarity:

(16) *A*: It was a good film
     B: / *p* Y̲E̲S̲ / *p* you're R̲I̲G̲H̲T̲/

In this example, high key *yes* is said to convey ' "yes-not-no" = "you are right": the speaker makes a judgment' (1980: 71). Elsewhere (1980: 36) we read that if high key *yes* is often construed as emphatic, this is 'because it means, in terms of a rather odd paraphrase, "You are not wrong!"'. The notion of contrastivity as a 'social construct', involving a 'closed set of items created by the participants as part of the common ground', seems to be of less obvious relevance here than in (14) and (15).

In other examples, the high key item is said to rectify a previous misapprehension:

syllables are capitalized and tonic syllables underlined. High, mid, and low pitch ranges are indicated by vertical arrangement on the page. All the quoted examples are taken from Brazil *et al.* (1980).

[3] There is a possibility of misunderstanding here. High key on *Bognor* signals that the speaker in this tone unit is selecting the lexical item *Bognor* and rejecting *Margate*. The choice of a linguistic form is not to be confused with the speaker's rejection of Bognor as the intended destination.

(17) / p i DIDn't TELL peter about it /

Here, high key implies 'you are wrong in thinking Peter knew' (1980: 49). Closely related is the use of high key to signal the speaker's expectation that the hearer will find the content of the tone unit surprising:

(18) / p i met henry's BROTHer / p he's a BANKer /

This sentence would be appropriate in the context of a presumption that Henry's family are pretty inept when it comes to money matters (1980: 35). We could still perhaps claim that these examples are contrastive, on a rather broad interpretation of Brazil's definition of the term. In (17) there is a closed contrast between the speaker's depiction of a state of affairs and the listener's presumed misapprehension, while in (18) the actual situation, i.e. the brother's financial expertise, contrasts with the expectation of his financial ineptitude. Brazil, however, goes on to use the term contrast to describe the following sentence, where *tennis gear* does not seem to contrast with anything in particular; rather, high key merely implies the unexpectedness, in the circumstances, of the event:

(19) / r as soon as he'd finished EATing / p he changed into TENnis gear /

Even more remote from the interactional definition of contrast are those cases where the high key item seems to be introducing new information into the discourse, as in the following examples:

(20) / p What happened at WIMbledon /

(21) / p this is eLIZabeth / p PEter's wife /

In order to retain the formula 'high key = contrast', Brazil is forced to claim that in cases like these, high key conveys 'an implied setting of the named object against all other possibilities'; (1980: 28). In other words, we witness a return to the very general, Saussurian sense of contrast, according to which every linguistic form is contrastive. Difficult to understand in terms of any operationally useful definition of contrast are cases like the following, where, it is claimed, high key 'enables a speaker to indicate that he has chosen a given word or phrase with great care' (1980: 28):

(22) / p the GOVernment / p have so ANGered / r the farmers of this COUNtry /

Finally, we come to one of the most important functions of high key, and again it is one which seems to have little to do with contrast, on any understanding of the term. This concerns the 'paragraphing' of spoken discourse. A speaker uses high key to open a new phonological paragraph, or, in Brown *et al.*'s (1980: 26) terminology, a new 'paratone'. Typically, a new phonological paragraph coincides with a change in topic:

(23) / r for my <u>MAIN</u> topic this evening / p i TURN to eco_{NOM}ic matters /

This brief review of the semantic contribution of high key in English has led to the same conclusion as our earlier examination of tone. Having identified the semantic contribution of high key in a limited range of utterances, Brazil and his co-authors feel compelled to apply their semantic formula to all instances of high key, no matter what the consequences for the original definition. This is not, of course, to deny that the monograph abounds in valuable insights into intonational meaning, not the least of which is to have isolated key as an important meaning-bearing component of English intonation. But high key is certainly not the monosemous element it is claimed to be. The examples discussed above suggest that high key has at least ten distinct meanings. These are:

(*a*) Explicit contrast involving the members of a closed set (13)
(*b*) Implicit contrast within a closed set, where the contrasting members are given by the context of situation (14)
(*c*) Implicit contrast between members of a closed linguistic system (15)
(*d*) Polarity contrast, as a special instance of the above (16)
(*e*) Emphasis (16)
(*f*) Rectification of a misapprehension (17)
(*g*) Unexpectedness (18) (19)
(*h*) Introduction of new information (20) (21)
(*i*) Careful choice of a linguistic item (22)
(*j*) Beginning of a new phonological paragraph, signalling change in topic (23).

Although it would be impracticable to extract a common core from these ten meanings, the meanings are nevertheless related, and appear to cluster in three major sense groups. Meanings (*a*) to (*d*), as well as (*f*), have to do with selection from a closed set; the closed set may be explicitly stated, it may be derivable from the context of the utterance, or it may be encoded in the linguistic system. A second group of meanings has to do with high information value. High key can be used for emphasis (*e*), to signal unexpectedness (*g*), or to show that a linguistic form has been selected with great care (*i*). Thirdly, high key accompanies the introduction into the discourse of new material, whether a new lexical item or a new discourse topic. This is the case with meanings (*h*) and (*j*). The second of these sense clusters, i.e. high information content, may be regarded as central. Contrastive uses of high key are related to the central cluster in virtue of the double information conveyed by a contrastive item: in selecting one term of a contrast, a speaker is necessarily also rejecting the other terms. In a rather different sense, new information, or a new topic of discourse, can likewise be regarded as a special instance of high informativity.

This approach to high key could be easily extended to examples of mid and low key. Low key, for instance, would signal in its central sense low informativity, its other meanings (e.g. continuation of the same phonological paragraph) being derivable from this central sense. Furthermore, the approach readily lends itself to a metaphorical interpretation, of the kind outlined earlier for tone. Key has to do with the height of a syllable relative to the terminating pitch of a preceding tone unit. Raised pitch lends perceptual prominence to a syllable. It is natural that the high information content of a tone unit should be signalled by its relative perceptual prominence.

10

Grammatical Categories

THE prototype model of categories was developed in the early 1970s as a response to empirical evidence concerning the way people categorize things in their environment. Important landmarks in this research were Labov's studies of the categorization of household receptacles, Berlin and Kay's findings on colour categories, and the work of Rosch and her associates, which refined and extended the insights of Berlin and Kay.

There were, from the outset, two orientations that prototype research could take. The direction of cognitive psychology (cf. Smith and Medin 1981) was to study the way concepts are structured and represented in the mind. Alternatively, research on categorization could be channelled into linguistics. Here the emphasis comes to be placed, not on concepts *per se*, but on the structure of the semantic pole of the linguistic sign, i.e. on the meanings of linguistic forms. The two orientations are closely intertwined. As we saw in the discussion of hedges (section 4.4), linguistic data and the psychologist's experimental findings mutually complement each other. Indeed, one of the main sources of evidence for conceptual structure is linguistic; conversely, any reasonable account of linguistic behaviour needs to make reference to the conceptual structures which linguistic forms conventionally symbolize.

Linguists, while keen to exploit the findings of the cognitive psychologists, were not likely to be content with data limited, in the main, to the names of natural kinds, like birds and fruit, and cultural artefacts, like vehicles and furniture. In the hands of linguists, the prototype model was rapidly extended so as to encompass concepts of increasing abstraction, not only notions like "murder" and "tell a lie", but also the meanings of grammatical formatives like prepositions and bound morphemes, and even the elusive nuances conveyed by intonation contours. And, of course, it was linguistic evidence (the all-pervasive presence of polysemy) that suggested that prototype categories can be co-ordinated in family resemblance structures.

Recent years have seen the extension of the prototype concept to ever more areas of linguistic research. Hudson (1980) has argued that many of the constructs of sociolinguistics—kinds of speech act (e.g. promise), types of interaction (e.g. business transaction), the parameters of power and solidarity, even the very concept of a speech community—can be usefully regarded as prototype categories, definable in the first instance in terms of clear cases. Another significant development has been the application of the prototype concept to the purely formal elements of linguistic description. Bybee and Moder (1983) claim that 'speakers of natural language form categorizations of linguistic objects in the same way that they form categorizations of natural and cultural objects', which suggests that 'the psychological principles which govern linguistic behavior are the same as those which govern other types of human behavior' (1983: 267). Bybee and Moder (see also Bybee and Slobin 1982) reached this conclusion from a study of certain morphological alternations in English. Amongst the strong verbs in English are those which, like *sing*, show the vowel alternation /ɪ/-/æ/-/ʌ/ in the present tense, past tense, and past participle. Others, like *cling*, have the pattern /ɪ/-/ʌ/-/ʌ/. The two classes have been moderately productive over the centuries, having extended their membership to include verbs originally in other classes, such as *ring*, *fling*, *stick*, and *dig*. Also, verbs which have a vowel other than /ɪ/ in the present tense have been added, e.g. *hang*, *strike*, and, for some speakers, *sneak*, *shake*, and *drag*. These latter, on account of their non-conforming present tense forms, clearly count as more marginal members of the classes. In other respects, too, the classes exhibit a prototype structure (Table 10.1). The majority of the verbs have as the final consonant of the stem a velar nasal (*sing*, *spring*, *cling*). Other verbs exhibit an only partial similarity to this characteristic of the central members. Some, for instance, have as their final consonant a non-velar nasal (*swim*, *win*, *spin*), others end in a non-nasal velar (*stick*, *dig*).

The extension of the prototype concept from word meanings to linguistic objects was perhaps inevitable, given the linguist's twofold interest in categories. As noted at the beginning of Chapter 1, not only do linguistic forms symbolically stand for conceptual categories, linguistic forms themselves constitute categories. It is with the categorization of linguistic forms that we will be concerned in this chapter, in particular the categories WORD, AFFIX, and CLITIC, as well as the grammatical categories traditionally known as parts of speech. We shall see that there is a very remarkable parallelism between the

TABLE 10.1 *Properties of English strong verbs having /æ/-/ʌ/ or /ʌ/-/ʌ/ in past tense and past participle.* Sing *and* cling, *which share a maximum number of properties typical of the verbs, have a more central status in the categories*

	/ɪ/ in present tense	Velar as final consonant	Nasal as final consonant
sing	yes	yes	yes
cling	yes	yes	yes
hang	no	yes	yes
swim	yes	no	yes
stick	yes	yes	no
strike	no	yes	no

structure of conceptual categories and the structure of linguistic categories. Just as there are central and marginal members of the conceptual category BIRD, so too a linguistic category like NOUN has representative and marginal members. And just as marginal instances of a conceptual category like CUP might overlap with marginal instances of neighbouring categories like BOWL or VASE—even though typical cups are quite distinct from typical bowls and typical vases—so too a category like WORD merges, at its boundaries, with categories like AFFIX and CLITIC. Facts like these provide further evidence against the view discussed in Chapter 4, i.e. that prototype effects are merely an aspect of so-called performance, and thus outside the scope of a narrowly defined autonomous linguistics. Rather, prototype effects permeate the very structure of language itself.

10.1 Words, affixes, and clitics

In pre-generative days, the working out of criteria for the identification and classification of linguistic units was one of the primary concerns of linguistic enquiry. With the advent of the generative paradigm in the late 1950s and early 1960s, the exercise of 'grouping and classification' (Robins 1964: 180) appeared at best superfluous; the grammar itself would 'automatically, by its rules, characterize any relevant class' (Householder 1967: 103). Consequently, there has been very little discussion in generative circles of an issue which used to be thought fundamental, namely, how to define the word, the noun, the verb, etc. In this respect, the subject-matter of the present chapter harks back to earlier concerns, viewing them in the light of the prototype model which has been elaborated in preceding chapters.

As an illustration of what is involved in attributing prototype structure to a linguistic category, I will focus in this section on one of the most basic, and intuitively most salient (yet controversial) of all linguistic categories, the word.[1] It is notoriously difficult to give an adequate definition of WORD, such that one can unhesitatingly delimit the words in any given stretch of language. (Yet this has not prevented linguists from using the word as a theoretical construct.) No one, presumably, would question the word status of _mother_ and _husband_ in expressions like _This is Jane's mother_, _Meet Jane's husband_. Less clear is the number of words in the expressions _mother-in-law_ and _ex-husband_. Problematic too is the number of words in contractions. How many words are there in the contracted form _there's_ in _There's a man been shot_? Suppose we decide that the contraction consists of two words. What, then, is the identity of the second of the two words? (Note that * _There is a man been shot_ and * _There has a man been shot_ are both ungrammatical; cf. Lakoff 1987: 562 f.)

The existence of intuitively clear cases alongside a number of not-so-clear cases strongly suggests that we are dealing with a prototype category. We can give more substance to this intuition by restricting our attention, in the first instance, to the typical members of the category. We may begin by listing some of the attributes shared by those linguistic forms which we would unhesitatingly characterize as words:

(_a_) Words in the stream of speech can be optionally preceded and followed by pauses. In the limiting case, a word can stand alone as an independent utterance. As Bloomfield (1933: 178) put it, the word is 'the minimum free form'.

---

[1] The term 'word' is ambiguous (Lyons 1977: 18 ff.). It can refer to a lexical item (in which case we would say that _run_ and _running_ are two forms of the same word), or to a segmentable portion of an utterance (in which case each occurrence of _run_ and _running_ in an utterance constitutes a separate word). Which sense is intended will hopefully be clear from the context.

(*b*) In a stress language like English, each word is eligible for stress, both salience and tonic prominence.

(*c*) Words possess a fair degree of phonological invariance. Many phonological rules, for example, operate preferentially within the domain of the word, rather than over sequences of words. Thus we find instances of obligatory assimilation between component parts of words (*im*possible, *in*sensitive),[2] while between-word assimilations (e.g. the pronunciation of *good boy* as [gʊb bɔɪ]) are often optional, and dependent on speech style and speaking rate. Again, the stress pattern of a word is fairly constant property of the word itself, and is determined in large part by the word's phonological and morphological structure (compare *réalist* and *realístic*). Only rarely is word stress affected by context (compare *He's only fourtéen* and *There are fóurteen people*).

(*d*) On the whole, words are rather unselective with regard to the kinds of item to which they may be adjacent. While we popularly think of adjectives as words which precede nouns, a moment's thought shows that an adjective can stand next to practically any part of speech.

(*e*) Under appropriate conditions, words can be moved around in a sentence. The word sequences XYZ and ZXY might be equally acceptable (*I like John, John I like*). Again, under appropriate conditions, the second occurrence of a word in a sentence can be deleted: *She can sing but I can't sing* → *She can sing but I can't.*

We could go on listing further characteristics of words, but the above selection will suffice for our purposes. The five characteristics effectively distinguish words from units larger than the word (i.e. phrases, which consist of more than one word), and from component parts of words (i.e. stems and affixes). Consider for example the characteristics of affixes:[3]

[2] Assimilation is the process whereby one phoneme becomes 'more similar', with respect to some aspect of its articulation, to an adjacent phoneme. In *impossible*, the nasal of the negative prefix takes on the place of articulation (bilabial) of the following /p/, while in *insensitive*, the nasal has the alveolar articulation of the following /s/.

[3] It is usual to distinguish between derivational, or word-forming affixes, and inflexional affixes. However, as Carstairs (1987: 4 f.) notes, the distinction may be more of a continuum than a matter of discreteness. (Is the adverb-forming *-ly* derivational or inflexional?) Derivational affixes are used to create new words, while inflexional affixes change the form of a word according to its syntactic role in a sentence. Examples of the former include the verb-forming *-ize* in *characterize* (> *character*) and the negative-forming *un-* of *untidy*. Examples of inflexional affixes include the number agreement *-s* of *says* and the participial-forming *-ing* of *saying*.

(*a*) Affixes cannot occur independently of the stems to which they attach, neither can a pause, not even a hesitation pause, be inserted between an affix and its stem.

(*b*) Affixes are generally unstressable.

(*c*) Affixes are generally integrated into the phonological shape of the word of which they are a part. The phonological shape of the affix may be affected by the stem to which it is attached (e.g. by assimilation), or the phonological shape of the stem (e.g. with regard to stress placement) may be affected by the affix.

(*d*) Affixes are highly selective with regard to the kind of stem to which they attach. The third-person singular marker *-s* and the participial-forming *-ing*, for instance, can only attach to a verb stem.

(*e*) Affixes cannot be moved around independently of their stems, neither can the second occurrence of an affix be deleted; *singing and dancing* cannot be reduced to **singing and dance*, neither can *sings and dances* be replaced by *sings and dance.

The various phonological and syntactic characteristics of words as opposed to affixes are analogous to the attributes on whose basis we decide membership of a conceptual category. In many instances, the attributes are correlated, and the word-affix distinction appears clear-cut. But just as there are entities which exhibit only some of the attributes typical of a conceptual category, with the consequence that these entities are accorded a more marginal status within the category, so sometimes an application of the tests for word and affix status can give ambiguous results. Consider the definite article *the*:

(*a*) Although the definite article alone cannot constitute a well-formed utterance, it may be separated from what follows by a hesitation pause.

(*b*) The definite article, although generally unstressed, can sometimes bear sentence stress.

(*c*) There is a degree of phonological integration between the article and an adjacent item, in that the phonetic form of the article is affected by the following sound: *the* [ðə] *man*, but *the* [ði] *earth*.

(*d*) *The* can stand in front of practically any part of speech: adjective (*the old man*), adverb (*the incredibly old man*), verb (*the—dare I say old—man*), preposition (*the in my opinion old man*), and so on.

(*e*) The definite article cannot be moved around by itself; if it moves, it moves along with the noun phrase of which it is a component. Often, a second occurrence of the article can be deleted (*the men and the women* → *the men and women*), but sometimes it cannot (*the old man and the sea* → **the old man and sea*).

What then is the status of *the*? Is it an affix? No, because it possesses a certain degree of autonomy: it can be preceded and followed by a pause, it can bear stress, and it is fairly unselective with regard to adjacent elements. Is it then a word? No, because it does not possess the full autonomy of a word: it cannot stand alone in an utterance, it cannot be moved independently of its host, and it is not always subject to deletion under identity. Probably, on the whole, *the* is more of a word than an affix—a fact reflected by our writing system. The main motivation for this decision is the freedom of *the* to stand adjacent to practically any part of speech. The importance of this criterion derives from the fact that the five tests for wordhood all point to the word as a syntactically and phonologically autonomous entity, intermediate in status between the minimally meaningful unit of language, the morpheme, and the complex units of phrase and sentence. Thus the concatenation of words is subject to syntactic constraints; at the same time the word is the domain for the operation of a number of phonological and morphophonological processes. The hierarchical structure of sentences is in turn consistent with a modular, or compartmentalized conception of grammar. One component of a grammar is responsible for word formation, through, for example, the combination of stems and derivational affixes. Words, in their appropriate phonological form, are listed in the lexicon. Another component is the syntax, which assembles words from the lexicon into well-formed syntactic units, while a further component puts words into their correct inflexional form. Within this kind of framework, it is clearly preferable to assemble noun phrases in the syntax, than to attach the article to all kinds of items in the word-formation or inflexional components. Hence the definite article, in spite of some affix-like properties, is best considered a word.

The distinction between words and affixes is complicated by the existence of another unit of linguistic structure, the clitic. In some respects, clitics are rather like words, in other respects they are like affixes. In addition, certain characteristics suggest that clitics form a category of their own. There are no really good examples of clitic in English, so I will illustrate from Zulu. Zulu has the morpheme *ke*, which attaches indifferently to practically any part of speech—noun, verb, adverb, etc.—generally at the end of whatever happens to be the first constituent of a clause. Its meaning corresponds roughly to English *and . . . then*. More precisely, it seems that *ke* underlines the given status of the sentence topic. Since only one element in any clause can be topicalized, it follows that *ke* can occur only once in a clause. Let us apply the word/affix tests to *ke*:

(*a*) *Ke* can never stand alone, neither can it be separated from its host by a pause.

(*b*) Zulu does not have sentence stress, so this test does not apply.

(*c*) There is obligatory phonological integration with the host. The penultimate syllable of a Zulu word is lengthened. For the purpose of the lengthening rule, *ke* is regarded as an integral part of the word, i.e. the addition of *ke* causes lengthening to shift one syllable to the right. The following examples illustrate the process (the colon represents vowel length, the hyphen indicates a morpheme boundary):

(1) (*a*) Ng-uba:ni igama lakho?
        It's-what name your
        "What's your name?"
    (*b*) Ng-ubani:-ke igama lakho?
        It's-what-then name your
        "And what's *your* name then?"

(*d*) Up to now, *ke* looks like an ordinary affix. One thing that distinguishes *ke* from affixes is the fact already noted, that *ke* can attach to practically anything, even to a word like *yebo* "yes" (*Yeboke* "OK, then"). Affixes, it will be recalled, are very highly constrained with regard to the stems to which they attach. Furthermore, there are often a number of arbitrary gaps in the distribution of affixes. While the past tense forming affix *-ed* only attaches to verb stems, not every verb stem can take the *-ed* suffix. There are no such restrictions on the occurrence of *ke*.

(*e*) Like affixes, *ke* cannot be moved around. Deletion of a second occurrence is not applicable, since *ke* can only occur once in a given sentence.

It is largely because of their freedom to attach to practically any part of speech that clitics are recognized as a special linguistic unit. Consistent with their special status, it has been proposed that clitics get inserted into a sentence by a special post-syntactic component of the grammar, distinct from both the word formation and the syntactic components (Zwicky 1985). This view is also supported by the fact that semantically clitics are usually different from affixes. Affixes change the semantic content and/or the syntactic function of a word. Clitics, on the other hand, do not affect word meaning or word function, but generally have to do with text structure or speaker attitude.

In spite of the general validity of the distinction, we again, not surprisingly, find borderline cases. Some putative clitics seem more like words, while others are not too different from affixes. Zulu has another morpheme, *nje*, which, like *ke*, attaches freely to different parts of speech; semantically it functions as a downtoner, with the meaning "only", "just". Unlike *ke*, however, *nje* is not phonologically integrated with its host, i.e. it does not affect the location of syllable lengthening; it can also stand as a one word utterance, with the meaning "so-so", "not bad". *Nje*, then, is a fairly word-like clitic. Or consider the possessive *'s* in English. If *'s* only attached to nouns denoting a possessor, it would constitute a fairly run-of-the-mill affix. But *'s* is not so tightly restricted, cf. *A friend of mine's house*, *Who the heck's book is this?* Consequently, *'s* could be regarded as a fairly affix-like clitic (or clitic-like affix). On the other hand the definite article, because of its freedom to attach to practically anything, might be categorized as a clitic-like word.

Table 10.2 displays the characteristics of words, affixes, and clitics. The table provides compelling evidence for graded membership of the categories in question. There are good, representative examples of words (*mother*), of affixes (*-ed*), and of clitics (Zulu *ke*); there are not such good examples (*the*), and there are borderline cases (*nje* and *'s*). That the categories have graded membership is not a new insight. It was clearly recognized by Robins in a passage which uncannily anticipates the terminology of the prototype theorists:

Words ... are the products of several different though related criteria. Thus they comprise nuclear members of the category, to which all the criteria apply, more peripheral or marginal ones to which only some apply, and very marginal or doubtful cases in which the criteria may conflict and different conclusions may be reached by the different weighting of the conflicting criteria. (Robins 1964: 194–5)

Even so, most linguists, past and present, have operated on the assumption that what counts as a word or an affix *is* a matter of either–or. Indeed, the modular conception of grammar, outlined in an earlier paragraph, presupposes this approach. To permit degrees of

TABLE 10.2 *Properties of words, affixes, and clitics*

	Can stand alone	Can be separated by pauses	Can be stressed	Phonological autonomy	Selectivity of adjacent item	Subject to movement and deletion
mother	yes	yes	yes	high	low	yes
nje (Zulu)	sometimes	sometimes	n/a	high	very low	no
the	no	sometimes	sometimes	low	fairly low	sometimes (deletion)
-ed	no	no	no	low	very high	no
possessive *'s*	no	no	no	low	fairly high	no
-ke (Zulu)	no	no	n/a	low	very low	no

membership in linguistic categories makes it necessary to revise, perhaps even to give up, the modular conception of grammar. The absence of a clear boundary between affixes and words (and between words and phrases) means of necessity that the grammar of the word (morphology) must merge into the grammar of the sentence (syntax). Both Lakoff (1987) and Langacker (1987) have argued that the lexicon and the syntax are not so much discrete components of grammar, but rather the ends of a continuum. For Hudson (1984), too, there is no natural division between the way a phrase is composed of words, and the way a word is composed of morphemes.

10.2 Grammatical categories[4]

I now turn to a discussion of word classes—the traditional parts of speech—and of syntactic categories like NOUN PHRASE. A useful starting-point is the definition of *noun* in Collins English Dictionary.

(2) *Noun*: a word or group of words that refers to a person, place or thing or any syntactically similar word

This definition consists of two parts. Firstly there is a semantic definition (nouns are defined in terms of what they mean) followed by a syntactic definition (nouns are defined in terms of their similar syntactic behaviour).

The inadequacy of an exclusively semantic definition of parts of speech has been recognized at least since the earliest days of structuralism. Thus Robins (1964: 228f.) warns us that 'extra-linguistic' criteria, like meaning, must play no role in the assignment of words to word classes. Although one might quibble at Robins's view of meaning as something extra-linguistic, the strict exclusion of semantic criteria would at first sight appear a *sine qua non* for the definition of parts of speech. *Teacher* and *table* are both pretty good instances of words that refer to persons and things. But what about *doorway* and *sky*? Arguably, these are also 'things', but things of a rather intangible nature. We need to relax further our notion of thing as a discrete concrete entity in order to be able to say that a period of time like *year*, a colour like *red*, a property like *height*, or a state of mind like

---

[4] I use the term 'grammatical category' to cover both lexical categories (i.e. parts of speech) and syntactic categories (i.e. NOUN PHRASE, SENTENCE, and other syntactic constructions).

happiness, are things. Nouns like *swim* (as in *have a swim*) and *arrival*, on the other hand, would appear to refer not to things at all, but rather to activities and events. Thus, on purely semantic grounds, we would have to recognize a gradience of nounhood. *Teacher* and *table* are good examples of nouns, *doorway* and *sky* are less good examples, *year*, *red*, *height*, and *happiness* are rather marginal examples, while *swim* and *arrival* would not appear to be candidates at all. Semantic definitions of other parts of speech turn out to be equally unsatisfactory. Collins defines *adjective* as 'a word imputing a characteristic to a noun or pronoun'. Apart from the fact that it is not nouns as such to which characteristics are imputed, but rather their referents, this definition would exclude from the class of adjectives the word *late* in the expression *my late husband* ('being late' is not a characteristic of 'my husband'), as well as e.g. *former* and *each* in *my former wife* and *each day*.

An alternative to a purely semantic approach is given in the second half of the Collins definition of *noun*. Words are assigned to classes on the basis of common syntactic properties. As Gleason put it, word classes must be characterized by 'maximum homogeneity within the class' (1965: 130). The aim is to set up classes in such a way as to maximize the correlation of syntactic properties over the members of the class, and to minimize the correlation of properties over members of different classes. 'Syntactic properties', as used here, is a cover term which includes at least three kinds of phenomena:

(*a*) Phonological. In some cases, a grammatical category may be regularly associated with a distinctive phonological structure. In English, compound nouns (*bláckboard*, *phýsics teacher*) are characterized by initial stress, in contrast to adjective-plus-noun combinations (*black bóard*, *American téacher*), which have final stress.

(*b*) Morphological. It frequently happens that words of a given class, and only words of that class, can take on the morphological trappings of the class. Thus, in English, only verbs can be marked for tense; only nouns can appear in singular and plural form; only adjectives and adverbs admit of degrees of comparison. The ability to be inflected for, e.g. tense, can thus serve as a heuristic test for verb status.

(*c*) Distributional. Typically, certain slots in a syntactic construction are reserved for words of a particular form class. A characteristic of adjectives, for example, is their possibility of occurring in the second place in the noun phrase construction DET ADJ N.

Before proceeding, we might note that the kinds of criteria listed above do not always yield unambiguous evidence for category membership. Consider again the adjective category. An adjective like *cheap* exhibits a number of typically adjectival properties. It may be used both attributively and predicatively (*the cheap book*, *the book is cheap*); it can be graded (*very*, *extremely cheap*) and admits both comparative and superlative forms (*cheaper*, *cheapest*); the modified noun may be replaced by pronominal *one* (*an expensive book and a cheap one*). Not all adjectives share all of these properties. Some can be used only in attributive position (*my former husband*, **my husband is former*), others only in predicative position (*the child is asleep*, **the asleep child*). Others cannot be graded, and do not have comparative forms (*each*, *first*). Consider, as a particularly problematic example, the status of *apple* in *apple pie*. At first glance, *apple* looks like a noun, and *apple pie* an N N compound, analogous to *physics teacher*. Yet some speakers accept the predicative construction (*This pie is apple*, cf. **This teacher is physics*), some even accept comparative and pronomial expressions (*This pie is more apple than that one*, *I wanted a meat pie, not an apple one*). Also, some speakers employ the stress pattern of an ADJ N phrase, not that of an N N compound, i.e. they say *apple píe* rather than *ápple pie*. Is *apple*, then, a noun or an adjective?

With the advent of the generative paradigm, a fourth kind of syntactic property has come to the fore; this concerns the ability of a string of words to undergo a transformation. Transformational rules (e.g. rules of movement and deletion) do not operate blindly on any random string of items; each rule requires as input an ordered string of constituents of the appropriate syntactic class. For instance, the rule of yes–no question formation converts a string of the form NP AUX VP into AUX NP VP, i.e. the rule inverts the subject NP and the auxiliary. The possibility of a rule applying to a given string of words (more precisely, to the phrase marker underlying the string) can thus provide evidence for the grammatical categories present in the input, i.e. yes–no question formation may be used as a test both for NP status, and for auxiliary-verb status.

Now, the transformational paradigm absolutely requires that membership in grammatical classes is a clear-cut matter. To see why this is so, let us briefly consider some of the properties of Chomsky's Extended Standard Theory (see e.g. Chómsky 1976). The EST model envisages a grammar consisting of a number of autonomous modules. One module is the so-called 'base component', responsible for generating 'initial phrase markers' (the 'deep structures' of earlier versions of the theory). Initial phrase markers are generated in two stages. Firstly, the 'categorial component' of the base generates, by means of rewrite rules of the kind S → NP AUX VP, NP → DET N, an 'abstract phrase marker', i.e. a string of category symbols with an associated structural description. The other module of the base, the 'lexical insertion component', slots items from the lexicon into the abstract phrase marker. Any item in the lexicon marked with an appropriate feature, e.g. [N], is a candidate for insertion into the N-slot of the abstract phrase marker. The output of the base is thus a string of items with an associated structural description. This initial phrase marker serves as input to the other components of the grammar, e.g. the transformational and phonological components.

Botha (1968: 67 f.) has pointed out that generative grammar offers an exclusively extensional characterization of word classes—which items count as members of a class is ultimately a matter of exhaustive listing. Nouns are simply those items in the lexicon which bear the feature specification [N], and which, in virtue of this feature specification, are candidates for insertion under the N-nodes generated by the categorial component. The further properties of nouns—their morphological characteristics, their distinctive distribution, their accessibility to transformational rules—are derivative, in that they fall out from the operation of the base component, and the manner in which its output is handled in the other components of the grammar. Further, the generative model presupposes a limited number of (putatively universal) categories, like NOUN, VERB, DETERMINER, as well as, of course, subcategories of these categories, e.g. COUNT NOUN and MASS NOUN as subcategories of NOUN (but these subcategories are subject to the same kind of extensional definition as the superordinate categories), the items in the lexicon being associated with the corresponding syntactic features, like [N], [V], [DET], and so on. These features are the syntactic counterparts of the classical phonological and semantic features discussed in Chapter 2. The features, that is, are construed as binary, primitive, universal, and (presumably) innate, and they necessarily establish either–or membership in the respective categories. As already mentioned, it is in virtue of their feature specification that lexical items can get inserted into the abstract phrase marker; the meaning of the lexical item is irrelevant in this respect. Similarly, transformational rules operate on underlying phrase markers, independently of the semantics of the lexical items which fill the category slots. As a consequence, not only are grammatical categories clear-cut entities, the category GRAMMATICAL SENTENCE has clear-cut boundaries too. A grammatical sentence is whatever string happens to be generated as output of the transformational component. Even a language has clear-cut boundaries, comprising all and only the grammatical sentences generated by the grammar. Sentences not generated by the grammar are, by definition, ungrammatical, and therefore not part of the language.

The far-reaching implications of the generative conception of grammatical categories—in particular the exclusion of semantic criteria from grammaticality, the postulation of a clear dividing line between the grammatical sentences of a language and non-grammatical sentences, and the related notion of a language as a well-defined set of grammatical sentences—have been queried by a number of scholars (e.g. Hockett 1968, Matthews 1979, Sampson 1980*a*). Here, I want to restrict my attention to the assumption that it is all-or-nothing membership in a grammatical category that determines syntactic behaviour. In fact, it has been known since the earliest days of generative grammar that category membership, as specified by a phrase marker, does not always guarantee the applicability of a transformational rule. The matter was investigated by George Lakoff in his 1965 dissertation (Lakoff 1970). Lakoff assembled numerous instances of rules which fail to apply to input strings, even though the inputs met the structural description of the rule. The phenomenon is particularly frequent with regard to the 'minor' rules of word derivation. Thus not all transitive verbs undergo agentive nominalization:

(3) (*a*) John is one who imports rugs →
John is an importer of rugs
(*b*) John was one who knew that fact →
*John was the knower of that fact

and not all verbs undergo able-substitution:

(4) (*a*) His handwriting can be read →
His handwriting is readable
(*b*) The lighthouse can be spotted →
*The lighthouse is spottable

'Major' rules are also implicated. For instance, not all transitive sentences of the form NP V NP undergo passivization:

(5) (*a*) John kicked the ball →
The ball was kicked by John
(*b*) John owes two dollars →
*Two dollars are owed by John

Such irregularities can be (and were) taken care of by the flagging of individual items in the lexicon; a verb, for example, could be marked [–PASSIVE], so as to block the application of the passive transformation. Alternatively—but given the extensional characterization of word classes, the alternative amounts to the same thing—word classes may be subcategorized such that one subcategory undergoes the rule in question, while the other does not. Even so, these solutions ignore the possibility that some items might be better candidates for a transformation than others, i.e. the putative subcategories might themselves have fuzzy boundaries. Consider passivization. Some transitive verbs (like *kick*) readily passivize, others (like *resemble*) do not passivize at all. With *owe*, the situation is not so clear. Lakoff's *Two dollars are owed by John* does seem odd. But what about *Millions of dollars are currently owed by third-world governments*?

The fuzziness of grammatical categories shows up very clearly in a series of papers by Ross (e.g. Ross 1972, 1973), which extended the approach taken by Lakoff in his dissertation. Ross showed that in many cases members of a category can be graded with respect to their ability to undergo a range of transformations. The transformations themselves can also be graded—some apply more or less across the board to all input strings of the appropriate structure, while others are much choosier in this regard. Consider, for example, the category NOUN PHRASE (Ross 1973). Only some NPs—preferentially those which designate humans—can undergo the rule of double raising,[5] as illustrated in (6):

(6) (*a*) It is likely to be shown that John has cheated →
John is likely to be shown to have cheated
(*b*) It is likely to be shown that no headway has been made →
*No headway is likely to be shown to have been made

Double raising is a fairly choosy rule, and *headway* (part of the idiom *make headway*) is not very accessible to it. Question tag formation, on

---

[5] Raising is a rule which moves a constituent from a 'lower' embedded sentence into a 'higher' sentence. Double raising involves two such movements.

the other hand, applies more or less across the board to any subject NP. Even here, though, there are some dubious cases:

(7) (*a*) Some headway has been made →
     Some headway has been made, hasn't it?
    (*b*) Little heed was paid to her →
     ?*Little heed was paid to her, was it?[6]

Not even one of the most robust properties of NPs—the fact that, in subject position, an NP determines the number of the auxiliary verb—shows up in all instances. By most of the criteria for subject NP status, such as inversion with the auxiliary in yes–no questions (8) (*b*), raising (8) (*c*), accusative-gerund complementation (8) (*d*), *there* in (8) (*a*) must be considered a subject NP. Yet it fails to determine the number of the verb in (8) (*e*):

(8) (*a*) There's a man at the door
    (*b*) Is there a man at the door?
    (*c*) There seems to be a man at the door
    (*d*) I was surprised at there being a man at the door
    (*e*) There are (*is) two men at the door[7]

Contrary to one of the major assumptions of the generative paradigm, it seems, then, syntactic rules *are* sensitive to the lexical content of a phrase marker. Furthermore, lexical items can be graded, according to how readily they undergo specific transformations. Neither Ross nor Lakoff employed the terminology of prototype theory, which was being developed independently by cognitive psychologists like Rosch. Yet when we read (Ross 1973: 98) of 'copperclad, brass-bottomed NP's', and of some noun phrases being 'more noun-phrasy' than others, we readily recognize the commonality with a prototype approach. Some NPs share a maximum number of typical noun phrase attributes; they constitute more central members of the category. Others—the more marginal members—display only a few of the attributes typical of the category.

The gradience of grammatical categories—like the gradience of the

---

[6] The acceptability judgements in (6) and (7) are Ross's.

[7] The case of subject *there* is actually more complicated. Plural verb agreement appears in the raised construction, e.g. *There seem (*seems) to be two men at the door*, suggesting that *there* copies, without overt morphological marking, the number of the following noun phrase (*a man, two men*) (cf. Lakoff 1987: 548). Even so, a noun phrase with no inherent number is a pretty untypical exemplar of the category!

category WORD—is not in itself a new discovery. The notion that word classes have central members, which satisfy a maximum number of criteria of the respective class, and more peripheral, borderline members, was fully articulated in Crystal (1967). With the almost total hegemony of the generative paradigm in the late 1960s and the 1970s, the insights of non-generative linguists on this topic tended to be ignored, or forgotten. The last few years, however, have seen a rediscovery of category gradience. Symptomatic is the importance assigned to degree of category membership in the recent *Comprehensive Grammar of the English Language* (Quirk *et al.* 1985), as compared with the earlier, 1972 grammar (Quirk *et al.* 1972). Interesting, too, is McCawley's recent comparison of parts of speech with the categories of biological natural kinds:

Parts of speech are much more like biological species than has generally been recognized. Within any part of speech, or any biological species, there is considerable diversity. Parts of speech can be distinguished from one another, just as biological species can be distinguished from one another, in terms of characteristics that are typical for the members of that part of speech (or species), even though none of those properties need be instantiated by all members of the parts of speech (or species). (McCawley 1986: 12)

This view is not quite so innovative as McCawley would have us believe; Botha (1968: 56) had mentioned (and, as a committed generativist, dismissed), the idea that word classes might exhibit the same kind of structure as biological natural kinds.

10.3 The semantic basis of grammatical categories

In the discussion so far I have endeavoured to adhere to the structuralist maxim of the irrelevance of semantic criteria for word class definitions, and considered grammatical categories solely in terms of their syntactic properties. Even this approach, as we have seen, strongly points to the prototype structure of the categories. I would now like to reappraise the semantic basis for category definition. Cognitive linguists reject the notion of a syntactic level of linguistic organization, autonomous of semantics. The aim, as Lakoff (1987: 491) puts it, is to 'show how aspects of form follow from aspects of meaning'. Langacker is even more explicit: 'Cognitive grammar makes specific claims about ... the notional basis of fundamental grammatical categories' (1987: 183), including the claim that 'all members of a given [grammatical] class share fundamental semantic properties' (1987: 189).

Clearly any attempt at a semantic definition of grammatical categories like NOUN and VERB will have to be more sophisticated than the traditional dictionary definitions cited earlier. If nouns and verbs do share semantic properties, these are obviously going to be of a highly abstract nature. Langacker discusses the issue at considerable length (1987: chs. 5–7). His proposal is that NOUN be defined as a linguistic unit which profiles a 'thing', where 'thing' is defined as a 'region in some domain' (1987: 189). Similarly, verbs are defined as linguistic units which profile a 'temporal relation', while adjectives, adverbs, and prepositions profile an 'atemporal relation'. Langacker's definition of NOUN readily incorporates the traditional notion of a noun as the name of a person or a concrete object. Persons and objects are bounded regions in the domain of three-dimensional space, while mass concrete nouns, like *water*, profile *un*bounded regions in three-dimensional space. But the definition does not give any priority to the spatial domain. *Red* shares the common property in that it profiles a region in the domain of colour, a year is a bounded region in the domain of time, C-sharp is a region in the domain of pitch, and so on. Langacker then goes on to characterize 'region' in terms of the 'inter-connectedness' of entities within a domain. In this way, nouns which refer to groups of discrete entities, like *archipelago*, *constellation*, and *team*, are brought under the schematic definition. Interconnectedness is inversely related to the 'cognitive distance' between entities within a domain, which is in turn a function of cognitive scanning over time. This understanding of interconnectedness makes it possible to account for the status of deverbal nouns like *arrival*. *Arrival* profiles, not a temporal relation *per se*, but a collectivity of temporally adjacent relations. The profile of a deverbal noun like *jumping*, on the other hand, is analogous, in the temporal domain, to that of a concrete mass noun like *water*. Jumping, as well as other abstracts like love and envy, is construed as a relatively homogeneous and unbounded 'substance', which is instantiated whenever some specific instance of the process or quality occurs.

An alternative to searching for what is common to all members of a grammatical class is to capitalize on traditional definitions, and to incorporate these into a prototype account. It may be noted that the manner in which Langacker takes his reader through his definition of

NOUN itself suggests the plausibility of a prototype account. Thus we may say, following tradition, that a noun designates, in the first instance, a discrete, concrete, three-dimensional entity (i.e. a bounded region in three-dimensional space). By a projection of the thing-schema on to non-spatial domains, linguistic units which profile regions in the other domains, e.g. colour, time, pitch, etc., get included in the noun category. Then, with a more sophisticated definition of region, we account for the noun-status of *archipelago*, *team*, *arrival*, and so on. Finally, we establish a metaphorical link between concrete substances and abstract qualities; Langacker himself needs to appeal to such analogies in order to account for the noun status of abstracts like *love* and *envy*.

A prototype view of a category is not necessarily incompatible with an account which attempts to capture what is common to all the category members (cf. Section 4.2). It would seem, though, that there are good reasons for assigning a certain primacy to the prototype account of NOUN. A prototype view of NOUN entails that some nouns are better examples of the category, while others have a more marginal status. Significantly, the closeness of an item to the (semantically characterized) prototype tends to correlate, in many instances, with its closeness to the prototype defined on purely syntactic criteria. This correlation emerges very clearly from Ross's paper on NPs (1973). As we saw, NPs can be hierarchically ordered according to their accessibility to various transformational rules. The most accessible (i.e. the most 'noun-phrasy') are those NPs which refer to conscious, volitionally acting, animate creatures, primarily human beings. Some-what lower on Ross's hierarchy are NPs which refer to concrete inani-mates, followed by those which refer to events and abstracts. Even lower are 'meteorological *it*' (*It's muggy*) and 'subject *there*' (*There's a man at the door*). The relevance of the semantic prototype will be obvi-ous. Interestingly, the syntactic criteria even suggest that our earlier characterization of the noun prototype may have been too broad. It seems that the best examples of the category refer, not to any concrete three-dimensional object, but, more specifically, to human beings.

The correlation of syntactic and semantic criteria for nounhood shows up in many places. For an illustration we may take the possessive genitive construction, as represented by the formula NP's N. Consider the kinds of noun which can serve as the head of the 'possessor' NP. A noun like *teacher* is readily available: *the teacher's house*, *the teacher's work*, *the teacher's arrival*, and so on. Nouns which are semantically more distant from the prototype are less satisfactory; *the table's surface* and *the building's age* are still (perhaps) OK, but *the sky's colour* and *the doorway's height* are more dubious. Some of the non-prototypical nouns behave rather erratically. *In a year's time* and *the year's work* are standard expressions. One would normally prefer *by the end of the year* to *by the year's end*, although the latter expression is sometimes encountered in journalistic texts. Yet analogous expressions like **before the year's middle* and **since the year's start* are impossible. Equally bad are possessive expressions with nouns like *arrival* and *swim*: **my arrival's time*, **the swim's place*. In brief, not any noun can be inserted with equal facility into the possessive construction. Some occur freely, some hardly at all, while with some insertion is dubious or sporadic. And the ease with which nouns can designate a 'possessor' appears to correlate with closeness to the *semantically* defined prototype.[8]

A prototype approach to word classes has been adopted (implicitly) by Givón (1979). Givón argues that the essential difference between nouns and verbs resides in the 'time-stability' of their referents. Time-stability constitutes a continuum. At one pole are those entities with the highest time-stability, i.e. entities which do not change their identity over time. These are (typically) referred to by nouns. Prototypical verbs, on the other hand, refer to entities which lack time-stability, i.e. events and rapid changes in state (1979: 14). A further corollary is that the referents of nouns are characterized in terms of their existence in space; the typical noun-referent is an identifiable, enduring thing. Verb-referents, on the other hand, typically have existence only at a certain point in time; the typical verb-referent is thus an identifiable event (1979: 320 f.).

Developing Givón's approach, Hopper and Thompson (1985) have pointed out that the status of a word within its respective grammatical category is by no means a fixed property of the word in question. The semantically relevant properties—in the case of nouns, the extent to which the noun refers to an identifiable, enduring thing, with verbs,

---

[8] A similar state of affairs holds with other uses of the *'s* morpheme. Optionally, the *'s* morpheme may be used in a gerundial expression following a preposition: *without the teacher('s) knowing*, *in spite of the teacher('s) being aware*, etc. As nouns diverge from the prototype, the possibility of using the *'s* morpheme declines much more rapidly than with the possessive construction: **without the table's being moved*, **in spite of the year's having started*, **as a result of his arrival's having been delayed*. The *'s* morpheme, then, only seems to attach to nouns of the very highest degree of (a semantically defined) nouniness, i.e. nouns which refer to human beings.

whether the verb refers to a specific dynamic event—can vary according to context. Consider the following sentences (based on Hopper and Thompson 1985):

(9) (*a*) We trapped a bear in the forest
    (*b*) Bear-trapping used to be a popular sport

In (*a*), both *trap* and *bear* are being used as prototypical members of their respective classes. Consistent with this function, both verb and noun can take on the whole range of typically verbal and nominal trappings. The verb is marked for tense (past rather than present), aspect (simple rather than progressive), polarity (affirmative rather than negative), mood (indicative rather than imperative), and voice (active rather than passive). Similarly, the noun can take on the various trappings typical of its class. It can appear as singular or plural, it can be preceded by a determiner, it can be modified by adjectives and relative clauses. The (*b*) sentence is very different. *Bear* in this sentence does not refer to a discrete identifiable object, neither does *trap* refer to a single identifiable event. Symptomatic of this loss of semantic categoriality is the fact that neither word can be inflected or modified. The potential oppositions between singular and plural, affirmative and negative, past and present, active and passive, and so on, are to all intents and purposes neutralized.

The phenomenon is quite general. As Hopper and Thompson (1985) document with data from a range of languages, when a noun which can potentially refer to a discrete entity does not in fact do so, it tends to lose the morphological and distributional attributes of the noun class. In the (*a*) sentences below, *fire*, *buffalo*, and *president* function, both syntactically and semantically, as highly representative examples of the noun class. The (*b*) sentences, in contrast, exemplify the partial decategorialization of the nouns. In (10) (*b*) the noun has been incorporated into a complex verb (*to make fire*), in (11) (*b*) the noun is modifying another noun, while in (12) (*b*) the noun does not refer to a specific individual, but designates a role in a social institution. In all three cases, the nouns cannot be inflected for number, neither can they be modified by adjectives.

(10) (*a*) We made a big fire
     (*b*) We made (*big) fire

(11) (*a*) We ate the meat from a slaughtered buffalo
     (*b*) We ate (*slaughtered) buffalo meat

(12) (a) Meet the new president of the society
        (b) He was elected (*the new) president

The decategorialization of nouns is paralleled by the case of verbs which, in certain contexts, loose the morphological trappings typical of their class. Givón (1984) makes an important distinction between 'realis' and 'irrealis' verb forms. The former—restricted in the main to affirmative, declarative main clauses in the present or a past tense—report on some state of affairs that actually exists, or existed. Irrealis forms, on the other hand, refer to some non-existing, or not-yet-existing, state of affairs. Irrealis forms include futures and negatives, and are typically found in counterfactual clauses and clauses expressing a wish, desire, or command. Very often, irrealis forms exhibit a neutralization of oppositions characteristic of realis. In English, tense contrasts are neutralized in the imperative; the demise of the past subjunctive in modern spoken French and Italian has left only one tense form in the irrealis subjunctive mood; in Zulu, the realis contrast between the recent past tense and the remote past tense gives place in the negative to a single past tense form (Taylor 1987).

The decategorialization of verbs is especially striking in subordinate clauses. It is here that verbs, in English, may appear as infinitives or gerunds. As such, the verbs lose many of their morphological and distributional characteristics, such as agreement with a third-person singular subject, and the ability to be preceded by auxiliaries. Givón (1980) has noted that the occurrence of these non-finite verb forms correlates strikingly with the extent to which the subordinate clause describes a state of affairs which is dependent on the wishes, intentions, or influence of the subject of the main clause. In (a) below, Peter's departure is an autonomous event, independent of John's act of reporting. The subordinate verb can realize any of the contrasts typically associated with categorial verbs. In the remaining sentences, Peter's departure is to a greater or lesser extent dependent on the wishes or action reported in the main clause.

(13) (a) John said that Peter would leave/had left/might leave, etc.
        (b) John enabled Peter to leave
        (c) John persuaded Peter to leave
        (d) John forced Peter to leave
        (e) John insisted on Peter leaving

To the question whether semantic criteria are relevant to grammatical categorization, the answer must be affirmative. Semantic criteria surely play a role in any intensional definition of word classes, so noticeably lacking in generative treatments of the subject. This is not to claim that all the members of a grammatical category necessarily share a common semantic content. (But neither do all the members of a grammatical category necessarily share the same syntactic properties.) Even less would one want to put forward semantic criteria as the sole basis for deciding category membership. Grammatical categories have a prototype structure, with central members sharing a range of both syntactic and semantic attributes. Failure of an item to exhibit some of these attributes does not of itself preclude membership.

11

Syntactic Constructions as Prototype Categories

IN reviewing the evidence for the prototype structure of grammatical categories, we saw in Chapter 10 that members of a grammatical category do not necessarily exhibit a common set of syntactic properties. Not every noun can be inserted with equal facility into the possessor slot of the possessive construction, not every transitive verb has a passive counterpart, and so on. Furthermore, it is not just that nouns and transitive verbs can be divided into two complementary sets—those that are candidates for insertion into the respective construction, and those that are not. Possibility of occurrence in a construction is more a matter of gradience, some items being readily available, others being totally excluded, with, in between, a range of items whose use is dubious or sporadic. As a consequence, constructions, no less than other kinds of linguistic object, also need to be regarded as prototype categories, with some instantiations counting as better examples of the construction than others.

Graded membership in constructions has always posed a problem for the generative paradigm, with its axiom of a language as a well-defined set of grammatical sentences (see Matthews 1979: 25 ff.). For the cognitive linguist, on the other hand, syntactic constructions provide some of the most compelling evidence for the similar structuring of linguistic categories on the one hand, and the categories of non-linguistic reality on the other. The main body of this chapter will be devoted to an examination of the prototype structure of a specific construction in English, namely the transitive sentence. First, however, it is necessary to say a few words about the notion of construction within cognitive grammar, and to explicate the prototype nature of constructions with the aid of one or two examples.

11.1 Constructions

As was the case with the grammatical categories of Chapter 10, the focus of this chapter harks back to one of the concerns of pre-generative linguistics. Robins (1964: 190), speaking for descriptivist structuralism, characterized grammar as the 'description and analysis of structures ... in terms of recurrent elements and patterns'. It was, furthermore, well known that structural patterns exhibited prototype effects (cf. Quirk 1965). But, with the advent of the generative paradigm, constructions ceased to be a focus of interest. One could even say that the paradigm denied to constructions the status of theoretical entities altogether. Constructions were merely 'epiphenomena' (Lakoff 1987: 467), the by-product, as it were, of phrase structure and transformational rules. Cognitive linguists, in contrast, recognize the syntactic construction as a fundamental unit of syntactic description. Important landmarks in the rediscovery of the construction are Lakoff's (1977) paper on linguistic gestalts and Fillmore's (1979*a*) notion of syntactic formulas. Perhaps the most extensive account to date is Lakoff's (1987: 462ff.) monumental analysis of some sixteen distinct constructions involving deictic and existential *there*, and the manner in which the constructions are related within an overarching family resemblance category.

Structuralist interest in constructions was largely restricted to purely formal aspects of linguistic patterning. Cognitive grammar, in contrast, views a construction as the pairing of a specification of form with a specification of meaning. With regard to the former, a construction can be thought of as a kind of formula consisting of an ordered sequence of slots. Some elements are obligatory to the construction, others might be optional. Each element carries a specification of the kinds of item that can instantiate it. In some cases, only very general grammatical categories might be specified, e.g. noun phrase, transitive verb. Alternatively, a small set of candidates might have to be exhaustively listed; in the limiting case, there may be only one possible candidate. For some constructions, the formal characterization may need to include prosodic and even paralinguistic information, e.g. regarding stress, intonation, voice quality, and accompanying gestures (cf. the raised forefinger which often accompanies the perceptual deictic; see Lakoff 1987: 509ff.). As mentioned, the statement of a construction's formal aspects is linked to a statement of its meaning, which may include information on conditions and context of use. Meaning is therefore to be understood in a rather broad sense, to embrace both pragmatic and discourse-related matters.

Various kinds of relation may exist between the different constructions of a language. Firstly, a construction may function as part of another construction. Take the possessive construction in English. The formal properties of the construction may be represented by the formula NP's N. The formula indicates that the first element in the construction is a noun phrase. But noun phrases themselves constitute constructions, one possibility being represented by the formula DET N. Secondly, it sometimes happens that a given construction may be regarded as an instantiation of another construction. For instance, a possessive expression of the form NP's N not only contains an NP, it also constitutes an NP, and may be analysed as an instantiation of the NP formula DET N, with NP's functioning as the determiner. Clearly, the interaction of the relationships of componentiality and instantiation may result in a number of alternative, and equally valid analyses of a given linguistic expression. Thus the noun phrase *The teacher's wife's car* may be represented by the formulas DET N, NP's N, NP's N's N, and DET N's N's N. A third kind of relationship between constructions is the 'based-on' relation discussed by Lakoff (1987). Lakoff identifies, amongst the various constructions exhibiting deictic *there*, a central deictic, as instantiated by the expression *There's Harry with his red jacket on*, and an activity start deictic, exemplified by *There goes Harry, meditating again*. The two constructions are formally and semantically distinct. Yet certain properties of the latter can be derived from properties of the former. The one, in fact, can be regarded as an extension of the other. The based-on relationship is not to be identified with the process of transformation, or derivation. There can be no question, in cognitive grammar, of one construction being transformed into, or derived from, another (Fillmore 1985). The exclusion of transformation and derivation from the cognitivist's arsenal follows from the claim that 'grammatical structure is almost entirely overt' (Langacker 1987: 46). Semantic content is structured and symbolized, not at the level of some abstract, unobservable underlying representation, but at the surface level of an utterance. This is not to deny the possibility of regular correspondences, both formal and semantic, between different constructions. One may readily pair off instantiations of the NP's N construction with instantiations of the NP of NP construction, for example *the country's president* vs. *the president of the country*. But similarity does not entail the need to posit identity, at some level of description.

A fully explicit constructionist grammar would have to incorporate a statement of these kinds of correspondence. This, and other issues, will not be dealt with in detail here. The main focus of the present chapter will be the prototype structure of grammatical constructions. Earlier, I characterized a construction as the pairing of a meaning with a form. Consistent with the prototype approach, both meaning and form need to be stated, in the first instance, in terms of central cases. Both may display prototype effects. A construction may be used to express meanings which differ to a greater or lesser extent from the central specification. Similarly, the items which fill the construction slots may diverge from the formal specification of the prototype. Obviously, the characterization of a construction needs to specify, not only the prototype, but also the manner and the extent of permitted deviation from the prototype. In other words, the degree of productivity of a construction needs to be stated as part of its characterization.

I have already given a brief account of a grammatical construction in prototype terms—I refer to the discussion of yes–no interrogatives at the close of Chapter 8. There, the focus was on semantic, rather than formal extension from the prototype. The example illustrates an important property of many of the more productive constructions, namely the tendency for some of the more peripheral members to acquire idiomatic, or formulaic status. Thus, from a purely syntactic point of view, the expression *Is that a fact?* is a regular instantiation of the yes–no interrogative. Semantically, however, the sentence is a rather marginal exemplar, in that it does not ask for polarity specification. Arguably, it is not even a question at all, instead, it serves purely as an expression of speaker surprise. (When used in its idiomatic sense, the sentence is also associated with a rather special intonation contour.) Neither is the meaning of the expression entirely predictable from the prototype specification. Thus *Is that a fact?* has dual allegiance. On the one hand, the sentence instantiates the yes–no interrogative. At the same time, we can regard the sentence as a construction in its own right. The formula for the construction would have to state the specific lexical items (including the required tense of the verb and the number of the noun) that may occur in the construction slots; the characteristic intonation and precise conditions on use would also have to be specified. Furthermore, the construction would have to be regarded as highly *un*productive, since extension from the central specification is hardly possible. For instance, one could not say, as expressions of speaker surprise, **Are those facts?*, ** Were these facts?*, and so on. The phenomenon is quite frequent. The greeting *How do you do?*, the challenge *Over my dead body!*, and the enthusiastic endorsement *You're telling me!* are, from one point of view, instantiations of the WH-interrogative, the prepositional phrase, and the transitive sentence construction, respectively. At the same time, the expressions instantiate highly unproductive, one-member constructions. *How do you do?* cannot be extended to encompass **How does she do?*, or even **How do you all do?*; *You're telling me!* is even constrained with regard to its intonation pattern, i.e. the construction requires falling tone on *tell* and *me* (*You're ˋTELLing ˋME*). With an alternative intonation, e.g. *You're ˊTELLing me*, the sentence is no longer interpreted in its idiomatic sense.[1]

Other formulaic expressions are productive, but to an extremely limited extent. Consider various means for expressing thanks: *Thanks*, *Thanks very much*, *Thanks a lot*, *Thanks a million*. The construction is not freely extendible. One might, as an expression of very enthusiastic gratitude, encounter *Thanks a billion*, but the insertion of other numerals, e.g. ** Thanks a hundred*, ** Thanks a thousand*, is impossible. Another construction of low productivity is that instantiated by the expression *day in day out* (Fillmore 1979*a*). The construction is used to express unchanging monotony. As such, it permits the insertion of alternative time units into the N slots. Predictably, these designate the time periods over which monotony is usually perceived: *week in week out*, *month in month out*, *year in year out*. Both very long and very short time units are not permitted: ** century in century out*, **millennium in millennium out*, **minute in minute out*, **second in second out*. The reason is, clearly, that monotony is not usually measured in terms of seconds and minutes, neither can human beings, with their limited life span, perceive monotony in the succession of centuries and millennia. (One could, however, imagine the writer of a science fiction tale expressing the boredom of a creature of extreme longevity by means of the expression *century in century out*). In this respect the construction provides a fine illustration of the interdependence of formal and semantic properties.

---

[1] On the frequent association of formulaic expressions with a fixed intonation pattern, see Bolinger (1986: 4 ff.).

11.2 The possessive genitive

In this and the following section I would like to examine two highly productive constructions in English. For our first example I return to the possessive genitive (*John's car*, *the year's work*, etc.). We have already discussed some aspects of the construction's formal properties (Sections 10.3 and 11.1). What about its semantics?

Let us start with the thesis that the possessive genitive, in its central sense, identifies one entity, the 'possessed', with reference to its possession by another, the 'possessor'. Possession is a difficult concept (see Miller and Johnson-Laird 1976: 558 ff. for some discussion). It is perhaps best thought of as an 'experiential gestalt', in the sense of Lakoff and Johnson (1980, especially chs. 14 and 15). On the one hand, possession is a 'basic' concept; people frequently appeal to it, without analysing it, in order to 'organize their physical and cultural realities' (Lakoff and Johnson 1980: 69). Yet possession is not a semantic primitive. It certainly is possible to identify a number of properties that are shared by instances of the possession relation. Some of the properties of typical possession are listed below:

(*a*) the possessor is a specific human being. Non-human animates, and even less, inanimates, cannot possess things;

(*b*) the possessed is a specific concrete thing (usually inanimate) or collection of specific concrete things, not an abstract;

(*c*) the relation is an exclusive one, i.e for each thing possessed there is only one possessor;

(*d*) the possessor has the right to make use of the possessed; other people can make use of the possessed only with the permission of the possessor;

(*e*) the possessor's rights over the possessed are invested in him in virtue of a transaction, i.e. through purchase, donation, or inheritance. The rights remain with him until a further transaction (sale, gift, bequest) transfers them to another person;

(*f*) the possessor is responsible for the possessed; he is expected to care for it, and to maintain it in good condition;

(*g*) in order that the possessor can exercise his rights and duties with respect to the possessed, possessor and possessed need to be in close spatial proximity;

(*h*) the relation of possession is a long-term one, measured in months and years rather than minutes and seconds.

The co-occurrence of the above constellation of properties con-stitutes cases of prototypical possession. Whenever a relation of prototypical possession, as characterized above, exists between two entities, the relation can be expressed by means of the possessive genitive construction. But the construction can also be used to encode many other kinds of relationship between two entities. These relation-ships can be regarded as extensions, some minimal, some more substantial, from the prototype. A minimal extension is exemplified by *the dog's bone*. A dog is not a prototypical possessor. Yet the relation of dog to bone comes close to the prototype case in that the dog, having found the bone, claims exclusive rights over it. Consider, as another example, *the secretary's typewriter*, in the sense "the typewriter that has been assigned to the secretary for regular use". The relation diverges from prototypical possession mainly with respect to the fact that the secretary has only limited rights over the typewriter; otherwise the relation exhibits considerable commonality with the prototype. With *John's train* (in the sense "the train John is travelling on"), it is again the possessor's right to use the possessed that is in focus; the rights are, however, limited and non-exclusive. A further important group of possessive expressions encodes the relation of a part to a whole: *John's hands*, *the cat's tail*, *the car's door*, *the play's final act*. Here we witness the perspectivization of spatial proximity of possessor and possessed (*g*), as well as the temporal duration of the relation (*h*)—a part is always and necessarily 'near' the thing of which it is a constituent; also, for each part, there is only one whole of which it is a constituent, cf. (*c*). By extension, the possessive construction comes to encode the long-term relation between a thing and its properties (*John's intel-ligence*, *the car's road-holding ability*).

Of special importance to a characterization of the possessive genitive is the exclusive nature of the relation between possessed and possessor (*c*). While a person (the prototypical possessor) may enter into a possession relation with many different things simultaneously, at a given time a thing may enter into a possession relation with only one possessor. Hence the possessive expression is a particularly suitable device for a speaker who wishes to uniquely identify an entity. And indeed, possessive expressions generally do have specific reference; *John's house*, for example, identifies a specific house in terms of its one (and only) possessor. This function of the possessive construction motivates the use of the possessive to encode relations which at first sight would appear to have very little to do with possession in the strict sense. Possessive expressions commonly invoke kinship and other interpersonal relationships: *John's wife*, *Mary's rival*, *my friends*. A person can only be described as a wife, a rival, or a friend from the vantage point of a second person. Different vantage points may lead one and the same person to be described, alternately, as wife or mother, rival or associate, friend or enemy. The genitive nominal makes it possible for a speaker to spell out from whose vantage point a given individual is so designated. A similar motivation lies behind expressions like *the company's director*, *the country's president*. Again, a person is a director or a president only from the vantage point of an institution in which he occupies a certain role. Even deverbal nouns (i.e. nouns like *arrival* and *invasion*, which are derived from the verbs *to arrive* and *to invade*) may be construed with genitive nominals, just in case the genitive nominal uniquely 'locates' the abstract entity with respect to one of its participants or circumstances: *the train's arrival*, *the prisoner's escape*, *Poland's invasion*, *yesterday's arrests*, *last night's performance*, etc.

In view of the multiplicity of relations that can be invoked by the possessive construction, some linguists have proposed that the semantics of the possessive are highly indeterminate. The claim is that the possessive simply identifies one entity by invoking *some* relation between that entity and another entity; otherwise, the meaning is 'quite indeterminate' (Kempson 1977: 125). And indeed, certain possessive expressions are open to multiple interpretations. *John's car* could identify the car as the one John is driving, the one he has rented, the one he owns, the one he has designed, the one he is always talking about—in fact, the expression can invoke just about any relation in terms of which a car can be plausibly identified with reference to a person. Similarly, *John's photograph* could be the photograph that John owns, the one he took, or the one that depicts him. There is, however, some evidence for the primacy of the relation of possession, in the strict sense. The interrogative *whose car?* is not a request to the hearer to name some person who stands in some indeterminate relation to the car; the expression is a request to name the possessor (in the prototypical, or close to prototypical sense) of the car. The possession relation is likewise invoked by contrastive uses of possessive expressions, of the kind *not John's photograph*, *Max's photograph*. Finally, consider the following scenario. Someone lends me his car, which I then smash. In approaching a passer-by for assistance, I could quite well say *I've just smashed my car*, meaning by *my car* no more than "the car I was driving". But it would be highly imprudent of me to report the incident to the friend who had lent me the car with the sentence *I've just smashed my car*. In such a context, the central, prototypical meaning of the possessive construction would very strongly come to the fore.

A prototype approach throws light on certain other matters. It will be appreciated that, semantically, the possessive genitive construction permits very considerable extension from its prototype characterization. Even so, extension from the prototype only goes so far. It is not the case that *any* entity can be identified in terms of *any* kind of relationship with any other entity. An important constraint is that the 'possessor' should not diverge too much from the prototype speci-fication, i.e. a human being. We saw in Section 10.3 that inanimates and abstracts cannot readily serve as 'possessors'; in these cases, full productivity gradually gives way to idiomaticity and dubious accept-ability. In comparison with the NP's N construction, other con-structions involving genitive nominals permit very little extension indeed from the prototype. Consider predicative genitives, of the kind *This car is John's*. This expression is not open to the multifarious inter-pretations of *John's car*. The expression invokes a relation of true possession, or possibly a relation which is very close to true possession (e.g. authorized usage, as sanctioned by an agreement with a car-hire company). Accordingly, NP's N expressions which invoke a relation which is rather distant from the possession prototype do not permit predicative genitive rewordings: *This rival is Mary's*, *This door is the car's*, *This invasion was Poland's*, *These arrests are yesterday's*. Another construction involving a genitive morpheme is the post-genitive construction: *a book of John's*, *a friend of Mary's*. Again the construction permits only limited extension from the prototype. For instance, non-human possessors are ruled out (*a bone of the dog's*). And while *John's photograph* is open to different semantic inter-pretations, *a photograph of John's* can only mean "a photograph that John owns".

To conclude this brief survey of the possessive genitive, I would like to repeat a point made earlier. Attempts have been made to capture semantic aspects of possessive expressions by deriving them from deep structures which allegedly correspond more closely to their semantic content (Jacobs and Rosenbaum 1968; Chomsky 1970). Derivational accounts go against the spirit of cognitive grammar. Even on its own terms, such an approach is far from unproblematic (see Hawkins 1981 for some discussion). This is not to deny that instantiations of the possessive construction may be regularly paired off with instantiations of other constructions, nor that an algorithm can be devised for converting the one set of expressions into the other. However, similarity (note: similarity, not identity) in meaning between *Eric's dictionary* and *The dictionary that Eric has* does not entail that the one construction is related, via transformation, to the other.

11.3 The transitive construction

I now turn to one of the most productive constructions in English, the transitive sentence construction. The following are typical instantiations:

(1) The child kicked the ball

(2) John moved the table

(3) Mary killed the intruder

The syntactic properties of the construction may be represented by the formula $NP_1 V_{TRANS} NP_2$, where NP_1 and NP_2 stand for the subject and direct object, and V_{TRANS} is a transitive verb. In its prototypical instantiations, both NPs have specific reference, while the verb is realis, i.e. affirmative and indicative, and in a reporting tense (either present or past). These latter characteristics fall out from the specification of the construction's meaning. Semantically, the construction is rather difficult to characterize in a few words. Drawing on Lakoff (1977) and Hopper and Thompson (1980), we can list at least eleven semantic properties of the construction, in its prototypical instantiations. The length of this characterization should not be taken to imply that the semantics of the transitive sentence are particularly complex. On the contrary, the meaning of the construction again has the status of an experientially primitive gestalt, cognitively simpler than any of its component parts. Indeed, it would probably be true to say that each of the following properties is understood relative to a prior understanding of the gestalt; the gestalt does not emerge from the summation of independently conceptualized attributes.

(*a*) The construction describes events involving two, and only two participants, encoded by the subject and direct object NPs respectively.

(*b*) The two participants are highly individuated, i.e. they are discrete, specific entities (from this it follows that both the NPs in the construction have specific reference), distinct both from each other, and from the background environment.

(*c*) The event is initiated by the referent of the subject NP, i.e. by the agent. Responsibility for the event thus lies exclusively with the agent. Furthermore, the subject NP is the sentence topic; the subject is what the sentence is about.

(*d*) The agent acts consciously and volitionally, and thus controls the event. Since consciousness and volition are typically human attributes, it follows that the agent is typically a human being.[2]

(*e*) As a consequence of the agent's action, something happens to the patient, i.e. the referent of the object NP. The effect on the patient is intended by the agent. Often, though by no means necessarily, the patient is inanimate.

(*f*) After the occurrence of the event, the patient is in a different state from before the event. Usually, the difference is one which would be highly perceptible to an onlooking observer.

(*g*) The event is construed as punctual. Even though the event necessarily has temporal extension, the internal structure of the event, and the intermediate states between its inception and termination, are not in focus.[3]

(*h*) The agent's action on the patient usually involves direct physical contact, and the effect on the patient is immediate.

(*i*) The event has a causative component—the agent's action causes the patient to undergo a change.

(*j*) Typically, agent and patient are not only clearly differentiated entities; often they also stand in an adversative relationship.

(*k*) Finally, the events reported by the construction are real, not imaginary, hypothetical, or counterfactual. Hence, central instantiations of the construction are realis.

The NP and V slots of the transitive construction can be filled by virtually any combination of items which meet the above semantic specification. But, like the possessive genitive, the transitive construction can

---

[2] With respect to this property, sentences (1)–(3) are each open to two interpretations, according to whether the action is carried out intentionally or accidentally. Only the intentional reading is consistent with prototypical transitivity.

[3] Again, sentences (1) and (2) are open to two interpretations with respect to this characteristic, the one punctual ("The child kicked the ball once"), the other iterative ("The child kicked the ball repeatedly").

be used to encode a wide range of states of affairs which differ, in one or more ways, from the paradigm specification. To begin with, we may note that the acceptability of a transitive sentence is not, in general, affected by the choice of tense, mood, polarity, or aspect of the verb, even though, cf. (*k*), only realis verb forms are consistent with prototypical transitivity. The NPs, too, may have generic, or non-specific reference:

(4) Elephants uproot trees

The following sentences illustrate other kinds of deviation, some minimal, others more extensive, from the central specification:

(5) The lightning destroyed the building

(6) We approached the city

(7) I dug the ground

(8) He brushed his teeth

(9) I carried the suitcase

(10) Mary helped John

(11) John obeyed Mary

In (5), the subject NP refers to an inanimate force, not a consciously and purposely acting agent. Otherwise, the event in (5) is highly transitive. (6) is rather less typical, in that the event is not punctual, and the patient does not undergo any change as a consequence of the agent's action. (7) is untypical in that only part of the patient undergoes change, while in (8) the patient, being part of the agent, is not maximally individuated. In (9) the event is temporally protracted, while in (10) the adversative component is missing from the agent–patient relationship. Finally, in (11), although an action is carried out by the agent, the event is arguably under the control of the patient rather than the agent.

With some of the above examples, we are already quite distant from the central semantic specification of the construction. Indeed, it is doubtful whether it is still legitimate to speak of the subject of (11) as the agent, and the direct object as the patient. Even further removed from the prototype are those transitive sentences which do not describe an event at all, but rather an act of perception on the part of the subject. In these cases, the role of the subject is better described as experiencer, and the direct object as stimulus:

(12) I watched the movie

Here, the act of watching is still under the control of the subject. In this respect, *watch* is a more transitive verb than *see* (as in *John saw Mary*). In other cases, the experiencer appears as the direct object, while the stimulus stands in subject position:

(13) The movie interested me

Again, it is still possible to claim that the event in (13) is 'initiated', in some metaphorical sense, by the subject, in that properties of the movie are 'responsible' for the event. However, when the verb encodes a mental state, even this property of the prototype is lost:

(14) I like John
      I've forgotten his name
      I regret the incident

Still further removed from the prototype are transitive sentences which describe a relation between entities, not some action performed by one entity with respect to another:

(15) John resembles his brother
      The book costs $20

What we can identify on semantic grounds as more central members of the transitive construction exhibit a number of syntactic and distributional characteristics not shared by more marginal members. Only sentences with agents which act volitionally can be embedded under *persuade*:

(16) (*a*) I persuaded Mary to kill the intruder
      (*b*) *Mary persuaded me to regret the incident

Only sentences which report on events (rather than states) can be inserted into the clefting expression *What happened was that S*:

(17) (*a*) What happened was that the lightning destroyed the building
      (*b*) *What happened was that John resembled his brother

Only actions allow clefting with *do*:

(18) (*a*) What elephants do is uproot trees
      (*b*) *What the movie did was interest me

The punctual nature of an event is consistent with the occurrence of temporal adverbials like *suddenly*, *at ten o'clock*; non-punctual events are odd in this context:

(19) (*a*) Suddenly, at 10 o'clock, John saw Mary
     (*b*) *Suddenly, at 10 o'clock, John obeyed Mary

Conversely, punctual events cannot be associated with adverbials expressing temporal extension, like *all morning*, *for hours on end*:

(20) (*a*) *Mary killed the intruder for hours on end
     (*b*) I carried the suitcase for hours on end

Patients which are affected by the action of the agent can readily stand as subject of a passive sentence; the ungrammaticality of a passive counterpart indicates that the object of a transitive sentence is in no way acted upon by the agent:

(21) (*a*) The ground was dug by me
     (*b*) *$20 have been cost by the book

Although many of the sentences cited so far have been rather distant, semantically, from the construction's prototype specification, the construction has retained a high degree of productivity, in that less central instantiations are subject to very few constraints of a non-predictable, idiomatic nature. Although *X saw Y* is not a very good example of a transitive sentence, it is still the case that practically any nominal denoting a sighted creature can stand as the subject of *see*, while the name of any visual stimulus can function as its direct object; the same applies, *mutatis mutandis*, to other verbs of perception, like *hear*, *feel*, *smell*, *taste*. In the next section we shall examine some more marginal members of the construction, where full regularity gives way to idiomaticity.

11.4 The transitive construction: more marginal members

A striking feature of English over the centuries has been the steady encroachment of the transitive construction to encode states of affairs which diverge increasingly from prototypical transitivity. A well-known example concerns the development of experience verbs like *think* and *like*. In Old English, the stimulus stood as the nominative-case subject of the verb, while the experiencer functioned as the dative-case indirect object:

(22) þam cynge licoden peran
   "to the king (DAT) like pears (NOM)"
   (cf. Hawkins 1986: 68)

The extension of the subject–verb–object pattern continues apace in modern English. Symptomatic is the possibility of deleting a path preposition from a prepositional phrase following an intransitive verb of motion:

(23) (*a*) He swam across the Channel →
   (*b*) He swam the Channel[4]

In (23) (*a*) the verb is intransitive. Swimming is an activity involving only one participant, namely the swimmer, with the prepositional phrase indicating the path the swimmer follows. In (23) (*b*), the path has been incorporated into the verb. *Swim* (a usage which according to the OED dates from the end of the sixteenth century) here means "swim across", with the consequence that the event is now encoded by a transitive sentence. That *the Channel* is now the direct object of *swim* is confirmed by the existence of a passive counterpart (*The Channel has been swum*). Other verbs, e.g. *fly*, behave in a similar way:

(24) He regularly flies across the Atlantic →
   He regularly flies the Atlantic

Yet this extension of the construction is not fully productive. A path preposition cannot always be deleted from a prepositional phrase following an intransitive verb of motion:

(25) The child crawled across the floor →
   *The child crawled the floor

(26) We drove across the Alps →
   *We drove the Alps

Not even all examples with *swim* (*across*) are fully acceptable:

---

[4] The arrow in this and following examples does not indicate the derivation of the one sentence from the other. The sentences on either side of the arrow, while systematically related in meaning and form, are instantiations of independent, autonomous constructions. See s. 11.2.

(27) ?He swam our new swimming pool

It would seem, then, that the possibility of using a verb of motion in a transitive sentence is an idiomatic property of individual lexical verbs; to judge from (27), which nominals are permitted as direct object is also a matter of idiom.

The transitive construction comes to be applied to other one-participant events through the use of a semantically (relatively) empty verb and a deverbal nominal as its direct object:

(28) We swam → We had a swim

(29) He walked → He took a walk

The status of these sentences as highly marginal members of the transitive construction is shown by the fact that passivization is not possible:

(30) *A swim was had

(31) *A walk was taken

Again, not all intransitive verbs have transitive empty verb-plus-deverbal nominal equivalents. There is no *to have/take/make/do a death* alongside *to die*.

There also exists in English the possibility of encoding a three-participant event as a transitive sentence, through the incorporation of the patient into the verb. Thus, in (32), a locative, and in (33), a benefactor, come to function as patients:

(32) He laid a carpet in the room →
     He carpeted the room

(33) The Government provided houses for the squatters →
     The Government housed the squatters

Again, the phenomenon is sporadic, rather than fully productive. Not all benefactors and locatives can be promoted to patient through incorporation of a direct object into the verb:

(34) He installed windows in the house →
     *He windowed the house

(35) He provided money for the orphanage
     *He moneyed the orphanage

The idiomatic nature of the phenomenon is well illustrated in (36), in the relative acceptability of (*a*) and *b*), in contrast with the ungrammaticality of (*c*) and (*d*):

(36) (*a*) He wined the guests
    (*b*) He champagned the guests
    (*c*) *He beered the guests
    (*d*) *He coffeed the guests

The encroachment of the transitive construction shows up again in the alternative ways of encoding three-participant events involving the transfer of a patient to a recipient. Usually, either patient or recipient can function as direct object:

(37) (*a*) John gave the book to Mary
    (*b*) John gave Mary the book

That both *the book* and, respectively, *Mary* function here as direct object is shown by the passive counterparts in (37):

(38) (*a*) The book was given to Mary
    (*b*) Mary was given the book

Often, the same choice exists with more abstract instances of transfer:

(39) (*a*) He showed the pictures to the children
    (*b*) He showed the children the pictures

With some verbs of abstract transfer, however, the alternative encodings are not available. Which verbs admit the recipient as direct object would appear to be a matter of idiom. In many dialects, (40) (*b*) is ungrammatical:

(40) (*a*) He explained the problem to the class
    (*b*) *He explained the class the problem

Sometimes the recipient can even stand as direct object without mention of the patient:

(41) Give me! Show me!

With these examples, we are approaching the outer limits of the transitive construction. The acceptability of such sentences appears to be crucially dependent on the mood of the sentence and the context in which it is uttered. The imperative forms in (41), spoken in the presence of the objects which would normally function as the patients of the verbs, are more acceptable than the past tense reports *?John gave me*, *?*Mary showed me*. (These latter sentences seem incomplete: What was given/shown?) It is here, also, that one encounters considerable between-speaker variation—another symptom of the highly marginal status of the phenomenon under discussion. Some speakers accept the transitive sentence *I'll write you*, others insist on *I'll write to you*. Even so, *I'll write you* seems better than the past tense report *John wrote Mary*.

The above discussion has shown how, in special cases, NPs referring to very unpatient-like entities can function as the direct object of a transitive sentence. Subjects with unagent-like properties are no less frequent. We have already seen how forces, experiencers, and stimuli can stand as subjects. Also unproblematic, in English, are sentences with the names of institutions as subjects. In such cases we can say that the name of the institution is being used metonymically for the human agent who holds an important position in the institution:

(42) This hotel forbids dogs

A relation of metonymy between an agent and the instrument he uses to affect the patient similarly sanctions the use of an instrument in subject position:

(43) The key opened the door

Further removed from the prototypical agent are subjects which designate the scope, or setting of an event:

(44) My guitar broke a string

(45) The stove has blown a fuse

Sometimes the scope subject almost has the role of a locative or temporal:

(46) This tent sleeps six

(47) The room seats 500

(48) The fifth day saw our departure

With these last examples, we have again approached the outer limits of the transitive construction. Symptomatic of the highly marginal status of (44)–(48) is the extremely low productivity of the construction with scope subjects. We cannot say, on analogy with *My guitar broke a string*, **The window cracked a pane*. Alongside *The tent sleeps six*, we do not have * *The house lives four*, nor can we say, on the model of *The fifth day saw our departure*, * *Midnight heard the explosion*, or * *Spring experienced his return to health*. Furthermore—and this is a property already noted in connection with (41)—the acceptability of these highly marginal sentences seems to be affected by the tense, aspect, and polarity of the verb, and by the number and specificity of the NPs. *All these tents have been sleeping six* and *May the fifth day see our departure* are both decidedly odd. Even *The key won't open the door* seems more usual than *The key opens the door*.

11.5 Metaphorical extension of syntactic constructions

Metaphor, as we saw in Chapter 7, is one of the principal means of category extension. Our earlier discussions of metaphor were restricted mainly to the meanings of lexical items. The question arises whether metaphor also motivates the semantic extension of a syntactic construction. Halliday, for one, explicitly deals with sentences like *The fifth day saw our departure* in terms of grammatical metaphor (1985: 321 ff.)—an approach endorsed by, amongst others, Dirven (1985). In this section, I would like to examine more closely the validity of this view. What exactly is meant by saying that non-central transitive sentences like *He swam the Channel*, *I took a walk*, *They carpeted the room*, *My guitar broke a string*, are metaphorical?

I have characterized metaphor as a process whereby one domain of experience is conceptualized in terms of another. To say that the transitive construction undergoes metaphorical extension would be to claim that the agent–action–patient schema, characteristic of transitive events, gets projected on to states of affairs which are not inherently transitive. These states of affairs thus come to be conceptualized in terms of an agent consciously acting in such a way as to cause a change in state in a patient. Some non-central transitive sentences certainly lend themselves to this kind of interpretation. The slogan of the pro-gun lobby, *Guns don't kill people, people kill people*, gets its effect precisely by denying the implication that, because *guns* can stand as the subject of the transitive sentence *Guns kill people*, guns therefore participate in the killing of people as consciously acting, responsible agents. Further indirect evidence for the power of the grammatical metaphor comes from a paper by Coleman (1980), in which she documents some characteristics of the speech of born-again Christians.

Reborn Christians deny the full agency of human beings; man's actions, it is believed, are ultimately God's work. This belief is reflected in the systematic avoidance of transitive sentences with first-person subjects. Sentences of the form *I did X* tend not to occur. Instead, circumlocutions like *I felt led to do X* and *I was enabled to do X*, are preferred.

For other, more marginal transitive sentences, the applicability of the transitive schema seems less appropriate. It does not, on the face of it, make much sense to say that *We had a swim* encodes a conceptualization of a state of affairs in terms of a consciously acting agent ('we'), whose action (that of 'having') causes a change in state in a patient ('a swim'). Neither is 'our departure' in any way affected by the action of 'seeing' on the part of 'the fifth day'. (By the same token, the use of the possessive construction in *John's wife* cannot reasonably be taken to imply that a man 'owns' his wife.) But if the use of the transitive construction does not always imply a projection of the full agent–action–patient schema, the choice of a transitive encoding might nevertheless serve to attribute selected aspects of prototypical transitivity to an otherwise non-transitive state of affairs. Indeed, the only partial applicability of the transitive schema would in itself point to a less central status within the construction. To the extent that a transitive sentence encodes a state of affairs which is only partially compatible with prototypical transitivity, that sentence will have the status of a more marginal member of the category.

We may note, to start with, that transitive sentences are rarely synonymous with non-transitive wordings. *We had a swim* does not mean the same as *We swam*. *We had a swim* conceptualizes the activity as a temporally bounded event, in contrast to *We swam*, where the activity is (potentially) unbounded. Thus one may readily say *We swam for hours on end*, but not * *We had a swim for hours on end*. In this respect, the transitive construction does impose one component of the transitivity schema, namely punctuality. A different component of prototypical transitivity, namely the adversative relationship between agent and patient, is involved in *He swam the Channel*. In contrast to *He swam across the Channel*, where *across the Channel* merely denotes the location of the swimming, *He swam the Channel* presents the Channel as a challenge to the swimmer's prowess. (It is along these lines that we may account for the oddity of *He swam our new swimming pool*.) To take another of our earlier examples: *He carpeted the room* focuses on the action of carpeting as a discrete, self-contained activity, while *He laid the carpet in the room* presents the carpet as an independent participant in the process.

Particularly interesting in this context is sentence (49), in which the subject NP refers to what looks like the patient of the action, not the agent:

(49) The book sold a million copies

Clearly, this sentence is a highly marginal example of the transitive construction. Passivization, for instance, is impossible (*A million copies were sold by the book*), and seemingly analogous sentences with *buy* (**The book bought a million copies*) are also ungrammatical. The possibility of a transitive encoding in (49) appears to depend on the fact that certain aspects of agency can be attributed to the subject (van Oosten 1977). This is not to say that the book is construed as a full-fledged agent; the book does not act volitionally and consciously, it does not by its actions effect a change in state of another entity. The true agent, in the act of selling, can only be the person who sells. Yet the seller does not have complete control over the act of selling. A successful sale depends, in no small measure, on the attributes of the thing that is sold. (49) seems to highlight the contribution of the merchandise itself (e.g. the fact that the book appeals to a wide audience) to the high sales figures. An analogous sentence with *buy* is not possible, precisely because the act of buying is to a much greater extent under the control of the buyer. Similar arguments to these have been used by Schlesinger (1981) in connection with the only limited productivity of the transitive construction with an instrument in subject position. *The key opened the door* is acceptable, since the successful opening of a door depends, in large part, on properties of the key. In contrast, **An ivory baton conducted the symphony* is bizarre, since conducting a symphony is the sole responsibility of the conductor, and the properties of his baton play no part in the event.

The reader may well be wondering which aspects of prototypical transitivity sanction the use of the transitive construction in *The fifth day saw our departure*. In fact, practically the only commonality between this sentence and more central members of the category is the status of the subject as sentence topic: the fifth day is what the sentence is about. The absence of any other aspects of prototypical transitivity is in itself symptomatic of the extreme marginality of the sentence.

11.6 A comparison with German

Evidence for the essential correctness of the prototype view of constructions comes from a rather unexpected source, namely from cross-language comparisons. We can hypothesize the following situation. Two languages, A and B, each have a construction whose semantics—at least with regard to the central instances—are very similar. In language A, the construction has undergone considerable extension, in B the construction is restricted to cases which are fairly close to the prototype. Consequently, all instantiations of the construction in B will have syntactically comparable translation equivalents in A; the converse will not hold. Furthermore, the lack of correspondence between A and B will not be random; only the more marginal members in A will not have simple translation equivalents in B. Such a situation exists with regard to the transitive construction in English and German. English is remarkable for the extent to which the construction has undergone extension. The transitive construction in German is much more restricted. As Hawkins (1986) amply documents, a transitive sentence in German requires, for its nominative-case subject, an NP with fairly typical agent properties; similarly, the accusative-case direct object must be a fairly typical patient, while the verb must denote a fairly typical action. Thus, only the more central members of the English construction have transitive equivalents in German. Some of the differences with regard to the less central members of the English construction may be summarized as follows:

(*a*) English readily encodes the experiencer of a mental state as a transitive sentence subject. In German, the experiencer often appears in the dative case, with stimulus as subject, rather as in Old English (cf. sentence (22)):

(50) Mir gefällt Mary
      "to me (DAT) pleases Mary (NOM)"

(*b*) If the agent–patient relationship is 'co-operative' rather than adversative, the patient in German may appear as a dative object, rather than as an accusative object:

(51) Er half mir; Er antwortete mir
      "He helped me (DAT)"; "He answered me (DAT)"

(*c*) The transitive construction is not possible in German if the agent performs some action on his own body, i.e. agent and patient are not maximally differentiated:

(52) Er hat sich die Zähne geputzt
"He brushed the teeth to himself (DAT)"
i.e. "He brushed his teeth"

(*d*) If the patient does not undergo any change in state as a result of the action of the agent, the verb in German is sometimes reflexive, and the patient may appear in a case other than the accusative:

(53) Ich erinnere mich seines Namens
"I remember myself (ACC) of his name (GEN)"
i.e. "I remember his name"

(54) Ich näherte mich der Stadt
"I approached myself (ACC) to the city (DAT)"
i.e. "I approached the city"

(*e*) Under no circumstances can German encode a recipient—cf. (41)—with an accusative object:

(55) *Zeig mich!; *Gib mich!
"Show me (ACC)"; "Give me (ACC)"

(*f*) In a limited number of lexically specified cases, transitive sentences are possible in German through the omission of a preposition (56), or through object-incorporation (57). In such cases, the verb requires a special transitive prefix:

(56) Wir wohnten im Hause → Wir bewohnten das Haus
"We lived in the house" → "We lived-in, i.e. inhabited, the house (ACC)"

(57) Er machte Bilder für das Buch → Er bebilderte das Buch
"He made pictures for the book" → "He pictured, i.e. illustrated, the book (ACC)"

(*g*) German does not, in general, permit instruments to function as subjects:

(58) ?Der Schlüssel öffnete die Tür
"The key opened the door"

(*h*) Not even institutional agents are possible:

(59) *Das Hotel verbietet Hunde
      "The hotel forbids dogs"

(*i*) Finally, it comes as no surprise that sentences at the very limit of
the English construction have no transitive equivalents in German:

(60) *Das Zelt schläft sechs
      "The tents sleeps six"

11.7 Concluding remarks

In the EST version of generative grammar outlined in Section 10.2,
the constructions of a language are the output of transformational
rules which operate on initial phrase markers, which in turn are the
output of the categorial rules of the base. On this view, knowing a
construction means, above all, knowing the rules which generate it. On
the constructionist account, constructions are not generated, they are
individually learnt as pairings of formal conditions with a semantic
specification. Also included in the knowledge of a construction is a
measure of the construction's productivity, as well as an indication of
its formal and semantic relationships with other constructions.[5]

In principle, the generative model foresaw only fully regular rule
applications, and hence, only fully productive constructions. Yet it is
doubtful whether any construction in a language is ever *fully*
productive, in the sense that all lexical items which satisfy the formal
requirements of the construction can be inserted with equal facility
into the respective construction slots. It may well be possible to
represent certain formal characteristics of the transitive construction
by means of the phrase structure rules S → NP VP; VP → V NP. Yet
not every random combination of NPs and V produce equally
acceptable transitive sentences. It was therefore necessary to limit the
power of phrase structure and other rules, by drawing on devices like
subcategorization and selection restriction. Ultimately, this kind of

---

[5] Although historical issues have not been our concern in this chapter, we may
observe that a speaker's linguistic creativity may extend a construction beyond its
conventional limits. Over the centuries, some such process has been at work in English,
and is no doubt still under way, with regard to the transitive construction. Conversely,
peripheral instantiations of a construction may fall into disuse, resulting in a contraction
of the category. Thus the dative-experiencer construction illustrated in (22) has been
restricted, in modern English, to a few verbs like *seem* and *appeal*.

information resided in the lexicon. It is significant that in his most recent writings, Chomsky (1986) envisages the virtual elimination of phrase structure and transformational rules, with a corresponding increase in the function and the scope of the lexicon. In this, Chomsky appears to be approaching the position where the permissible constructions of a language are nothing other than generalizations over properties of lexical items. What is missing in this approach is the grounding of transitivity in the experiential gestalt discussed in Section 11.3. In the last analysis, transitivity is a property of the clause, not of lexical items, and of the construal of the world which the clause symbolizes.

12

Prototype Categories in Phonology

In this chapter I discuss a topic of crucial importance for the coherence of the thesis presented in this book, namely the possibility of attributing non-classical structure to phonological categories. I drew attention in Section 2.3 to the role of the structural analogy assumption in twentieth-century linguistic research. To recapitulate: the structural analogy assumption states that a linguist will expect the same kinds of structure to show up at different levels of linguistic description. Now, taking a rather broad view of the recent history of linguistics, it is probably true to say that it was in the study of phonology that modern linguistics first came of age. There are many reasons why this should have been so. The sounds of a language are concrete and observable in a way in which meanings and syntactic structures are not; the number of entities (e.g. phonemes and features) which need to be posited for any one language is small and manageable; and linguists were able to draw on the findings of a highly sophisticated tradition of articulatory phonetics. Be that as it may, the descriptive apparatus first worked out for phonology came to be applied to other areas of linguistic description, especially morphology and syntax, and somewhat later, semantics. As argued in Chapter 2, it was above all the phenomenal success of the classical model in phonology, with phonological categories being represented in terms of a small set of binary atomic primitives, that encouraged the use of criterial features in the characterization of syntactic and semantic categories.

A striking characteristic of the cognitive paradigm has been that it has reversed this pattern of development. Cognitive linguistics is associated, first and foremost, with an area of linguistic analysis which other schools of linguistics have dealt with last, namely semantics, more particularly lexical semantics. Certainly, it was with regard to the meanings of lexical items that the prototype model scored its first successes. The organization of this book has traced the application of this model to other areas of analysis, to bound morphemes like the diminutive, to the units of intonation description, and to the formal elements of language description, such as parts of speech and syntactic constructions. There remains the area of phonology. It would be counter to the spirit of the structural analogy assumption if the units of phonology needed to be categorized according to principles unique to this level of analysis. Indeed, such a state of affairs would seriously threaten the status of the prototye model as a valid alternative to classical models of linguistic categorization.

In our treatment so far we have not, of course, totally neglected phonological matters (see the account of intonational categories in Chapter 9). The discussion in Chapter 9 emphasized the analogies between the categories of intonation analysis and other meaning-bearing elements of language. In this respect, intonational categories are untypical of phonological categories as a whole. Phonology is concerned, primarily, with the patterning of elements which are in themselves meaningless. To what extent is it feasible and, more importantly, insightful, to attribute prototype structures to these kinds of elements?

12.1 Phoneme categories

The salient aspects of the classical approach to the phoneme were reviewed in Chapter 2. Phonemes, as we saw, were characterized in terms of a conjunction of primitive, abstract features; furthermore, by focusing on the relations between categories, and on the value of categories within the phonological system as a whole, classical phoneme theory tended to disregard the concrete phonetic instantiations of the categories. For a valuable antidote to this approach, we cannot do better than turn to Daniel Jones's characterization of the phoneme. A phoneme, Jones wrote at the beginning of the century, can be described as 'a family of sounds consisting of an important sound of the language (generally the most frequently used member of that family) together with other related sounds which "take its place" in particular sound-sequences or under particular conditions of length or stress or intonation' (Jones 1964: 49).

It will be appreciated that this definition, with its reference to a family of sounds which are related in some way, is immediately suggestive of a prototype approach. Let us consider a case in point. The /t/ phoneme in English constitutes a category made up of a large number of members, i.e. the allophones of /t/.[1] Amongst these, we can list the following:

(*a*) In onset position[2] in a stressed syllable, /t/ is articulated as a voiceless aspirated alveolar plosive: [tʰ].

(*b*) In the speech of some speakers, the aspiration in the onset of a stressed syllable is so heavy that the sound is affricated. This articulation may be represented [tˢ].

(*c*) When /t/ occurs in coda position, a great many articulations are possible. If the /t/ is utterance-final, both the aspirated and the affricated articulations may occur. Utterance-final /t/ may also be unreleased: [tº].

(*d*) In utterance-final position, the alveolar closure of /t/ may be released ejectively: [tˈ]. This is particularly common in highly emphatic utterances like *What!?*.

(*e*) As a variant of (d), the ejective /t/ may be affricated: [tˢˈ].

(*f*) Alternatively, /t/ in the coda position of a stressed syllable may be glottalized, i.e. closure in the alveolar region occurs simultaneously with a glottal closure [ʔt]. This pronunciation is especially frequent in southern England.

(*g*) If the glottal closure mentioned in (*f*) momentarily precedes alveolar closure, and if, furthermore, the /t/ is utterance-final and unreleased, the alveolar closure makes no acoustic contribution to the sound produced. In other words, post-vocalic, pre-pausal /t/ is heard as a glottal stop [ʔ]. The glottal stop pronunciation generalizes, especially in southern British English and some kinds of Scottish speech, to codas of stressed syllables, even when these are not utterance-final.

(*h*) A number of articulations are possible if /t/ occurs in the onset of an unstressed syllable following a vowel. The /t/ in this environment might have less aspiration than in onset position, or it may be articulated with no audible closure. In this case, /t/ is realized by an /s/-like fricative, which may be represented [ʂ]. The spirantization of /t/ is particularly common in rapid speech.

(*i*) Alternatively, in the environment described in (*h*), a /t/ may be articulated as a flap: [ɾ], especially in American English. Another possibility is a voiced articulation, i.e. /t/ is spoken as [d].

---

[1] The following discussion develops a number of points in Nathan (1986).
[2] Roughly speaking, the onset of a syllable comprises the consonantal elements which precede the vocalic nucleus, while the coda consists of consonantal elements following the nucleus. For a more precise characterization, see below, s. 12.2.

(*j*) In certain non-standard northern varieties of British English, an intervocalic /t/, especially if it follows a short stressed vowel, is pronounced as [ɹ]. *I've got to go* is heard as *I've gorra* [gɒɹə] *go*, and *Get up* as *Gerrup* [geɹʊp]. The 'r'-variant is also common in the unmonitored speech of South Africans.

(*k*) In rapid, relaxed speech, an intervocalic, post-stress /t/ may even be elided. Thus one might hear *What's the matter* [mæ:] *with you?*. In certain consonant clusters in a syllable coda, elision of /t/ is probably the norm, e.g. *prints* [prɪns].

(*l*) The place of articulation can vary. Before /r/ a more retracted articulation is common. A retracted articulation is also characteristic of the affricate [tʃ], while a dental articulation is likely before a dental fricative, as in *eighth*.

(*m*) Utterance internally, /t/ may be released in different ways, depending on the characteristics of the following sound: nasal release before a nasal (*mutton*), lateral release before a lateral (*little*).

(*n*) /t/ obligatorily loses its characteristic aspiration in the syllable-initial cluster /st/. As already mentioned, loss of aspiration is also common if /t/ constitutes the onset of an unstressed syllable.

Before turning to the way the members of the /t/ phoneme are structured, a few preliminary remarks are called for. It will be observed that in listing the members of the /t/-family of sounds, I have referred to different regional varieties of English (southern British, Scottish, American, South African). I have also included examples from different stylistic levels (rapid, emphatic). This reflects the view that there is no such thing as a 'completely homogeneous speech community' (Chomsky 1965: 3). Chomsky's idealization might perhaps be justified in certain kinds of syntactic description, as a basis for describing a speaker's phonological ability, however, it goes counter to even the most superficial observation of speech behaviour. Every speaker of a natural language commands a range of stylistic variants, and most speakers have at least a passive knowledge of different regional accents. The heterogeneity of the members of /t/ listed above should therefore not be exaggerated. With the exception of the flaps, all the listed articulations are employed, some perhaps not very frequently, by the present writer, a native of the north-east of England who speaks in formal situations a reasonably close approximation to standard British English.

It will also be noted that certain sounds have *not* been included as members of /t/. These are sounds which replace /t/ in certain morphological environments. For instance, the /t/ of *president* is replaced by /ʃ/ in *presidential* and by /s/ in *presidency*. The exclusion of [ʃ] and [s] as members of /t/ is in line with the distinction between what Bloomfield called 'automatic' alternations and 'non-automatic', or 'grammatical' alternations (Bloomfield 1930: 211ff.), i.e. between phonological alternations proper, and morphophonological alternations. It is well known that generative phonology has tended to handle phonological and morphophonological alternations by the same component of the grammar; it has regarded them, in other words, as the same kind of phenomena. The distinction, however, was taken as self-evident in pre-generative days (although, as with so many other distinctions, there are borderline cases which are difficult to classify), and it has recently been revived by proponents of so-called natural phonology. Morphophonological alternations—Bloomfield's non-automatic processes (the /t/-/ʃ/ alternation in *president–presidential* is an example)—are sensitive to the morphosyntactic structure of a linguistic form. Purely phonological alternations, on the other hand, reflect exclusively prosodic aspects of an utterance, i.e. such things as the phonetic environment of a segment, its position in a syllable, the position of the syllable relative to pauses, the degree of stress of the syllable, as well as speech style and speaking tempo.

After these preliminary considerations, let us now turn to the structuring of the sounds which make up the /t/ phoneme. The analogy with the family resemblance structure of semantically polysemous items is indeed striking. Just as there are no criterial semantic features common to all the meanings of *climb* and *over*, so there are no phonetic features which unify all the members of the /t/ phoneme and which jointly distinguish the /t/ phoneme from contrasting phoneme categories. English /t/ would normally be described as a voiceless aspirated pulmonic alveolar stop; yet some allophones of /t/ are voiced, some stop realizations are unaspirated, pulmonic air-stream mechanism is absent in the ejectives, dental and glottal articulations defeat the characterization alveolar, and not all members of /t/ are stops. Symptomatic of this state of affairs—and again the parallelism with the meanings of polysemous forms will be obvious—is the fact that some allophones of /t/ have practically nothing in common, phonetically, with others. Consider in this regard the [ʂ]-articulation and the glottal stop allophone, or the 'r'-variant and the ejective. Continuing the analogy with polysemous categories, it is possible to establish chaining relationships on the basis of phonetic similarity between individual members of /t/. For instance, glottalized [ʔt] can be considered the chaining link between non-glottalized [t] and the glottal stop articulation [ʔ]. As a final point of comparison, it will be observed that the /t/ phoneme, in some of its instantiations, encroaches on the phonetic space of other phoneme categories. We have encountered analogous instances of category overlap in earlier chapters, e.g. the encroachment of *over* on the semantic space of *across*. The glottal stop realization of /t/ overlaps, in some dialects, with the glottal stop allophones of /p/ and /k/ (thus, for some speakers, *boot* and *book*, *pip* and *pit* are homophones); the flap is a possible instantiation of both /t/ and /d/ (some American speakers do not distinguish *rider* and *writer*); the [ʂ] allophone encroaches on the phonetic space of the sibilants, while the 'r'-variant of /t/ is phonetically identical with an important member of the /r/ phoneme.

The similar structure of phoneme and semantic categories prompts, in the case of phoneme categories, the same questions as were raised in connection with polysemous items (cf. Section 6.4). Are there limits on the extension of a phoneme category? Do certain members of the category have a central status, and if so, on what basis? And what motivates the extension of the category in the first place? As regards the first question, we might suppose, as we did in the case of semantic categories, that the extension of a category will be constrained by the presence of neighbouring categories. In general, this principle seems to hold—most members of the /t/ phoneme do not in fact trespass on the phonetic space of other categories. Yet some do—cf. the examples of overlap discussed above. As was the case with polysemous categories, the principle of category distinctiveness, intuitively appealing as it is, fails as an absolute constraint on category extension.

The second question concerns the centrality of certain members of the category. Daniel Jones, it will be recalled, suggested frequency of occurrence as a decisive factor. I have no statistical data on the incidence of the different allophones of /t/, averaged over different speakers for different speaking styles and speaking rates. As was the case with prototypical members of semantic categories, I suspect that the impression of a higher frequency of the central allophone may well be a consequence of its central status, and not a defining characteristic of it. There are two other approaches to this issue, one structuralist, the other psychological. Structurally, we can understand centrality as a function of the relations between categories and of the internal structure of the categories. In this respect the central members of phoneme categories are akin to the central members of basic level categories (see Section 3.3). Although the referential range of basic level terms might overlap, the central members of the categories are kept perceptually and cognitively maximally distinct. Thus the putative central member of /t/—say, the voiceless aspirated alveolar plosive—enters into a number of highly salient perceptual and articulatory contrasts with the putative central members of neighbouring categories, such as the unaspirated alveolar plosive of /d/, the voiceless aspirated velar plosive of /k/, and so on. Furthermore, the centrality of [tʰ] is confirmed by the fact that the chaining relationships between the members of /t/ do seem to radiate out from this central member.

If the structuralist approach to centrality is more in keeping with the ideas of Saussure, Trubetzkoy, and Jakobson, the psychological approach harks back to Sapir. For Sapir, the phoneme was a unitary mental entity, allophonic variation being the effect of subconscious adaptations of a speaker's intentions to the phonetic environment in which a speech sound occurs (1970: 55 f.). As a corollary, phonetically naïve speakers are typically unaware of the extent of allophonic variation in their language, phonetically distinct allophones generally being perceived as the 'same sound'. Needless to say, the psychological and the structuralist approaches are not necessarily in conflict. It is quite plausible to maintain that a speaker's mental image of /t/ as a voiceless aspirated alveolar plosive reflects the structural properties of the category in question. The mentalistic approach, however, does provide a starting-point for explaining the process of category extension.

In an earlier paragraph, I briefly mentioned the recent development of natural phonology. The allusion was not fortuitous. Of the various trends in modern phonology, it is perhaps natural phonology which in its aims and assumptions comes closest in spirit to the cognitive approach to syntax and semantics. The basic thesis of natural phonology is that the sound patterns of a language 'are governed by forces implicit in human vocalization and perception' (Donegan and Stampe 1979: 126). Just as cognitive linguistics rejects the notion of an autonomous faculty of language and attempts instead to ground the structure of language in more general processes of cognition and conceptualization, so natural phonology argues against the thesis that human beings are born with a unique phonological competence, in the sense of the generativists. Rather, from their earliest age, human beings apply to their vocalizations a set of universal natural processes which derive, as the above quotation indicates, from universal facts of articulation and perception. The phonological system of a language, it is proposed, results from the suppression of some of these natural processes and the exploitation of others, together with the imposition of a set of non-natural, language-specific rules. These latter correspond, in the main, to the non-automatic morphophonological alternations referred to earlier. Morphophonological alternations have various sources. Very often, they are the result of the telescoping of several individually natural processes, whose combined effect is no longer natural. As a consequence, morphophonological rules have a very different cognitive status from the natural processes which constitute the proper object of phonological enquiry.[3]

Donegan and Stampe (1979: 142f.) draw attention to two particularly important natural processes, and both are operative in the extension of the /t/ category. These are fortition (or strengthening), and lenition (or weakening). Fortitions serve to make a segment perceptually more prominent, e.g. by increasing the acoustic energy associated with the segment, by exaggerating the phonetic characteristics of a segment, by increasing the phonetic distance between the segment and adjacent segments, or by maximizing the contrast with other categories in the system. In English, fortition processes apply especially in stressed syllables—indeed, the extra energy associated with stress prominence makes stress a fortition process *par excellence*. Accordingly, it is the /t/s in the onsets of stressed syllables which are particularly liable to be heavily aspirated, and the /t/s in the codas of stressed syllables which are likely to be glottalized. Aspiration and glottalization each emphasizes, in different ways, the contrast between the voicelessness of /t/ and the voicing of an adjacent vowel, the former by interposing a segment of highly audible noise between the stop and the vowel, the latter by abruptly cutting short the vocal cord vibration of the vowel. The syllable-final ejective articulation, being based on a glottal air-stream mechanism, may also be regarded as the consequence of a fortition. Lenition processes, on the other hand, downplay the characteristics of a segment, by reducing the

---

[3] There is a further respect in which cognitive linguistics can find an ally in natural phonology: each in its different ways develops ideas which were very much alive in earlier linguistic traditions. Natural phonologists, perhaps, have emphasized the historical roots of their approach to a greater extent than cognitive linguists.

articulatory distance between the segment and adjacent segment or the contrast with other elements in the system. Lenitions occur, typically, in unstressed syllables, and in casual, inattentive, and allegro speech styles. Symptoms of lenition are the spirantization of /t/ (the speech organs fail to achieve complete closure), voicing in intervocalic position, flapping (the speaker merely initiates a ballistic movement of the tongue rather than carefully co-ordinating the movement of the tongue with the offset and onset of voicing), and the fricative [ɹ]-variant. The glottal stop articulation may be seen as the consequence of a lenition process (the elimination of an oral closure) applying after a fortition (glottalization) has taken place. The ultimate lenition process, of course, is elision.

12.2 The gradience of phoneme categories

In the preceding section I examined in some detail the internal structure of a phoneme category in English. The discussion clearly showed that the family of sounds comprising the phoneme category cannot be characterized in terms of a conjunction of categorial features. There still, however, remains the possibility of a feature-based definition of some abstract representation of the category. I would now therefore like to reappraise the status of features which characterize a speech sound. As was pointed out in Chapter 2, the classical model of categorization rests on the assumption that a given feature either is or is not present in any particular instance, and that features, either singly or in combination, define clearly circumscribed classes of sounds, i.e. those that possess the feature(s) in question, and those that do not. The class of voiced sounds, for example, all possess the feature [VOICE], while the complementary class of voiceless sounds are characterized by [-VOICE].

The basis for this kind of clear-cut distinction between classes of sounds has been questioned by Jaeger and Ohala (1984). Jaeger and Ohala trained groups of phonetically naïve speakers of English to classify the initial sounds of English words according to the parameters [±ANTERIOR], [±SONORANT], and [±VOICE]. In a subsequent testing session, subjects were required to categorize the initial sounds (some of which had not been presented during the training sessions) of English words according to the relevant parameter. It was found that each of the three parameters appeared to define, not two mutually exclusive categories, but rather a continuum, the opposite ends of which constituted the best examples of the categories in question. Results for the voicing dimension are shown in (1). Of the sounds tested, /r,m,n/ were the best examples of voicing, while /p,t,k/ were the best examples of voicelessness. The so-called voiced stops /b,d,g/ turned out to occupy an intermediate position between voicing and voicelessness.

(1)

most voiced ←   → *least voiced*

/r,m,n/   /v,ð,z/   /w,j/   /b,d,g/   /f,θ,s,h,ʃ/   /p,t,k/

It would seem, then, that phonetic features are not too different from the attributes which characterize cognitive categories. Features are not so much binary classificatory devices, but merely embody dimensions of perceived similarity between different speech sounds.

Jaeger and Ohala, in a reference to Jaeger's doctoral dissertation (1980), claim that degree of membership in phonological classes, as illustrated in (1), is a relevant factor in such diverse areas as speech errors, memory confusions, similarity judgements, and language acquisition. Dissatisfaction with the binary classifications of the classical approach may be inferred from other recent trends in phonology. Consider, for example, the treatments of vowels in dependency phonology. Dependency phonology (for an overview, see Anderson and Durand 1986, and Lass 1984: 271 ff.) postulates four components of vowel quality: |i| (i.e. frontness, or labiality), |u| (backness), |a| (openness), and |ə| (centrality). The quality of any given vowel is represented by various admixtures of these components, and of the dependency relations which exist among them. Within this framework, vowels do not fall into mutually exclusive classes, e.g. those which are [+LOW] and those which are [−LOW]. Rather, differences in vowel height are treated as a function of differences in the predominance of the |a| component. Dependency phonology has provided a particularly suitable model for the description of historical processes. For instance, the gradual raising of vowels over time—a rather common process of language change—can be easily captured in terms of a gradual weakening of the |a| component. Needless to say, the description of this kind of gradual process in terms of binary features proves extremely cumbersome.

The gradience of phonological features is relevant to another area of phonology, namely syllable structure. Recent work in metrical phonology has suggested that syllables in all languages conform to a universal syllable template (for a brief overview, see Lass 1984:

248 ff.). The template attributes to syllables a constituency structure which mediates between the category symbol σ (= syllable) and the syllable's terminal elements, i.e. phones. (The analogy with the familiar phrase structure description of syntactic analysis will be obvious.) All syllables consist of an obligatory rhyme optionally preceded by an onset. The rhyme in turn consists of an obligatory nucleus followed by an optional coda. Each of the three elements—onset, nucleus, and coda—may itself branch, i.e. may consist of more than one terminal element. The universal template is represented in (2).

(2)

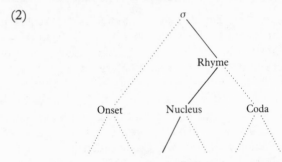

Not any random selection of segments are eligible for insertion into the terminal slots of (2). In any language, [pam] is likely to be a better syllable than [ltakr]. Underlying this judgement is a universal sonority hierarchy. The most sonorous sounds in a syllable occupy the nucleus position, while the sounds flanking the nucleus exhibit a progressive decline in sonority. The syllable template given in (2) can thus be elaborated as shown in (3).

(3)

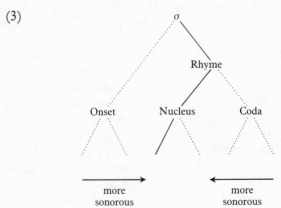

The notion of sonority, as used here, refines the well-known articulatory-acoustic characterization of the major phonological categories of vowel and consonant. As a parameter for the two-way classification of speech sounds, sonority was already invoked by Daniel Jones. Two factors are involved. One has to do with voicing. All other things being equal, a voiced sound (in the light of the earlier discussion, we should perhaps say 'a sound which exhibits a higher degree of voicing') is more sonorous than a voiceless one. The other factor concerns the degree of constriction of the vocal tract. From this point of view, the most sonorous sounds—the ones with the greatest carrying power—are the vowels. Vowels are articulated with minimum constriction of the vocal tract: 'the air issues in a continuous stream through the pharynx and mouth, there being no obstruction and no narrowing such as would cause audible friction' (Jones 1964: 23). All other sounds, i.e. the consonants, being articulated with varying degrees of vocal tract constriction, exhibit lower degrees of sonority.

While sonority certainly makes possible a two-way classification of speech sounds into vowels and consonants, it will be clear that sonority is not a matter of either–or, but of more-or-less. As a class, vowels are more sonorous than consonants. But within the class of what we traditionally call vowels, some are more sonorous than others. The most sonorous of all—the most 'vowel-like', if one wishes—is the maximally open /ɑ/, while the high vowels /u/ and, especially, /i/, are somewhat lower on the sonority scale. Similarly with the consonants. The least sonorous consonants are those which are voiceless and which are articulated with maximum constriction of the vocal tract, i.e. the voiceless stops. Progressively more sonorous are the voiced stops, the voiceless and the voiced fricatives, the nasal stops, the liquids, and the glides. Sonority relations are illustrated in (4):

(4)

most sonorous ←						→ *least sonorous*
low vowels	high vowels	glides	liquids	nasals	fricatives	stops

In an earlier chapter (Section 3.2), I raised the question whether certain vowels may be considered better examples of the category than others. To the extent that the category is defined in terms of the binary feature [VOCALIC], the answer is clearly negative; all members of the category VOWEL necessarily have equal status. However, if we take sonority to be a defining attribute of vowels, vowels and consonants do not emerge as two clearly circumscribed, mutually exclusive classes. /ɑ/ is indeed a more central member of the category than /i/, while the glides, liquids, and nasals have a somewhat ambiguous status as vowel-like consonants (or consonant-like vowels). This example, together with the ones discussed at the beginning of this section, strongly suggests that the sounds of a language are to be categorized along substantially the same principles as other elements of linguistic structures. The fuzzy demarcation of vowels and consonants, of voiced and voiceless, of high and low, is exactly analogous to the absence of a clear boundary between words and clitics, words and affixes, nouns and adjectives (and between cups and bowls).

12.3 The syllable as a construction

Let us now return to the syllable template given in (3). We can regard the syllable template in (3) as the phonological analogue of the syntactic constructions studied in Chapter 11. Like the formula for a syntactic construction, the syllable template specifies the kind of items which can fill the available slots; in the former case, items are available for insertion on the basis of their syntactic and/or semantic properties, in the case of syllables the relevant properties are phonetic. Syntactic constructions may have central and more marginal instantiations, according to the closeness of the filler items to the specification of the construction formula. We can likewise distinguish optimal and more marginal instantiations of the syllable template, according to the phonetic characteristics of the sounds which fill the syllabic slots. Let us consider, in illustration, the kinds of sounds which can occupy the nucleus position.

Optimal instantiations of the syllable template have in the nucleus position a sound which is very close to the sonorous end of the sonority continuum, i.e. a vowel. Indeed, in the overwhelming majority of cases, in English and other languages, a syllable consists, obligatorily, of a vowel, optionally flanked on either side by progressively less sonorous consonants. But sounds which are somewhat lower on the sonority scale can also occupy the nucleus position. A number of cases may be distinguished, at least for English. In most dialects of English, /l/ and /n/ can function as syllabic nuclei, in certain environments: *mutton* [mʌtn̩], *little* [lɪtl̩]. A second class of cases occurs in fast speech, where the elision of an unstressed vowel may thrust a sound which is rather low on the sonority hierarchy into the nucleus slot. Thus, the elision of the first schwa in *photography* may result in the initial syllable of the word having as its nucleus the fricative /f/: [ftɒgɹəfɪ]. Lass (1984: 261) claims that in fast speech *university* retains its five syllables, with /n/ and /s/ functioning as nuclei in place of the elided vowels: [juŋvɜʂtɪ]. Thirdly, highly emphatic speech may lend nucleus status to certain non-vowel segments. The first syllable of *brilliant* would usually be [bɹɪl]; in emphatic speech the word may be pronounced [bɹɪliənt], with the 'r' acquiring nucleus status. The final, and somewhat marginal class of cases concerns a small number of ideophone-like vocalizations. The attention-grabbing *psst!*, or the shivering *brr!*, may both be regarded as instantiations of the syllable template, the former having /s/ as its nucleus, while in the latter a rolled /r/ functions as nucleus.

It will be noted that, in each of these four cases, the possibility of a non-vowel occurring in nucleus position is subject to various restrictions. With the exception of the ideophones, the phenomenon is found only in unstressed syllables; syllabic /f/ in *photography* occurs only in fast speech; syllabic /r/ in *brilliant* is characteristic only of highly emphatic speech; syllabic /n/ and /l/ in words like *little*, *mutton*, demand an unstressed environment following an obstruent. These very restrictions point to the marginal status of the phenomenon in question. As sounds get progressively less sonorous, their general availability for insertion into the nucleus slot declines, in accordance with the reduced productivity of the syllable template.

I would like, in the remaining pages of this chapter, to pursue the analogy between syllabic and syntactic constructions. As already mentioned, the syllable template in (3) is claimed to have universal validity. Clearly, different languages do not exploit to an equal degree the possibilities offered by the universal template. Some languages— those which permit only open syllables—do not exploit the potentiality of the coda, others have restrictions on the branching of the onset and the coda, i.e. on the occurrence of consonant clusters at syllable boundaries. Each language, it seems, has a number of preferred syllable structures, analogous, I would suggest, to the highly productive syntactic constructions of the language. Other syllable constructions, on the other hand, are either not attested, or have only a marginal status within the language. The latter are the analogues of the syntactic constructions with only a low degree of productivity. The topic is a vast one, and I can only offer a highly programmatic illustration of the kinds of issues involved. Consider, as a starting-point, the fact that English, in common with some other Germanic languages, has co-occurrence conditions on branching within the rhyme. It is well known that in stressed monosyllables in English, a long vowel or a diphthong (both may be represented by means of a branching nucleus) may be followed, either by an empty coda or by a coda consisting of one or more elements. Short vowels in stressed monosyllables, on the other hand, must be followed by a filled coda; */bæ/, */be/, */bɪ/, etc. are unacceptable as English monosyllables. The condition is that the rhyme must contain at least one branching node; if the rhyme itself does not branch, then the nucleus must branch (cf. Lass 1984: 255). (5) (*a*), (*b*), and (*c*) are possible, and highly productive syllable constructions in English; (5) (*d*) is impossible.

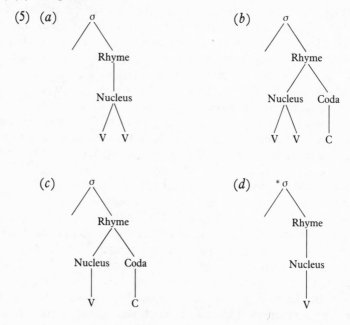

The same restriction holds in other Germanic languages, e.g. Dutch. In Dutch—as well as, to a less marked extent, in English—there is in addition a tendency to limit to two the number of branchings dominated by the rhyme. Clusters of two consonants (dominated by a branching coda) freely occur after short vowels; long vowels (dominated by a branching nucleus), on the other hand, tend to be followed by at most one consonant. This pattern presents itself more strongly if we accept Moulton's (1962: 303) distinction between final consonants proper, and post-final /s, t, st, ts/; in more recent terminology, we would say that these alveolar consonants have extra-metrical status outside the structure of a syllable. (6) takes account of this distinction; (6) (*a*) and (6) (*b*) are productive syllable structures in Dutch, while (6) (*c*) is not.

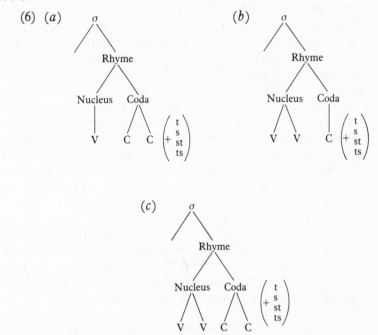

Examples (taken from Moulton) of instantiations of (6) (*a*) include *terp*, *werpt*, *dorps*, *tact*, and *scherpst*; examples of (6) (*b*) include *hoop*, *doopts*, *loops*, and *diepst*. The structure in (6) (*c*), however, is not totally excluded from Dutch. Moulton mentions, as 'exceptions' to the regularity he had pinpointed, *deern*, *hielp*, and *bedierf*. The syllable construction in (6) (*c*) is thus not ruled out by Dutch phonology; only, the construction has very limited productivity.

It will be noted that instantiations of (6) (*c*) all have, in the first consonant slot of the coda, a liquid, i.e. /r/ or /l/. It is of interest to observe that in the course of the 300 year evolution of Dutch into Afrikaans, many consonant clusters which are acceptable in coda position in Dutch have undergone simplification. As a consequence, the constructions in (6) (*a*) and (6) (*c*) have acquired a rather different status in Afrikaans. Consonant clusters in the coda are rather rare, especially after long vowels; furthermore, such clusters are virtually restricted to sequences of two consonants, the first of which is a liquid or nasal. As a consequence, (6) (*a*) has suffered a dramatic decline in productivity, while (6) (*c*) is of even more marginal status than in Dutch (see Taylor and Uys 1988).

Certain characteristics of syllable onsets can also be understood in terms of degrees of productivity. In standard German, there is a very strong tendency to avoid stressed syllables which lack an onset. If the onset does not contain a phonemic element, the onset is filled, by default as it were, by a glottal stop. Speakers of standard varieties of English also tend to avoid stressed syllables with empty onsets. Again, glottal stops may be inserted; alternatively, for speakers of standard British English, an empty onset may be filled in certain environments by a linking or intrusive /r/. Even so, stressed syllables with empty onsets are rather more frequent in English than in German, especially word-internally. We would say that the syllable construction permitting empty onsets is slightly more productive in English than in German. This statement does not, however, apply to all varieties of English. Many broader varieties of South African English resemble German in their virtual prohibition of empty onsets. The otherwise empty onsets are filled, as in German, by a glottal stop, or, in some instances, by the so-called voiced (actually, breathy-voiced) 'h'. These insertions may even occur word-internally. Thus *create* may be heard either as [kriʔeɪt] or [krifieɪt].

To summarize: syllable structures of a given language differ, like syntactic constructions, in their productivity. Some are highly productive, others are forbidden. Between these two extremes are structures which, while attested in a language, tend to be of rather restricted occurrence. As the Dutch-Afrikaans example suggests, historical change can also be understood, in part, in terms of a fluctuation in the productivity of syllable constructions. To our introductory question, whether it is feasible and insightful to attribute non-classical categorization principles to the units of phonology, the answer to both must be yes.

13

The Acquisition of Categories

ONE of the stated aims of the Chomskyan paradigm (at least in its more recent formulations) is to account for the process of language acquisition; conversely, alleged facts of acquisition are continuously, even monotonously, invoked as evidence for the correctness of the paradigm. The form of the argument is familiar. An examination of syntactic, semantic, and phonological phenomena leads to the postulation of abstract entities which are not visible in the surface sentences of a language. These entities, and the rules which manipulate them, cannot therefore be learnt by any process of induction or generalization from mere exposure to the surface forms. This is the 'logical problem' of language acquisition, which, it is argued, can only be solved if the child is credited with a rich initial state of the language faculty. The child, that is, succeeds in acquiring a Chomsky-style grammar because the scaffolding of the grammar is genetically inherited. Acquisition is seen as the unfolding of the innate potential; only the arbitrary facts of the target language (the phonological shape of morphemes, for example) need to be learnt.

Cognitive grammar eschews abstract entities. The claim instead is that semantic content is structured and symbolized overtly, in the surface forms of a language, not at the level of abstract underlying representations (see Section 11.1). In this respect, language acquisition does not present a logical problem to the cognitive linguist. Nevertheless, the Chomskyan paradigm teaches a valuable methodological principle. Any attempt to characterize the (relatively) steady state of language knowledge presumed to be present in the mind of a mature speaker needs to consider whether the facts of acquisition accord with an account of how the steady state could be plausibly achieved. As far as the present discussion is concerned, this means, above all, inquiring into the development of categories in child language. We need to examine in this connection not only the acquisition of semantic categories symbolized by the meaningful morphemes of a language, but also data pertaining to the development of the formal categories of linguistic structure.

Although it has not taken place within an explicitly cognitive framework, much recent work in language acquisition is consonant with many of the principles and assumptions of cognitive linguistics (see for example the various contributions to Wanner and Gleitman 1982). The reasons for this convergence are not hard to find. Anyone studying the development of language in the young child is hardly likely to be able to find much inspiration in a theoretical model which makes a clean division between syntax and semantics, and between semantic structure and conceptualization. The child's emerging skill in the manipulation of the formal elements of language cannot reasonably be separated from the increasing range of meanings that he is able to express. By the same token, his growing ability to use language meaningfully cannot be isolated from the development of more general cognitive skills. It is in child language, in fact, that we are particularly likely to find confirmation for the cognitive hypothesis of the grounding of language structure in non-linguistic cognition.

This chapter does not intend to offer a comprehensive overview of recent research into language acquisition. Rather, I will focus on a limited number of topics which are of particular relevance to the arguments of the preceding chapters. It will be appropriate to begin by considering some general implications of a non-classical model of categorization for category acquisition. Assuming the essential correctness of the views presented so far in this book, how might we expect prototype and family resemblance categories to be learnt, in contrast to categories structured on purely classical principles?

13.1 Hypothesized acquisition routes

Classical and non-classical models of categorization give rise to different expectations as to the course that category acquisition will take. Let us consider, first of all, classical categories. Classical categories, it will be recalled, are defined in terms of a conjunction of necessary and sufficient features for membership. A realistic hypothesis is that a classical category will be acquired through the gradual assembling of the appropriate feature set. Initially, we may assume, the child's specification of the category will be incomplete; one or more of the criterial features defining the category will be missing. The effect of this incomplete specification will be overextension. A lexical item will have a much wider denotational range than the adult word, grammatical categories will include items excluded from the adult category, and so on. As further features are added to the child's definition, overextension will be curtailed, presumably in quantal jumps, until eventually the child's representation of the category coincides with the adult's.

This rather simple model (a detailed version was proposed by Clark 1973*b*) assumes that at every stage in the child's development the features defining the child's category form a proper subset of the features defining the adult category. We should not, however, exclude the possibility that the child at some stage incorporates into his category specification features which are absent from the adult category, or gives a feature the wrong value (e.g. [+] rather than [-]). Such spurious feature specifications will lead, not to overextension, but to varying degrees of overlap between the child and the adult category. The model is open to refinement in other respects. Consider, for example, the nature of the features. If features are taken to be abstract primitives, as the pure classical model requires, then it is clear that the semantic content of a feature will remain unchanged as the child moves towards adult competence. [MALE] will 'mean' the same thing for the two-year-old as for the mature adult. If, on the other hand, we accept that features might be cognitively quite complex, the possibility arises that features themselves might undergo development. Initially, [MALE] might be understood in terms of perceptual characteristics, the biological understanding emerging only later.

Less strong versions of the classical model might thus be compatible with a course of acquisition which diverges in minor details from the hypothesized initial overextension, followed by contraction, in discrete steps, of the category boundaries. In contrast, the prototype model makes a clear prediction of initial underextension. Prototype categories will initially crystallize around a mental representation of a prototype. This may take the form of a cluster of perceptual and functional attributes; alternatively, and perhaps more realistically, the prototype may be understood as a holistic gestalt. Further acquisition will proceed by extension from the prototype. Things will get assimilated to the category on the basis of some kind of perceived similarity to the prototype. The dimensions of similarity exploited by the child may not, of course, be the same ones that underlie the extension of the adult category, neither need the child's representation of the prototype exactly coincide with the adult's. The child's emergent prototype category need not, therefore, at every stage be properly included in the adult category. Gradually, however, the child will adjust his prototype representation in accordance with adult norms, and will learn to select the appropriate dimensions of similarity as criteria for category membership. Eventually, after perhaps intermediate periods of overextension or overlap with respect to the adult category, his category will become roughly isomorphic with the adult category. A similar process is indicated for family resemblance categories. Initially, while the central member is being acquired, the child will underextend with respect to the adult category. This stage will be followed by a stepwise extension along the chaining links which hold the adult category together; alternatively, the child may experiment with chaining extensions which are not sanctioned by adult usage.

It will be noted that both the classical and non-classical models can accommodate category overextension during the acquisition process. Overextension, however, takes a rather different form in the two cases. Overextension of a classical category is due to the fact that membership in the category has not yet been narrowed down sufficiently; one or more criterial features defining the adult category have not yet been added to the child's specification. Symptomatic of this state of affairs will be the use of a lexical item corresponding to the adult use of a superordinate term. As the appropriate criterial features are added to the child's specification, the range of things which pass as members of the category will contract, in quantal steps. Overextension of a prototype or family resemblance category, on the other hand, will proceed outwards from a conceptual core; extension and subsequent contraction will be gradual rather than quantal; usage at the periphery of the category may well be vacillating, in contrast to the stability of the category centre.

The models for category acquisition sketched out here presuppose that adult categories are acquired through a process of accretion to the nascent child category, with minor adjustments along the way. Only thus is it possible to make inferences from the structure of adult categories to the manner of their acquisition, and vice versa. One cannot, however, rule out a priori the possibility of category restructuring during the acquisition process. We have, in fact, already hinted at such a possibility in Section 4.2. The extraction of schemas (in Langacker's sense), and the imposition of expert definitions during the course of formal education, may effectively trigger a redefinition of erstwhile prototype categories in terms of a set of criterial properties.

13.2 Grammatical categories

Some of the clearest evidence for non-classical category structure comes from the acquisition of grammatical categories. Roger Brown (1973: 233) observed that 'the productive acquisition of a syntactic construction seldom at first entails using it over the full semantic range to which it applies'. Amongst the examples he gives, two have to do with categories already studied in earlier chapters, namely the past tense and the possessive.

In Section 8.2 I proposed a family resemblance structure for the meanings of the past tense; the central sense involved reference to past time, while the counterfactual and pragmatic softening senses had a more peripheral status. As one would expect, it is the hypothesized central sense which first emerges in child language; indeed, according to Brown, counterfactual past tenses do not occur at all until a comparatively late stage of development, namely from the age of about six. (Brown gives no data on the use of the past tense as a pragmatic softener.) Brown's data, however, not only lend support to our proposed family resemblance structure of the category, they also suggest that our original account of the past tense needs to be considerably refined. Brown noted that the first instances of the past tense refer exclusively to the immediately preceding past; only later does the child extend the meaning of the past tense to include the more distant past. Secondly, the past tense is not initially applied across the board to all the verbs in the child's lexicon. Earliest uses are restricted to items like *fall*, *drop*, *slip*, *crash*, *break*,[1] which designate highly punctual events; furthermore, the events involve a highly salient change in state—usually a change for the worse—for one of their participants, i.e. for the thing or person that falls, drops, slips, is broken, etc. Only later does the child extend the past tense to verbs denoting non-punctual events and non-visible mental states, like *see*, *watch*, *know*, etc. It seems, then, that the central meaning of the past tense is not simply pastness with reference to the moment of speaking, as suggested in Chapter 8. The central meaning is much more specific, namely 'completion in the immediate past of a punctual event, the consequences of which are perceptually salient at the moment of speaking'.

---

[1] At issue here is not the child's mastery of the appropriate morphological marking of the past tense, but merely the past tense use of the verbs, irrespective of the morphological correctness (by adult standards) of the child's forms.

Brown's other example concerns the possessive. We saw in Section 11.2 that the genitive construction can denote many different kinds of semantic relation between a 'possessor' and a 'possessed', and proposed, as the central member of the category, a relationship based on a common law notion of property. Brown notes that in the overwhelming majority of genitive constructions in early speech— examples include *Daddy chair*, *Eve seat*,[2] etc.—the possessor noun of the construction serves as a kind of modifier, which enables the speaker to identify an object in terms of either a long term or a more transitory relation to a human being. These uses, according to Brown, reflect 'primitive local notions of property and territoriality', which give the possessor 'prior rights' of access to the possessed (1973: 233). Significantly, such uses of the possessive in early speech far outweigh cases like *Daddy nose*, where the genitive is used to denote a whole– part relationship.

Many other cases of initial underextension of grammatical and morphological categories could be cited. To take another example relevant to our earlier discussion (cf. Section 8.1): Bates and Rankin (1979) found that, at age three, Italian children were making extensive use of diminutive and augmentative suffixes. Mostly, the suffixes were being used in their central senses, i.e. they referred only to the physical size of concrete objects. The full range of affective meanings, so characteristic of the adult language, had yet to be acquired. Of particular interest is the acquisition of the transitive construction. Slobin (1981) speculated that, in the early experience of the child, certain constellations of circumstances in the world come to acquire the status of prototypical transitive events. Highly transitive events then get mapped on to the transitive sentence construction, realized in English by means of word order (subject–verb–object) or, in some other languages, by case marking, usually also in association with word order preferences (nominative–verb–accusative). The corre- spondence between the event and the construction is established by age two.

The transitive construction emerges out of earlier two-word combinations, i.e. agent-action and action-object, which themselves embody components of prototypical transitivity. Evidence for the correctness of Slobin's thesis comes from the fact that transitive sentences involving non-punctual events and non-perceptible mental

---

[2] See n. 1 above. At issue is not the child's acquisition of the genitive morphology, but the construal of two nouns in a possessive relationship.

states occur later than examples of prototypical transitivity. Slobin cites the case of a Russian child who first applied accusative case marking only to the direct objects of action verbs (*put*, *throw*, *give*), only later marking for case the objects of mental experience verbs (*read*, *see*, *know*). It is also significant for Slobin's thesis that the child's productive mastery of active transitive sentences predates by a long period the first passive sentences; furthermore, the first passive sentences to be comprehended are those which involve reversals of prototypical transitivity. The salience of prototypical transitivity is also suggested by the fact already noted, that the past tense is first applied to the kinds of verbs which are likely to participate in highly transitive sentences.

Slobin suggests that the full range of transitive sentences is acquired through a process of 'metaphorical and semantic extension' from the prototype. The process has been discussed by Schlesinger (1981). Schlesinger proposes that gradually instruments and experiencers, as well as agents, come to be used as subjects of transitive sentences, the instruments and experiencers thereby taking on 'the semantic flavour of agency' (1981: 241). In a sense, the instrument also 'performs' an action, analogous to the agent; in a different kind of way, a person directing his attention to a state of affairs is also engaged in an 'action'. In this connection, Schlesinger makes the highly pertinent observation that the semantic role categories of agent, instrument, experiencer, etc. are by no means as clear-cut as most expositions of case grammar (e.g. Fillmore 1968) would have us believe. A mother handing a bottle to the child is clearly an agent performing an action. But what if the mother merely holds the bottle? And what about the bottle holding the milk? There is, in these cases, no clear cut-off point which separates agent-action from a stative relation. Or consider, as another of Schlesinger's examples, the gradience between action-verbs and experience-verbs manifested in the series *Tom writes down/figures out/ guesses/recalls/remembers/knows the date*.

The semantic-based approach to grammatical categories has been strongly criticized by Maratsos, in various publications (e.g. Maratsos and Chalkley 1980). Maratsos points to the impossibility of a purely semantic definition of lexical and grammatical categories like NOUN, VERB, ADJECTIVE, SUBJECT, etc. *(To) please, (to) like*, and *(to be) fond (of)* are roughly equivalent, semantically. Yet *fond* is an adjective, *please* and *like* are verbs; *like* takes as its subject the experiencer, while with *please* the experiencer appears as the direct object. If the child were to

build up his categories on the basis of a common semantic denominator, Maratsos argues, one would expect, initially at least, a large
number of form class errors, i.e. the semantic similarity of *like* and
fond would give rise to errors of the kind **He fonds her*, on analogy
with *He likes her*. Such errors are vanishingly rare. Maratsos and
Chalkley also discuss (and reject) a prototype view of grammatical
categories, according to which 'people both analyse and permanently
represent major categories ... according to the statistically modal or
"core" semantic analysis of their members' (1980: 177). The facts of
semantic overlap between categories, however, preclude such an
approach:

[T]he term *careful* functions grammatically as an adjective but semantically it
very closely resembles the 'best' examples of an action term prototype (i.e.,
physical contact can be involved, an animate entity intentionally controls the
activity; it can refer to a brief event). There exists, simply, no semantic
boundary which can adequately deal with the profligate crossover of meanings
of terms of different syntactic categories. Thus, the hypothesized semantic-
based prototype should result in errors such as incorrectly labeling ... *careful*
as a 'good' action term; and lead to errors of use like ... **He carefuls the toy*. If
one uses only semantic criteria (even in the form of a prototype) for determining how to cluster grammatical privileges to terms, one would never be able to
achieve adult linguistic competence. (Maratsos and Chalkley 1980: 178)

Maratsos thus claims that grammatical categories need to be
defined in purely formal terms; an item is assimilated to the category
VERB, not because of what it means, but simply in virtue of the fact that
it can be inflected for past tense and for subject agreement. That even
very young children are able to manipulate formal categories—that
they in fact latch on to formal properties earlier than semantic
commonalities—is shown by the acquisition of gender. In languages
like French and Hebrew, every noun is obligatorily categorized as
masculine or feminine, and every pronoun must be marked according
to the gender of its antecedent; other languages, like German and
Russian, have a three-way gender system (masculine, feminine, and
neuter). As far as inanimate nouns are concerned, assignment of
gender is arbitrary; in these cases, gender categories may be seen as
nothing other than highly correlated distributional patterns, with no
semantic base. In German, being of masculine gender simply means
that when a noun is nominative singular, it is preceded by the *der*-form
of the definite article, when accusative singular by the *den*-form, and
so on. Semantic motivation does, however, enter into the gender of

nouns and pronouns referring to humans; here gender does correlate in the vast majority of cases with sex. If the child learner were looking for semantic commonalities in grammatical categories, one would expect that gender assignment would first manifest itself for human nouns and pronouns, gender assignment for non-human nouns being at first random and error-prone. The opposite, however, seems to occur (cf. Levy 1983). Children master arbitrary gender assignment of nouns during their second year of life, well before they learn to select the appropriate sex-marked personal pronouns.

There are several flaws in Maratsos's argumentation. Firstly, Maratsos accepts without question traditional views on the semantic motivation (or the lack of it) of grammatical categories. In the case of German, at least, the received view that the gender of non-animate nouns is arbitrary has been questioned by Zubin and Köpcke (1981, 1986), while Langacker's (1987) more abstract characterization of NOUN, VERB, etc. goes a long way towards capturing the common essence of the categories. A related fact is that although *like, please*, and *fond* might be similar in meaning, they are not identical, and do structure a perceived state of affairs in slightly different ways. Secondly, there is nothing in the prototype approach to categories which demands that only semantic criteria be employed for the characterization of the prototype; I argued extensively in Chapters 10 and 11 that the prototypes of grammatical categories need to be specified in terms of both semantic and formal criteria. Furthermore, purely formal properties considered by themselves are not, in general, consistent with all or nothing membership in grammatical categories; in this respect, gender categories (where membership *is* a clear matter of either–or) are rather untypical of grammatical categories as a whole. A final point is that the role of semantic criteria needs to be seen in the context of the child's more general cognitive development. It is to this issue that we now turn.

13.3 Conceptual development

Cognitive linguistics takes a broad, encyclopaedic view of meaning. Axiomatic for the cognitive paradigm is the thesis that the meaning of any linguistic form can only be characterized relative to an appropriate cognitive domain, or set of domains (see Chapter 5). Domains encapsulate knowledge and beliefs about the world, and may vary in complexity from a basic apperception of time and oriented space, through to highly sophisticated scientific theories about the nature of matter. Given the role of domain-based knowledge in the characterization of meanings, it is clear that the child's grasp of the semantic import of a category distinction is necessarily dependent on a prior understanding of the domain against which the semantic distinction is to be drawn. It may well be the case that in languages with gender systems the overwhelming majority of human nouns are assigned non-arbitrarily to gender classes on the basis of the sex of their referents. Notions such as male and female, however, are anything but semantic primitives; they are, as Susan Carey (1982: 368) puts it, highly 'theory-laden' concepts. Initially, no doubt, the child can rely on perceptual differences between men and women—things like hair length, voice pitch, and kind of clothing worn. However, an adequate understanding of these notions presupposes, if not a fully articulated biological theory, at least a fairly sophisticated folk theory of sex differences and sex roles. The incorporation of sex differences into the specification of linguistic categories must necessarily await the development of the appropriate domain-based knowledge. Such a development, it seems, does not take place before age three (see Levy 1983).

Arguably, one of the most fruitful points of interaction between the cognitive paradigm and child language research is likely to concern the relationship of the child's language to the current state of his cognitive development. Many of the young child's lexical errors *vis-à-vis* the adult language would seem to be traceable to the non-availability of the relevant cognitive domains. Consider, for example, the frequent misuse in early speech of *old*; applied to human beings, the word is often used as if it were synonymous with *big*. Now, *old* can only be adequately characterized against the domain of the life cycle. Until the notion of the life cycle is grasped, there can be no basis for knowing what it means to say that one person is old, or getting old, or that another is not old. The young child merely associates being old with one of the perceptual attributes of old people, namely their fully grown size. Young children similarly fail to understand what it means to say that one person is the brother or sister of someone else. In early speech, before the notions of birth and parenting have been understood, *brother* and *sister* tend to be used as equivalents of *boy* and *girl* (Carey 1982: 373 f.).

The role of domain-based encyclopaedic knowledge in language mastery goes much deeper than these few lexical examples might suggest. Let us look in more detail at the notion of prototypical transitivity. A (usually human) agent performs some action which affects a patient; a boy, for instance, kicks a ball. The event is construed as a unitary, punctual happening. Yet the event of kicking a ball may be arbitrarily decomposed into any number of subevents: balancing one's weight on one leg, raising the other leg from the ground, flexing the leg at the knee, and so on. Conversely, the action of kicking a ball may itself be seen as a component part of a larger event, say a ball game. Prototypical transitivity, then, presupposes a conceptualization of events at a certain level of categorization, rather than at subordinate or superordinate levels. The same applies to the participants in a transitive event. One may focus attention on any arbitrary part of the agent or patient, and agent and patient may themselves be seen as parts of larger conglomerations of entities. Yet agent and patient are not conceptualized as conglomerations of parts, nor as parts of larger configurations, they are conceptualized as gestalts, functioning within a unitary event. How does the child know, when learning the word *kick*, that the word refers to the punctual act of kicking, and not to some arbitrary component of the event? How does he know that *fall* encompasses the total trajectory followed by a falling object, such that a ball falling from a table on to the floor instantiates only one instance of falling, and not, say, two or more successive instances? And on what basis does he infer that a ball rolling away after it has fallen instantiates a separate, though temporally contiguous event? Similarly with nouns. On hearing the word *ball* in conjunction with the presence of the referent, how does the child correctly conclude that the meaning of the word has to do with the whole entity, and not with a portion of its curved surface?

We are touching here on Quine's celebrated thesis of the 'indeterminacy of translation' (see e.g. Quine 1960: 51ff.). Quine posed the problem in terms of a field linguist attempting to break into the semantic system of a totally alien language. On hearing the native speaker of the language utter the word *gavagai* as he points to a rabbit running across his path, the linguist would no doubt infer that *gavagai* means "rabbit". But on what basis? Could not *gavagai* mean "rabbit parts attached to each other", or "temporally transient instance of rabbithood"? These meanings would be equally consistent with the use of the word *gavagai* in the presence of a rabbit. In fact, there would be no fully reliable basis whatsoever for preferring the one translation of the word over another. And yet we feel, intuitively, that "rabbit" is the only plausible meaning; the other translations are simply bizarre.

Quine's problem repeats itself whenever a young child infers the meaning of a term from its use in a specific context. The very fact that learners do not make bizarre inferences of the kind discussed by Quine strongly suggests that learners are cognitively biased towards certain conceptualizations of entities, and not towards other conceptualizations which, from a logical point of view, would be equally plausible. Pre-eminent, in this connection, seems to be the deeply engrained notion of what it means for something to be a physical object. Physical objects stand out as gestalts against their surroundings; they can be handled and can be moved independently of their environment; they possess a characteristic shape and texture. Even though they are typically made up of parts, they are not seen as configurations of parts, but as wholes, with a fairly homogeneous internal constitution. Even though their appearance might change relative to the location of a viewer, and the objects might even disappear for a time from the viewer's field of vision, they are nevertheless thought of as enduring, unchanged, over time. Pulman (1983: 56ff.), drawing on the relevant developmental research, points out that the notion of physical object as something permanent, detachable, observable, and feelable is already present in the child by age one. It is, *pace* Quine, a basic element of a person's folk ontology. It is also, we may suppose, the locus for the emergence of the notions of event. Crucially, events involve a change in state of a physical object. Such changes in state are likewise conceptualized as unitary, and fairly homogeneous in their internal constitution, being bounded on either side by the relative stability of the object, or by sudden discontinuities in the manner of change. Thus not any randomly segmented change can qualify as an event: a ball falling from a table on to the floor is seen as one event, the rolling away of the ball after it has fallen is seen as a second event.

The child's early prototypes of physical object and event are part of that encyclopaedic knowledge of the world which is a precondition for the understanding of word meanings, and for the emergence of proto-typical transitivity as a cognitive unit. In the course of the child's development, these notions will need to be extended from the early proto-type. The category of physical object, for example, will have to be extended so as to include, at the very least, parts of wholes ('wing', 'leg', 'handle', etc.), invisible and non-manipulable substances ('air', 'fog'), things characterized against domains other than three-dimensional space (noises, emotions, thoughts), institutional things (countries, national frontiers), as well as things consisting of non-contiguous parts ('fence', 'archipelago'). Likewise, the notion of event will need to be extended from the prototype, so as to include activities, mental states, and stative relations.

The interplay between the child's emerging knowledge of the world and his developing linguistic skills may be illustrated by a further example, namely the expression of spatial relations. In a well-known paper, Clark (1973*a*) studied the understanding of the static spatial concepts "in", "on", and "under" in children aged 1;6 to 6;11. The children were asked to place a given object (the trajector, or TR; cf. Section 6.3) in a relation of in, on, or under with respect to another object, the landmark (LM). It was found that if the LM could function as a container, the youngest children invariably placed the TR inside the LM, irrespective of the instructions given to them. If the LM did not have a clearly defined inside, the TR was placed on its upper horizontal surface, again irrespective of the experimenter's instructions. Only rarely did the children position the TR under the LM, even when explicitly asked to do so. This suggests that below age three (by which time they seem to have worked out the different meanings of *in*, *on*, and *under*) children have very clear ideas about where objects 'belong'. The relationship of inclusion is the most salient; if inclusion is not possible, because of the shape of the LM, the positioning of a TR on top of the LM is preferred. A further experiment reported in Clark (1973*a*) required the child to position a TR with respect to a LM in imitation of a model set up by the experimenter. The children's responses again suggested the salience of in- and on-relationships. A configuration consisting of a small toy placed beside an upright glass was imitated by the toy being placed inside the glass; the child would place the toy on top of a block when imitating a configuration consisting of the toy placed beside the block. A further interesting finding was that children tended to imitate a configuration of proximity by positioning the TR in contact with the LM. Clark and Clark (1976: 504) also note certain preferences with regard to the understanding of dynamic spatial relationships. Just as relationships of in and on are more salient to the two-year-olds than a relationship of under, so three-year-olds seem to have clear notions of how objects should move with respect to each other. Irrespective of whether the instructions were to move an object towards or away from the LM, the children invariably moved the TR towards the LM.

These experimental findings may be put alongside Slobin's (1985) observation that in languages where place and goal are encoded differently (such as German, Slavonic, and Turkish), it is a common error for young children to use place marking for both relationships, while the source relationship, although acquired later, is never conflated with place or goal. If a young child knows that one object exists in a spatial relationship to another object, he initially assumes that either the relationship is static, or, if it is dynamic, that it will continue until a static relationship of contact is achieved. Thus goal comes to be conflated with place, both relationships being encoded by the same linguistic form, while the source relationship remains cognitively and linguistically distinct. It is significant that this state of affairs, typical for the acquisition of German, Slavonic, and Turkish, persists to some extent in adult English. As noted in Section 7.1, many place prepositions in English can also express a goal relationship, while the polysemy of place and source is comparatively rare.

13.4 Word meanings

I have argued that the acquisition of grammatical categories provides strong evidence for the correctness of a prototype view. The relevant point was that grammatical categories seem to be restricted, initially, to a small range of central instances, the category gradually being extended to encompass the full range of adult uses. With word meanings the situation is somewhat different. Superficially, at least, the well-known phenomenon of semantic overextension in very early speech would seem to support the classical theory, according to which word meanings are built up feature by feature. For instance, the fact that *doggie* is typically used by the young child to refer, not only to dogs but to all small four-legged animals, would suggest that the child's feature specification for the word is still incomplete, that his word roughly corresponds, in fact, to the superordinate term *animal* in adult language. Similarly, that *Daddy* is used not only of the child's father but of all adult males might suggest that the child is operating with the incomplete feature specification [ADULT] and [MALE], the feature [PARENT OF] still needing to be added.

The classical view predicts that the first categories to be learnt by the child will be those specified by a minimum number of features. These categories will, perforce, be categories at a very high level of abstraction, like PHYSICAL OBJECT, ANIMAL, etc. There is strong evidence, however, that abstract categories emerge relatively late in the child's development, well after the acquisition of categories at the basic level (Brown 1958). The matter was investigated by Rosch *et al.* (1976). Children were presented with groups of three pictures, and asked to say in each case which pair of pictures went together. In some of the picture triads, pictures could be paired with regard to common membership in a basic level category (e.g. types of car), while in other triads only categorization at a superordinate level (e.g. types of vehicle) was possible. The youngest of the children studied (three-year-olds) were able to sort into basic level categories virtually without error. When pairing at superordinate level, however, three-year-olds scored only 55 per cent correct; by age four, though, performance on superordinate sorting had risen to 96 per cent correct. Interestingly, the youngest subjects could sort correctly at the basic level even though they might not be able to name the depicted objects, or to give other reasons for their categorizations.

The salience of basic level categories, even in very young children, is fully in accord with Rosch's hypothesis that basic level categories maximize the perceptual, functional, and other attributes of the things which occur in the world (Section 3.3). The delayed development of superordinate categories, on the other hand, contrasts strikingly with the course of development predicted by the classical theory. On the classical theory, the feature specification of a higher-order category is included in the feature specification of each subordinate category. The category ANIMAL is defined by means of the feature [ANIMAL], and kinds of animals, e.g. DOG and CAT, are specified by the feature [ANIMAL] in association with further distinguishing features, like [CANINE], [FELINE]. Featurally, the basic level categories are more complex than the superordinate category. On the assumption that feature specifications are acquired one by one, we would expect—indeed, the assumption requires—that superordinate categories are learnt before subordinate ones.

The delayed acquisition of higher-order categories needs to be seen in the context of the young child's inability to abstract from a range of diverse entities those properties which the entities have in common. (It is the relatively late emergence of this ability which supports my earlier contention—see Section 4.2—that categorization by schema, as postulated by Langacker, occurs subsequent to a prior categorization by prototype.) Consider in this connection Piaget's well-known 'bead-problem' (Piaget 1947: 133). Children are shown a box containing a number of wooden beads. Some of the beads are white, while most of them are brown. In response to the question 'Which are there most of, brown beads or wooden beads?', children below the age of about seven almost invariably respond that there are more brown beads. For children who give this response, the brown beads and the white beads constitute two mutually exclusive classes. Only at a comparatively late stage of development (i.e. from seven upwards) does the ability emerge to abstract from these two classes a common schema, characterized by the attribute which the classes have in common, i.e. [wooden]. In view of these considerations, it seems more plausible that the young child's failure to use words like *Daddy* and *doggie* in their restricted adult sense reflects semantic extensions from a prototype, ones not sanctioned by adult usage, rather than categorization at a more abstract, featurally more impoverished level.

Detailed, longitudinal studies of children's early vocabulary development (e.g. Bowerman 1978, Rescorla 1980) seem to bear out this hypothesis. These studies suggest, firstly, that dramatic overextension *vis-à-vis* the adult system is by no means typical of all, or even the majority of the words in the child's early vocabulary. In fact, the words most likely to be overextended are the dozen or so which are acquired very early. Rescorla's data for these words (collected in the main by parents in naturalistic settings) allowed a number of temporal patterns to be distinguished. In some cases, a word was used for a gradually narrowing range of referents. A more common pattern was for a word to be extended first in one direction, then in another, with varying degrees of temporal overlap between successive extensions. Consider the data for *Daddy*. Overextensions for one child took the following sequence: the child's mother (age 1;1–1;2), other fathers (1;3–1;4), her father's possessions (1;4–1;5), and pictures of men and animal fathers (1;5–1;6). A rather more complex example concerns the word *clock*:

One child used the word *clock* first for an unfamiliar picture of a cuckoo clock and immediately after for his parents' alarm clock; he then extended the word within a month to many clocks and clock pictures, watches and watch pictures, meters, dials, and timers of various sorts, bracelets, a buzzing radio and telephone, and a chevron-shaped medallion on his dishwasher; finally he limited the word to clocks and watches, saying *clock-buzz* for the alarm clock and *clock-ticktock* for watches. (Rescorla 1980: 331–2)

Initially, *clock* was used to refer only to clocks, more specifically, a buzzing alarm clock (presumably, the buzzing alarm clock formed the centre of the child's representation of the category). Things were then assimilated to the category on the basis of shared attributes with the prototype—watches on account of a common function, a buzzing radio and the telephone on account of the sound they made, dials and the dishwasher medallion on account of their circular shape. The inclusion of bracelets in the category was presumably mediated by initial extension to watches. The child's category thus exhibits the same kind of internal structure as the complex adult categories studied in Chapters 6 and 8. Of course, the child's clock-category does not enjoy conventionalized status in the English language (or presumably in any other adult language). Not infrequently, however, a child's apparently idiosyncratic extensions in his mother tongue do happen to correspond with conventionalized polysemy in other languages. A typical semantic extension amongst English-speaking children is the use of *open* and *close* in the senses "switch on/off" and "turn on/off"; that is to say, the words refer to the operation of electric lights, television sets, and water taps, as well as to the opening and closing of doors and windows (Bowerman 1978). These metaphorical senses (the schemas of gaining and closing off access to a three-dimensional container are transferred from the spatial domain to the domains of the functioning of electrical and water devices) are not conventionalized in adult English. The translation equivalents of *open* and *close* in some other languages, e.g. French, Italian, and Russian, do however include "switch on/off" and "turn on/off" amongst their conventionalized senses.

In the discussion of natural phonology in Chapter 12, I referred to the thesis that acquiring the phonology of a language involves the suppression of certain natural phonological processes and the exploitation of others. There is perhaps a parallel to be drawn with the acquisition of semantic categories. The example of "open" and "close" suggests that the acquisition of adult word meanings might consist, not so much in the child learning to make a set of semantic extensions from a prototype, but rather in the restraining of natural processes of category extension, and the channelling of these in accordance with adult norms. By the same token, the creative extension of a category in adult speech, e.g. by novel metaphor, may be seen as a regression to an earlier stage of language development, where word meanings are fluid, and subject to uninhibited and idiosyncratic extensions in all directions. The emergence of adult categories is thus testimony to the dialectic of convention and motivation that has been implicit throughout the course of this study. The semantic categories of adult language are conventionalized, and rarely stand in one-to-one correspondence to the categories of other languages. Yet the categories are not arbitrary, but are structured along natural principles of category formation.

14

Recent Developments (1995)

SINCE this book was first published, in 1989, prototype categorization has received a fair amount of attention in the linguistic literature. There is, now, the monograph of Kleiber (1990), the review article of MacLaury (1991), a special issue of the journal *Linguistics* (Vol. 27(4), 1989) on the theme 'Prospects and problems of prototype theory', and scheduled for 1995 is a special issue of *Rivista di Linguistica*. Collected volumes edited by Corrigan *et al.* (1989), Tsohatzidis (1990), and Geiger and Rudzka-Ostyn (1993) contain many chapters of immediate relevance. Mention should also be made of the publication, in 1991, of the second volume of Langacker's *Foundations of Cognitive Grammar*. This applies the theoretical principles developed in Langacker (1987) to a wide range of phenomena, in English and other languages, and tackles, alongside much else, such fundamental issues as the categories of noun and noun phrase, tense and modality, transitivity and case relations, and, in a final chapter, situates the goals and methods of 'cognitive grammar' within the current theoretical landscape. Readers interested in pursuing this approach to language might also wish to consult the contributions to the journal *Cognitive Linguistics*, founded in 1990, as well as the volumes of the book series 'Cognitive Linguistic Research', published by Mouton de Gruyter, also from 1990.

In this chapter, written for the second edition of *Linguistic Categorization*, I want to draw attention to more recent discussions of the issues raised in the book, especially as these pertain to word meanings. My presentation will, of necessity, be selective, and focus on issues that I personally find interesting and/or important. The reader needs to be aware, however, that there are many trends in current linguistics, trends which one might qualify as 'formalistic' and which in one way or another are heirs to the structuralism of the early decades of the century, which remain sceptical, not to say hostile, to the approach developed in this book. Substantive criticism has been raised by a group of German scholars, all strongly influenced by the work of Manfred Bierwisch, to which I return in later sections of this chapter.

14.1 Overview of prototypicality

It has been aptly said (Geeraerts 1989: 592) that the very notion of prototypicality is itself a prototype concept. This is not, after all, too surprising. If, as argued in this book, so many of the categories in the linguist's theoretical arsenal—categories such as the word classes, and notions such as 'grammaticality', 'transitivity', and the like—exhibit prototype structure, it would be odd indeed if prototypicality should turn out to be classically definable.

The situation is due, in part at least, to the fact that the term proto-type was initially applied to a very restricted set of data, and then was gradually extended to encompass a range of rather different, though related, kinds of phenomena. In the process, the term prototype category has come to have a range of applications which stand more in a family resemblance relation, than exhibiting a common set of defining properties.

The primary use of the term prototype in the past was in connection with the 'focal reference' of colour terms, and the 'best examples' of certain natural and cultural kind terms, such as *bird* and *vehicle*. As documented in the earlier chapters of this book, the work of Berlin and Kay (in the domain of colour), and Eleanor Rosch (initially in the domain of colour, subsequently in connection with natural and cultural kinds) was crucial to the empirical validation of the notion. However, even here, the notion of prototype category is not a perfectly homogeneous construct. Although for both colour and kind terms we can identify 'best examples' of the categories in question, and, more generally, can distinguish various degrees of representativity in the categories, degree of representativity does not always correlate with fuzziness of category boundaries. In the case of colour, it is evident that adjacent categories may merge into each other, with some colour samples having a somewhat indeterminate or ambiguous status between categories. With cultural, and especially natural kind terms, on the other hand, boundaries are often rather clearly demarcated. Kiwis, ostriches, penguins, and the like may not be particularly good examples of the bird category, but they are birds (100% birds!), none-theless, not birds 'to a certain degree'. On the other hand, bats and flying insects, although they may resemble birds in some respects, are definitely not birds at all. Neither are the natural and cultural kinds exactly comparable with respect to the possibility of stating a set of necessary and sufficient conditions for membership in the categories. Arguably, *toys* may be characterized in terms of the essential (and sufficient?) property [something that a child can play with] (which is not to deny that some toys may be more representative than others); such a possibility is not available (at least, not on the folk understanding of the category) with a natural kind like *bird*.

From these beginnings, the notion of prototype category was extended to cover many different kinds of phenomena. One of my aims in this book was to show that the basic insight of prototypes, originally worked out in the domain of colour, might be insightfully applied to a great many aspects of natural language, most obviously to various issues in semantics (especially lexical semantics), but also to matters of syntax, phonology, and sociolinguistics. In fact, the idea that such notions as 'agent', 'transitivity', 'subject', and so on are to be understood in terms of 'good examples' is rather well established in many quarters. Indeed, it seems safe to say that *any* theoretical construct (in whatever domain of enquiry, not just linguistics) that is characterized by a set of not necessarily correlated properties will be open to prototype effects, in that some manifestations of the construct will exhibit a good many of the characteristic properties, whereas other putative manifestations will exhibit significantly fewer. In some cases, even, it might actually be a matter of very fine judgement whether a particular instance does, or does not, instantiate the category in question.

A nice example from the recent linguistic literature concerns the notion of 'syntactic head'. The notion of head is fundamental to just about all syntactic theories, whether these be phrase-structure theories in the X-bar tradition, dependency theories, or indeed Langacker's cognitive grammar (Langacker 1991: 6). Closely tied up with the notion of head are the related notions of complement and modifier. In *the cat on the mat*, we would say that the preposition *on* heads the prepositional phrase *on the mat*, with *the mat* as complement of *on*, whilst the noun *cat* heads the nominal phrase *cat on the mat*, with *on the mat* a modifier of *cat*.

In a very real sense, the identification of heads, complements and modifiers, for any given expression, will fall out from the specifics of a given syntactic theory. Matters become somewhat problematic, though, when different theories come up with radically different analyses! A notorious example concerns the proper analysis of nominal phrases. In traditional phrase-structure theories (and on this, 'traditional' grammar would no doubt concur), a determiner-plus-noun expression, of the kind *the cat*, is unproblematically a noun phrase, headed by the noun *cat*, with the article as 'specifier'. Following Abney (1987), more recent versions of X-bar theory construe the expression very differently, namely as a determiner phrase, DP, headed by the determiner *the*, with *cat* as its NP complement. Linguists working within other theoretical frameworks, for example Hudson (1984: 90–2) and Hewson (1991), have independently come up with the 'determiner as head' analysis. On the other hand, Giorgi and Longobardi (1991), working within a Government and Binding framework, still adhere to the traditional analysis. Van Langendonck (1994) also argues for the traditional view of the noun as head.

The arguments for headhood within different theories are complex, and would take us beyond the scope of the present discussion; the interested reader is referred to the texts cited in this and the preceding paragraph. Suffice it to say that the matter becomes especially delicate when one tries to decide between diametrically opposed analyses on the basis of a more general consideration of what 'heads', 'complements', etc. actually *are*, independently, as it were, of any specific theory. Such attempts generally involve setting up a list of typical properties of heads, established on the basis of intuitively clear cases, and which are to be invoked to decide the more problematic or controversial cases. This, for example, was the procedure of Zwicky (1985*b*), Hudson (1987), and, more recently, Zwicky (1993). Nevertheless, even with the battery of tests that these texts provide (it should be noted, also, that Hudson's and Zwicky's criteria by no means coincide), there still remains a residue of ambiguous cases, that is, phrases, none of whose constituents turns out to be a very good example of a head, and where it even seems impossible to decide conclusively which constituent actually is the head. An example of just such a situation is documented by Corbett (1993), in his close analysis of number phrases in Russian. The trouble is, most syntactic theories are predicated on clearly definable categories. It is anything but obvious how phrase-structure grammars could handle a situation in which the headedness of a phrase is actually unclear. In Taylor (1995*a*), discussing another example of syntactic fuzziness, I suggest that the notion of 'syntactic construction'—itself understood as a prototype category (see Section 11.1)—might be well suited to handling such cases.

As documented especially in Chapter 6, the notion of prototype has proved especially useful in studies of word meaning. In particular, the prototype idea was extended to encompass aspects of lexical polysemy, whereby the various senses of a word may be related to a putative 'central' or basic sense (that is, 'prototype', in a derived sense of the word). In this book, I was careful to distinguish between 'prototype categories', narrowly construed, and 'family resemblance categories', the latter corresponding to Lakoff's (1987) 'radial categories'. A principal difference is that, as already hinted, a radial category comprises a number of distinct senses of a linguistic unit, whilst prototype categories in the narrow sense are monosemous. Although *bird* may refer to different species of creature, we would not for this reason want to identify a range of distinct senses of *bird*. On the other hand, prepositions such as *over* and *round* may designate a number of different kinds of spatial relation, and in these cases we would want to identify a number of distinct senses of these words, related in a radial category.

Radial categories—and indeed the very basis for their identification, namely, polysemy—raise a number of complex and difficult issues, to be addressed in due course. In the meantime, I want to draw attention to some recent work—in particular, the important study by Geeraerts *et al.* (1994)—which has a bearing on the notion of prototype category in the earlier, narrower sense of the term, that is, in relation to words which one would unquestionably want to regard as monosemous.

14.2 Prototypes and basic level terms

Geeraerts *et al.* (1994) confined their study to a single lexical field, and to a single domain of discourse, namely terms for outer clothing garments as used in a selection of Dutch-language magazines. A distinctive feature of the corpus was that it included only linguistic tokens that could be unambiguously paired with a visual representation of the intended referent. On the basis of its pictorial representation, each referent, after having been assigned to one of several garment types, such as 'trouser-like garment', 'jacket-like garment', and so on, was described in terms of a set of 'features' appropriate to that garment type. Thus, for trouser-like garments, the relevant features included such aspects as length of leg, broadness/tightness of fit, and so on.

This set-up permitted a systematic combination of the semasiological and the onomasiological perspectives. The *semasiological* perspective asks, for a given linguistic expression, what range of entities or situations may be named by it. The *onomasiological* perspective is the converse, and asks, for any given entity or state of affairs, what range of linguistic expressions may be used to denote it. With respect to the clothing corpus, therefore, Geeraerts and his colleagues were able, for any term, to list all the features, and feature combinations, of the garments which this term was used to denote; conversely, for any garment, described in terms of a combination of feature values, they were able to list all the linguistic expressions which were used to refer to it.

One significant outcome of the dual perspective was that it served to confirm the strong interdependence, noted in Section 3.3, between the twin notions of prototype and basic level. The identification of a prototype relies on the semasiological perspective, in that a prototype may be characterized in terms of *semasiological salience*. For terms such as *broek* 'trousers', *jeans*, *legging*, it was possible to list the most frequent features, and feature combinations, of the referents, and so to come up with detailed specifications of the prototypical instances of the categories. The methodology also, of course, made it possible to plot the usage range of a given term outside the prototypical core. The data confirmed that for many (though by no means all) of the terms investigated, the categories could not be adequately delimited from neighbouring categories on the basis of a set of necessary and sufficient features. *Onomasiological salience*, on the other hand, defines the notion of basic level term. A term is basic level to the extent that *this* term, rather than another, is selected with greater frequency to refer to a certain entity. One important aspect of the study, therefore, is that it offers a refinement, and operationalization, of the notion of basic level term.

The study also makes very clear that the semasiological and onomasiological perspectives are not necessarily mirror images of each other. Given that linguistic expression l is typically used to denote entity e, it does not follow that e will typically be denoted by l; nor, given that e is typically denoted by l, does it follow that the typical use of l is to denote e. Exclusive concern with only one of the perspectives could therefore lead to an impoverished, and distorted, account of linguistic meaning.

Most semantic studies have been confined, willy-nilly, to the semasiological perspective. Lexicographers, for example, generally must infer the meaning of a word solely from the linguistic context of its use; there is, in most cases, no chance of pairing each use of a word with an independent account of the word's reference. In an important sense, therefore, lexicography is, and will presumably remain, a predominantly hermeneutic (a subjective, interpretative) activity. Indeed, for many conceptual domains, it is difficult to imagine how the onomasiological approach could be implemented at all. One cannot hold up an exemplar of an emotional state, and ask how this emotional state may be named. The only way of 'holding up' an emotional state is to name it with a linguistic expression such as *anger, rage, annoyance, irritation*, and it would not really make sense to ask people how they would call 'anger'! Other domains could well be amenable to a combination of the two perspectives. One example that comes to mind is the domain of spatial relations, as expressed by prepositions and other resources. In point of fact, most of the numerous studies on prepositional semantics that have appeared over the past decade or so—for some recent additions to the literature, see the edited volumes of Rauh (1991) and Zelinski-Wibbelt (1993)—have adopted the semasiological perspective. Whatever the source of the data—whether introspected, attested, or elicited—researchers have typically relied on their own intuitions, and/or the responses of informants, in order to ascertain the spatial configurations denoted by an expression. The trouble is, there is every reason to suspect that intuitions in this regard may pertain only to the prototypical configurations, and may say little about the full range of referential possibilities. Only an implementation of the onomasiological perspective could give reliable information on this score.

There is one domain, however, in which a combination of the semasiological and the onomasiological has been systematically pursued, namely, colour. (Colour once again turns out to be an 'ideal testing ground'—see p. 2—for semantic theories!) MacLaury, extending the methodology of Berlin and Kay (1969), developed a three-part elicitation procedure for use in the field.[1] In a first part, subjects are required to *name* each of 330 colour chips presented in random sequence; then to *select* on a colour chart the best example of each of the colour terms they had earlier proffered; and finally to *map* each of their colour terms on the colour chart, by indicating which colours on the chart could be named by the respective terms. One finding was that naming and mapping ranges more often than not do not coincide; that colour

---

[1] For a succinct exposition, see MacLaury (1987); for more comprehensive accounts of the methodology, and for the wider significance of the findings for theories of categorization, see MacLaury (1995*a*, 1995*b*).

sample *c* is named by colour term *t* does not entail that *t* will be mapped so as to include *c* ... and vice versa.[2] Furthermore, the combination of the naming and mapping procedures (which implement the onomasiological and semasiological approaches, respectively) enabled MacLaury to identify with considerable precision a number of special semantic relations holding between neighbouring terms. One such relation is the one called by MacLaury the relation of 'coextension'. The characteristics of coextension are, first, that on the naming task, two colour terms appear to be in free variation, that is, they appear to be synonyms. However, the focal reference of the two terms is not identical, as might be expected if the two terms were true synonyms; furthermore, the mapping of one of the two terms is more restricted, being 'skewed' towards one side of the mapping range of the other term. As far as I am aware, the relation of coextension, as characterized by MacLaury, has not been documented elsewhere (even under a different name) in the semantic literature. It is interesting to speculate, therefore, whether the relation of coextension may not have more general significance outside the domain of colour, especially with regard to alleged synonyms, or partial synonyms. For an exploratory application of the notion to the domain of spatial terms, see Taylor (1992*b*).

14.3 Polysemy and the two-level approach

The question of polysemy looms large in any study of word meaning, if only because of the ubiquity of the phenomenon. In Chapters 6 and 7 I argued for the relevance of a prototype approach to polysemy. However, the nature of polysemy, the criteria for its identification, and its proper treatment in semantic theory are far from settled. To some extent, the problem lies in the fact that polysemy is a graded notion; inevitably, therefore, demarcation disputes will arise.

It is probable that the overwhelming majority of words in a natural language are polysemous to a greater or lesser degree, in that a word may typically denote different kinds of entities, or different kinds of situation, in different contexts of its use. Or, as some semanticists

---

[2] Another of MacLaury's findings that is worth mentioning concerns the considerable between-speaker variation—even for speakers of the 'same' language—on the various tasks. MacLaury's protocols, in fact, provide convincing evidence of the uniqueness of each person's linguistic knowledge, a matter briefly touched on above, p. 56.

might prefer to put it, a word typically contributes different sets of truth conditions to the complex expressions in which it occurs.

For some words, such as *bank*, *punch*, *port*, and so on, that is, words traditionally regarded as homonymous, the different readings have so little in common that we would not hesitate in associating each of the words with more than one distinct sense. At the other extreme are rather subtle meaning variations, where the case for recognizing distinct senses is much less compelling. Compare *break the window* and *paint the window*, on their normal interpretations. Strictly speaking, *window* does refer to different entities here. In the first case, what is broken, probably, is a glass panel (but not the surrounding frame), in the latter case, what is painted is the surrounding frame (but not the enclosed glass). Other readings are possible, of course. *Break the window* could denote the breaking of the frame plus the glass, *paint the window* could denote the painting of the glass but not the frame! Yet neither *break the window* nor *paint the window* is felt to be *ambiguous* because of these different readings. Rather, the favoured readings seem to emerge from general knowledge of what windows are, and of what is conventionally involved in 'breaking' as opposed to 'painting a window'. In contrast to Lakoff (1987: 416), therefore, who does indeed take the line that the different referential possibilities of *window* are evidence for the polysemy of the word, we might prefer to handle these examples in terms of Cruse's (1986) notion of the 'conceptual modulation' of a unitary meaning of *window*, as suggested in Section 7.1. Langacker (1990) has also addressed this kind of phenomenon. When an entity e is involved in some predication, normally only some aspect of e—the 'active zone'—participates in the relation. Langacker points out that the active zone phenomenon is ubiquitous; only in very rare circumstances do all parts of an entity participate equally in a predication.

One interesting aspect of these examples concerns the issue of semantic compositionality, that is, the question of the computation of the meaning of a complex expression from the meanings of its parts. If we regard *window* as genuinely polysemous, we are able to guarantee the compositionality of *break the window* and *paint the window* by selecting highly specific senses of *window* (and, presumably, highly specific senses of *break* and *paint*, also). On the contextual modulation analysis, however, compositionality will not be guaranteed. The complex expressions will have meanings that are more specific than the compositionally derived meanings. A person intent on preserving strict compositionality might therefore be tempted to favour the polysemy analysis. On the other hand, the absence of full compositionality, as Langacker (1987: 281) has pointed out, is an all-pervasive phenomenon, and recourse to polysemy is unlikely to restore it completely. *The football under the table* (Langacker 1987: 280 f.) would normally be taken to mean that the table was in its canonical standing position, with the football on the ground between its legs. (Again, other, less normal interpretations are conceivable: the table could be upside down, with the football squashed beneath it.) Yet the 'normal' and 'less normal' interpretations are not compositionally derivable. We should scarcely want to say that *table* is associated with a range of polysemes, each designating a different orientation of a table!

I have mentioned the extreme ends of the polysemy continuum: homonymy and contextual modulation. Between these extremes stand a whole range of examples where the different readings of a word may diverge to a greater or lesser extent. But just as the phenomenon of polysemy itself is graded, so too are linguistic treatments of it. Two broad kinds of approach can be distinguished.

One approach happily allows the proliferation of the number of senses of a word, on the ground that different uses refer to different kinds of situation. The other approach attempts to maximally restrict polysemy by bringing as many different uses as possible under a single common representation; senses that cannot be so treated are assigned to homonymous semantic entries.

The first kind of approach was exemplified in Chapter 6, on the example of *over*. There, more than a dozen separate senses of the word were identified. One of these, it was suggested, might plausibly be singled out as 'central' (or, in a somewhat extended sense of the term, as the 'prototype'), with the other senses having the status of extensions from it. Thus arise the 'radial categories', called, in Chapter 6, 'family resemblance categories'. The phenomenon is not peculiar to word meanings. As argued in later chapters of this book, the meanings of such things as inflexional and derivational morphemes, syntactic constructions, even intonation contours may exhibit a radial structure.

The approach is not without its problems. For example, if we allow the multiplication of the senses of a word, where do we stop? Since no two tokens of a word will refer to *exactly* the same situation, there will always be *some* difference between two uses of the same word. But how different do the uses have to be, in order for us to be sure that we are dealing with two distinct polysemes? Where, and on what grounds, do we draw the line between polysemy and contextual modulation? A further aspect is that as the number of senses proliferates, we may lose sight of the essential unity of a lexical-semantic category. On the other hand, for those who wish to restrict polysemy as much as possible, the problem becomes, how to state the meaning of a word with sufficient generality so as to cover the full range of different uses (and, at the same time, with sufficient specificity so as to distinguish that word from its conceptual neighbours). Proponents of general meanings are also under the obligation to account for the full usage range of an item, by spelling out how a unitary, and presumably fairly schematic meaning can come to be instantiated in a range of sometimes very different usage situations.

It would probably be true to say that the weight of tradition (at least in theoretical semantics) favours the single meaning approach. (One recalls the structuralist slogan of 'one form—one meaning'.) Barring obvious cases of homonymy, it is necessary to search for a single meaning for each distinct phonological form. Jakobson's (1936) defence of the one form—one meaning postulate has already been mentioned (p. 142f.). A recent and noteworthy implementation of the principle is Ruhl (1989). Ruhl makes a valiant attempt to bring even such an apparently multi-valued word as the verb (*to*) *bear* under a single abstract definition. On the other hand, those engaged in what one might call practical semantics (for example, lexicographers) have generally had few qualms about listing large numbers of different senses. Indeed, the kinds of highly general meanings advocated by Ruhl would be quite useless in lexicography, in that the dictionary user (a foreign learner, for example) would still need information on the specific range of uses sanctioned by linguistic convention. Thus the COBUILD dictionary lists nineteen different senses of the verb *bear* (not counting phrasal expressions), with no attempt to offer a unifying definition; even for such an apparently unproblematic verb as *open*—although on closer examination the word is by no means so unproblematic (Taylor 1992*a*)—COBUILD has no fewer than twenty-nine separate entries.

In this and the following section, I focus on one specific implementation of the one form—one meaning principle. This is the so-called 'two-level approach', associated especially with the work of Manfred Bierwisch and his disciples. The approach is of interest, not only because it offers an alternative account of the kinds of data that have been handled in prototype accounts, but also because some of its adherents have been openly critical of prototype approaches.

The 'classic' statement (in German) of the two-level approach is Bierwisch (1983); a brief account, in English, is contained in Bierwisch (1981), whilst a more recent presentation may be found in Bierwisch and Schreuder (1992). The approach has enjoyed considerable favour, especially amongst German-speaking linguists, and has been applied mainly, though by no means exclusively, to the study of spatial predicates, that is, prepositions and dimensional adjectives.[3]

The term 'two-level' alludes to a proposed distinction between a linguistic-semantic level of meaning, and an essentially non-linguistic, conceptual level.[4] Exactly how this works will be illustrated in the next section. The basic idea is that the 'semantic form' of a lexical item specifies the purely linguistic meaning of the item, as stored in the mental lexicon; it is this semantic content that the item contributes to the meanings of complex expressions in which it occurs. Semantic form is subject to conceptual interpretation, relative to conceptual knowledge, in the context of the word's use. (The approach, therefore, is firmly grounded in a modular conception of human cognition—see Section 1.4—with linguistic-semantic knowledge being essentially autonomous of conceptual knowledge.) In this way, a lexical item can come to have a range of contextually specified meanings which are not actually part of the linguistic meaning of the word. Consider the following sentence.

(1) John left the University a short time ago

This sentence has two clearly distinct readings. On the one, John moved away from the University premises, on the other, he severed a

[3] The term 'two-level' appears to have been made popular by Lang, cf. the title of Lang (1991). As far as I am aware, Bierwisch himself has not used the term. Studies conducted within the framework of the two-level approach include Herweg (1988), Lang (1991), Wunderlich (1991, 1993), and several contributions to Habel *et al.* (1989), especially Herweg (1989). The most extensive implementation to date of the approach is the formidable Bierwisch and Lang (1987). For a critical appraisal of the two-level approach, see Taylor (1994).

[4] The 'conceptual level' is not to be equated with the illocutionary force of an utterance. Bierwisch (1983: 65) proposes to handle this aspect in terms of a level of interactional meaning. Consider the sentence in (1).

(1) This is the University

The fact that *the University* might be taken to refer to the building rather than to the institution, is, for Bierwisch, a matter of conceptual interpretation of a unitary semantic meaning; that (1) could be used as a request for payment (if spoken, for example, by a taxi driver, on arrival at the client's destination) is a matter of interactional interpretation of a conceptual meaning. Strictly speaking, therefore, we ought to be talking of the 'three-level' approach to meaning, the three levels being the semantic, the conceptual, and the interactional.

relation of association with the University—he graduated, or resigned his position. The two readings involve different readings of each constituent of the sentence. *The University* denotes either the building or the institution; *leave* denotes movement away from a place or the severing of a relation of association; *a short time ago* invokes different time scales: 'not many hours/minutes ago' as opposed to 'not many weeks/months ago'. Even *John* has slightly different readings: a person *qua* mobile physical object versus a person *qua* student or employee. All these differences, Bierwisch maintains, are matters of conceptual interpretation, relative to a conceptual domain (location versus institutional affiliation), of unitary semantic representations.[5]

A central claim of the two-level approach, therefore, is that much of what passes as polysemy, or meaning variation (as treated, for example, in prototype accounts, or as reflected in, say, the COBUILD dictionary), is not in fact a linguistic-semantic phenomenon at all, but reflects alternative conceptual interpretations, relative to context, of unitary semantic representations. As I have already said, adherents of the two-level approach have been explicitly critical of the prototype approach. The substance of the criticism[6] appears to be that prototype theory fails to constrain, in a principled way, the range of possible senses that a lexical item may have; that, consequently, prototype accounts tend to be purely descriptive, rather than explanatory, in that they merely list the various senses, rather than deriving them from general principles; also that the meanings postulated by prototype theorists are unnecessarily rich in detail, in that they contain all manner of conceptual information which, it is claimed, is supplied only in the process of interpretation in context, and which therefore does not belong to the linguistic meaning of a word. In contrast to what Herweg (1988: 106) calls the 'polysemy inflation' promoted by prototype theorists, the two-level approach seeks linguistic-semantic representations which are of maximum generality and economy, leaving to conceptual interpretation the kinds of meaning variation which words generally exhibit in their usage contexts. Thus both Bierwisch (1983: 76) and Wunderlich (1991: 593) subscribe to the 'methodological principle' that one should try to bring as many different senses of a lexical item as possible under a single semantic entry.

[5] See Bierwisch (1981: 348; 1983: 77) and Bierwisch and Schreuder (1992: 31 f.). For an account of these kinds of effects within an encyclopaedist semantics, see Croft (1993).

[6] See, for example, Herweg (1988: 53–8, 1989: 104–6), Lang (1991: 145 f.), Wunderlich (1993: 132).

One scholar whose approach to meaning variation turns out to be very similar to that of Bierwisch is John Searle. Searle (1983: 145 ff.) pointed out that different uses of the verb *open* (*open the door*, *open the book*, *open the wound*, and so on—note that all of these constitute 'literal', that is, non-metaphorical, uses of the word) denote different kinds of activities, and determine different sets of truth conditions. A person who proceeds to 'open the door' in the way in which a surgeon would 'open a wound', that is, by making incisions in it with a scalpel, could not be said to have 'opened the door' at all! (Searle (1980) had argued much the same point on the example of the verb *cut*, observing that you do not 'cut the cake' in the same way as you 'cut the grass', namely, by running the lawnmower over it.) Yet Searle is reluctant to conclude that *open* is polysemous. Such a move could end up with our having to recognize as many different senses of *open* as there are kinds of things that may be opened; since the number of things that may be opened is indefinite, we could end up by having to say that *open* is indefinitely polysemous, and indefinite polysemy Searle (1983: 146) finds 'absurd'. On the contrary, Searle insists that *open* has but a single sense, and makes exactly the same semantic contribution to each expression in which it occurs. Searle squares this position with the phenomenon of meaning variation by appeal to a construct which he calls 'the Background of meaning'. The Background comprises those beliefs, practices, assumptions, and so on that make it possible for a person to interact with the world. Linguistic expressions do not normally designate aspects of the Background; rather, expressions are *interpreted* relative to the Background. In the case of *open*, the different truth conditions for various uses of the verb come about when expressions are interpreted against background knowledge of different practices. To illustrate the point, Searle (1983: 147) cites the expression *Sam opened the Sun*. We are able to fully *understand* this expression, Searle maintains, on the basis of our knowledge of the linguistic-semantic meaning of *open* (and of other elements in the sentence). But we can have no idea at all of what Sam actually *did*, hence we can have no way of verifying the truth of a statement that he 'opened the Sun'. This is because we have no background knowledge of the practice of 'opening the Sun', against which to interpret the expression.

Searle is actually quite vague as to the mechanics of sentence interpretation. (Also, in spite of his insistence that *open* has a unitary semantic meaning, he fails to state what this unitary meaning might be.) Undoubtedly, one achievement of the two-level theorists has been to make explicit proposals in this regard, for a certain range of data, at least.

14.4. Two illustrations: *in* and *round*

The two-level theorists assume semantic representations which decompose a word's meaning into predicate-argument format. The representations contain semantic primitives, whose actual value may be determined only at the conceptual level. The semantic entry thereby specifies 'conditions for the identification of conceptual elements' (Lang 1991: 146). By way of illustration, I would like to consider some two-level accounts of prepositions. I begin with a fairly simple case, which is not, however, without its interest. The following exemplify some uses of the preposition *in*.

(2) (*a*) The water in the vase
    (*b*) The crack in the vase
    (*c*) The flowers in the vase

(3) (*a*) The coin in my hand
    (*b*) The splinter in my hand
    (*c*) The umbrella in my hand

Taking these on their normal interpretations, it is apparent that the (*a*), (*b*), and (*c*) expressions denote three different kinds of spatial arrangement. In (*a*), the one object—the trajector (TR)—is (wholly) located within a hollow internal region defined by the exterior sides of the landmark (LM) object; in (*b*), the TR is located within the material substance of the LM object; whilst in (*c*) the TR is supported, or held in position, by partial containment within the LM.

In spite of these differences, Herweg (1988)—from whom the examples have been adapted—has insisted that the three uses of *in* exemplify the very same semantic sense of the preposition. In common with other two-level theorists, he assumes (4) as the general format for the semantics of a spatial preposition.

(4) $\lambda y \, \lambda x [\text{LOC}[x, \text{REG}[y]] \ldots]$

Roughly: *x* is located in the region of *y*. ('...' in (4) allows for the possibility of some further conditions.) The different prepositions impose different conditions on the specification of REG[y]. For *in*, Herweg proposes (5).

(5) $\lambda y \, \lambda x \, [\text{LOC}[x, \text{PLACE}[y]]]$

That is, *x* is located in a region characterized as the space occupied by *y*.

Observe that this formula states purely geometrical conditions for the *in* relation; there is no hint of 'functional' or 'experiential' aspects, such as containment, holding, or support. The formula also says nothing about the topological properties of the space occupied by *y*, for example, whether the space is the hollow internal region of a container-like object, or whether it is the space occupied by the material substance of an object. These aspects are specified only in the process of conceptual interpretation of the semantic primitives LOC (= Location) and PLACE, by reference to conceptual knowledge of the entities that instantiate the variables *x* and *y*, and of the kinds of relation that may normally hold between these entities. Thus, given conceptual knowledge of what a crack is, *the crack in the vase* (2) (*b*) comes to have a different reading from *the water in the vase* (2) (*a*). The account certainly captures the intuition that the special reading of (2) (*b*) may be due as much to the semantics of *crack* as to the semantics of *in*. Consider also, in this light, the contrast between *the coin in my hand* (3) (*a*) and *the splinter in my hand* (3) (*b*). The contrast appears to be due, in part, to the fact that a 'hand' may be conceptualized in slightly different ways, as a flexible object that can be shaped into a fist, or as an object that can be penetrated. Even so, it is not impossible to imagine that the coin is lodged inside the flesh of my hand, nor that the splinter is held in the hollow of my hand. It was with these effects in mind that I introduced the examples in (2) and (3) by referring to the 'normal interpretations' of the expressions. Adherents of the two-level approach would claim that the 'normality' of an interpretation reflects purely conceptual aspects, not the semantic meanings of the constituent expressions.

Somewhat problematic, for the two-level approach, are the (*c*) examples. In terms of the formula in (5), the TR entity has to be totally included within the LM entity. Clearly, an umbrella can be 'in my hand', without it being the case that the umbrella is totally included within the space defined by 'my hand'. One possibility might be to appeal to some notion of 'pragmatic tolerance', which permits some deviation from the strict requirement of total inclusion. For Wunderlich (1993: 125), 'pragmatic tolerance' smacks too much of prototype theory; appeal to such an 'unrestricted' notion, in order to 'explain everything we are not able to explain otherwise', would be methodologically 'bad'. Moreover, this kind of pragmatic tolerance would conflict with what is claimed to be 'a quite general semantic requirement', namely, the 'homogeneity presupposition of predication' (6).

(6) Homogeneity presupposition: If we predicate P of *x* we assume *x* to be homogeneous with respect to P (Wunderlich 1993: 125)

A statement to the effect that *x* is 'in *y*' entails that *all of x* is in *y*. *The chickens are in the yard* is true, only if *all* the chickens are in the yard. Likewise, *My car is in the garage* is true, only if my car is *completely* in the garage. If the homogeneity requirement is not met, we need some kind of quantifying expression, such as *most, some, partly*, and the like. However, the use of quantifying expressions with the kinds of situations denoted by (2) (*c*) and (3) (*c*) does not result in more fully specified descriptions of the situations. Rather, we get descriptions of other kinds of situations—or expressions which are simply anomalous. *The flowers are partly in the vase* does not mean that only part of each flower is 'in the vase', it means that some of the flowers are in the vase, the others are not in the vase. And *The umbrella is partly in my hand* is simply bizarre. Wunderlich therefore concludes that the homogeneity principle is not being violated in the (*c*) expressions.

Still, the fact remains that in (2) (*c*) not all of each flower is in the vase, and that in (3) (*c*) not all of the umbrella is in my hand! To explain these facts—which some might want to take as a good indication that the (*c*) uses do exemplify a sense of *in* which is distinct from that of the (*a*) and (*b*) uses—Wunderlich (1993: 124f.), developing the discussion in Herweg (1989), appeals to a 'conceptual focusing strategy'. He points out that the special notion of 'holding', or 'support', is brought to bear on the interpretation. This notion is not present in the semantic form (the semantic form contains only geometrical notions, not functional or experiential notions), it is supplied only in the process of conceptual interpretation. Given that a holding or support relation is involved in the (*c*) examples, we conceptually focus only on that part of the TR entity that is involved in the relation. It is this part of the TR that is (completely) 'in' the LM. Consequently, the semantic condition of interiority 'is satisfied literally' (Wunderlich 1993: 125).

The affinity of Wunderlich's notion of 'conceptual focusing' with the Langackerian notion of the 'active zone' will be obvious. (A crucial difference, though, is that for Wunderlich, 'focusing' is a purely conceptual, that is, a non-linguistic, non-semantic phenomenon, whereas for Langacker, active zone phenomena 'go right to heart of critical grammatical issues'.)[7] On a more polemical note, one might ask why Wunderlich should regard the strategy of conceptual focusing as exempt from the kinds of criticism that he levelled at the notion of deviation from a prototype. Given the homogeneity presupposition principle (6) as a strict condition on semantic representations, the focusing strategy (or some similar device) will need to be invoked rather often. Consider (7):

(7) (*a*) My new car got dented in the accident
     (*b*) Johnny fell and cut himself

According to the homogeneity principle, (7) (*a*) would be true only if the total surface of my car ended up dented. But (7) (*a*) could be asserted even if only a tiny dent had been made in some obscure part of the bodywork. Likewise, for (7) (*b*) to be true, it is not necessary for the whole of Johnny's body to be lacerated; a tiny cut on the elbow would suffice. Neither does quantification appear to be indicated in such circumstances. *Johnny fell and partly cut himself* is just bizarre. (Rather, the 'active zone' is likely to be spelled out in a prepositional adjunct: *He cut himself on the elbow.*) Cases like these are probably the norm, not the exception. Wunderlich, as we have seen, is sceptical of the notion of deviation from a prototype, partly on the grounds that we have no principled way of predicting which deviations will be tolerated, also because of the desire to preserve intact the homogeneity principle and the strict satisfaction of semantic conditions; allowing prototypes and deviations therefrom 'would undermine our whole endeavor for a combined semantic and conceptual approach' (p. 125). But, equally, given the ubiquity and diversity of focusing effects, one wonders why these effects, which seem to be no less 'unrestricted' in their operation than 'deviations from prototypes', should not also, in the long run, also undermine the two-level endeavour.

Be that as it may, the device of conceptual focusing plays a crucial role in Wunderlich's (1993) account of the German preposition *um* "(a)round". In this case, we have available, for comparison, a prototype account of the English equivalent of *um* (Schulze 1991, 1993). It

---

[7] Langacker (1991: 189). Thus, Langacker applies the notion of active zone to such a quintessentially grammatical phenomenon as so-called 'object-to-subject raising'.

should be pointed out that the usage range of German *um* does not exactly coincide with that of English (*a*)*round*, a point we return to later. On the other hand, the German examples that Wunderlich discusses do have English equivalents with (*a*)*round*, and to this extent we may be justified in applying Wunderlich's account to the English preposition.

On the face of it, (*a*)*round* presents the two-level theorist (and indeed anyone intent on deriving the various uses of the word from a unique definition) with a considerable challenge. Consider the following sentence with *round*.

(8) The boy ran round the playing field

There are at least three markedly different interpretations of this sentence. These are illustrated diagrammatically in (*a*)–(*c*) of Fig. 14.1. In both (*a*) and (*b*) of Fig. 14.1, the TR, i.e. the boy, moves along a path whose general shape follows the boundary of the LM entity, i.e. the playing field. The difference is that in (*a*), the path is external to the LM's boundary, whereas in (*b*) it is internal to the boundary. The third reading, (*c*), is similar to (*a*), in that the path is external to the LM. An extra component is that the LM is presented as an obstacle on the TR's path from some unspecified origin to some unspecified destination, whereby the TR makes a detour, circumventing the LM. In this case, the path 'round' the playing field does not completely enclose it; in all probability, it goes only about 'half way round'. But even in (*a*) and (*b*), it is not clear whether the boy ran 'all the way round' the field, or only 'part of the way round', or even whether he went round several times. There could be grounds, therefore, for claiming that the notion of complete as opposed to partial enclosure is not actually intrinsic to the meaning of *round*, but is induced by contextual factors.

In this connection, note that the choice between readings (*a*) and (*b*) may be closely bound up with the lexical context in which *round* occurs. Compare:

(9) (*a*) The boy ran round the lake
    (*b*) The boy sailed round the lake
(10) (*a*) The boy sailed round the island
    (*b*) The boy ran round the island

Given what we know about lakes and islands, and about running and sailing, it is obvious that the (*a*) sentences can only be interpreted

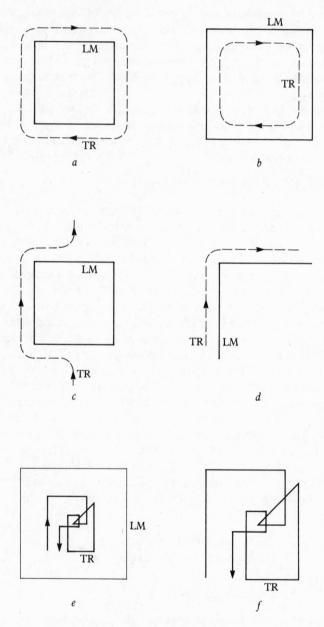

FIG. 14.1 *Some meanings of* round

according to diagram (*a*) in Fig. 14.1, whereas the (*b*) sentences can only be interpreted according to (*b*).

The issue of complete or partial encirclement may also be settled, in some instances, by the nature of the LM entity. One interpretation of (11) (*a*) is that the boy went full circle round the block, finishing at the place where he started. In (11) (*b*), however, the TR's path goes through only approximately 90 degrees. This reading—sketched in (*d*) of Fig. 14.1—seems to be dependent on the fact that the LM object, *corner*, denotes a part of a larger entity, and thus cannot, of itself, be fully surrounded.

> (11) (*a*) The boy ran round the block
>   (*b*) The boy ran round the corner

There are many other uses of the *round* in English, but let us pause here. The question is how to handle these different uses. One approach might be to recognize a particular usage variant—(*a*) of Fig. 14.1, for example—as 'basic', or prototypical, and to see the other uses as extensions from it. (*Pace* Wunderlich, these extensions are not 'pragmatically tolerated deviations' from the prototype, they constitute independent, established senses of the word.) Another approach might be to identify what is common to the various uses, and to propose this as the general meaning of *round*. One possibility that I have hinted at could be to say that the path of the TR roughly follows the (non-rectilinear) boundary of the LM. (Still, the postulation of a general meaning of this nature does not remove the need for specifying the conventionalized instantiations of this meaning; it is, I would maintain, a *particular fact* about English *round*, and German *um*, that they may denote the specific configurations in (*a*)–(*d*) of Fig. 14.1.) Wunderlich's solution is different. He proposes a semantic representation (12) that appears to correspond rather closely to (*a*) of Fig. 14.1, but which is claimed, nevertheless, to be subject to general processes of conceptual interpretation, giving rise to the configurations sketched in (*a*)–(*d*).

> (12) *um* "(a)round"
> $\lambda y \, \lambda x \, [\text{LOC}[x, \text{EXT}[y]]] \, \& \, \text{ENCL}[\text{D}[x], y]]$

Roughly, x is located in the proximal exterior of y, and $D[x]$, the dimensional extension of x, encloses y.

This semantic formula requires that the TR be external to the LM, and that it completely encloses it. Apparent violations may be due, in the case of partial enclosure (11) (*b*), to special properties of the LM entity. For an entity such as a corner, the exterior region EXT[*y*] only partially surrounds the entity. For the circumventing sense (*d*), the device of conceptual focusing is called upon. Given a conceptual focus on the route that the TR takes in getting from some place of origin to some intended destination, only a half-plane of the LM object is under observation. Within this focused region, D[*x*] has the ideal gestalt of a semicircle. Hence, Wunderlich asserts, the semantic conditions of the preposition are strictly observed; 'nothing must be changed in the semantic condition ... to arrive at the desired result' (i.e. the strict observation of semantic conditions).

The case of interiority, as in (*b*) of Fig. 14.1, Wunderlich also derives through conceptual focusing. On the case of it, sense (*b*) clearly conflicts with the semantic condition of exteriority contained in (12). Wunderlich's solution is to claim that certain entities, such as a pond or lake, can be conceptualized in two different ways. Looking at them from the outside, they constitute 'closed regions', with a clearly marked external boundary; in the case of a lake, this external boundary would be the shore. If you 'run round' a lake, your path is external to this boundary. On an alternative conceptualization, the 'lake proper' is the central, deep part of the lake; the lake becomes an 'open region', whose rather vaguely demarcated boundary is the shallow water surrounding the deep central area. While wading or swimming in the shallow border region, you could still refer to the central region as 'the lake', and conclude that it might be dangerous for you to swim across it. By the same token, 'swimming round the lake' involves conceptual focusing on the central portion of the lake, and your path is strictly external to this central area.

The idea is not as far-fetched as it might at first sight appear. One piece of evidence (not cited by Wunderlich) concerns the use of *into*. Normally, to 'go into' a region means to cross an external boundary. If you 'walk into' the room, your path begins outside the room, and terminates inside it. But *into* can also be used to denote motion towards the centre.

(13) We drove deeper into the forest

This sentence does not entail that our journey began outside the forest. It could be that we started our journey somewhere on the periphery of the forest (but still at a place which is 'in' the forest), and proceeded towards the central region. One might therefore argue, with Wunderlich, that (13) conceptually focuses on the dense internal region of the forest as the 'forest proper', which is bounded by the peripheral, and less dense region. What is crossed, in (13), is the rather vaguely demarcated boundary between the peripheral and the central region.

So far, then, so good. The snag is, German *um*, and English *round*, have uses which cannot plausibly be brought under the semantic representation in (12). Wunderlich (1993: 131) cites the use of the verb particle *um* in (14) (*b*), which contrasts with the preposition *um* in (14) (*a*).

(14) (*a*) Sie fuhr um die Absperrung
"She drove round the barrier"
(*b*) Sie fuhr die Absperrung um
"She ran over the barrier", i.e. "She drove over the barrier and knocked it down"

Particle *um* denotes, according to Wunderlich, 'some change in position'. He notes (p. 132) that the syntactic and semantic differences between particle *um* and prepositional *um* are so great, that it would be impossible to derive both from a 'common, even more abstract semantic source'. Consequently, particle *um* has to be regarded as a separate lexical item from prepositional *um*; *um* thus turns out to be homonymous, associated with two quite unrelated semantic entries.

I will not go into the question of whether the meaning of particle *um* may not in fact be related to that of prepositional *um*. The situation is probably not too dissimilar to that of English *over*, discussed in Section 6.3. There, we traced a chain of meanings which related the spatial preposition, as in *fly over the city*, to the change in position sense of the particle/adverbial, as in *turn over the stone* (as well as, of course, in *run over the barrier*).

The case of English *round*, however, seems quite clear. Consider the following use of the preposition.

(15) We spent half an hour driving round the city centre, trying to find a parking place

On its normal interpretation, (15) does not mean that our path followed the boundary of the city centre, whether external to the boundary or internal to it, but rather that our path had a random, convoluted shape, criss-crossing the area of the inner city. This use is illustrated in (*e*) of Fig. 14.1. There is a certain affinity between (*e*) and (*b*), in that in both cases the path is confined within the boundary of the LM.

There is, though, virtually no affinity at all between (*e*) and (*a*), apart from the notion of the bounded LM entity. Even this aspect may disappear. In (16), illustrated in (*f*) of Fig. 14.1, all that is at issue is the random, convoluted nature of the path; the enclosing space is not specified.[8]

(16) We spent half an hour driving round, trying to find a parking place

Some further extensions might be briefly mentioned. Consider (17) and (18).

(17) There were people standing round the room, talking

(18) There were people standing round, talking

These exemplify positional variants of the meanings exemplified in (15) and (16). Whereas in (15) the TR moves along a random path within a bounded region, in the positional variant (17) a multiplex TR is randomly distributed within a bounded region, while in (18) it is only random distribution, within an unspecified region, that is at issue.

Senses (*e*) and (*f*) of Fig. 14.1 are not shared with German *um*; these would be expressed, in German, not by the simple preposition *um*, but by *herum*, or even *um herum*. Thus, (15) might be rendered as *Wir sind eine halbe Stunde im Zentrum herumgefahren, auf der Suche nach einem Parkplatz*. A direct application of Wunderlich's analysis to the English preposition is therefore not entirely legitimate. Still, looking at the English data in the spirit of the two-level approach, we may ask whether it might be possible to derive variants (*e*) and (*f*) from a unique semantic representation like that in (12). For myself, I see no way in which this could be managed, even with a liberal dose of conceptual focusing! One solution could be to take our cue from Wunderlich, and recognize two homonyms, *round*[1], with readings (*a*)–(*d*), and *round*[2], with readings (*e*) and (*f*). This, however, would ignore the obvious affinity between (*b*) and (*e*), both of which involve a non-rectilinear path within a bounded region. The English data, it seems to me, clearly demand a radial category account, of the kind proposed by

---

[8] Traditionally, *round* in (16) would be described as a particle or an adverbial, not as a preposition. Jackendoff (1973) advanced a number of reasons why certain adverbials, particles, and even conjunctions should be assimilated to the category of preposition. Thus, we could say that (16) exemplifies an 'intransitive' use of the preposition— intransitive, since its complement remains unexpressed. Jackendoff's arguments had been prefigured by Jespersen (1924: 87 ff.).

Schulze (1991; 1993), and on whose work the drawings in Fig. 14.1 are based.[9]

14.5 Polysemy and the network model

An evaluation of the two-level approach involves several issues. One of these concerns the proposed distinction between a level of linguistic-semantic meaning, and a level of non-linguistic, conceptual meaning. Logically independent of the semantic-conceptual split is the issue of the legitimacy, in principle, of abstract schematic representations of word meanings.

On the first issue, it should be borne in mind that the two-level approach is by no means unique in proposing a bifurcation of meaning into a purely linguistic component, and a non-linguistic, or encyclopaedic, component. On the contrary, the bifurcation is a common thread running through much semantic theorizing of the last couple of decades. The distinction is fundamental to Montague grammar,[10] it turns up in Jackendoff's recent work,[11] Sperber and Wilson's (1986) relevance theory is predicated upon it, Searle (1980 and 1983) appealed to it in his analysis of *cut* and *open*, as did Katz and Postal (1964) with their distinction between semantic markers, which are responsible for systematic contrasts in a language, and distinguishers, which capture the idiosyncratic residue (see Chapter 2, p. 33 f.).

[9] A question not addressed by Schulze is the possible differentiation of *round* and *around*. (He chooses to see them as synonyms, in free variation.) It is my impression, supported by some informal questionnaires, that different speakers may differentiate the words in slightly different ways. For myself, I prefer *around* when the randomness of the TR's motion/position is at issue (though *round* is not impossible in such contexts), and use *round* when an encircling motion/position is denoted (though, again *around* is not excluded, here, either). In fact, a close investigation, combining the semasiological and onomasiological perspectives, of *round* and *around* might show that the two terms stand in the relation of coextension, mentioned in Section 14.2 in connection with MacLaury's findings in the domain of colour.

[10] Thomason (1974), in his introduction to a collection of Montague's papers, insisted that semantic theory should be clearly demarcated from lexicography. (Hence, for Thomason, lexicography would not be a semantic pursuit at all!) The proper object of semantic theory, Thomason asserts, is the different kinds of meanings that attach to different syntactic categories; semantics is not at all concerned with 'an account of how any two expressions belonging to the same syntactic category differ in meaning' (p. 48). The difference in meaning between the verbs *run* and *walk* is therefore not a semantic issue, but the concern of the lexicographer, who, unlike the semanticist, may freely appeal to 'concepts from all areas of knowledge and practice' (p. 49).

[11] See Taylor (1995c) for the role of the semantic/encyclopaedic bifurcation with special reference to Jackendoff (1990).

Indeed, the very postulate of an autonomous language faculty (see Section 1.4) entails the distinctiveness of linguistic knowledge *vis-à-vis* conceptual, and encyclopaedic knowledge. Equally, a number of linguists, of various theoretical persuasions, have been highly sceptical of the very basis of the linguistic-conceptual bifurcation. Critics have included Bolinger (1965), Sampson (1980*a*), Haiman (1980), Geeraerts (1985*b*), Langacker (1987), and many others. In fact, the thesis that meaning is inherently and essentially encyclopaedic in scope has become a kind of hallmark of the cognitive linguistic approach advocated in this book (see especially Chapter 5).

The second issue, the legitimacy, in principle, of highly schematic representations of word meanings, is perhaps less controversial. I imagine that a good many linguists—including many of those who subscribe to an encyclopaedist semantics—might well endorse the 'methodological principle' of trying to cover as many uses as possible by a unique semantic representation. Even Langacker might not be entirely unsympathetic. Whilst Langacker (1991: 194) takes it for granted that polysemy is 'the normal state of affairs' in lexical semantics, he has also devoted considerable attention to the search for maximally general characterizations of such things as the semantic import of word classes (alluded to in Section 10.3), the meaning of the possessive morpheme in English (Langacker 1991: 172), and a general characterization of that most elusive of the English prepositions, *of* (Langacker 1992).

There can therefore be no quarrel in principle with the idea of general characterizations of words such as *in* and *round*, which propose to capture what is common to many different uses of the words. (This said, I doubt, in the case of *round*, whether *all* uses could be subsumed under a single entry; and, as already pointed out, the general characterizations will in any event need to be supplemented by information on the range of accepted and language-specific instantiations of the general meanings.) A general notion of containment, say, for *in*, or a general notion of encirclement for (some uses of) *round*, are unobjectionable. But I see no reason why these general characterizations should be any less 'conceptual' in content than the more specific readings; it is just that the general meanings lack the detail associated with the more specific meanings. The more abstract senses are therefore not ontologically distinct from the specific senses; they are still understood in experiential, imaginistic terms, just like the specific readings, rather than in terms of a disembodied logic of space.

Over and above the legitimacy, in principle, of general as opposed to specific semantic statements, there is an empirical question. This concerns the level of abstraction at which word meanings actually *are* stored in the mind of a speaker, and the level at which speakers actually *do* access word meanings in the process of producing and understanding language.

It is commonly agreed that a word may typically be used in a variety of contexts, to denote a range of different kinds of situation. It does not follow that each of these different contextual variants is separately stored in the mind of the speaker/hearer; it could be that a person accesses a rather more abstract representation, and derives contextual variants by some general processes of conceptual elaboration, possibly along the lines suggested by the two-level theorists.

On the other hand, the fact that an ingenious linguist may be able to come up with a maximally general semantic statement which covers a wide range of different uses does not entail that speakers of a language do store the word meaning in the abstract format, and that they do implement a process of conceptual elaboration, on each occasion of the word's use. It could be that at least some of the variants are mentally stored and can be directly accessed in the production and comprehension of language.

Neither do we have to regard the two perspectives as mutually exclusive. It seems to me perfectly plausible that a speaker can store *both* a range of specific uses of a word, *and* a more abstract representation that captures what is common to the more specific uses. Indeed, there seems no a priori reason why a speaker should not store a number of representations of varying degrees of abstraction.

Methodological objections might be raised against such a proposal. If different uses of a word *can* be covered by a single semantic entry, why clutter up the grammar with a list of specific and more or less predictable instantiations of the general entry? Surely, the very essence of linguistic enquiry (as we tell our first-year students) is, precisely, the formulation of general statements, not the listing of specific instances covered by the general statements![12]

Yet there is considerable circumstantial evidence that speakers of a language do associate words with a range of rather specific readings.

[12] Langacker (1987: 29) discusses these issues under what he calls the 'rule/list fallacy'. This is 'the assumption, on grounds of simplicity, that particular statements (i.e. lists) must be excised from the grammar of a language if general statements (i.e. rules) that subsume them can be established'. But, he adds, 'for anyone taking seriously the goal of "psychological reality"', the simplicity thereby achieved is 'specious'.

To the extent that a linguist's description of a language is meant to model the native speaker's acquired knowledge of the language—to the extent, that is, that a linguist's grammar is supposed to be 'psychologically real'—it will need to take account of this evidence. A major weakness of the two-level approach, it seems to me, is that it denies in principle the possibility of stable mental representations of specific meanings. To allow that more specific readings (such as the 'circumvent-a-hindrance' sense of *round*) are separately stored in the mental lexicon would threaten the very architecture of the two-level model.

(*a*) There are, first of all, the well-known and well-documented prototype effects. If a person is asked to come up with sentences exemplifying a target word, then, with remarkable consistency, certain uses will be cited earlier, and more frequently, than others. I have already mentioned (pp. 117 f.) the results of a small investigation with *over*. Similar tests with *round* consistently generated instances of sense (*a*) in Fig. 14.1, of the kind *The Earth goes round the Sun*. These results suggest that certain readings of a word have a privileged status in the mental lexicon, and can be accessed more easily than others. Such a possibility is incompatible with the assumption that each reading of a word is generated from a unique representation.

(*b*) Speakers of a language are generally hard put to state the general meaning of a word, the more so if the word is one in common use. A person has no problems at all to explain what *open the door* means. But ask someone for the general meaning of *open*, abstracted away from various uses of the verb (*open the door, open the office, open a newspaper, open a parcel, open a penknife, open a zip*), and they find the task embarrassingly difficult. It might be premature to conclude from this that the mental lexicon contains only the specific readings of the word, to the exclusion of a general characterization. The generative paradigm (of which the two-level model is an offshoot) accepts that people do not have conscious access to the rules and representations which underlie their linguistic performance. Still, it seems rather perverse to insist that speakers and hearers, in their everyday use of language, *do not* access specific senses that are readily available to introspection, and that they *do* access an abstract sense that is hardly available at all to introspection.

(*c*) Speakers of a language are able to give quite reliable judgements of degrees of similarity between the different senses of a word. This is true not only of words such as *body*, whose different meanings ('physical being', 'main part') are markedly dissimilar (Durkin and Manning 1989), but also for the more closely related meanings of a preposition such as *round*. Schulze (1991) reports a number of experiments investigating similarity judgements pertaining to twenty different uses of (*a*)*round*. These judgements were subjected to the statistical procedure of hierarchical cluster analysis. The clusters that emerged can plausibly be taken as indications of the salience, at varying levels of abstraction, of different senses of the preposition. Of special interest is the emergence of clusters that appear to correspond, rather closely, to the distinct senses sketched in Fig. 14.1. One such cluster corresponds to the 'circumvent-a-hindrance' sense of *round*; this sense, then, appears to be more than just a 'conceptual variant', induced by a context-specific focusing strategy. A further point: Inspection of Schulze's results lends little support to the thesis, which we briefly entertained as one which the two-level approach might favour, that *round* might be homonymous; the 'random path/location within a bounded area' sense does *not* emerge as totally unrelated to the other uses of *round*.

These findings are just what we should expect, given the assumption that different readings of *round* are structured in a radial category. But the findings are quite inexplicable on the assumption that the mental lexicon contains only the most abstract representation, and that *all* senses of a word derive equally, by a process of conceptual interpretation, from this abstract representation.

(*d*) Processes of metaphorical extension typically apply to a rather specific sense of a word, not to the most general. *The boy got round his mother*, in the sense 'the boy got his mother to let him have his own way', conceptualizes a person's actions as a path, and circumstances that frustrate the achievement of an intended action as obstacles on the path.[13] The metaphor is sanctioned by the specific 'circumvent-a-hindrance' sense of *round*, not by the general encirclement sense, or whatever. The very existence of the metaphor, and the fact that it is so readily understood along the lines suggested, suggests that speakers have access to a stable mental representation of this specific sense of *round*.

(*e*) Very important is the evidence of semantic change, a topic not touched on, to my knowledge, by the two-level theorists. Semantic

---

[13] The expression is therefore based on the 'image schema' (Johnson 1987) of the journey; see above, p. 134.

change typically involves a shift in the relative frequency and relative salience of different readings. What might start out as a one-off, context-dependent extension acquires, through time, and with repeated use, the status of an established sense, perhaps even the prototypical sense, whereby the original sense(s) may get pushed to the periphery, and eventually fall into disuse. Geeraerts (1985a) documents just such a process.[14] The process presupposes that speakers can keep track of the different readings of a word, with respect to frequency and centrality. This, as Geeraerts (1993) has also pointed out, in turn presupposes that speakers have access to stable mental representations of these specific readings.

(f) Even assuming that speakers do store highly abstract representations of the words of their language, we need to ask how a language learner could acquire these abstractions in the first place. Words—it seems safe to say—are learned on examples of their use. It seems rather implausible that the child language learner (or an adult learner, for that matter—for it is not just pre-school children who learn new words, adults do so too), after having encountered a new word for the first time, will instantaneously construct a highly abstract sense. On the contrary, the initial representation, we may suppose, will be rather specific, and rich in contextual detail. Acquisition then proceeds both *horizontally* (new uses are associated through similarity with already familiar uses) and *vertically* (as different uses become familiar, a more schematic representation may be abstracted, which captures the commonality of known uses, and which also sanctions a range of new usage possibilities). There is no reason to suppose, however, that as more schematic representations emerge, the more specific representations on which they are based will necessarily be erased.

Just this possibility is foreseen by Langacker's *network model* of category structure. The model was introduced in Section 4.2, on the example of the word *tree*; for a fuller account and for more detailed illustration, see Langacker (1988). According to the model, the established senses of a word constitute the nodes of a possibly complex, extended network. The senses are linked, horizontally by relations of similarity, and vertically by the relation of a schema and its instantiations. The nuclear structure of the network is depicted in Fig. 14.2. Sense [B] is an extension of sense [A], that is, [B] is perceived to be

---

[14] A veritable mine of information on semantic change is C. S. Lewis's *Studies in Words* (Lewis 1960). What makes this book especially valuable is the fact that Lewis had no theoretical-linguistic axes to grind!

similar, in some respects to [A]; sense [C] is schematic for both [A] and [B], that is, it captures, at a level which abstracts away from the specific differences between [A] and [B], the commonality between them. We can imagine that the lowest nodes of a network might comprise specific collocations (and their conventionalized meanings) of a lexical item, which may be accessed as preformed chunks; but the possibility of more abstract representations, perhaps even of a 'super-schema', which covers the full range of particular uses of an item, is not denied. What the network model does deny is that the most abstract representation is always and necessarily invoked in the understanding of contextual variants.

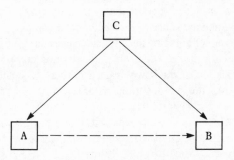

FIG. 14.2 *The network structure*

Consider what it means for a person to know the meaning of a word. (*Mutatis mutandis*, the following remarks apply also to knowing the meaning of a bound morpheme, a syntactic construction, an intonation melody.) Take Searle's example of the verb *open*. A person encounters the word in a wide range of contexts. Some of these may be perceived to be similar in some respects. *Open the office, open a parcel, open an envelope*, all have the idea of gaining access to the interior of a closed container. Other uses focus on the manner in which access is gained, namely by manoeuvring some device in order to create an aperture: *open the door, open the lid, open the cork*. Yet again, other uses focus on the moving apart of the component parts of an entity: *open one's shirt, open a zip, open a penknife*. Other uses have to do with making something accessible, for example to the general public: *open an exhibition, open a nature reserve, open a road*; others, yet again, have more to do with the initiation of an interactional process: *open a discussion, open a debate, open a conference*. These are all conventionalized

uses of the verb. Any adult speaker of English will surely be familiar
with them, and will have learned the kinds of situation to which the
expressions may be applied. Together, they form a coherent category,
not so much because of some overarching common element which
they each instantiate, but through criss-crossing networks of similarities, at various levels of generality. The category, it also needs to be
stressed, is peculiar to English. Approximate translation equivalents of
open in other languages may have more restricted, or more extended,
usage ranges. Italian *aprire* can probably be used in all circumstances
in which English *open* can be used. But in addition, *aprire* is conventionally used in contexts in which *open* is not appropriate: *aprire la
radio*, 'turn on the radio', *aprire la luce*, 'turn on the (electric) light',
aprire il riscaldamento, 'turn on the central heating'. These uses are
unified by a schematic sense (which bears a resemblance to other uses
of the verb), 'render some (especially electrical) device operative'.

On the network model, the problem of the non-compositionality of
complex expressions, which was raised earlier, dissipates. A person
does not compute the compositional meaning of *open the window* from
the constant meanings of its component parts; any competent speaker
of English already knows this expression, and knows what it means.
And what about expressions with which a speaker is not familiar, such
as Searle's *open the Sun*? I would dispute Searle's claim that a person
can *understand* this expression, while failing to *interpret* it. A person
tries to understand it, certainly, by trying to assimilate it to an already
familiar use, that is, by trying to establish some kind of similarity
between it and an established use. Persons with vivid imaginations,
nurtured on science fiction, may be able to come up with various
coherent scenarios, in which case they may be said to both understand
and be able to interpret it. But if a person's imagination is insufficient
to this task, then I think one should have to conclude that the person
does not understand the expression, for the very reason that he fails to
interpret it; the person would declare that he has no idea at all what
'open the Sun' could possibly mean!

One consequence of adopting the network model is that the question of whether a word is polysemous or not turns out to be incapable
of receiving a definite answer. The answer will depend on the level of
abstraction at which the word's meaning is accessed. As the focus
descends to more specific senses, the word will be increasingly polysemous; with focus on the more schematic senses, the word is much
less polysemous, even monosemous. Yet neither of these perspectives

can be regarded as inherently more correct than the other. To consider only the particular to the neglect of the schematic—and vice versa—impoverishes our understanding of word meaning. The point has been made by Geeraerts (1992), at the conclusion of his detailed study of the Dutch preposition *over*.

The various tests for polysemy that were mentioned in Section 6.1 may be brought into the picture here. The possibilities of co-ordination and anaphoric cross-reference require that different uses of a word instantiate one and the same sense. But if polysemy is a function of the level in the network at which meanings are accessed, the results of these polysemy tests ought to be highly variable. This is indeed the case. (19) only makes sense if Jane and I both live, either near a financial institution, or near a river; a 'crossed' interpretation is not possible. This fact could be taken as evidence of two distinct readings of *bank*.

(19) I live by a bank, and so does Jane

But now consider (20). (The sentence is due to Deane 1988: 345; Geeraerts 1993 cites some similar examples.)

(20) Financial banks resemble those you find by rivers; they control, respectively, the flow of money and of water

This sentence, unlike (19), invites us specifically to focus on the resemblance between the two kinds of things called *bank*; it forces us to access (or even to create) a schematic sense unifying the two readings of *bank*. Or take a couple of Tuggy's (1993) examples with the verb *paint*.

(21) I have been painting, and so has Jane
(22) When I'm painting I try to get the colour on evenly, and so does Jane

If I have been painting white stripes on a parking lot, and Jane has been doing a portrait in oils, (21) would be at best facetious. This suggests the existence of two discrete senses of *paint*, each associated with a different kind of situation. The zeugmatic effect completely disappears in (22). The sentence compels us to shift our attention to what is common between a workman painting stripes on a parking lot and an artist painting a portrait; in both cases, a person is engaged in putting colour on a surface.

14.6 The historical perspective

I have been discussing some issues from the recent linguistic literature which have a bearing on the topics treated in this book. But it is also instructive to look backwards and sidewards—backwards into the historical antecedents of prototype categorization, and sidewards into other disciplines. For the idea of categorization by prototype did not emerge suddenly in the early 1970s in the wake of Rosch's studies of colour categorization, neither was the family resemblance idea uniquely Wittgenstein's brainchild. On the contrary, there appears to have been a convergence, around the middle of the century, in the life and the human sciences, on the idea of a category structured around resemblances between instances, in contradistinction to the scholastic view of categories as defined by necessary and sufficient conditions for membership.

One person whose writings deserve a close rereading in the light of subsequent developments, especially in linguistic semantics, is John Austin. I am thinking not so much of his well-known work on speech acts, as of the perhaps lesser known *Sense and Sensibilia* (1962), and the *Philosophical Papers* (1961). Austin, the 'ordinary language philosopher', was concerned with the meanings of words, and his acute observations are still pertinent. Consider, as an example of the prototype notion *ante litteram*, the following remarks on the concept of 'cause', from his essay 'A plea for excuses'.[15]

Going back into the history of a word, very often into Latin, we come back pretty commonly to pictures or *models* of how things happen or are done.... We take *some very simple action*, like shoving a stone, usually as done by and viewed by oneself, and use *this*, with the features distinguishable in it, as our model in terms of which to talk about other actions and events: and we continue to do so, scarcely realizing it, even when these other actions are pretty remote and perhaps much more interesting to us in their own right than the acts originally used in constructing the model ever were, and even when the model is really distorting the facts rather than helping us to observe them.... 'Causing', I suppose, was a notion taken from a man's own experience of doing simple actions, and by primitive men every event was construed in terms of this model: every event has a cause, that is, every event is an action done by somebody—if not by a man, then by a quasi-man, a spirit. When, later, events which

---

[15] For some further reflections on the current relevance of Austin, see Taylor (1995*b*).

are *not* actions are realized to be such, we still say that they must be 'caused', and the word snares us: we are struggling to ascribe to it a new, unanthropological meaning, yet constantly, in searching for its analysis, we unearth and incorporate the lineaments of the ancient model. (Austin 1961: 202–3)

The passage is of interest for several reasons. Observe, for example, that Austin sees the original, or primordial, notion of cause in experiential terms—in image-schematic terms, one might say—not as a disembodied logical predicate. A person shoves a stone, and the stone moves—he 'causes' the stone to move. But when a stone moves without the agency, or without the direct agency, of a human being, what do we say then? We still say that something caused the stone to move— but now, Austin cautions, we are using *cause* in a slightly different, extended sense, removed from the original experiential scene, but nevertheless still coloured by it.

The 'therapeutic' import of Austin's remarks is still valid, especially when we realize that 'cause' plays a crucial role in many decompositional theories of semantics. 'Cause', in fact, has acquired the status of a semantic primitive *par excellence*, featuring prominently in formalistic semantic analyses, including those of Bierwisch and the two-level theorists. Thus, Bierwisch (1981: 344 f.) decomposes the transitive use of *melt*, as in *x melts y*, into something like '*x* does *z*, and *z* causes *y* to go from being rigid to being liquid'. But Austin warns us that 'cause' is not a simple, undifferentiated concept. There are many different kinds of cause, some closer to the primordial concept, some more distant. To postulate an invariant element in the semantic representations of different lexical items could therefore easily 'snare' us (to use Austin's word) into seeing identity where there is only similarity, or family resemblance. The legitimacy of this point is confirmed by Dirven (1995), who shows that what we loosely call 'cause' in fact comprises a family of distinct cause concepts. Comparisons between English and two languages closely related to English, namely Dutch and German, suggest also that the construal of a situation in terms of a particular kind of cause may well be language-specific.

It is not only linguists, and linguistically oriented philosophers, who became dissatisfied with 'classical' categories, defined by a list of necessary and sufficient features. Rodney Needham, a social anthropologist, reports (Needham 1975) how, 'in the empirical practice of anthropological comparison' (p. 350), he came to question the scholastic view of categorization. A detailed study of the ethnographic facts, he tells us, convinced him that what might in various societies be described as, for example, 'patrilineal' or 'matrilineal descent' was not a unified concept at all, but needed to be characterized by 'a set of criteria which might be matched only sporadically, and in highly various combinations, by the jural institutions of real societies' (p. 351). Patrilineal descent, therefore, turned out to be a thoroughly Wittgensteinean family resemblance category (Needham 1974).

But Wittgenstein was not the only one who, some thirty years earlier, had proposed the idea of categorization by overlapping similarities. Needham (1975: 350) points to a 'remarkable parallel' between Wittgenstein's notion of family resemblance (see Section 3.1) and Vygotsky's 'chain complexes', in which the defining attribute 'keeps changing from one link to the next', with 'no consistency in the type of bonds' between the links, and hence with no overarching attribute defining the whole class.[16]

Thus by an intriguing convergence of psychological and philosophical analyses, reported independently in Russia and England respectively in 1934, the traditional common-feature definition of a class was demonstrated to be both empirically and formally defective. (Needham 1975: 350)

Needham draws attention to some further remarkable convergences. Like Lakoff (1987: Ch. 12) over a decade later, he reviews the establishment, in the life sciences (biology, botany, zoology, microbiology), of the notion of 'polythetic' classification. A polythetic class comprises organisms whose members share a large number of properties, but no property is necessarily shared by each member. The idea, in botany, he adds, goes back to the eighteenth century. Whilst recognizing the affinity between these developments and his own independent work in anthropology, Needham also draws attention to some crucial differences between the life sciences on the one hand, and the human sciences on the other.

In classifying living organisms, the criteria for classification—the

[16] See Vygotsky (1962: Ch. 5). In addition to chain complexes, Vygotsky also identifies 'associative complexes' (p. 62) and 'diffuse complexes' (p. 65). He discusses (pp. 61–6) these various kinds of 'thinking in complexes' (p. 61), which all involve relations between individual instances, rather than overarching commonalities, as a developmental stage between 'unorganized congeries' of objects and the attainment of abstract, generalizing concepts. Vygotsky states, however, that 'remains' of categorization by complexes persist in adult language (p. 61). He cites (p. 73) the example of the diachronic development of the Russian word *sutki*, from "seam joining two pieces of cloth", through "junction (e.g. of two walls)", to "corner", and metaphorically, to "twilight"; then, by metonymy, to the present meaning of "24-hour day".

classificatory features—can generally be reliably identified and quant-
ified; they 'have generally a real, distinct, and independent character,
and they can be clearly stipulated in advance' (p. 363). The features
include, in zoology, such matters as skeletal structure (how many
bones arranged in which configuration), or, in bacteriology, chemical
substances and their reactions. But in anthropology, that is, 'in the
realm of social facts', the ground is inherently unstable.

The determination of the constituent features of a polythetic class cannot be
carried out by reference to discrete empirical particulars, but entails instead a
reliance on further features *of the same character which themselves are polythetic*. In social life, there are no established phenomena, in the form of isolable
social facts for instance, which correspond to the elements and particles in
nature.... This contrast [with the natural sciences] is the most marked when
the materials for an anthropological classification are collective representations. (p. 364; emphasis added)

Even a polythetic conception of marriage, characterized by 'sporadic
likenesses' (p. 364), will not carry the guarantee that some feature,
regarded by an indigenous population as essential to the institution,
will not have been left out (p. 363). In brief:

human affairs are semantically so very complex that it must be difficult in the
extreme (if it is even conceivable) either to stipulate significance as a polythetic
feature or to assess the degree of similarity amongst the meanings or values
attached by different civilisations to any kind of institution that is the subject
of a comparative proposition. (p. 363)

The very basis for postulating a classification thus becomes inherently unstable. Neither can the social scientist, unlike the life scientist,
appeal to the evolutionary perspective. The notion of phylogenetic
descent cannot be meaningfully applied to social facts. In the life
sciences, a common ancestor may suggest a 'natural' classification of
organisms which subsequently became variegated by natural selection,
whereby the descendants may indeed share some common genetic
traits. But the origin of social institutions is irrelevant to their synchronic classification. The diachronic transformation of social facts is
'causally different' (p. 361) from the evolution of natural species.

If we admit that language is a 'social fact', and that the categories
conventionally symbolized by a community's linguistic resources are
'collective representations', Needham's remarks will be pertinent also
to linguistic enquiry. For the very reasons that Needham states, we
have to be sceptical about the alleged universality of the 'classificatory

concepts' of linguistic theory, and of the 'features' which are claimed to enter into their definitions.

Yet if the traditional classificatory concepts of anthropology are 'worse than unserviceable' (p. 365), Needham still sees the possibility of meaningful discussion and comparison of social facts at a much higher level of abstraction, in terms of 'formal properties' and 'relational concepts'. Again, a linguistic analogy may be pertinent. We may seek linguistic universals, not in the conceptual content of any specific feature, such as [CAUSE], but in terms of the architecture of the conceptualizations symbolized by linguistic resources, and in the mechanics of their combination. Some might see the predicate-argument format, abstracted away from the content of any specific predicates and arguments, as a possible candidate. My own preference would be for various 'structural' notions inherent to Langacker's (1987, 1991) work—notions such as profile and base, thing and relation, the mechanics of valence, and the attendant notions of head, modifier, and complement.

14.7 Epilogue: on zebras and quaggas

In 1926, that *enfant terrible* of South African letters, Herman Charles Bosman, was condemned to hang for the murder of his stepbrother. His sentence was commuted to ten years hard labour, subsequently reduced to four and a half. Some twenty years later, Bosman recounted his prison experiences in a 'chronicle', entitled *Cold Stone Jug*.

He tells us that after he had completed about three years of his sentence, 'a wave of culture-consciousness swept through the prison'. One of its manifestations lay in the ability of a convict to state the difference between a zebra and a quagga.

Nobody knew who started that teaser. But in no time everybody took it very seriously. It was regarded as a mark of educational attainment to be able to recite straight out, word perfect, just as it was in the dictionary, the definition of, respectively, a zebra and a quagga. (Bosman 1969: 162)

Mysteriously, the Z and Q pages of the prison dictionaries had the respective definitions cut from them. Groups of convicts had to rote-learn the definitions from an inmate already conversant with them.

The narrator affects an attitude of intellectual superiority to these goings-on. If he really wanted to know the difference, he says, he would go and look it up in a book. 'You won't look it up in no book', though, he is told, aggressively, 'Not in this boob you won't. Them words is cut out of the dictionaries, see? And if you want to know the difference you got to keep it in your blooming head, see?'

He takes the blue-coat (prisoner serving an indeterminate sentence) to task on his understanding of the definition of *quagga* that he recited.

'You've recited the whole thing,' I said, 'But now what does it mean?'

'Well, it's a quagga, ain't it?'

'Yes,' I answered, 'I know it's a quagga. But from what you've recited, all those words, if you were to see a quagga, would you know if it was a quagga?'

The blue-coat sneered.

'I stayed on a farm once, where there was quaggas,' he announced, 'And of course I knows a quagga when I sees one. A quagga is like a big buck, with stripes all over his backside, like he got lashes. That's a quagga. You can't fool me, you can't. You got to go and learn, that's what. You got no brains, that's that.'

He had me licked, all right.

'But if you know what a quagga is,' I pursued, weakly, 'What do you want to go and learn the definition out of a dictionary for?'

The blue-coat looked at me in scorn.

'That's eddication,' he replied, 'Ain't you never heard of eddication?' (pp. 164 f.)

The episode is an object lesson for many issues in lexical semantics. It would be tedious to spell them all out, and in any case, this chapter is already much longer than I intended it to be.

References

Abbreviations

BLS: Proceedings of the Berkeley Linguistic Society
CLS: Proceedings of the Chicago Linguistic Society
LAUD: Linguistic Agency, University of Duisburg

ABNEY, S. (1987). The English noun phrase in its sentential aspect. Ph.D. diss. MIT.

ALLERTON, D. J. (1979). *Essentials of Grammatical Theory: A Consensus View of Syntax and Morphology*. London: Routledge & Kegan Paul.

ANDERSON, J., and DURAND, J. (1986). Dependency phonology. In J. Durand (ed.), *Dependency and Non-linear Phonology*, 1–54. London: Croom Helm.

ANDRÉ, J. (1949). *Étude sur les termes de couleur dans la langue latine*. Paris: Klincksieck.

ARISTOTLE (1933). *Metaphysics*. Translated by H. Tredennick. London: Heinemann.

ARMSTRONG, S. L., GLEITMAN, L. R., and GLEITMAN, H. (1983). What some concepts might not be. *Cognition* 13: 263–308.

AUSTIN, J. L. (1961). *Philosophical Papers*, ed. J. O. Urmson and G. J. Warnock. Oxford: Oxford University Press.

—— (1962). *Sense and Sensibilia*. Reconstructed from the manuscript notes by G. J. Warnock. Oxford: Oxford University Press.

BAILEY, C.-J. N., and SHUY, R. W. (eds.) (1973). *New Ways of Analysing Variation in English*. Washington: Georgetown University Press.

BATES, E., and RANKIN, J. (1979). Morphological development in Italian: Connotation and denotation. *Journal of Child Language* 6: 29–52.

BATTIG, W. F., and MONTAGUE, W. E. (1969). Category norms for verbal items in 56 categories. *Journal of Experimental Psychology Monograph* 80: No. 3, Pt. 2.

BEAUGRANDE, R. DE, and DRESSLER, W. (1981). *Introduction to Text Linguistics*. London: Longman.

BERLIN, B., and KAY, P. (1969). *Basic Color Terms: Their Universality and Evolution*. Berkeley: University of California Press.

BICKERTON, D. (1981). *Roots of Language*. Ann Arbor: Karoma.

BIERWISCH, M. (1967). Some semantic universals of German adjectivals. *Foundations of Language* 3: 1–36.

—— (1970). Semantics. In J. Lyons (ed.), *New Horizons in Linguistics*, 166–84. Harmondsworth: Penguin.

BIERWISCH, M. (1981). Basic issues in the development of word meaning. In Deutsch (1981), 341–87.

—— (1983). Semantische und konzeptuelle Repräsentation lexikalischer Einheiten. In R. Růžička and W. Motsch (eds.), *Untersuchungen zur Semantik* (= *studia grammatica* XXII), 61–99. Berlin: Akademie-Verlag.

—— and LANG, E. (1987). *Grammatische und Konzeptuelle Aspekte von Dimensionsadjektiven.* Berlin: Akademie-Verlag. English translation: *Dimensional Adjectives: Grammatical Structure and Conceptual Interpretation* (1989). Berlin: Springer.

—— and SCHREUDER, R. (1992). From concepts to lexical items. *Cognition* 42: 23–60.

BLACK, M. (1962). *Models and Metaphors.* Ithaca: Cornell University Press.

BLOOMFIELD, L. (1933). *Language.* London: George Allen & Unwin.

BOLINGER, D. (1965). The atomization of meaning. *Language* 41: 555–73.

—— (1980). *Language: The Loaded Weapon.* London: Longman.

—— (1986). *Intonation and its Parts: Melody in Spoken English.* London: Edward Arnold.

BORNSTEIN, M. H. (1975). The influence of visual perception on culture. *American Anthropologist* 77: 774–98.

BOSCH, P. (1985). Context dependence and metaphor. In Paprotté and Dirven (1985), 141–76.

BOSMAN, H. C. (1969). *Cold Stone Jug.* Cape Town: Human and Rousseau.

BOTHA, R. P. (1968). *The Function of the Lexicon in Transformational Generative Grammar.* The Hague: Mouton.

—— (1984). *Morphological Mechanisms: Lexicalist Analysis of Synthetic Compounding.* Oxford: Pergamon.

—— (1989). *Challenging Chomsky: The Generative Garden Game.* Oxford: Blackwell.

BOWERMAN, M. (1978). The acquisition of word meaning: An investigation into some current concepts. In N. Waterson and C. Snow (eds.), *The Development of Communication.* New York: Wiley.

BRAZIL, D., COULTHARD, M., and JOHNS, C. (1980). *Discourse Intonation and Language Teaching.* London: Longman.

BROWN, G., CURRIE, K. L., and KENNWORTHY, J. (1980). *Questions of Intonation.* London: Croom Helm.

—— and YULE, S. (1983). *Discourse Analysis.* Cambridge: Cambridge University Press.

BROWN, R. (1958). How shall a thing be called? *Psychological Review* 65: 14–21.

—— (1973). *A First Language: The Early Stages.* Cambridge, Mass.: Harvard University Press.

—— and LENNEBERG, E. H. (1954). A study in language and cognition. *Journal of Abnormal and Social Psychology* 49: 454–62.

BRUGMAN, C. (1981). Story of OVER. MA thesis, University of California, Berkeley. Reproduced by LAUD (1983).

BYBEE, J. L., and MODER, C. L. (1983). Morphological classes as natural categories. *Language* 59: 251–70.

—— and SLOBIN, D. I. (1982). Rules and schemas in the development and use of the English past tense. *Language* 58: 265–89.

CAREY, S. (1982). Semantic development: The state of the art. In Wanner and Gleitman (1982), 347–89.

CARSTAIRS, A. (1987). *Allomorphy in Inflexion*. London: Croom Helm.

CHOMSKY, N. (1965). *Aspects of the Theory of Syntax*. Cambridge, Mass.: MIT Press.

—— (1972). Remarks on nominalization. In R. A. Jacobs and P. S. Rosenbaum (eds.), *Transformational Grammar*, 184–221. Waltham, Mass.: Ginn.

—— (1976). *Reflections on Language*. London: Fontana.

—— (1980). *Rules and Representations*. Oxford: Basil Blackwell.

—— (1982). *The Generative Enterprise: A Discussion with Riny Huybregts and Henk van Riemsdijk*. Dordrecht: Foris.

—— (1986). *Knowledge of Language: Its Nature, Origin, and Use*. New York: Praeger.

—— and HALLE, M. (1968). *The Sound Pattern of English*. New York: Harper and Row.

CLARK, E. V. (1973*a*). Non-linguistic strategies and the acquisition of word meanings. *Cognition* 2: 161–82.

—— (1973*b*). What's in a word? On the child's acquisition of semantics in his first language. In Moore (1973), 65–110.

CLARK, H. H., and CLARK, E. V. (1976). *Psychology and Language*. New York: Harcourt Brace Jovanovich.

CLAUDI, U., and HEINE, B. (1986). On the metaphorical base of grammar. *Studies in Language* 10: 297–335.

COLEMAN, L. (1980). The language of 'born-again' Christianity. *BLS* 6: 133–42.

—— and KAY, P. (1981). Prototype semantics: the English word *lie*. *Language* 57: 26–44.

COLOMBO, L., and FLORES D'ARCAIS, G. B. (1984). The meaning of Dutch prepositions: A psycholinguistic study of polysemy. *Linguistics* 22: 51–98.

COOPER, D. E. (1986). *Metaphor*. Oxford: Basil Blackwell.

CORBETT, G. C. (1993). The head of Russian numeral expressions. In Corbett *et al.* (1993), 11–35.

——, FRASER, N. M., and McGLASHAN, S. (eds.) (1993). *Heads in Grammatical Theory*. Cambridge: Cambridge University Press.

CORRIGAN, R., ECKMAN, F., and NOONAN, M. (eds.) (1989). *Linguistic Categorization*. Amsterdam: John Benjamins.

CRAIG, C. (ed.) (1986). *Noun Classes and Categorization*. Amsterdam: John Benjamins.

CROFT, W. (1993). The role of domains in the interpretation of metaphors and metonymies. *Cognitive Linguistics* 4: 335–70.

CRUSE, D. A. (1986). *Lexical Semantics*. Cambridge: Cambridge University Press.

CRUTTENDEN, A. (1981). Falls and rises: Meanings and universals. *Journal of Linguistics* 17: 77–91.

—— (1986). *Intonation*. Cambridge: Cambridge University Press.

CRYSTAL, D. (1967). English, in *Word Classes*. *Lingua* 17: 24–56.

CULLER, J. (1976). *Saussure*. London: Fontana.

DAHL, Ö. (1985). *Tense and Aspect Systems*. Oxford: Basil Blackwell.

DEANE, P. (1988). Polysemy and cognition. *Lingua* 75: 325–61.

DEUTSCH, W. (ed.) (1981). *The Child's Construction of Language*. London: Academic Press.

DIRVEN, R. (1981). Spatial relations in English. *anglistik & englischunterricht* 14: 103–32.

—— (1985). Metaphor as a basic means for extending the lexicon. In Paprotté and Dirven (1985), 85–119.

—— (1987). Diminutives in Afrikaans and Dutch. In Lörscher and Schulze (1987), 100–9.

——, GOOSSENS, L., PUTSEYS, Y., and VORLAT, E. (1982). *The Scene of Linguistic Action and its Perspectivisation by Speak, Talk, Say and Tell*. Amsterdam: John Benjamins.

—— and TAYLOR, J. (1988). The conceptualization of vertical space in English: The case of *tall*. In Rudzka-Ostyn (1988*b*), 379–402.

—— (1995). The construal of cause: The case of cause prepositions. In Taylor and MacLaury (1995), 95–118.

DOKE, C. M. (1981⁶). *Textbook of Zulu Grammar*. Cape Town: Longman. 1st edn.: 1927.

DONEGAN, P. J., and STAMPE, D. (1979). The study of natural phonology. In D. A. Dinnsen (ed.), *Current Approaches to Phonological Theory*, 126–73. Bloomington: Indiana University Press.

DOWNING, P. (1977*a*). On 'basic levels' and the categorisation of objects in English discourse. *BLS* 3: 475–87.

—— (1977*b*). On the creation and use of English compound nouns. *Language* 53: 810–42.

DURKIN, K., and MANNING, J. (1989). Polysemy and the subjective lexicon: Semantic relatedness and the salience of intraword senses. *Journal of Psycholinguistic Research* 18: 577–612.

ECO, U. (1979). *The Role of the Reader*. Bloomington: Indiana University Press.

FILLMORE, C. J. (1968). The case for case. In E. Bach and R. Harm (eds.), *Universals in Linguistic Theory*, 1–88. New York: Holt, Rinehart & Winston.

—— (1979*a*). Innocence: A second idealization for linguistics. *BLS* 5: 63–76.

—— (1979*b*). On fluency. In C. J. Fillmore, D. Kempler, and N.S.-Y. Wang (eds.), *Individual Differences in Language Ability and Language Behavior*, 85–101. New York: Academic Press.

—— (1982). Towards a descriptive framework for spatial deixis. In R. J. Jarvella and W. Klein (eds.), *Speech, Place, & Action: Studies in Deixis and Related Topics*, 31–59. Chichester: John Wiley.

—— (1985). Syntactic intrusions and the notion of grammatical construction. *BLS* 11: 73–86.

GEERAERTS, D. (1985*a*). Cognitive restrictions on the structure of semantic change. In J. Fisiak (ed.), *Historical Semantics*, 127–53. Berlin: Mouton de Gruyter.

—— (1985*b*). *Paradigm and Paradox: Explorations into a Paradigmatic Theory of Meaning and its Epistemological Background*. Leuven: Leuven University Press.

—— (1988*a*). Cognitive grammar and the history of lexical semantics. In Rudzka-Ostyn (1988*b*), 647–77.

—— (1988*b*). Where does prototypicality come from? In Rudzka-Ostyn (1988*b*), 207–29.

—— (1989). Introduction: Prospects and Problems of Prototype Theory. *Linguistics* 27: 587–612.

—— (1992). The semantic structure of Dutch *over*. *Leuvense Bijdragen* 81: 205–30.

—— (1993). Vagueness's puzzles, polysemy's vagaries. *Cognitive Linguistics* 4: 223–72.

——, GRONDELAERS, S., and BAKEMA, P. (1994). *The Structure of Lexical Variation: Meaning, Naming, and Context*. Cognitive Linguistics Research, 5. Berlin: Mouton de Gruyter.

GEIGER, R. A., and RUDZKA-OSTYN, B. (eds.) (1993). *Conceptualizations and Mental Processing in Language*. Cognitive Linguistics Research, 3. Berlin: Mouton de Gruyter.

GIORGI, A., and LONGOBARDI, G. (1991). *The Syntax of Noun Phrases: Configuration, Parameters and Empty Categories*. Cambridge: Cambridge University Press.

GIVÓN, T. (1979). *On Understanding Grammar*. New York: Academic Press.

—— (1980). The binding hierarchy and the typology of complements. *Studies in Language* 4: 333–77.

—— (1984). *Syntax: A Functional–Typological Introduction*, i. Amsterdam: John Benjamins.

—— (1986). Prototypes: Between Plato and Wittgenstein. In Craig (1986), 77–102.

GLEASON, H. A. (1955). *An Introduction to Descriptive Linguistics*. New York: Holt, Rinehart & Winston.

—— (1965). *Linguistics and English Grammar*. New York: Holt, Rinehart & Winston.

GUSSENHOVEN, C. (1983). Focus, mode, and the nucleus. *Journal of Linguistics* 19: 377–417.

302 *References*

GUSSENHOVEN, C. (1985). Intonation: A whole autosegmental language. In H. van der Hulst and N. Smith (eds.), *Advances in Nonlinear Phonology* 117–31. Dordrecht: Foris.

HABEL, CH., HERWEG, M., and REHKÄMPER, K. (eds.) (1989). *Raumkonzepte in Verstehungsprozessen*. Tübingen: Narr.

HAIMAN, J. (1980). Dictionaries and encyclopaedias. *Lingua* 50: 329–57.

—— (ed.) (1985). *Iconicity in Syntax*. Amsterdam: John Benjamins.

HALLIDAY, M. A. K. (1970). *A Course in Spoken English: Intonation*. Oxford: Oxford University Press.

—— (1985). *An Introduction to Functional Grammar*. London: Edward Arnold.

HAMMOND-TOOKE, W. D. (1981). *Patrolling the Herms: Social Structure, Cosmology and Pollution Concepts in Southern Africa*. 18th Raymond Dart Lecture. Johannesburg: Witwatersrand University Press.

HAWKINS, B. (1984). The Semantics of English Spatial Prepositions. Ph.D. diss., University of California, San Diego. Reproduced by LAUD (1985).

—— (1988). The natural category MEDIUM: An alternative to selection restrictions and similar constructs. In Rudzka-Ostyn (1988*b*), 231–70.

HAWKINS, J. A. (1986). *A Comparative Typology of English and German: Unifying the Contrasts*. London: Croom Helm.

HAWKINS, R. (1981). Towards an account of the possessive constructions: *NP's N* and *the N of NP*. *Journal of Linguistics* 7: 247–69.

HAYDEN, D. E., and ALWORTH, E. P. (eds.) (1965). *Classics in Semantics*. London: Vision.

HEIDER, E. R. (= Rosch) (1971). 'Focal' color areas and the development of color names. *Developmental Psychology* 4: 447–55.

—— (1972). Universals in color naming and memory. *Journal of Experimental Psychology* 93: 10–20.

HERRMANN, L. (1975). On 'in that'. *BLS* 1: 189–95.

HERWEG, M. (1988). Zur Semantik einiger lokaler Präpositionen des Deutschen: Überlegungen zur Theorie der lexikalischen Semantik am Beispiel von 'in', 'an', 'bei' und 'auf'. LILOG-Report 21, IBM Deutschland.

—— (1989). Ansätze zu einer semantischen Beschreibung topologischer Präpositionen. In Habel *et al.* (1989), 99–127.

HEWSON, J. (1991). Determiners as heads. *Cognitive Linguistics* 2: 317–37.

HEWSON, M., and HAMLYN, D. (1983). Cultural metaphors: Some implications for science education. *Anthropology and Education Quarterly* 16: 31–46.

HOCKETT, C. F. (1968). *The State of the Art*. The Hague: Mouton.

HOFFMAN, R. R. (1985). Some implications of metaphor for philosophy and psychology of science. In Paprotté and Dirven (1985), 327–80.

HOPPER, P. J., and THOMPSON, S. A. (1980). Transitivity in grammar and discourse. *Language* 56: 251–99.

—— and —— (1985). The iconicity of the universal categories 'noun' and 'verb'. In Haiman (1985), 151–83.

References   303

HOUSEHOLDER, F. W. (1967). Ancient Greek. In *World Classes*. *Lingua* 17: 103–28.

HUDSON, R. (1980). *Sociolinguistics*. Cambridge: Cambridge University Press.

—— (1984). *Word Grammar*. Oxford: Basil Blackwell.

—— (1987). Zwicky on heads. *Journal of Linguistics* 23: 109–32.

JACKENDOFF, R. (1972). *Semantic Interpretation in Generative Grammar*. Cambridge, Mass.: MIT Press.

—— (1973). The base rules for prepositional phrases. In S. Anderson and P. Kiparsky (eds.), *A Festschrift for Morris Halle*, 345–56. New York: Holt, Rinehart & Winston.

—— (1983). *Semantics and Cognition*. Cambridge, Mass.: MIT Press.

—— (1990). *Semantic Structures*. Cambridge, Mass.: MIT Press.

JACOBS, R. A., and ROSENBAUM, P. S. (1968). *English Transformational Grammar*. Lexington. Xerox College.

JAEGER, J. (1980). Categorization in Phonology: An Experimental Approach. Ph.D. diss., University of California, Berkeley.

JAEGER, R. and OHALA, J. J. (1984). On the structure of phonetic categories. *BLS* 10: 15–26.

JAKOBSON, R. (1936). Beitrag zur allgemeinen Kasuslehre: Gesamtbedeutungen der russischen Kasus. In *Selected Writings*, ii. 23–71. The Hague: Mouton.

——, FANT, G., and HALLE, M. (1951). *Preliminaries to Speech Analysis*. Cambridge, Mass.: MIT Press.

JESPERSEN, O. (1924). *The Philosophy of Grammar*. London: George Allen & Unwin.

JOHNSON, M. (1987). *The Body in the Mind: The Bodily Basis of Meaning, Imagination, and Reason*. Chicago: University of Chicago Press.

JONES, D. (1964⁹). *An Outline of English Phonetics*. Cambridge: Heffer. 1st edn., 1918.

JONGEN, R. (1985). Polysemy, tropes and cognition, or the non-Magrittian art of closing curtains whilst opening them. In Paprotté and Dirven (1985), 121–39.

KATZ, J. J. and FODOR, J. A. (1963). The structure of a semantic theory. *Language* 39: 170–210.

—— and POSTAL, P. M. (1964). *An Integrated Theory of Linguistic Descriptions*. Cambridge, Mass.: MIT Press.

KAY, P. (1975). Synchronic variability and diachronic change in basic color terms. *Language in Society* 4: 257–70.

—— (1983). Linguistic competence and folk theories of language: Two English hedges. *BLS* 9: 128–37.

—— and McDANIEL, C. K. (1978). The linguistic significance of the meanings of basic color terms. *Language* 54: 610–46.

KEMPSON, R. M. (1977). *Semantic Theory*. Cambridge: Cambridge University Press.

KEMPTON, W. (1981). *The Folk Classification of Ceramics: A Study of Cognitive Prototypes*. New York: Academic Press.

KLEIBER, G. (1990). *La sémantique du prototype: Catégories et sens lexical*. Paris: Presses Universitaires de France.

KRISTOL, A. M. (1980). Color systems in Southern Italy: A case of regression. *Language* 56: 137–45.

KUČERA, H., and FRANCIS, W. N. (1967). *Computational Analysis of Present-day American English*. Providence: Brown University Press.

LABOV, W. (1973). The boundaries of words and their meanings. In Bailey and Shuy (1973), 340–73.

LADD, D. R. (1980). *The Structure of Intonational Meaning: Evidence from English*. Bloomington: Indiana University Press.

LADEFOGED, P. (1975). *A Course in Phonetics*. New York: Harcourt Brace Jovanovich.

LAKOFF, G. (1970). *Irregularity in Syntax*. New York: Holt, Rinehart & Winston.

—— (1972). Hedges: A study in meaning criteria and the logic of fuzzy concepts. *CLS* 8: 183–228.

—— (1977). Linguistic Gestalts. *CLS* 13: 236–87.

—— (1978). Some remarks on AI and linguistics. *Cognitive Science* 2: 267–75.

—— (1987). *Women, Fire, and Dangerous Things: What Categories Reveal About the Mind*. Chicago: University of Chicago Press.

—— and BRUGMAN, C. (1986). Argument forms in lexical semantics. *BLS* 12: 442–54.

—— and JOHNSON, M. (1980). *Metaphors We Live By*. Chicago: Chicago University Press.

LAKOFF, R. (1975). *Language and Woman's Place*. New York: Harper and Row.

LANG, E. (1991). A two-level approach to projective prepositions. In Rauh (1991), 127–67.

LANGACKER, R. W. (1987). *Foundations of Cognitive Grammar*, i, *Theoretical Prerequisites*. Stanford: Stanford University Press.

—— (1988). A usage-based model. In Rudzka-Ostyn (1988*b*), 127–61.

—— (1990). Active zones. In *Concept, Image, and Symbol: The Cognitive Basis of Grammar*. Cognitive Linguistics Research, 1. Berlin: Mouton de Gruyter, 189–201. First published in *BLS* 10 (1984), 172–88.

—— (1991). *Foundations of Cognitive Grammar*, ii. Stanford: Stanford University Press.

—— (1992). The symbolic nature of cognitive grammar: The meaning of *of* and of *of*-periphrasis. In M. Pütz (ed.), *Thirty Years of Linguistic Evolution: Studies in Honour of René Dirven on the Occasion of his Sixtieth Birthday*, 483–502. Amsterdam: John Benjamins.

LASS, R. (1984). *Phonology: An Introduction to Basic Concepts*. Cambridge: Cambridge University Press.

LEACH, E. (1964). Anthropological aspects of language: Animal categories and verbal abuse. In E. H. Lenneberg (ed.), *New Directions in the Study of Language*, 23–63. Cambridge, Mass.: MIT Press.

—— (1982). *Social Anthropology*. London: Fontana.

LEECH, G. (1981²). *Semantics*. Harmondsworth: Penguin. 1st edn., 1974. Harmondsworth: Penguin.

LEES, R. B. (1960). *The Grammar of English Nominalizations*. The Hague: Mouton.

LEPSCHY, A. L., and LEPSCHY, G. (1977). *The Italian Language Today*. London: Hutchinson.

LEVY, Y. (1983). It's frogs all the way down. *Cognition* 15: 75–93.

LEWIS, C. S. (1960). *Studies in Words*. Cambridge: Cambridge University Press.

LIEBERMAN, P. (1967). *Intonation, Perception and Language*. Cambridge, Mass.: MIT Press.

LINDNER, S. (1981). A Lexico-Semantic Analysis of English Verb-Particle Constructions with UP and OUT. Ph.D. diss. University of California, San Diego. Reproduced by LAUD (1985).

LÖRSCHER, W., and SCHULZE, R. (eds.) (1987). *Perspectives on Language in Performance. Studies in Linguistics, Literary Criticism, and Language Teaching and Learning. To Honour Werner Hüllen on the Occasion of His Sixtieth Birthday*. Tübingen: Narr.

LYONS, J. (1968). *Introduction to Theoretical Linguistics*. Cambridge: Cambridge University Press.

—— (1977). *Semantics* (2 volumes). Cambridge: Cambridge University Press.

McCAWLEY, J. D. (1986). What linguists might contribute to dictionary making if they could get their act together. In P. C. Bjarkman and V. Raskin (eds.), *The Real-World Linguist: Linguistic Applications in the 1980s*, 3–18. Norwood: Ablex.

MacCORMAC, E. R. (1985). *A Cognitive Theory of Metaphor*. Cambridge, Mass.: MIT Press.

MacLAURY, R. E. (1987). Coextensive semantic ranges: Different names for distinct vantages of one category. *CLS* 23(I): 268–82.

—— (1991). Prototypes revisited. *Annual Review of Anthropology* 20: 55–74.

—— (1995*a*). *Color Categorization in Mesoamerica: A Cross-Linguistic Survey and Cognitive Model*. Austin: University of Texas Press.

—— (1995*b*). Vantage theory. In Taylor and MacLaury (1995), 231–76.

McNEILL, D. (1972). Colour and colour terminology. Review of Berlin and Kay (1969). *Journal of Linguistics* 8: 21–34.

MALINOWSKI, B. (1937). The dilemma of contemporary linguistics. Review of M. M. Lewis (1936), *Infant Speech: A Study of the Beginnings of Language*, London: Kegan Paul. *Nature* 140: 172–3.

MARATSOS, M. P., and CHALKLEY, M. A. (1980). The internal language of children's syntax: The ontogenesis and representation of syntactic categories. In K. Nelson (ed.), *Children's Language*, ii. 127–213. New York: Gardner Press.

MATTHEWS, P. H. (1979). *Generative Grammar and Linguistic Competence*. London: George Allen & Unwin.

MILLER, G. A., and JOHNSON-LAIRD, P. N. (1976). *Language and Perception*. Cambridge, Mass.: Harvard University Press.

306   *References*

MOORE, T. E. (ed.) (1973). *Cognitive Development and the Acquisition of Language*. New York: Academic Press.

MOULTON, W. G. (1962). The vowels of Dutch: Phonetic and distributional classes. *Lingua* 11: 294–312.

NATHAN, G. S. (1986). Phonemes as mental categories. *BLS* 12: 212–23.

NEEDHAM, R. (1974). Remarks on the analysis of kinship and marriage. In *Remarks and Inventions: Skeptical Essays about Kinship*, 38–71. London: Tavistock. First published 1971.

—— (1975). Polythetic classification: Convergence and consequences. *Man* (New Series) 10: 349–69.

NIDA, E. A. (1975). *Componential Analysis of Meaning*. The Hague: Mouton.

NUNBERG, G. D. (1978). The Pragmatics of Reference. Ph.D. diss. City University of New York.

OAKESHOTT-TAYLOR, J. (= Taylor) (1984*a*). Factuality and intonation. *Journal of Linguistics* 20.: 1–21.

—— (1984*b*). On the location of 'tonic prominence' in English. *Linguistische Berichte* 91: 3–24.

ORTONY, A. (ed.) (1979). *Metaphor and Thought*. Cambridge: Cambridge University Press.

OSGOOD, C. E., SUCI, G. J., and TANNENBAUM, P. H. (1957). *The Measurement of Meaning*. Urbana: University of Illinois Press.

OSHERSON, D. N., and SMITH, E. E. (1981). On the adequacy of prototype theory as a theory of concepts. *Cognition* 9: 35–58.

PAIVIO, A., and BEGG, I. (1981). *Psychology of Language*. Englewood Cliffs: Prentice Hall.

PALMER, F. R. (1974). *The English Verb*. London: Longman. First published as *A Linguistic Study of the English Verb* (1965).

PAPROTTÉ, W., and DIRVEN, R. (eds.) (1985). *The Ubiquity of Metaphor*. Amsterdam: John Benjamins.

PIAGET, J. (1947). *The Psychology of Intelligence*. London: Routledge & Kegan Paul.

PIKE, K. L. (1945). *The Intonation of American English*. Ann Arbor: University of Michigan Press.

PULMAN, S. G. (1983). *Word Meaning and Belief*. London: Croom Helm.

PUTNAM, H. (1975). *Mind, Language and Reality: Philosophical Papers*, ii. Cambridge: Cambridge University Press.

QUINE, W. V. O. (1960). *Word and Object*. Cambridge, Mass.: MIT Press.

QUIRK, R. (1965). Descriptive and serial relationship. *Language* 41: 205–17.

——, GREENBAUM, S., LEECH, G., and SVARTVIK, J. (1972). *A Grammar of Contemporary English*. London: Longman.

—— —— —— and —— (1985). *A Comprehensive Grammar of the English Language*. London: Longman.

RADDEN, G. (1985). Spatial metaphors underlying prepositions of causality. In Paprotté and Dirven (1985), 177–207.

RAUH, G. (ed.) (1991). *Approaches to Prepositions*. Tübingen: Narr.

REDDY, M. J. (1979). The conduit metaphor: A case of frame conflict in our language. In Ortony (1979), 284–324.

RESCORLA, L. A. (1980). Overextension in early language development. *Journal of Child Language* 7: 321–35.

RHODES, R. A., and LAWLER, J. M. (1981). Athematic metaphors. *CLS* 17: 318–42.

RIPS, L. J., SHOBEN, E. J., and SMITH, E. E. (1973). Semantic distance and the verification of semantic relations. *Journal of Verbal Learning and Verbal Behaviour* 12: 1–20.

ROBINS, R. H. (1964). *General Linguistics: An Introductory Survey*. London: Longmans.

ROSCH, E. (1973a). Natural categories. *Cognitive Psychology* 4: 328–50.

—— (1973b). On the internal structure of perceptual and semantic categories. In Moore (1973), 111–44.

—— (1975a). Cognitive reference points. *Cognitive Psychology* 7: 532–47.

—— (1975b). Cognitive representations of semantic categories. *Journal of Experimental Psychology: General* 104: 192–233.

—— (1975c). Universals and cultural specifics in human categorisation. In R. W. Brislin, S. Bochner, and W. J. Lonner (eds.), *Cross-cultural Perspectives on Learning*, 177–206. New York: John Wiley.

—— (1976). Structural bases of typicality effects. *Journal of Experimental Psychology: Human Perception and Performance* 2: 491–502.

—— (1978). Principles of categorization. In E. Rosch and B. B. Lloyd (eds.), *Cognition and Categorization*, 27–48. Hillsdale: Lawrence Erlbaum.

—— and MERVIS, C. B. (1975). Family resemblances: Studies in the internal structure of categories. *Cognitive Psychology* 7: 573–605.

—— —— GRAY, W. D., JOHNSON, D. M., and BOYES-BRAEM, P. (1976). Basic objects in natural categories. *Cognitive Psychology* 8: 382–439.

ROSS, J. R. (1972). Endstation Hauptwort: The category squish. *CLS* 8: 316–28.

—— (1973). A fake NP squish. In Bailey and Shuy (1973), 96–140.

RUDZKA-OSTYN, B. (1985). Metaphoric processes in word formation: The case of prefixed verbs. In Paprotté and Dirven (1985), 209–41.

—— (1988a). Semantic extensions into the domain of verbal communication. In Rudzka-Ostyn (1988b), 507–53.

—— (ed.) (1988b). *Topics in Cognitive Linguistics*. Amsterdam: John Benjamins.

RUHL, C. (1989). *On Monosemy: A Study in Linguistic Semantics*. Stony Brook: State University of New York Press.

SADOCK, J. (1972). Speech act idioms. *CLS* 8: 329–39.

SALMOND, A. (1982). Theoretical landscapes: On cross-cultural conceptions of knowledge. In D. Parkin (ed.), *Semantic Anthropology*, 65–87. London: Academic Press.

SAMPSON, G. (1980a). *Making Sense*. Oxford: Oxford University Press.

—— (1980b). *Schools of Linguistics*. Stanford: Stanford University Press.

SAPIR, E. (1970). *Language: An Introduction to the Study of Speech*. London: Rupert Hart-Davis. 1st pub., 1921.

DE SAUSSURE, F. (1964³). *Cours de linguistique générale*, ed. C. Bally and A. Sechehaye. Paris: Payot, 1st edn., 1916.

SCHLESINGER, I. M. (1981). Semantic assimilation in the development of relational categories. In Deutsch (1981), 223–43.

SCHULZE, R. (1991). Getting round to (*a*)*round*: Towards the description and analysis of a 'spatial' predicate. In Rauh (1991), 253–74.

—— (1993). The meaning of (*a*)*round*: A study of an English preposition. In Geiger and Rudzka-Ostyn (1993), 399–431.

SEARLE, J. (1975). Indirect speech acts. In P. Cole and J. Morgan (eds.), *Syntax and Semantics*, 3. New York: Academic Press.

—— (1979). Metaphor. In Ortony (1979), 92–123.

—— (1980). The background of meaning. In J. R. Searle, F. Kiefer, and M. Bierwisch (eds.), *Speech Act Theory and Pragmatics*, 221–32. Dordrecht: Reidel.

—— (1983). *Intentionality: An Essay in the Philosophy of Mind*. Cambridge: Cambridge University Press.

SKINNER, B. F. (1957). *Verbal Behavior*. New York: Appleton Crofts.

SLOBIN, D. I. (1981). The origin of grammatical encoding of events. In Deutsch (1981), 185–99.

—— (1985). The child as a linguistic icon-maker. In Haiman (1985), 221–48.

SMITH, E. E., and MEDIN, D. L. (1981). *Categories and Concepts*. Cambridge, Mass.: Harvard University Press.

SPERBER, D., and WILSON, D. (1986). *Relevance: Communication and Cognition*. Oxford: Blackwell.

TALMY, L. (1978). The relation of grammar to cognition—a synopsis. In D. Waltz (ed.), *Proceedings of TINLAP-2 (Theoretical Issues in Natural Language Processing)*. Urbana: University of Illinois. Repr. with revisions in Rudzka-Ostyn (1988*b*), 165–205.

TAYLOR, J. (1987). Tense and metaphorisations of time in Zulu. In Lörscher and Schulze (1987): 214–29.

—— (1988). Contrasting prepositional categories: English and Italian. In Rudzka-Ostyn (1988*b*), 299–326.

—— (1992*a*). How many meanings does a word have? *Stellenbosch Papers in Linguistics* 25: 133–68.

—— (1992*b*). A problem with synonyms. *South African Journal of Linguistics* 10: 99–104.

—— (1994). The two-level approach to meaning. *Linguistische Berichte* 149: 3–26.

—— (1995*a*). Fuzzy categories in syntax: The case of possessives and compounds. *Rivista di Linguistica* 7.

—— (1995*b*). On construing the world. In Taylor and MacLaury (1995), 1–21.

—— (1995*c*). On running and jogging. *Cognitive Linguistics* 6.

——, and MacLaury, R. (eds.) (1995). *Language and the Construal of the World*. Berlin: Mouton de Gruyter.

—— and Uys, J. Z. (1988). Notes on the Afrikaans vowel system. *Leuvense Bijdragen* 77: 1–25.

Thomason, R. H. (1974). *Formal Philosophy: Selected Papers of Richard Montague*. New Haven: Yale University Press.

Trubetzkoy, N. S. (1939). *Grundzüge der Phonologie. Travaux du Cercle Linguistique de Prague* 7.

Tsohatzidis, S. (ed.) (1990). *Meanings and Prototypes: Studies in Linguistic Categorization*. London: Routledge.

Tuggy, D. (1993). Ambiguity, polysemy, and vagueness. *Cognitive Linguistics* 4: 273–90.

Tversky, A. (1977). Features of similarity. *Psychological Review* 84: 327–52.

Vandeloise, C. (1984). Description of Space in French. Ph.D. diss. University of California, San Diego. Reproduced by LAUD (1985).

Van Langendonck, W. (1994). Determiners as heads? *Cognitive Linguistics* 5: 243–59.

van Oosten, J. (1977). Subjects and agenthood in English. *CLS* 13: 459–71.

Vygotsky, L. S. (1962). *Thought and Language*. Trans. E. Hanfmann and G. Vaker. Cambridge, Mass.: MIT Press.

Wanner, E., and Gleitman, L. R. (eds.) (1982). *Language Acquisition: The State of the Art*. Cambridge: Cambridge University Press.

von Wattenwyl, A., and Zollinger, H. (1979). Color-term salience and neurophysiology of color vision. *American Anthropologist* 81: 279–88.

Wierzbicka, A. (1980a). *The Case for Surface Case*. Ann Arbor: Karoma.

—— (1980b). *Lingua Mentalis: The Semantics of Natural Language*. Sydney: Academic Press.

—— (1985). *Lexicography and Conceptual Analysis*. Ann Arbor: Karoma.

Wittgenstein, L. (1978). *Philosophical Investigations*. Translated by G. E. M. Anscombe. Oxford: Basil Blackwell.

Wunderlich, D. (1991). How do prepositional phrases fit into compositional syntax and semantics? *Linguistics* 29: 591–621.

—— (1993). On German *um*: Semantic and conceptual aspects. *Linguistics* 31: 111–33.

Zelinski-Wibbelt, C. (ed.) (1993). *The Semantics of Prepositions: From Mental Processing to Natural Language Processing*. Berlin: Mouton de Gruyter.

Ziervogel, D. J., Louw, A., and Taljaard, P. C. (1967). *A Handbook of the Zulu Language*. Pretoria: Van Schaik.

Zubin, D. A., and Köpcke, K.-M. (1981). Gender: A less than arbitrary grammatical category. *CLS* 17: 439–49.

—— and —— (1986). Gender and folk taxonomy: The indexical relation between grammatical and lexical categorization. In Craig (1986), 139–80.

Zwicky, A. M. (1985a). Clitics and particles. *Language* 61: 283–305.

ZWICKY, A. M. (1985 b). Heads. *Journal of Linguistics* 21: 1–29.

—— (1993). Heads, bases and functions. In Corbett *et al.* (1993), 292–315.

—— and SADOCK, J. M. (1975). Ambiguity tests and how to fail them. In J. P. Kimball (ed.), *Syntax and Semantics*, 4, 1–36. New York: Academic Press.

Index